THE CROSS-CULTURAL STUDY OF WOMEN

A Comprehensive Guide

Edited by Margot I. Duley
and Mary I. Edwards

THE FEMINIST PRESS
at The City University of New York
New York

Library of Congress Cataloging-in-Publication Data

The Cross-cultural study of women.

1. Women—Cross-cultural studies—Study and
teaching (Higher) I. Duley, Margot I. II. Edwards,
Mary I.
HQ1206.C755 1986   305.4'07'11   83-14209
ISBN 0-935312-45-5
ISBN 0-935312-02-1 (pbk.)

First edition
90 89 88 87 86 5 4 3 2 1

Cover photographs: © Robert Rattner: Kenyan woman, front upper right;
Guatemalan women, back upper left; Berber women in Tunisia, back bottom.
Used with permission. © Martha Stuart Communications, Inc.: Indian woman,
front lower right; Chinese woman and child, front left; Javanese woman, back
upper right. Used with permission.

Text design by Lea Smith
Cover design by Lucinda Geist
Typeset by Coghill Book Typesetting
Manufactured by Haddon Craftsmen

CONTENTS

Preface, ix
Introduction, xiii

"Women and Nature" Debate—Public Versus Private
Domain—Lesbianism and Gender Stratification

Cultural Values—Obstacles, Opportunities, and Strategies
in Colonial and Modern Africa: Methodological Issues
and Approaches; Economic Change and Social Status;
Legal and Property Rights Changes; Marriage, Kinship,
and Urbanization; Political Representation and Strategies;
Beliefs, Rituals, and Cultural Adaptation—Concluding
Note

PREFACE

This guide to research and issues in the cross-cultural study of women is intended for a variety of uses. It can be readily used by instructors in colleges, community colleges, and universities as a core curriculum for women's studies courses and as supplemental material on women for courses in the traditional curriculum. Part I, "Theoretical Perspectives," contains twenty-four lecture outlines; Part II, "Area Studies," about thirty-six plus bibliographical materials. With the addition of classroom discussions, quizzes, and audiovisual materials, the format presented here probably lends itself to a two-semester or two-term course. The format is not intended as a rigid sequence but as a framework readily adaptable to a "mix and match" approach, by which instructors may select what seems most useful from the theoretical material in Part 1 and in the area outlines in Part II. Through selective editing, however, this instructor's text can also be used in faculty curriculum integration workshops, and by specialists who wish to expand their interdisciplinary knowledge. The discussion questions range in sophistication from those that can be used in the classroom to those that pose basic questions for future research. Thus, this is a sourcebook and critical guide with a variety of intended audiences.

These materials were initially developed through a National Endowment for the Humanities Educational Program Grant. Research and writing centered at the University of Michigan, with participation by graduate students and faculty members from Eastern Michigan University, Central Michigan University, Western Michigan University, and Schoolcraft College. The purposes of the project were to integrate the new scholarship on women, to develop women's studies courses that would introduce and critique the concepts and methods of the disciplines involved, and to offer to teachers trained in one discipline a means of grasping the interdisciplinary debátes central to the study of women in the social sciences and the humanities. *The Cross-Cultural Study of Women* is one of four interdisciplinary curricula developed under the series editorship of Mary I. Edwards.

The original task force that worked on the cross-cultural project in 1978 consisted of Margot Duley (chair), Charlotte Staelin, Karen Sinclair, Norma Ware, Martha Brown, and Ann Munster. All contributed to a greater or lesser extent with preliminary materials. Since that time the new scholarship on women has burgeoned, and the curriculum has been substantially rewritten, revised, and updated. It now represents most centrally the work of Margot Duley with special contributions from Karen Sinclair together with new sections from Lance Morrow, Muriel Nazarri, and the additional assistance of Susan Diduk on the "Women and Development" chapter. Throughout this lengthy process Mary Edwards has continued to give editorial guidance.

Many people offered useful advice, suggestions, and encouragement over the years. We would like to especially acknowledge the role of Professor Louise Tilly who was responsible for initiating the National Endowment for the Humanities project during her first year as Director of the Women's Studies Program at the University of Michigan. Professor Sherry Ortner of the University of Michigan Department of Anthropology as well as Professor Louise Lamphere of the Department of Anthropology of Brown University provided helpful general critiques during the revision of these materials for publication. Many scholars provided incisive and detailed comments on particular chapters: Michele Dominy (Indiana University) on Oceania and anthropological segments; Helen Safa, University of Florida, on Latin America; Carol Haddad (Michigan State University), Marlee Meriwether (Denison University), and Dr. Azizah al-Hibri on the Middle East and North Africa; Hanna Papanek (Boston University) on India, Pakistan, and Bangladesh, as well as the Middle East; Govind Kelkar (Centre for Women's Development Studies, New Delhi) on China; Kathleen Staudt (University of Texas at El Paso) on development issues, state formation, and Africa; Judith Bruce (The Population Council) on overall perspectives but especially on religions and cultural variability; and Sue-Ellen Jacobs (University of Washington) on theories of gender stratification. Conversations with other scholars provided crucial insights, among them Hemalata Dandekar (University of Michigan) on development issues in South Asia; Bahram Tavakolian (Denison University) on materialist versus idealist interpretations of purdah; and Evelyn

Blackwood (San Francisco State University) on cross-cultural perspectives on lesbianism. Early drafts of sections and chapters were contributed by Ann Munster, Charlotte Staelin, and Norma Ware, then graduate students of the University of Michigan, Ann Arbor. The discussion of contemporary Arab feminism in the Middle East was informed in part by a lecture given by Yvonne Haddad (Hartford Seminary) on "Women in the Arab World" at the University of Michigan in September 1982. It should be obvious from this lengthy list that a general work of this sort that crosses many disciplinary and ideological bridges is a collective work of construction and dialogue. The remaining deficiencies should be placed on the doorsteps of the editors and contributors who will claim them without undue defensiveness.

We would also like to thank past and present members of the staff of The Feminist Press for their advice and assistance, namely, Florence Howe, Joanne O'Hare, Jo Baird, Elsa Dixler, and especially Sandy Weinbaum for her enthusiasm and intelligent queries at a critical stage in the manuscript.

INTRODUCTION

Those who study the status of women cross-culturally are immediately confronted with questions that are both analytically complex and emotionally compelling. Why, in so many cultures, have men been dominant and women subordinate? How does one measure dominance and subordination—indeed, are they measurable? Is gender inequality a constant of human social organization, or have there been societies in which women have shared power equally with men or exercised power over them? How does one make meaningful cross-cultural comparisons of "power"? Do the origin and perpetuation of gender inequalities lie in biology, in culture, or in a complex interaction of both? In the realm of culture, what is the role of social organization, and particularly of economics and religion, in gender stratification?

In constructing this text we thought it essential to examine these broad theoretical questions at the outset before turning to the study of the history and status of women in particular cultures. Accordingly, Part I develops theoretical perspectives on the status of women, drawing freely from the discipline of anthropology, with additional help from psychology, biology, economics, history, politics, and religion.

There are no easy or obvious answers to the issues addressed here. Indeed, in exploring this material students will find themselves in the midst of an intellectual war zone. Crouching in one set of trenches are the biological and psychological determinists, who see male dominance rooted in unalterable laws of nature, such as a greater male capacity for aggression. Hurling fusillades from opposite trenches, with such vigor that one might suppose that the determinists would reconsider their premises, are feminist scholars who see the role of culture as primary in explaining gender inequality. Yet even among the "culturalists" there is no general agreement about the relative importance of economics, state formation, socialization, religion, parenting, family structures, and other cultural influences. The authors of this text believe the weight of evidence is clearly on the side of those who emphasize the importance of culture. Even so, we have not structured the material to lead to simple conclusions, but have tried to present problems and issues for the instructors' and students' consideration.

The treatment of theory in this volume occurs largely in an historical and developmental framework. Students are able to see how one theory builds upon another, how one scholar's work raises questions of fact, methodology, or interpretation that others then pursue. Where gaps exist in the literature, or existing interpretations seem inadequate, we have felt free to point this out, and at times to suggest some leads of our own.

The curriculum encourages students to think analytically and critically for themselves. The work of the scholar is presented as part of a constantly interacting and organic whole, cross-fertilized and modified by the insights and work of others. Through discussion questions students are encouraged to struggle to their own informed conclusions. This, we think, is part of the finest tradition of feminist pedagogy.

The ongoing debate about the origin and perpetuation of male dominance is of more than theoretical interest. The practical implications of the answers for those who advocate equality for women and a reshaping of society to achieve that goal are immense. As Gayle Rubin has colorfully put it:

> If innate male aggression and dominance are at the root of female oppression, then the feminist program would logically require either the extermination of the offending sex, or else a eugenics project to modify its character. If sexism is a by-product of capitalism's relentless appetite for profit, then sexism would wither away in the advent of a successful socialist revolution. If the world historical defeat of women occurred at the hands of an armed patriarchal revolt, then it is time for Amazon guerrillas to start training in the Adirondacks.*

In studying and discussing theories of male dominance, students are participating in one of the most significant and exciting debates in the humanities and social sciences today.

Part II surveys the history and status of women in six cultural areas. Wherever relevant, we have integrated references to the earlier theoretical discussion to enhance students' understanding

---

*Gayle Rubin, "The Traffic in Women: Notes on the 'Political Economy' of Sex," in Rayna R. Reiter, ed., *Toward an Anthropology of Women* (New York: Monthly Review Press, 1975), 157–58.

of the specific society under consideration. Three areas—India, China, and Oceania—are presented in the form of lecture outlines. Three others—Sub-Saharan Africa, Latin America, and the Islamic Middle East and North Africa—are presented as annotated bibliographies to help instructors construct their own lectures and discussions.

Because of the number of fine curricula on Western women already available, and because of constraints of time and space, we have deliberately excluded the Western world from consideration here. We have also excluded discussions of women of color in the United States. Our exclusion of Western examples was not made without misgivings. As any instructor of non-Western materials is acutely aware, the typical Euro-American tribal consciousness too often perceives the rest of the world as totally "other." Indeed, the very phrase "non-Western" betrays its bias. Therefore it is pedagogically advisable that instructors highlight the similarity of means whereby patriarchal societies around the globe have exercised control over women. The distance separating the ERA debate in the United States from the controversy surrounding the role of women in contemporary Iran may not be as great as students imagine.

Conversely it is important not to conflate all women's experiences to the same reductionist point. This curriculum stresses the diversity of women's lives, which springs from many factors—race, sexual orientation, material wealth (both personal and national), religious views, kinship patterns, environmental conditions, family structures, effects of technology, and legal systems to mention just some of the dividing lines. We hope students will see women's experiences in their full complexity, and that they will not assume (as, unfortunately, some Western feminists at international getherings have done) that their priorities, based on their cultural experiences, will necessarily be those of others. Some of the discussion questions are framed to foster reflection on these differences. It is our hope that this process will also increase students' sensitivity to the ethnic, racial, sexual preference, and class differences in our own society.

Looking, then, at the variety and complexity of women's lives across many continents and many centuries, is there no "sisterhood of woman"? Perhaps not "a" sisterhood, but, as we hope to show, many sisters.

Margot I. Duley

THE CROSS-CULTURAL
STUDY OF WOMEN

PART ONE
THEORETICAL PERSPECTIVES

CHAPTER ONE

BIOLOGY VERSUS CULTURE

Margot I. Duley, Karen Sinclair, and Mary I. Edwards

The central question at issue in this section is whether inequality between the sexes can be attributed to biology, culture, or to a complex interaction of these forces. We will examine the arguments of biological and psychological determinists, briefly survey the current research on sex differences, and examine the writings of theorists who believe that culture is of prime importance in shaping gender inequalities and in forming male and female personalities.

THE BIOLOGICAL DETERMINISTS

The most commonly cited "cause" of male dominance is biology. In this section we critically survey several biological explanations, particularly those that have become well known through popularized books on sociobiology. Students should be made aware of the political and social inferences frequently drawn from these works (i.e., defenses of the sexual and racial status quo), whether or not such implications are intended by the authors.

In this lecture we provide only a short overview of the arguments of sociobiologists, together with critiques mostly in the form of questions. For instructors who wish guidance on a more extended treatment we recommend consulting Anne Fausto-Sterling's excellent course outline, "The Biology of Gender," in *Women's Studies Quarterly* 1, no. 2 (Summer 1982): 17–19.

Out of several possibilities for a basic student text we have recommended Janet Sayers's *Biological Politics* for its lively juxtaposition of sociobiological and feminist arguments. She herself is critical of both sides, faulting "social constructionist" feminists for denying any role to biology, a characterization that not all in this feminist school would agree with. Nevertheless the book is certain to cause lively discussion. Oakley's excellent work is another possibility, though it needs updating.

Readings for Students
Leibowitz, Lila. "Perspectives on the Evolution of Sex Differences." In *Toward an Anthropology of Women,* edited by Rayna R. Reiter, 30–35. New York: Monthly Review Press, 1975.

Oakley, Ann. *Sex, Gender and Society,* Chap. 1. New York: Harper Colophon Books, 1972.

Sayers, Janet. *Biological Politics: Feminist and Anti-Feminist Perspectives.* New York: Methuen, 1982.

Readings for Instructors
Bleier, Ruth. *Science and Gender: A Critique of Biology and Its Theories on Women.* New York: Pergamon Press, 1984.

Collins, Randall. "A Conflict Theory of Sexual Stratification." In *Family, Marriage and the Struggle of the Sexes,* edited by Hans Peter Dreitzel. New York: Macmillan, 1972.

Goldberg, Steven. *The Inevitability of Patriarchy.* New York: William Morrow & Co., 1974.

Harris, Marvin. *Cows, Pigs, Wars and Witches.* New York: Vintage, 1974.

Hrdy, Sarah Blaffer. *The Woman That Never Evolved.* Cambridge: Harvard University Press, 1981.

Hubbard, Ruth, Mary Sue Henefin, and Barbara Fried, eds. *Women Look at Biology Looking at Women: A Feminist Critique.* Cambridge, Mass.: Schenkman, 1979.

Keller, Evelyn Fox. *Reflections on Gender and Science.* New Haven: Yale University Press, 1985.

Leacock, Eleanor Burke. "Review of Steven Goldberg's *The Inevitability of Patriarchy,*" 264–79 and "Social Behavior, Biology and the Double Standard," 280–301. In *Myths of Male Dominance.* New York: Monthly Review Press, 1981.

Scheinfeld, Amram. *Women and Men.* London: Chatto & Windus, 1947.

Tanner, Nancy. *On Becoming Human.* Cambridge: Cambridge University Press, 1981.

Tiger, Lionel. *Men in Groups.* New York: Random House, 1969.

Tiger, Lionel, and Robin Fox. *The Imperial Animal.* New York: Holt, Rinehart & Winston, 1971.

Wilson, Edward O. *Sociobiology: The New Synthesis.* Cambridge: Harvard University Press, 1975.

Lecture Topics

Some sociobiologists contend that all human behavior, including the dynamics of male-female relationships, is biologically based. This branch of sociobiology (for not all sociobiologists assume such an extreme position) we have termed the "biological determinists." Edward O. Wilson, for example, argues that all social behavior is rooted in biology, and that it can be analyzed across phylogenetic lines. A fully articulated science of sociobiology, according to Wilson, is one in which the social behavior of termite colonies, rhesus monkeys, and humans is seen to be grounded in the same biological principles.

Arguments for biologically based male dominance can be grouped into certain common themes:

Aggression Arguments. Males have greater innate aggressive tendencies, leading to dominance (Goldberg, Wilson).

Male Bonding Arguments. Males have genetically programmed bonds, close to men and exclusive of women, which evolved over centuries of hunting. Females have no such bonding (Tiger and Fox).

Physical Strength Arguments. The male's greater strength led to his dominance (Goldberg, Tiger and Fox, Harris). Harris, for example, argues that in "primitive warfare" the stronger male has the advantage, and successful warriors (who have to be motivated to risk their lives) are rewarded with the services and subordination of women.

Reproductive Arguments. Women's childbearing role removes them from nondomestic spheres, leading to male dominance (Scheinfeld); or, alternatively, females are made more vulnerable by childrearing, and the stronger male is more successful at sexual aggression and domination (Collins).

Discussion Questions

1. Discuss the following statement: "Biologists may tell us that men are, on the average, stronger than women, but

they cannot tell us why male strength and activities in general seemed to be valued by peoples in all cultures" (Michelle Zimbalist Rosaldo and Louise Lamphere, "Introduction," *Woman, Culture, and Society* [Stanford: Stanford University Press, 1974], p. 4.)

2. A number of the biological determinists use primate studies to support their arguments. How valid is evidence based on different species of primates? On invertebrates?

3. Discuss from your own experience whether males have bonds while females do not. Evaluate the role of culture in bonding.

4. Many of the determinist arguments are based on average differences between the sexes. Discuss whether this is a valid basis for making distinctions.

5. Many feminists argue that even if the determinist position can be used as an historical explanation for male dominance, it is irrelevant in an era of advanced technology (machines replacing muscle power, birth control, etc.). Discuss.

6. If anthropologists "discovered" the existence of egalitarian societies or matriarchies, what implications would this have for biological determinism?

CURRENT RESEARCH INTO BIOLOGICAL AND PSYCHOLOGICAL SEX DIFFERENCES

Much of the writing of the biological determinist school makes such sweeping assertions that it is essential to present a careful survey of the most recent research on biologically based sex differences. The works by Maccoby and Jacklin, and Money and Ehrhardt survey and evaluate the complex literature in the field. Bleier exposes the conceptual flaws in how much of the sociobiological case is framed and tested, while the articles by Rossi and her critics highlight the debate among feminist scholars about the relative importance of biology and culture in explaining human social organization.

Readings for Students
Gross, Harriet Engel. Introduction to "Considering 'A Biosocial

Perspective on Parenting.'" *Signs* 4, no. 4 (Summer 1979): 695–717.

Lambert, Helen H. "Biology and Equality: A Perspective on Sex Differences." *Signs* 4 (Autumn 1978): 77–117.

Oakley, Ann. *Sex, Gender and Society,* Chaps. 2, 3, 5, 6. While generally sound, Oakley's views on the origin of homosexuality should be read with some skepticism.

Rossi, Alice. "A Biosocial Perspective on Parenting." *Daedalus* 106, no. 2 (Spring 1977): 1–22.

Sayers, Janet. *Biological Politics.*

Tavris, Carol, and Carole Offir. *The Longest War: Sex Differences in Perspective.* New York: Harcourt Brace Jovanovich, 1977.

Readings for Instructors

Baker, Susan W. "Biological Influences on Human Sex and Gender." In *Women: Sex and Sexuality,* edited by Catharine R. Stimpson and Ethel Spector Person. Chicago: University of Chicago Press, 1980.

Bleier, Ruth. *Science and Gender.*

Hrdy, Sarah. *The Woman That Never Evolved.*

Leibowitz, Lila. *Females, Males, Families: A Biosocial Approach.* North Scituate, Mass.: Duxbury Press, 1978.

Lloyd, Barbara, and John Archer. *Exploring Sex Differences.* New York: Academic Press, 1976.

Maccoby, Eleanor Emmons, and Carol Nagy Jacklin. *The Psychology of Sex Differences,* Chap. 7. Stanford: Stanford University Press, 1974.

Moncy, John, and Anke A. Ehrhardt. *Man and Woman: Boy and Girl,* Chaps. 6–8. Baltimore: Johns Hopkins University Press, 1972.

Sherman, Julia. *Sex-Related Cognitive Differences: An Essay on Theory and Evidence.* Springfield, Ill.: Charles C. Thomas, 1978.

Tanner, Nancy. *On Becoming Human.*

Lecture Topics

The Psychology of Sex Differences (Maccoby and Jacklin). A review of over 1,200 works, covering such key areas as intellect and achievement (perception, learning, memory, intellectual abilities, cognitive styles, achievement motivation, and self-concept) and social behavior (temperament, social-approach-avoidance, and power relationships), reveals that measurable and proven sex differences are few. Maccoby and Jacklin conclude that boys may be more aggressive and excel in visual-spatial ability, while girls excel in verbal abilities. Helen Lambert's article assesses the most recent research in this area in a form useful for students. Teachers desiring a more detailed study should turn to Lloyd and Archer.

Endocrinologic Studies (Money and Erhardt). Studies of biological abnormalities are crucial in illuminating the relative roles of biology and culture (or environment) in shaping gender identity and behavior. Studies of hermaphrodites, for example, show the enormous power of childrearing practices in masking the effects of genetic sex coding.

Biological Critiques of Sociobiology (Tanner, Hrdy, Bleier). Much of the case against biological determinism will be developed in subsequent sections on anthropology. Ruth Bleier's key work, a feminist critique of biology, should be mentioned at the outset. Bleier details the influence of contemporary culture on so-called "objective" biological science, in its conceptualizations, hypotheses, observations, and conclusions. She also analyzes logical leaps and flaws in sociobiological arguments, and surveys current research on the evolution and development of the human brain.

Feminists, including Bleier, have also attempted alternative reconstructions of the sex roles of our Upper Paleolithic ancestors. Tanner and Hrdy have tackled evolutionary theory with stimulating though controversial reformulations.

Feminist Biosocial Science: Alice Rossi and the Parenting Controversy. The relative importance of "nature versus nurture" in shaping human behavior is an unsettled issue among feminist scholars. While most feminists writing about sex differences have tended to assign secondary or, occasionally, no importance, to nature or biology as an explanation for differential male-female status, there are those like Alice Rossi who dissent from the mainstream feminist view. In a provocative essay, Rossi argues that there are real and important biological differences between the sexes that cannot be minimized when interpreting the past or developing future policy. She cites what she believes to be a hormonally or chemically based maternal-infant bond as an example of a biological determinant of differential sex roles in parenting. Some of Rossi's critics question the research findings on which her assertions are based. Others argue against her conclusions on political grounds: They view her theory as a new formulation of the old notion that, for women, biology is destiny. Depending on the sophistication of the students, the Rossi controversy may be easily adapted to a discussion format.

Discussion Questions

1. What parts of the biological determinist argument, if any, hold up to the conclusions of Maccoby and Jacklin and of Money and Erhardt? Are Rossi's arguments supported or invalidated by these works?

2. Assuming that Maccoby and Jacklin's conclusions are correct, in what areas would you expect males and females to excel? Does this assumption correspond to reality? Why or why not?

3. What are the stereotypes of male and female behavior in American society? How do you conform to or deviate from them? Why? What cultural forces or particular family dynamics may have shaped your sex-role behavior?

4. Compare Oakley's conclusions with those of Maccoby and Jacklin on sex differences. Where do they differ? Where do they agree? What tests might be conducted to evaluate who is right in areas of disagreement?

5. Discuss Lambert's assertion that "the important matters for feminists to address would seem to be not the cause of sex differences, but how much of our collective resources should be devoted to equalizing and in what respects . . ." ("Biology and Equality," 116).

6. If Rossi is correct in arguing that there are real and important biological factors underlying differential male-female roles, what can or should social policy do to ensure equal status for men and women?

FREUD AND HIS FEMINIST CRITICS

For decades, Freud's theories of female sexuality and associated psychological development have been used as "scientific" justification for male domination and female subordination, despite Freud's own admission that his analysis of female development was unsatisfactory and incomplete. The following brief analysis of Freud is intended to provide an understanding of the context in which Margaret Mead and others argued for the importance of cultural conditioning in personality development.

Readings for Students

Freud, Sigmund. "Some Psychical Consquences of the Anatomical Distinction Between the Sexes" (1925), and "Femininity" (1933). In *Women and Analysis*, edited by Jean Strouse. New York: Grossman, 1974.

Mead, Margaret. "On Freud's View of Female Psychology." In *Women and Analysis*.

Mitchell, Juliet. "On Freud and the Distinction Between the Sexes." In *Women and Analysis*.

Readings for Instructors

Chodorow, Nancy. *The Reproduction of Mothering: Psychoanalysis and the Sociology of Gender*. Berkeley: University of California Press, 1978

Gallop, Jane. *The Daughter's Seduction: Feminism and Psychoanalysis*. Ithaca, N.Y.: Cornell University Press, 1983.

Masson, Jeffrey. *The Assault on Truth: Freud's Suppression of the Seduction Theory*. New York: Farrar, Straus and Giroux, 1984.

Mitchell, Juliet. *Psychoanalysis and Feminism*. New York: Random House, 1974.

Lecture Topics

Freud's Concept of Female Personality Development.[1] In the same years in which Margaret Mead conducted her path-breaking cross-cultural studies of sex and temperament, Sigmund Freud published his mature deliberations on the nature of woman, derived from years of observation of his female patients. Freud articulated a brand of anatomical determinism, reverberations of which are still felt in the psychoanalytic profession. Central to Freud's theory of female development is the concept of woman as castrated male.

According to Freud, two complex processes mark the progress of the girl-child into a mature woman. The first of these involves a shift in the girl's "erotogenic zone" from the clitoris to the vagina. The second, and linked process, is marked by a shift in the object of a girl's love from her "pre-Oedipal" love of her mother to Oedipal love of her father. Sometimes Freud distinguished these stages as an early masculine phase followed by the mature feminine phase of personality. The "fantasy of being seduced by the father (is) the expression of the typical Oedipus complex in women," declared Freud.

The traumatic event that impels a girl to rearrange her affection is the sight of the genitals of the opposite sex. "They at once notice the difference. . . . They feel seriously wronged, often declare they 'want to have something like it too,' and fall victim to 'envy for the penis.'" The girl in short, discovers she is castrated, and she holds her mother responsible for her castration, feeling that she is being punished for something. She turns to father for the gift of the missing penis; she reaches maturity when the wish for a penis is replaced with a wish for a baby. At the same time, "mortified by the comparison with the boy's far superior equipment and in consequence, she renounces her (childhood) masturbatory satisfaction for her clitoris." She reaches a vaginal stage of sexuality, and "passivity now has the upper hand."

Deprived of the superior penis, "envy and jealousy play an even greater part in the mental life of women than of men," Freud claimed. He also saw "shame" as intrinsic to the female character, the origin of which is concealment of genital deficiency. Shame, masked as modesty, also drove women to make their own historical mark: "Women have made few contributions to discoveries and inventions in the history of civilization; there is however, one technique which they may have invented—that of plaiting and weaving" in order to cover their embarrassing lack. The anatomical differences between the sexes thus expresses itself in both psychical consequences and social evolution.

Critics of Freud's Methodology. The collection of essays in Strouse's *Women and Analysis* provides an excellent dialogue between Freud and his critics, including feminist and contemporary responses. The points of attack have been multifaceted: Freud's culturally biased viewpoint in which he saw late Victorian stereotypes of female behavior as normal; the limited sample—women who had sought psychoanalytic help—on which he based his theory; his lack of evidence for bold assertions; his now clinically disproven theory of female sexual development from clitoral to vaginal; and, most recently, his scientific objectivity and even honesty have come under scrutiny.

In *The Assault on Truth: Freud's Suppression of the Seduction Theory,* Jeffrey Masson challenges the foundations of psychoanalysis by a bold claim: that Freud abandoned his belief in female patients' stories of seduction by their male relatives in order to protect his friend, Dr. Wilhelm Fliess. The story centers on one of Freud's first analytic patients, Emma Eckstein, who was suffering from painful menstrual symptoms. Fliess, whom Freud consulted for medical expertise, subscribed to the theory that sexual problems could be cured through nasal surgery. According to Masson, Fliess botched an operation on Emma's nose, resulting in severe hemorrhaging. Instead of criticizing Fliess's surgical skills, Freud came to the defense of his friend, ultimately deciding that Emma's nosebleed was an hysterical reaction from past traumas rather than a physical reaction to present events. Thus Masson's thesis: that Freud abandoned his seduction theory for personal reasons, and in doing so denied the validity of the real experience of Victorian women:

> In fact, in my opinion, Freud had abandoned an important truth: that sexual, physical, and emotional violence is a real and tragic part of the lives of many children.

Masson goes on to link Freud's denial of reality to that of modern psychoanalysts, who continue to interpret women's memories of abuse as Oedipal fantasy.

Reclaiming Psychoanalysis. Juliet Mitchell's reexamination of Freud presents a complex argument that runs counter to the usual feminist critique of psychoanalytic theory. She attempts to reclaim psychoanalysis as an intellectual instrument to be used in the analysis of women's oppression: "Psychoanalysis is not a recommendation for a patriarchal society, but an analysis of one" (xv).

The book is divided into two main parts. The first contains a highly detailed explication of Freud's overall work, with his theory of femininity understood in that general context. The second part turns to a critique of Wilhelm Reich and of R. D. Laing, and concludes with an examination of contemporary feminist critiques of Freud. The book closes with Mitchell's own historical analysis of patriarchy.

While students will find this work to be difficult reading, it remains an original and insightful contribution to feminist thought. Mitchell shows that we can use the understanding developed by Freudian psychoanalysis to explain the condition of women in patriarchy and to fully appreciate "how femininity is lived in the mind."

Another imaginative reworking of a psychoanalytic framework may be found in Nancy Chodorow's work.

Discussion Questions
1. Assuming Freud's observations of female personality to be accurate, what cultural explanations might also explain the behavior and attitudes he witnessed?

2. Discuss Freud's methodology. Does his focus on disturbed individuals who had come to him for treatment affect the generalizability of his conclusions? Why or why not?

3. According to Mead's essay, how have her views of Freud changed? What does she see as his essential error?

4. Why does Mitchell conclude that Freud's 1925 essay provides the key to understanding the oppression of women under patriarchy?

5. Compare Masson's view of Freud with Mitchell's critique. How do their conclusions differ?

ESTABLISHING THE ROLE OF CULTURE: THE WORK OF MARGARET MEAD

Margaret Mead was among the first anthropologists to demonstrate the importance of cultural factors in human development. Inspired by Franz Boas, her teacher at Columbia University, Mead's early work was an explicit attempt to deny the inevitability of biology and inherited characteristics.

To accomplish this, she set off for Samoa in 1925 to study female adolescence. There she discovered that adolescent behavior differed considerably from that found among American teenagers. While Americans made a difficult transition into adulthood, Samoans moved through this part of the life cycle relatively effortlessly. The ultimate reason for these differences was to be found not in biology but in culture. Similarly in New Guinea, where she found many definitions of masculinity and femininity, Mead once again demonstrated the range and importance of cultural variability. Thus, in *Sex and Temperament* and in *Male and Female,* Mead not only questioned the validity and revealed the narrowness of Freudian concepts, she also made the point that culture as well as biology had an important role to play in the determination of sex differences in personality. However, while her work has revealed the importance of culture as a determinant of human behavior, neither Mead nor most other so-called cultural determinists overlooked the constraints imposed by biology.

Mead's autobiography, *Blackberry Winter,* provides some insight into the early influences on her career. Her descriptions of her fieldwork, if less than candid or complete, are nevertheless fascinating reading. Moreover, it becomes clear that Mead was always comfortable adopting and advocating controversial positions. From her early work on adolescence and sex-role socialization to her later years when she assumed the stance of cultural critic, Mead was lively and outspoken. While an early round of the nature/nurture debate took place in the twenties and thirties, the current interest in sociobiology demonstrates that for many there has yet to be a conclusive resolution. Mead's work has come under renewed scrutiny. Recently, her methods, conclusions, and theoretical biases have been attacked by Derek Freeman. She has had no dearth of passionate, articulate defenders.

Readings for Students
Mead, Margaret. *Coming of Age in Samoa.* New York: William
      Morrow & Co., 1973.
————. *Sex and Temperament.* New York: Dell, 1963.

Readings for Instructors
Mead, Margaret. *Blackberry Winter.* New York: Simon and
      Schuster, 1972.
————. *Letters from the Field 1925–75.* New York: Harper and
      Row, 1977.
"In Memoriam Margaret Mead." *American Anthropologist* 82, no. 2
      (June 1980).

Biological Determinism and Cultural Variability

Mead's autobiography, *Blackberry Winter,* demonstrates what Mead was to devote her life to proving—the significance of the environment in shaping and molding the individual. While less than totally honest or revealing of her private life, and especially of her loving relationship with Ruth Benedict, as recently revealed by the latter's daughter, *Blackberry Winter* nevertheless vividly portrays the individuals and events that influenced and channelled the young Mead's intellectual development. Her commitment to understanding cultural differences can be more clearly understood in light of her early experiences at home, at school, and later at Columbia. In her letters, her published accounts of her fieldwork, and in her autobiography, Mead emerges as a strong, decisive personality, committed to making a contribution.

Mead's early fieldwork was undertaken at a time when biological determinism and eugenics (programs for the genetic "improvement" of humanity) dominated American intellectual circles. Such biological determinism ran counter to both her earlier experiences and her formal anthropological training, where she had learned of cultural variability, not biological inevitability. Her Samoan study, reaching a large and diverse audience, scored a decisive victory for the cultural determinists.

Reading for Students
Mead, M. *Coming of Age in Samoa.*

Readings for Instructors
Barnouw, V. *Culture and Personality.* 3d ed. Homewood, Ill.: The
   Dorsey Press, 1979.
Freeman, Derek. *Margaret Mead and Samoa: The Making and
   Unmaking of an Anthropological Myth.* Cambridge: Harvard
   University Press, 1983.
Mead, M. *Blackberry Winter.*
————. *Social Organization of Manua.* Repr. of 1930 edition.
   Millwood, N.Y.: Kraus Reprint.
Shore, Bradd. *Sala'ilua: A Samoan Mystery.* New York: Columbia
   University Press, 1982.

Lecture Topics

Mead's Early Life. In *Blackberry Winter,* Mead emphasizes the importance of her grandmother and father. Receiving scant formal education until she entered college, Mead was encouraged to learn a variety of skills in her early years, all the while revelling in her family's conviction that there was "nobody quite like Margaret." The young Mead observed and recorded the behavior of her younger siblings and participated in her mother's study of Italian immigrants. Mead thus had early influential experiences of understanding and documenting cultural differences.

Cultural relativism and variability were to become even more important to her as she undertook her studies with Boas and Benedict at Columbia. It was to demonstrate the importance of culture that Mead traveled to Samoa.

Mead's Samoan Research. In the two monographs that resulted from her Samoan research, Mead provided an ethnographic description of a South Seas culture that captivated the American public. She asserted that in this culture, life was undemanding and noncompetitive; young adolescent girls had no more onerous responsibilities than to dance and to make love. In the concluding chapters of *Coming of Age in Samoa,* she attributed the differences between American and Samoan adolescence to differences in the social structure and demands of the two cultures. Thus she made it clear that there was no biological mandate for the course of the life cycle.

The instructor should also emphasize Mead's field methods, a point that concerns Mead in her autobiography. While innovative, they have become an issue raised by several anthropologists, particularly Derek Freeman (see discussion below).

Critiques of Mead's Samoan Studies. The major criticisms of Mead's early work raise questions about her methodology. She lived in a naval dispensary for a very short period of time (by modern standards) without adequate language proficiency. Moreover, the historical context is never fully set out in Mead's writings. Samoa was far from untouched and unaffected by Western contact. Braroe (cited by Barnouw) suggests that the casual, easygoing Samoans depicted by Mead may well have been reacting to the collapse of the social structure in the face of Western contact. In other Pacific societies, deeper scrutiny often reveals tensions and conflicts beneath the surface serenity.

Discussion Questions
1. What particular questions did Mead address in *Coming of Age in Samoa?*
2. What conclusions does Mead reach on the basis of her study? Do you agree with her conclusions? Do her data provide an adequate base from which to draw the conclusions that she does? What other conclusions might she have drawn?
3. Compare Samoa with Ifaluk. Do you think there might be similar conflicts in Samoa?
4. What is the role of the *taupo* in Samoan society? How is her experience related to that of the adolescent girls?
5. What concerns about field methods does Mead express in *Blackberry Winter?* Does she resolve these successfully in her Samoan researches?

6. Discuss the early influences on Mead's life. What effect did these have on her later intellectual development? What biases do you as an individual bring to your current study? How may biases be minimized? Should they be?

7. Why was Mead drawn to Boas and Benedict? What intellectual position(s) did they hold? How did these coincide with her earlier beliefs?

8. It has been argued that Mead could have reached the same conclusions had she studied American adolescents. Why did Mead select Samoa? Discuss her disagreement and ultimate compromise with Boas.

Men and Women

Mead's work was often directed toward issues that occupied the public mind. By travelling overseas to produce evidence from an exotic culture or by adducing examples from the seven societies in which she had done fieldwork, Mead consistently demonstrated the relevance of cross-cultural knowledge and the primacy of cultural forces. In *Sex and Temperament* (a study of three New Guinea societies) and in *Male and Female* (a discussion of the seven Oceanic cultures in which she had worked) Mead discussed the interrelationship between gender, biology, culture, and personality. It is clear from these studies that Mead is far from being a rigid cultural determinist; on the contrary, she maintains that biological considerations impinge heavily on gender ideology. While Mead championed the importance of culture and sought to deny biological tyranny, she was far from being an explicit advocate of women's causes.

Readings for Students
Mead, Margaret. *Sex and Temperament.*

Readings for Instructors
Barnouw, Victor. *Culture and Personality,* Chap. 5.
Gewertz, Deborah. "A Historical Reconsideration of Female Dominance Among the Chambri of Papua New Guinea." *American Ethnologist* 8, no. 1 (1981): 94–106.
Mead, Margaret. *Male and Female.* New York: William Morrow & Co., 1975.
Sanday, Peggy. "Margaret Mead's View of Sex Roles in Her Own and Other Societies." *American Anthropologist* 82, no. 2 (1980): 340–48.

Lecture Topics

Sex and Temperament. In *Sex and Temperament* Mead demonstrated that temperament is neither instinctive nor innate, but is rather a matter of cultural conditioning. Her three examples—the Arapesh, the Mundugumor, and the Tchambuli—demonstrate that differences in personality vary cross-culturally and would appear not to be gender linked. Moreover she also provided examples of the variety of tasks each sex is capable of assuming. Such variety provided conclusive evidence for the importance of cultural factors. She writes, "The material suggests that we may say that many, if not all, of the personality traits which we have called masculine or feminine are as lightly linked to sex as are the clothing, the manners, the form of headdress that a society at a given period assigns to either sex." Yet even here, Mead recognized the interaction of biology and culture.

The neat fit between her conclusions and her data have raised some serious concerns (see Barnouw). Once again her methodology is open to question. But as Mead matured, and as anthropology became more rigorous, she was aware of her own limitations and often acknowledged them.

Male and Female. In the 1950s Mead addressed the problem of cultural variation within a distinctly biological framework. While still admitting variation, Mead concluded that it is men's work that universally bears the seal of cultural legitimacy. Her analysis is complex, depending on, but ultimately inverting, Freudian notions. Girls learn early that they will be mothers. For boys, the realization that they cannot procreate in the same manner leads them to turn their attention to achievement. Masculine cultural elaborations are then male compensations for not being able to reproduce.

Feminism and American Sex Roles. As an anthropologist Mead felt it was essential to use her experience of the exotic to inform American society. As a columnist for *Redbook* and in a variety of public forums Mead discussed contemporary America. She eschewed labels, writing "In a sense I was never a feminist. I made friends of women. I stood by women and if I was asked to do something that might improve the position of women in general I did, but I've never had a chip on my shoulder." In *Sex and Temperament* she tells us that it would be a mistake to deny or attempt to eradicate sexual differences. Instead, she suggested that we increase the number of individual options, rather than limit potential through rigid stereotyping.

Peggy Sanday has written,

> Margaret Mead was, still is and will continue to be as Betty Friedan puts it "the symbol of the woman thinker in America." Her writing influenced American popular thinking at many levels . . . Had Mead retained the position of *Sex and Temperament,* she might have passed on to the popular culture a truly revolutionary vision of women finally free to realize their full capabilities. Mead did not fully abandon her earlier point of view; she simply did not speak as vigorously for sex-role choice in her later years" (347).

Discussion Questions

1. What specific questions does Mead address in *Sex and Temperament?* What relevance did she attach to her findings for American sex roles?

2. How does Mead account for the differences in standardized personality types that she found in the three societies she studied in *Sex and Temperament?* Evaluate her explanation.

3. What cultural factors in Samoa or New Guinea reinforce or suppress male aggression?

4. Is there evidence of male bonding in these societies? Describe. Does bonding lead to dominance as Lionel Tiger suggests? Is there evidence of female bonding? Describe.

5. Does woman's reproductive role necessarily remove her from economic production in these societies? Compare your findings with those of Scheinfeld.

6. What correlations do these societies show between physical strength and status? Compare your findings with those of the biological determinists.

7. What do you see as the key factors leading to high or low female status in each society? When women's roles are devalued, is this culturally or biologically determined?

8. In the last chapter of *Sex and Temperament,* Mead suggests that American society has granted dominance to women. What do you think she means by this? Do you agree? Why or why not?

9. What do you see as the intellectual, political, or other significance of Mead's data and her theoretical explanation of the data for women's lives today? Do you think her work is less significant for women in the eighties than for women in the thirties?

10. What roles do women play economically in the societies described by Mead? Do economic contributions, or control of resources, affect female status?

Derek Freeman and Margaret Mead: Biology and Culture Reconsidered

In 1983, amid much attention in the national media, Derek Freeman published *Margaret Mead and Samoa: The Making and Unmaking of an Anthropological Myth*. Were this simply another critique of Mead, it could easily be subsumed under the earlier discussion of Mead's critics. However, as the book makes somewhat larger claims and has received so much attention, the instructor should examine both Freeman's purpose in writing this book at this time and his critical review of Mead's work.

Readings for Instructors
Freeman, Derek. *Margaret Mead: The Making and Unmaking of an Anthropological Myth*. Cambridge: Harvard University Press, 1983.
Marcus, George. "One Man's Mead." *The New York Times Book Review*. March 27, 1983.
Rensberger, B. "Margaret Mead: The Nature-Nurture Debate: From Samoa to Sociobiology." *Science '83* (1983): 28–46.
Schneider, David. "The Coming of a Sage to Samoa." *Natural History* 92, no. 6 (June 1983): 4–10.

Lecture Topics

The Foundations of Freeman's Critique. Freeman argues that in the midst of the nature/nurture debate in the twenties and thirties Mead produced her Samoan case study as a negative instance of the importance of biology as a determinant for human behavior. Thus, he maintains that cultural determinists subsequently had a clear field upon which to promulgate their doctrines. His goal is to prove Mead incorrect and to assert therefore that cultural determinism enjoyed an illegitimate ascendancy.

To this end Freeman divides his book into four parts. In the four introductory chapters Freeman traces the emergence of cultural determinism and Mead's contribution to the renunciation of a biological model. Part two summarizes Mead's work and her methods, while part three refutes her findings by placing them against data that have been gathered by other anthropologists. Part four is a two-chapter conclusion.

In sum, he presents a picture of Samoa very much at odds with Mead's portrayal in *Coming of Age in Samoa*. Freeman's Samoans are fierce, competitive, and puritanical. According to Freeman, Mead's methods were far from adequate for the task she set herself. He further maintains that in her determination to assert the primacy of culture, she was led astray by the counterfeit exaggerations of young Samoan girls. What does Freeman hope to prove? Schneider has written: "I think we must conclude that the main if not the only object of this book is to attack Margaret Mead and that the method for doing that is to show, first that other people did not agree with many of her findings on Samoa and second, that she reached conclusions with which Freeman disagrees."

How Successful Is Derek Freeman's Criticism? It is significant that when two anthropologists have reviewed the book in the popular media they have started off their reviews with "this is a work of great mischief" (Marcus) and "This is a bad book" (Schneider). Freeman has angered rather than convinced anthropologists. There are several reasons for this:

1. He oversimplifies and misrepresents the anthropological position on biology. Far from being contentious, the position that he advocates is largely accepted by the anthropological establishment. Moreover, the notion that biology and culture are separate but interrelated is, as Marcus points out, a legacy of the victory of Franz Boas over the extreme hereditarians.

2. While he may demonstrate that Samoans are different from the way in which Mead depicted them, he ultimately attributes Samoan behavior not to biology, but to socialization. Is he not then reaffirming the position he has set out to attack?

3. Mead's methods were not without their weaknesses; Freeman's no doubt are better (although Schneider raises some questions about this). Schneider points out that faulty data need not necessarily produce faulty con-

clusions. By debunking Mead's data, Freeman is not
necessarily discrediting her view that cultural factors
shaped Samoan adolescence.

The Importance of Freeman's Work. Recently, sociobiology has
received considerable attention. Its major proponents claim that
human behavior can be understood in terms of genetic guidelines.
In the public mind, Freeman's book has become the major work to
deny the contribution of culture. It is essential that students realize that the book does no such thing. The book attacks Margaret
Mead by offering another interpretation of Samoan behavior and
cultural practices. The explanation provided by Freeman is preeminently cultural. Moreover, even were he to have demonstrated
that Mead's work was unequivocally invalid, he has still left untouched generations of cultural determinists who have made quite
enduring contributions. Finally, if Mead was the product of a
particular political climate, Derek Freeman represents another.
Freeman, as well as Mead, demonstrate that the questions we ask
and the answers we find are functions of particular historical and
social contexts. Schneider writes: "Freeman's book is not a serious,
scholarly work but an unscientific personal attack on Margaret
Mead, who stands, in the eyes of many, for rationalist values. It is a
work that celebrates a particular political climate by denigrating
another."

Questions for Discussion
1. Why do you think Freeman wrote this book? In what
   ways does he challenge Mead?

2. Compare Freeman's and Mead's views on the relative
   importance of biology and culture. How much of a
   cultural determinist is Mead and how much of a biological determinist is Freeman?

3. It is relatively rare for anthropological arguments to be
   fought in the mass media. Why do you think Derek
   Freeman's book has received so much attention?

4. Are there alternative explanations for the different descriptions of Samoan behavior offered by Freeman and
   Mead?

5. Examine the development of Mead's methods. How do
   her later studies differ from her Samoan study?

FEMINIST PERSPECTIVES ON PERSONALITY

In recent years feminist psychologists have suggested new approaches to the general question of the role of culture in the determination of sex differences in personality. Among many recent scholars, we have selected Nancy Chodorow both for the intrinsic interest of her ideas, especially as a critic of Freud, and for her cross-cultural approach to personality development. In studying Chodorow's work, and the other supplementary articles included in the readings, students should begin to understand how this scholarship differs from and builds upon the work of Mead and Freud. Although we have presented Chodorow's work here within the context of psychoanalytic theory and the work of culture and personality theorists, it could just as easily be included with the gender stratification theories developed in Chapter Four.

Supplementing the Chodorow article in the Readings for Students is an ethnographic counter-argument by Alice Schlegel, based upon her work among the Hopi. We have also included an article by Bardwick and Douvan on American male/female socialization for those who wish to promote discussion based on the students' own experiences.

Readings for Students

Bardwick, Judith M., and Elizabeth Douvan. "Ambivalence: The Socialization of Women." In *Woman in Sexist Society,* edited by Vivian Gornick and Barbara K. Moran. New York: New American Library, 1972.

Chodorow, Nancy. "Family Structure and Feminine Personality." In *Woman, Culture, and Society,* edited by Michelle Zimbalist Rosaldo and Louise Lamphere. Stanford: Stanford University Press, 1974.

Schlegel, Alice, ed: Male and Female in Hopi Thought and Action." In *Sexual Stratification: A Cross-Cultural View,* 245–69. New York: Columbia University Press, 1977.

Readings for Instructors

Chodorow, Nancy. "Being and Doing: A Cross Cultural Examination of the Socialization of Males and Females." In *Woman in Sexist Society.*

O'Leary, Virginia. *Toward Understanding Women.* Monterey, Cal.: Brooks/Cole Pub. Co., 1977.

Lecture Topics

The Intellectual Problem. While Chodorow accepts Mead's argument that cross-culturally there are no constant personality differences among men and women, she nevertheless argues that to a greater or lesser extent each society differentiates on the basis of sex. The criteria may differ, but they do differentiate. Deliberate socialization, therefore, is a deficient explanation for the persistence of differences in male and female personalities. Nor does socialization, according to Chodorow, account "for the extent to which psychological and value commitments to sex differences are so emotion laden and tenaciously maintained" ("Family Structure," 43). She suggests the following explanation of why a distinction between "male" and "female" is central to the individual's sense of self in any culture, and also why the female is consistently devalued.

Role of Mothering in Personality Formation. Chodorow argues that universally women are largely responsible for early child care. Depending upon the culture, men may play some part in childrearing, but comparatively speaking they are more remote than the mother. Because boys lack a readily and consistently observable sex-role model, and parts of their father's lives, especially work, are not directly observable in the early years, the development of a secure gender identity is more problematic for boys than for girls. Masculinity is "elusive," and boys often come to define their masculinity "largely in negative terms, as that which is not feminine or involved with women" ("Family Structure," 50). Feminine identity, in contrast, is more easily learned by direct observation and identification with the mother. Dependency and difficulty in developing a sense of an autonomous self become difficult issues for girls, but their gender identity is secure.

Devaluation of the Female. Masculine gender identity involves, among other things, a denial of attachment to the mother, and repression and devaluation of female aspects of the male's personality. This accounts for the devaluation, dread, and fear of women found in many cultures that are dominated by men.

Discussion Questions
1. Discuss Chodorow's view that "It is easier for girls to achieve a feminine identity than boys to attain a masculine identity."

2. What solutions to the problem of the devaluation of femininity does Chodorow propose? Do you think they will work? Why or why not?

3. How do Bardwick and Douvan's views, as presented here, compare with those of the biological determinists? Of Freud?

4. What similarities and differences do you see between Bardwick and Douvan's arguments and those of Chodorow? What does your own experience tell you?

5. Test Chodorow's theory against any ethnographic studies you have read, including the Schlegel article. How are women and men viewed among the Hopi? What are Hopi childrearing practices? Are the Hopi egalitarian?

6. Discuss the relationship of Chodorow's views to those of Mead and Freud. How does she differ from or expand upon earlier work?

7. Discuss the stereotypes of male and female present in American society as outlined by Bardwick and Douvan. Are they still prevalent in the '80s? Are there differences by race and class?

Notes

1. All quotes are from Sigmund Freud, "Femininity" (1933), in *New Introductory Lectures on Psychoanalysis*, trans. James Strachey (New York: W.W. Norton and Co., 1965). Reprinted in Rosemary Agonito, *History of Ideas on Woman: A Source Book* (New York: Putnam's, 1977), pp. 299–322.

CHAPTER TWO

MALE DOMINANCE: MYTH OR REALITY?

Margot I. Duley and Karen Sinclair

Considerable controversy surrounds the debate over whether male dominance has been a universal historical and cross-cultural feature of societies. A minority viewpoint asserts that matriarchies existed in the past, but despite the popularization of this theory among some sectors of the American feminist movement, many feminist anthropologists are not convinced. We shall examine the nineteenth-century origins of matriarchy theory, and the ideological biases that underlie the debate.

The existence of egalitarian societies in the past is only slightly less disputed. Feminist scholars, especially those influenced by Marxist socioeconomic analysis, are forcing a serious debate on the issue. We examine their assertions and the counter-reply. Then, while acknowledging that universal male dominance may well be disputed, we trace its apparent emergence or intensification in a variety of societies. This approach, which attempts to relate women's status to varying levels of food technology, while common in anthropological literature, has recent challengers as well. We shall briefly consider some reformulations.

The instructor should stress to students that in examining the issue of male dominance and its origins there are no easy answers. Indeed there are important differences on the questions that should be asked, and many disputes about "fact." This presents many opportunities to encourage critical thinking, and to help students to see both the power and limitations of particular modes of analysis.

By way of introduction it would be well to define the technological typologies used by anthropologists. They are: hunting-gathering (including fishing); horticultural (gardening by clearing land through slash and burn techniques, and planting and harvesting by hand tools); agricultural (based on cultivation by plows on land that is terraced, drained, or irrigated); pastoral (based on herding and, usually, trade); and industrial.

BIAS IN ANTHROPOLOGY

Anthropology's development as a discipline was influenced by the prevailing intellectual and political assumptions of Victorian England. Evolutionary theory was used to support the argument that the social order of Victorian England, as well as her ascendancy as a colonial power, represented the triumph of civilization over man's natural baseness. These views were of course androcentric as well as ethnocentric, and assumed the subordination and domestication of women to be part of this natural order. Feminist anthropologists now argue that the development of anthropology in this cultural milieu explains, in part, why men were thought to be the only significant social actors. They have reexamined and reinterpreted old data in light of this hypothesis, considered the ways in which Western values may distort the contribution of women in other cultures, and discussed the particular problems women anthropologists confront.

General Readings on Bias in Anthropology
Ardener, Edward. "Belief and the Problem of Women." In *Perceiving Women*, edited by Shirley Ardener. New York: Wiley, 1975.
Fee, Elizabeth. "The Sexual Politics of Victorian Social Anthropology." *Feminist Studies 1* (Winter/ Spring 1973): 23–39.
Rogers, Susan Carol. "Woman's Place: A Critical Review of Anthropological Theory." *Comparative Studies in Society and History* (January 1978): 123–73.
Tiffany, Sharon. "Models and the Social Anthropology of Women: A Preliminary Assessment." *Man* 13 (1978): 34–51.

Readings for Students
Bujra, Janet. "Women and Fieldwork." In *Women Cross-Culturally: Change and Challenge*, edited by Ruby Rohrlich-Leavitt. The Hague: Mouton, 1975. The section on "Women in Anthropology" contains a number of useful articles.
Nelson, Cynthia. "Public and Private Politics: Women in the

Middle Eastern World." *American Ethnologist* 1 (1974): 551–
63.
Rohrlich-Leavitt, Ruby, Barbara Sykes, and Elizabeth Weather-
ford. "Aboriginal Woman: Male and Female Anthropological
Perspectives." In *Toward an Anthropology of Women,* edited by
Rayna R. Reiter. New York: Monthly Review Press, 1975.

Readings for Instructors
Bovin, Mette. "The Significance of the Sex of the Fieldworker
for Insights into the Male and Female Worlds." *Ethnos* 31,
Supplement (1966).
Etienne, Mona, and Eleanor Leacock, eds. *Women and Coloniza-
tion: Anthropological Perspectives.* New York: Praeger Pubs.,
1980.
Golde, Peggy, ed. *Women in the Field.* Chicago: University of
Chicago Press, 1966.
Goodale, Jane. *Tiwi Wives.* Seattle: University of Washington
Press, 1971.
Kaberry, Phyllis. *Aboriginal Woman: Sacred and Profane.* London:
Routledge & Kegan Paul, 1939.
Powdermaker, Hortense. *Stranger and Friend: The Way of an
Anthropologist.* New York: W. W. Norton & Co., 1966.
Scheper-Hughes, Nancy. "Introduction: The Problem of Bias in
Androcentric and Feminist Anthropology." *Women's Studies*
10, no. 2 (1983): 109–16.
Strathern, Marilyn. *Women in Between: Female Roles in a Male
World: Mount Hagen, New Guinea.* London: Seminar Press,
1972.
———. "Domesticity and the Denigration of Women, or Nature
and Culture out of Place." In O'Brien, Denise, and Sharon
Tiffay. *Rethinking Women's Roles.* Berkeley: University of
California Press, 1984.
Sutton, Constance, Susan Makiesky, Daisy Dwyer, and Laura
Klein. "Women, Knowledge and Power." In *Women Cross-
Culturally: Change and Challenge.*
Weiner, Annette B. *Women of Value, Men of Reknown: New Perspec-
tives in Trobriand Exchange.* Austin: University of Texas Press,
1976.

Lecture Topics

New Interpretations of Old Data. As the new scholarship began
to suggest the variety of roles women assumed in different

cultures, older material was reexamined and reanalyzed. Certain cultures in which women were presumed to be submissive pawns in extensive male manipulations proved, upon reexamination, to reveal hitherto unnoticed or unreported dimensions of female participation.

Western Bias and the Status of Women. Some scholars argue that paradigms used to explain female status may be biased by certain assumptions. For example, the concept of universal female subordination may in part reflect Western cultural bias, with its denigration of domesticity and devaluation of informal power. Recent studies argue that the imposition of Western values on non-Western cultures has led to an underestimation of the impact of women on social life.

Ahistorical Biases. Several Marxist anthropologists, of whom Eleanor Leacock is the leading spokesperson, criticize the basically ahistorical approach of anthropology. There is a tendency to treat the present circumstances of so-called traditional cultures as if they were identical to past circumstances, and to assume that these societies are static. In fact, hunting-gathering, horticultural, and traditional peasant societies have been altered by many years of direct and indirect contact with the outside world. We cannot assume, as many have done, that the present set of relationships between men and women are necessarily those of the past, and efforts to analyze the origins of gender stratification may be seriously flawed by failing to recognize this fact. Leacock and others assert that there were hunting-gathering peoples in Australia and Canada, and horticultural people in the eastern United States, West Africa, and the lowland forests of South America who were egalitarian in both their socioeconomic and gender systems in precolonial times. This ahistorical approach has warped our understanding of the central role played by women in "simple" societies. (See also the discussion of egalitarian societies, below.)

Women as Anthropologists. The study of women has often been accorded second-class status within anthropology. Bujra describes the problems involved both for women field workers and for anthropologists who chose to study women's issues:

> We assumed that studying a society did *not* mean studying women because *men* were the only real actors in important spheres of social activity. We greeted with hostility the suggestion that we study

women for it carried the implication that we were second-rate researchers, not fit for anything else, not capable of dealing with men's
worlds.

Many professional women caught in similar dilemmas have found
themselves alienated from the study of women's experience.

Discussion Questions
1. Do Victorian views of other cultures, women, and progress continue to shape the world view of the Euro-
   American West?

2. Can scholarship be "culture-free"? If it can't be, is one
   view simply as good as another? What values, especially
   unexamined ones, do you bring to the study of other
   cultures? Of women? Of men?

3. What biases might feminist anthropologists bring to their
   subject? Would radical feminists, liberal feminists, Marxist feminists, etc. have different stakes in particular
   findings?

METHODOLOGICAL ISSUES

A further difficulty in discussing the status of women is methodological. How does one measure status? What are the
determinants of status? How reliable are anthropological data?
Students might be encouraged to tackle these questions by attempting to build a simple model of female status and the factors
affecting it, based on their cross-cultural reading to date and on
their knowledge of United States society. This material lends itself
to discussion, which should occur before students tackle any of
the technical and statistically sophisticated articles listed below.
Teachers might caution students about some of the methodological difficulties of model-building, such as understanding
the difference between cause and effect and between dependent
and independent variables, and remembering to interpret data
within the context of the culture from which it came.

Readings for Students and Instructors
Sanday, Peggy R. *Female Power and Male Dominance: On the Origins
of Sexual Inequality.* Cambridge: Cambridge University Press,
1981.

————. "Female Status in the Public Domain." In *Woman, Culture, and Society,* edited by Michelle Zimbalist Rosaldo and Louise Lamphere. Stanford: Stanford University Press, 1974.
Stewart, Abigail J., and David G. Winter. "The Nature and Cause of Female Suppression." *Signs* 2 (Spring 1977): 531–53.
Whyte, Martin King. *The Status of Women in Preindustrial Societies.* Princeton: Princeton University Press, 1978.

Each of the suggested readings approaches the question of the status of women from a different perspective. Stewart and Winter, through factor analysis and multiple regressions, illustrate a standard statistical method for testing various theories about female status. More recently, Whyte, taking a broader sweep, statistically analyzes various hypotheses about female status, using data from ninety-three societies, ranging from hunting-gathering bands to peasant communities. His largely negative results suggest that no single factor determines the status of women cross-culturally. However, critics have questioned Whyte's conclusions, based as they are on a restricted sample of societies that largely omits African examples, where the correlation between status, economic contribution, and control of property seems clearer.

In discussing these articles, instructors might point out the limitations of the Human Relations Area Files on which most statistical surveys are based. Data on over 250 societies have been coded for the running of cross-tabulations. However, generalizations about preindustrial societies based on this data are suspect for reasons we have already discussed; most of these societies have in fact already been altered by outside influences, and observer bias in evaluating the position of women is pervasive in anthropological studies.

Sanday (1981), among others, also raises a basic methodological issue that goes beyond the deficiencies of the data base. She finds in her more recent work that "examining various patterns of male dominance and female power in particular historical and cultural settings told me a great deal more than the skeletal information contained in statistical associations" (xvi). Yet the statistical findings helped to inform the questions raised in her contextualized work, which we will examine in greater depth. Meanwhile Sanday's early work remains important. In a pioneering approach she attempted to correlate the status of women with their contributions to subsistence. She found that female production is a "necessary but not sufficient condition for the development of (high) female status." Women must not simply work, for that can imply an exploitive situation: they must control some valued resource, good, or service. These qualifications are important for Sanday has had many misinterpreters.

Finally the usage of the word "status" itself must be analyzed carefully. Status is scarcely a concrete, fixed attribute. Many have suggested it really is a composite and interactive concept. Sanday, for example, suggests a series of dimensions along which it can be considered: female authority/power in the domestic domain; female authority/power in the public domain; respect accorded to females in the domestic/public spheres; and differential treatment of females/males in the public domain. An individual woman's "status" may also vary with age or economic circumstance. These definitional issues are of central importance.

Discussion Questions

1. Stewart and Winter use the nation-state as a unit of comparison. How might this frame of reference affect their results?

2. Compare Sanday's and Whyte's findings. Are they consistent? Why or why not?

3. Discuss the possible effects of observer bias on all of these studies.

4. How are "status" and "power" defined in each of the studies? How do these definitions affect the conclusions reached? What is the difference between "power" and "authority" and "influence"? How might women have one but not another?

5. What are some of the strategies that "powerless" women might use to manipulate or to survive in an oppressive social system? Can informal power be quantified?

6. Is there such a thing as a comprehensive status or are there only separate statuses in a number of spheres (domestic, religious, political, etc.)?

7. What specific problems do women field workers face? How does gender sometimes work to their advantage?

8. Is there any validity to the assertion that the informal power often wielded by women is commensurate with the formal authority of men?

9. Why is the bias of Victorian anthropology so clear today, and so unclear to those nineteenth-century Victorian gentlemen? Might studies done in the 1980s be as seriously flawed? What biases might Marxist anthropologists bring to their studies? What of "mainstream" anthropologists? Feminist anthropologists? How can we minimize our biases?

MATRIARCHAL SOCIETIES

This section will assess the continuing debate over the existence of matriarchal societies in which women rule over men. The debate has polemical overtones in that the existence of matriarchies would, of course, refute the universal male dominance theories of the biological determinists. Special attention will thus be paid to the ideological presuppositions of writers on both sides of the controversy.

Reading for Students
Bamberger, Joan. "The Myth of Matriarchy: Why Men Rule in Primitive Society." In *Woman, Culture, and Society.*

Readings for Instructors
Bachofen, J. J. *Myth, Religion and Mother Right.* Translated by Ralph Mannheim. Bollinger Series, vol. 84. Princeton: Princeton University Press, 1967.
Borun, Minda et al. *Women's Liberation: An Anthropological View.* Pittsburgh: KNOW, Inc., 1971.
Cavin, Susan. *Lesbian Origins.* San Francisco: Ism Press, 1986.
Davis, Elizabeth Gould. *The First Sex.* New York: Putnam's, 1971.
Diner, Helen. *Mothers and Amazons.* New York: Julian Press, 1975.
Gough, Kathleen. "The Origin of the Family." In *Toward an Anthropology of Women.*
Hammond, Dorothy, and Alta Jablow. *Women: Their Familial Roles in Traditional Societies.* A Cummings Module in Anthropology, no. 57. California: Cummings Pub. Co., 1975.
Mellaart, James, *Catal Hüyük: A Neolithic Town in Anatolia.* New York: McGraw-Hill, 1967.
Pomeroy, Sarah B. "A Classical Scholar's Perspective on Matriarchy." In *Liberating Women's History,* edited by Berenice A.

Carroll. Urbana: University of Illinois Press, 1976.
Rorhlich, Ruby. "State Formation in Sumer and the Subjugation
of Women." *Feminist Studies* 6, no. 1 (Spring 1980) 76–102.
Spretnak, Charlene, ed. *The Politics of Women's Spirituality.* Garden
City, N.Y.: Doubleday Anchor Press, 1982.

Lecture Topics

Nineteenth-Century Anthropological Findings on Matriarchy.
The idea of a matriarchal society in which women dominated men
dates back to the work of several nineteenth-century anthropologists, most notably J. J. Bachofen, whose *Das Mutterrecht*
first appeared in 1861. Bachofen argued that in an early stage of
society, associated with the invention of agriculture by women,
women ruled both the private and public domains, while religion
was centered upon the Earth Goddess. Property passed to children through their mothers. This "primitive" matriarchal stage
was, according to Bachofen, replaced by a "higher" stage of
cultural evolution—patriarchy.

Twentieth-Century Feminist Cultural Nationalists. Although
most modern anthropologists reject the idea of matriarchy and
argue that Bachofen and others confused the existence of matrilineal inheritance with matriarchy, a number of current feminist writers have revived the idea. Both Davis and Diner, for
instance, claim that women were dominant in earlier times. Their
conclusions are cited by some feminists in making demands for
contemporary female liberation. Neither Davis nor Diner is an
anthropologist. The work of most of their feminist colleagues who
are anthropologists suggests that their case is built on shaky
ground.

Feminist Scholarship on Matriarchy. A number of feminist anthropologists and historians have resifted the evidence for matriarchal societies and have found it wanting. Hammond and
Jablow argue that the nineteenth-century use of the concept of
matriarchy was as biased, from an opposite perspective, as that of
modern pro-matriarchists. They argue that the concept of a lower
order of matriarchy, which was replaced by a superior patriarchal
system, was popular because it reinforced Victorian notions of
male superiority.

Pomeroy's more restricted study examines evidence for matriarchy in the Heroic or late Bronze Age of Greek history (2100–
1400 B.C.), whose classical legends, including those about Ama-

zons, influenced Bachofen. She finds the data inconclusive at best. Casting a wider net, Bamberger, Gough, and the KNOW group critically survey the anthropological evidence for matriarchal and/ or egalitarian societies and find it deficient. Finally the pioneering and widely respected study of prehistoric Anatolia by Mellaart, whom Davis selectively mined for evidence, may usefully be read by the instructor in the original to reveal some of the flaws in Davis's reasoning. The most that Mellaart's meticulous scholarship shows is that neolithic Anatolian children were buried with their mothers, and that mother goddesses were worshipped. From this one may be justified in concluding that the society was matrilineal and matrilocal. Rohrlich, a much more careful researcher than Davis, asserts it was egalitarian.

On balance, the evidence seems to suggest that feminists should not rely on matriarchies to bolster their case against biological determinists. However, the debate over matriarchies is not a static one. A new work, *Lesbian Origins*, by Susan Cavin musters enough empirical evidence to inject a note of rigor into the matriarchal side. Cavin argues for the existence of all-female societies at the dawn of human history, building her hypothesis on variables (sex-ratios, sex segregation, incest taboos) found in the Human Relations Area Files. Thus, the debate continues to be a lively one.

Discussion Questions
1. Discuss the difference between matriarchal, matrilineal, patriarchal, and patrilineal societies. How would you expect the status of women to differ in each system?

2. After evaluating the evidence for and against the existence of a matriarchal society, what is your conclusion?

3. It has been said that the matriarchy controversy is a lesson in the distorting effects of ideology on scholarship. Do your own ideological biases affect the way you evaluate data and reach conclusions?

4. What positive and negative purposes might the "myth of matriarchy" serve?

EGALITARIAN SOCIETIES

Some anthropologists, including some who reject the idea of matriarchy, nevertheless believe that a rough equality between males and females has existed, especially in hunting-gathering societies. In this section we will examine both the proponents and the opponents of this view.

Readings for Students
Bacdayan, Albert S. "Mechanistic Cooperation and Sexual Equality among the Western Bontoc." In *Sexual Stratification: A Cross-Cultural View,* edited by Alice Schlegel. New York: Columbia University Press, 1977.

Etienne, Mona, and Eleanor Leacock, eds. *Women and Colonization.*

Friedl, Ernestine. *Women and Men: An Anthropologist's View.* Basic Anthropology Units. New York: Holt, Rinehart & Winston, 1975.

Leacock, Eleanor Burke. "Women in an Egalitarian Society: The Montagnais-Naskapi of Canada." In *Myths of Male Dominance,* 33–81. New York: Monthly Review Press, 1981.

Rosaldo, Michelle Zimbalist. "Women, Culture and Society: A Theoretical Overview." In *Woman, Culture, and Society.*

Sacks, Karen. "The Case Against Universal Subordination." In *Sisters and Wives: The Past and Future of Sexual Equality.* Urbana: University of Illinois Press, 1982.

Shostak, Marjorie. *Nisa: The Life and Words of a !Kung Woman.* New York: Vintage, 1983.

Tiffany, Sharon W. *Women, Work and Motherhood: The Power of Female Sexuality in the Workplace.* Englewood Cliffs, N.J.: Spectrum Books, Prentice-Hall, 1982.

Readings for Instructors
Collier, Jane F., and Michelle Zimbalist Rosaldo. "Politics and Gender in Simple Societies." In *Sexual Meanings: The Cultural Construction of Gender and Sexuality,* edited by Sherry B. Ortner and Harriet Whitehead. Cambridge: Cambridge University Press, 1981.

Dahlberg, Frances, ed. *Woman the Gatherer.* New Haven: Yale University Press, 1981.

Draper, Patricia. "!Kung Women: Contrasts in Sexual Egalitarianism in Foraging and Sedentary Contexts." In *Toward an Anthropology of Women.*

Kehoe, Alice B. "The Shackles of Tradition." In *The Hidden Half,* edited by Patricia Albers and Beatrice Medicine. Washington, D.C.: University Press of America, 1983.

Lamphere, Louise. "Review Essay: Anthropology." *Signs* 2, no. 3 (Spring 1977): 612–27.

Martin, M. Kay, and Barbara Voorhies. *Female of the Species,*
   Chap. 7. New York: Columbia University Press, 1975.
O'Kelly, Charlotte G. *Women and Men in Society.* New York: Van
   Nostrand, 1980.
Rapp, Rayna. "Review Essay: Anthropology." *Signs* 4, no. 3
   (Autumn 1979): 497–513.
Reiter, Rayna Rapp. "The Search for Origins: Unraveling the
   Threads of Gender Hierarchy." *Critique of Anthropology* 3, no.
   9–10 (Spring 1975): 5–24.
Sanday, Peggy R. *Female Power and Male Dominance.*

Lecture Topics

Egalitarian Societies: Fact or Fiction? The issue of egalitarian
societies is a lively one, with many "established facts" now open to
question. Much of the debate revolves around whether some
hunter-gatherers provide illustrations of societies in which women
and men have equal and complementary power. The received
view that male dominance is universal is reflected in Ernestine
Friedl's widely adopted text *Women and Men*. We use this interpretation as a baseline for subsequent discussion. A more recent
treatment by Sharon Tiffany provides an alternative avenue to
getting at the same issues. Tiffany's short, well-written text presents the debate over egalitarianism, and she is sympathetic to the
questioners of universal subordination. Like Friedl, however, she
utilizes the common technological classifications of societies as the
framework in which to analyze women's status. She sees the interrelationship between women's work as mothers (which varies
widely throughout the world) and work outside the home as
critical analytic categories within the technological framework in
explaining women's status. This framework is also undergoing
challenge. For the moment, however, we will consider the case
that stratification intensifies with increasing complexities of social
organization, following Friedl's general line of reasoning.

Hunting-Gathering Societies. Stratification in general is limited
in such societies because nomadism sets limits upon accumulations
of wealth. Inheritance is not significant and in most such societies
a high degree of sexual freedom is permitted to both sexes; men
and women can engage in premarital sex, choose their own
spouses, and take lovers after marriage or even separate from
their spouses. Leadership is vested in persuasive, gifted, skillful,
or forceful individuals, regardless of sex, and is based on consent
rather than coercion. However, there is one important area of

gender-based advantage: males monopolize large game hunting when it is done in groups. This sexual division of labor Friedl attributes not to men's size, running ability, or aggressiveness— characteristics in which there is overlap between the sexes—but to women's function as childbearers: gathering is more compatible with the care of young children or pregnancy. Meat is a unit of extradomestic exchange; it is valued more highly than gathered foods; and through the hunt men are more likely to come into contact with the outside world and monopolize trade or external relations. Male dominance is greatest where the highest percentage of total food is provided by hunting (for example among the Eskimo).

Horticultural Societies. Stratification increases. The major strategic resource is land or rights to the use of land. Population density is higher, and protecting the land at its borders from encroachment by neighboring groups is crucial. Organized warfare is common, and much male energy is expended in war or in preparation for war. Because women are the bearers of children, men's lives are more expendable. Hence men dominate warfare. Because warfare is a life and death activity on which the group's survival depends, it acquires high prestige.

However, there are significant variations in the status of women and the quality of male-female relationships according to how a society reckons descent and residence rules for married couples. In patrilineal descent-reckoning with virilocal residence, the bride enters her husband's household, and she adds by childbearing to her husband's kin group. She is an outsider and is subject to controls. In matrilineal groups with uxorilocal residence, men strengthen their wives' lines; they are dependent upon their sisters and their sisters' husbands to strengthen their own kin group. Women are entitled to support from brothers and fathers, as well as from their husbands in return for sexual services. They also establish long-term cooperative relationships with their own sisters and mothers. There is less hostility and tenseness in male-female and female-female relationships. Overall, however, Friedl sees increased sexual stratification in horticultural societies—external relations, extradomestic exchanges of food, and trade are more likely to be dominated by men.

Critiques of the Friedl Position. A number of anthropologists have challenged the view that all hunter-gatherers and horticulturalists have had gender hierarchies. The most thoroughgoing critiques have come from Eleanor Leacock, Mona Etienne, contributors to the *Women and Colonization* volume, Karen Sacks, Peggy Sanday, Alice Kehoe, and Albert Bacdayan. These anthropologists assert that there were egalitarian hunting-gathering and horticultural societies, in terms of both gender and socioeconomic structures, prior to colonial contact. A substantial amount of work has been done that attempts to reconstruct the egalitarian basis of North American Indian Society. Leacock's own work documents how seventeenth-century Jesuit missionaries made the introduction of the European family structure and the importation of "chiefs" part of their "civilizing mission" to the Naskapi, whom she claims were hitherto egalitarian. Other researchers outline similar developments, stemming from the growth of trade, among the Algonkian (Robert Grumet), the Seneca (Diane Rothenberg), and the Bari of Columbia (Elisa Buenaventura-Posso and Susan Brown).

The growth of trade, it is argued, is crucial to the growth of hierarchy, bringing with it economic specialization (as certain people produce valued goods for exchange), and economic dependence (as the household or clan is no longer economically self-sufficient). Coupled with the arrival of the modern trader was the importation of European notions of hierarchy through legal codes, religious ideology, the expropriation of land forcing many people into wage labor, and systems of land tenure based on individual ownership. The resulting hierarchy affects many men. However, women are particularly damaged because men are favored in land tenure, technology, education, and access to cash and loans.

The assertion that hunting-gathering societies are egalitarian is included in the studies of Martin and Voorhies, who selected ninety foraging societies from Africa, Australia, and the Americas as their cross-cultural laboratory; and Draper, who examined the hunting and foraging !Kung of the Kalahari Desert of southwest Africa. Lamphere, however, challenges Draper's views by pointing to what she believes is incipient and actual gender stratification among the !Kung.

On the other hand, Friedl's assumption that men inevitably control big game hunting has recently been undermined by the discovery of women hunters among the Agra Negritos of northeast Luzon, the Phillipines (see "Woman the Hunter: The Agta" by Agnes Estioko-Griffin and P. Bion Griffin in Dahlberg).

The debate over egalitarianism continues. Leacock and others have undoubtedly demonstrated the intensification of stratification and the profound alteration of hunting-gathering horticultural societies by the penetration of capitalism and market

forces. But the historical documents available to precisely reconstruct precolonial social structures are far from satisfactory. The
traveller and missionary accounts, as well as oral traditions on
which the researcher must rely, contain important gaps and many
biases. Much work remains to be done.

Critiques of Technological Classifications. Instructors should
also be aware that although most anthropological literature relies
on technological classifications of societies (i.e., hunting-gathering, horticultural, agricultural, pastoral, and industrial), there are
inadequacies in this approach when correlations are drawn to
women's status. The categories are imprecisely defined: the term
horticultural, for example, subsumes a wide variety of ecological
demands (from root crops in West Africa to rice growing in Asia
to cereal crops in North America, to mention just a few). More
precise work by cultural geographers on the sexual division of
labor is needed.

Peggy Sanday's stimulating work (1981) illustrates a new conceptual approach that bypasses existing technological frameworks. Rejecting the notion of universal male dominance, she
instead poses the question, under what circumstances do female
power and male power arise? She finds evidence of female power
(domestic and public) in fairly diverse societies including the
foraging Mbuti and the Ashanti Kingdom, based on matriclans.
She argues, refining Sherry Ortner (see Chapter 4, "Toward a
Theory of Gender Stratification," above), that where the forces of
nature are sacrilized, women's maternal role is valued, and women
are seen as having "inherent power." She finds male power in
societies dominated by environmental stresses. Throughout she
distinguishes between an ideology or myth of male dominance,
and the actual situation.

Egalitarianism as a Concept. Finally we must be alert to the
cultural blinders we wear in searching for evidence of
egalitarianism. Those influenced by mainstream Euro-American
culture may look for indications of the existence of individual
autonomy, personal choice, freedom from exclusive family responsibilities, mobility, and independence (financial and otherwise) in deciding whether women are equal to men. These,
however, may be wholly inappropriate concepts when studying a
society constructed upon principles of interdependence and collective identity. As Sharon Tiffany puts it, women in many societies "are not totally 'free' to do exactly what they want at
anytime; but, neither are men" (121). In a sense this is a good case

for interactive gender studies. It is also a warning that the concept of equality must be examined subtly in culturally specific ways, and that a feminist prescription to achieve equality in one context may well have to be reformulated for another.

Discussion Questions

1. Tiger and Fox argue that our sex roles have been set by early hunting societies and there have been too few subsequent generations for significant behavioral changes to have occurred. Current sex roles are in this sense seen as natural. Evaluate this argument in light of male and female roles and personalities depicted in the hunting-gathering societies you have studied.

2. If the factors isolated by Draper and Martin and Voorhies do in fact lead to egalitarianism in hunting-gathering societies, what changes in our own society might similarly promote the equality of women?

3. Does Draper's work support a biological determinist, interactionist, or cultural model of sex-role development? What conclusions would you reach based solely on Leacock's work?

4. Evaluate Lamphere's criticism of Draper's work, particularly her assertion that "the !Kung may not be as egalitarian as Draper suggests, and that these inequalities could be explained by economic or social factors without resorting to biological explanations" ("Review Essay," 615).

5. How does the life of Nisa confirm or refute the arguments of those who believe hunter-gatherers are egalitarian? What evidence, if any, is there of sexual stratification? How are men valued? How are women valued? Has this society been changed from the outside?

6. What do women in this country and Nisa have in common? Where do they differ?

7. How compelling is the evidence of precolonial egalitarian societies presented by Leacock and Etienne? How are precolonial societies reconstructed methodologically? Evaluate this methodology.

8. Compare and contrast Friedl's explanation of male control of the hunt with that of the biological determinists. Which account is more convincing? Why?

9. How does the discovery of women hunters among the Agta Negritos modify Friedl's theory, if at all?

10. How comprehensive are Bacdayan's measures of equality among the Bontoc? How compelling is the evidence of egalitarianism in his article and in Sacks?

11. If Bacdayan's assertion that "mechanistic cooperation" is a key element in sexual equality, what public policy implications might this have in our own society?

12. Discuss the implications of Sacks's argument that part of the conceptual problem in recognizing that sexual equality existed is that many sociologists have been "defining or conceptualizing equality in a slippery way: whatever women lack is the critical marker" (94).

13. Compare Sack's evidence of female power, and the cultural adaptations made to female reproduction with Alice Rossi's views above.

14. How compelling is Sanday's evidence of egalitarianism?

15. Sanday argues that "male dominance evolves as resources diminish and as group survival depends increasingly on the aggressive acts of men" (210). Are we back to a form of biological determinism (Chapter 1)? Why or why not?

16. We have used the phrase "hunting-gathering" societies. Given women's maternal roles and contributions to subsistence, should we instead have said "gathering-hunting" ones? Discuss this and any other examples of how an assumption of male importance shapes societal descriptions.

AGRICULTURAL AND PASTORAL SOCIETIES

If the existence of egalitarian hunting-gathering and horticultural societies is debatable, there is nonetheless widespread agreement about the existence and elaboration of gender inequalities in more complex forms of social organization. Here we will give a brief overview of the status of women in agricultural and pastoral societies. This should provide a broad context for students to use in interpreting traditional cultures discussed in

Part II. The status of women in modernizing societies will be discussed in the next chapter, "Women and Development."

Readings for Students
Any field study of an agricultural or pastoral society that gives particular attention to the role of women in that society.

Readings for Instructors
Eisenstein, Zillah R., ed. *Capitalist Patriarchy and the Case for Socialist Feminism*. New York: Monthly Review Press, 1979.
Friedl, Ernestine. *Women and Men*, Part I; or Tiffany, Sharon. *Women, Work and Motherhood*, Chaps. 3–5.
Mackinnon, Catharine A. "Feminism, Marxism, Method, and the State: Toward Feminist Jurisprudence." *Signs* 8, no. 4 (1983): 635–58. See also "Comments." *Signs* 10, no. 1 (1984): 168–88.
Martin, M. Kay, and Barbara Voorhies. *Female of the Species*, Chaps. 8–10.
Ortner, Sherry, and Harriet Whitehead, eds. *Sexual Meanings*.
Rapp, Rayna Reiter. "Gender and Class: An Archeology of Knowledge Concerning the Origin of the State." *Dialectical Anthropology* 2, no. 4 (1977): 309–16.
———. "Women, Religion and Archaic Civilizations: An Introduction." *Feminist Studies* 4, no. 3 (1978): 1–6.
Rohrlich, Ruby. "State Formation in Sumer and the Subjugation of Women." *Feminist Studies* 6, no. 1 (1980): 76–102.
Sacks, Karen. *Sisters and Wives*.
Sanday, Peggy R. *Female Power and Male Dominance*.

Lecture Topics

Agricultural Societies. The great traditional civilizations of the West, the Middle East, China, India, and Latin America were based on this form of food production. Agriculture is distinguished from horticulture by the use of draft animals (or machines) rather than the simple hoe or digging stick. Food production yields are higher, permitting higher population densities.

In agricultural societies we see a growing complexity of social organization. Large agricultural surpluses permit the formation of state systems with bureaucracies and centralized political controls. Complex patterns of socioeconomic stratification arise, such as caste and class. There is a growth (some would argue an emergence) of gender stratification. Among the areas in which the form and symbols of gender hierarchy arise are:

1. Increased sexual division of labor;

2. Growth of differential control over exchange, political power, land, property, and participation and control of ritual;

3. Decreasing female contributions to subsistence, and a food surplus produced and distributed by males. (There are, however, class differences in female labor contributions);

4. Increased restriction of women to the domestic sphere and non-wage labor;

5. Increased restrictions, indeed control, of women's sexuality and reproductive functions, and increased concern with inheritance rights;

6. Growth in differential patterns of boy-girl role socialization;

7. Growth of differential personal autonomy and self-esteem in general between men and women;

8. Growth of an elaborate ideology of female subordination and submissiveness, embodied and sanctioned by religion.

Pastoral Societies. These societies are found in central and southwest Asia, the northern Sahara, and Sudanic and eastern areas of Africa. Pastoral societies tend to be male-dominant, although variations in female status do occur. Characteristically, males control the ownership, distribution, and tending of animals, while women make only a small contribution to subsistence (dairying and farming), if any.

State Formation. The importance of state formation is alluded to in a number of the studies we have already mentioned. Some scholars have attempted to probe the issue more deeply. Rayna Rapp writes that "kinship structures were the great losers in the civilizational process" (1977: 310). She, Karen Sacks, and Ruby Rohrlich, among others, have analyzed from varying ideological perspectives the complications of this for the status of women. Sacks gives a Marxist-feminist interpretation: "Where strong ruling classes eclipse the control of kin groups over productive means, they erode women's claims as sisters (i.e., women's relations to production based on kin group membership) and lead thereby to women's exclusive dependence as wives" (243). Rohrlich presents what might broadly be termed a radical feminist perspective in state formation arguing that "a critical factor in state formation is the emergence of patriarchy," taking as a case in point the development of gender stratification in Sumer, the earliest state society thus far unearthed. She does not, however, diminish the importance of class. Rohrlich sees class and gender stratification going hand in hand: As class society "became increasingly competitive over the acquisition of commodities, primarily luxury goods for elites, and for control over the trade routes, warfare became endemic, and eventually led to the centralization of political power in the hands of a male ruling class" (99).

Rapp, while acknowledging the importance of centralized authority replacing smaller kinship structures and its control of resources formerly vested in a kin group, is cautious about any simple correlations based on a limited sample of case structures. She points to instances (Sparta, Rome during the Second Punic War) where women gained during prolonged warfare, and where trade has not always existed in male hands.

These studies focus on archaic state formation and many more specific case studies are needed. There are of course numerous theoretical studies of the influence of modern state structures on women. Radical feminists see the modern state as an epiphenomenon, produced by the patriarchal base of society, the rule of the father writ large. To socialist feminists, the capitalist state is embedded in the patriarchal nuclear family wedded to the needs of capitalism (Mackinnon, Eisenstein).

Over the past few centuries the Third World has become what Rapp describes as "a bloody laboratory in which stratification by culture, class and gender occurred." The study of women in what is euphemistically termed "development" in the Third World provides telling and sometimes tragic insights into the relationship between new centralized bureaucracies, collapsing kinship systems, market economies, and gender stratification. These processes are in many instances different than archaic state formation, but they do illustrate the connection between alterations in state structures, cosmologies, local economies, and the status of women.

Discussion Questions

1. Friedl argues that men dominate warfare, not because of greater average physical strength but because society can better survive the loss of men than women. Can this assertion be proven? Does it matter to the outcome of the debate over biology versus culture?

2. Compare the status of the "nonworking" housewife in the United States with that of the Eskimo women mentioned by Friedl, who contribute negligible amounts to the food supply. Compare Friedl's view of the status of Eskimo women with that of Sacks (89). What might account for the differences?

3. Friedl argues that "the Women's Movement which stresses equality of opportunity for women in managerial and administrative positions is profoundly right from the standpoint of equalizing the public power of the sexes" (*Women and Men*, 136). Discuss in light of correlations between economic and political power and the status of women suggested in the readings.

4. Compare the status of women as described in any field study of an horticultural, agricultural, or pastoral society with the model presented in the instructor's lecture. What are the similarities and differences? What explains them?

5. Some people regard the progression from hunting-gathering and horticultural to agricultural societies as just that—"progression." What is meant by progress? What has been the effect of this "progress" on women?

6. What accounts for the apparent increasing subordination of women in hunting-gathering, horticultural, and agricultural societies?

7. Compare Sanday's findings (1974) on women in the public domain with actual female status in any hunting-gathering, horticultural, agricultural, or pastoral society you have studied.

8. Sanday (1981) argues: "Give women access to sacred roles and much else will change" (12). Discuss.

9. Is the state an epiphenomenon of economics, patriarchy, religious ideology, or what?

10. Do women invariably have more input into decision making in kin-based groups than in elaborated states?

11. What class-based status differences are to be found among women in any of the field studies you have read?

CHAPTER THREE

WOMEN, COLONIALISM, AND DEVELOPMENT

Margot I. Duley and Susan Diduk

The impact of modernization, especially on women, is literally a life and death issue for millions. United Nations statistics put the current status of women in stark perspective: "While they represent 50 per cent of the world population and one-third of the official labor force, they [account] for nearly two-thirds of all working hours, receive only one-tenth of the world income and own less than one percent of world property." Almost two out of every three illiterates in the world are female.[1] An indispensable guide to these and other statistics on the global condition of women is to be found in:

Boulding, Elise, and Shirley Nuss, et al. *Handbook of International Data on Women*. Beverly Hills: Sage Publications, 1976.

The history of how this situation has come to pass is a complex one. The risk of overgeneralization is large, and at times discussion is best grounded in area studies. However, in the contemporary period a common theme emerges in many parts of the Third World: The cultural and economic forces of industrialization and Western imperialism interacted with the existing social order in ways that often increased stratification along gender (and class) lines. In fact, the economic decline of many societies brought under the embrace of the world capitalist economy has been well documented. The Area Studies in this volume contain historically and culturally specific examples. We will, however, deal with the more general themes in this chapter.

For many years, during colonialism and in the post-independence period, little or no attempt was made to integrate women into development plans. Planners directed their attention to industrialization, rural development, educational expansion, and even family planning, with little regard for the consequences of their policies on women. Improvements in the lives of women were—and in many cases still are—assumed to be largely by-products of general national development. Where improvements did not occur for women, the problem was seen to be a consequence of imperfect integration of women into development. Those operating within this mental framework, capitalist and socialist planners alike, often dismissed demands for women's programs as special pleading, a mechanical imitation of Western "women's lib," needlessly divisive and even antinationalist. "As the nation progresses, so will women," the argument went, and some development agencies still echo this refrain.

This chapter first analyzes the progressive assumptions of early modernization theorists, and then surveys more recent feminist research that challenges the belief that general economic growth is a sufficient condition for the betterment of women's lives. Dependency theory offers persuasive support to this latter argument. Also the demands articulated by women in international forums suggest that despite the differences of race, class, ideology, and national power that divide women, a profound worldwide revolution of expectations is underway. We also consider the different priorities that Third World and Western feminists may have. Finally, the chapter reviews some of the obstacles to the integration of women into development plans. This chapter completes our survey of the status of women in a variety of social structures.

Studies of women in development that call many of the early theoretical assumptions into question have proliferated during the 1970s and 1980s, largely as by-products of the United Nations Decade on Women. For the instructor who wishes to go beyond the readings suggested here, we recommend the following bibliographical sources:

Al-Rihani, Mary. *Development as if Women Mattered: An Annotated Bibliography with a Third World Focus.* Washington, D.C.: Overseas Development Council, 1978.

Bibliographical Guide to Studies on the Status of Women, Development and Population Trends. London: Eastern Press, 1983.

Buviníc, Mayra. *Women and World Development, an Anotated Bibliography.* 2 vols. Washington, D.C.: Overseas Development Council, 1976.

Cebotarev, E. Z. (Nona), and Frances M. Shaver. *Women and Agricultural Production*. Special Edition: *Resources for Feminist Research/Documentation sur la Recherche Feministe*. Toronto: Ontario Institute for Studies in Education 2 (March 1982).

Charlton, Sue Ellen M. *Women in Third World Development*. Boulder, Colo.: Westview Press, 1984. A quick reference to key concepts and debates, Charlton provides a well-balanced discussion and chapter-by-chapter lists of supplementary readings.

Nwanosike, Eugene O. *Women and Rural Development: A Select and Partially Annotated Bibliography*. Buea, Cameroon: Regional Pan African Institute for Development, West Africa, 1980.

Saulniers, Suzanne Smith. *Women in the Development Process: A Select Bibliography on Women in Sub-Saharan Africa and Latin America*. Austin: Institute of Latin American Studies, University of Texas, 1977.

University of Wisconsin. *Women in Rural Development: A Bibliography*. Madison: Land Tenure Center, University of Wisconsin, 1979.

Vavrus, Linda Gire, with Ron Cadieux, comp. *Women in Development: A Selected Annotated Bibliography and Resource Guide*. East Lansing, Mich.: College of Education, Non-Formal Education Information Center, 1980.

WIN News. Edited by Fran P. Hosken, Women's International Network, 187 Grant St., Lexington, Mass. 02173. Though occasionally polemical, *WIN News* provides a very useful compilation of news items and publications, including official reports, from around the world that might otherwise be missed by the nonspecialist.

TRADITIONAL MODERNIZATION THEORY AND THE STATUS OF WOMEN

There has been widespread disagreement about what happens to women in non-industrialized societies facing fundamental social change. Before the 1970s modernization theory, premised upon "social evolutionary" suppositions, argued that such societies could improve the standard of living of their inhabitants by emulating the industrialized world. Its proponents saw industrialization as coterminous with modernization. Societies following the path of Western industrial modernization would open greater opportunities and participation to men and women alike in all aspects of contemporary society. The work of C. E. Black and S. N. Eisenstadt is typical of this position, and indeed reflects a more general bias in contemporary Euro-American thought that history is ultimately progressive and that the West provides *the* model of progress. For if Western industrialized societies are seen to have achieved development in the form of improved living standards, educational access, and the like, then their agenda for progress and development needed only to be emulated. Feminist scholars have also on occasion shared the assumption that "modernization" would bring improved options for women, and we have included an early essay of Janet Giele's as representative of such arguments. Development planning that was based largely on these assumptions rarely examined the possible impact of such policies upon women, whether in the colonial or post-independence period, nor did it critically examine the real position of women in the West.

Readings for Students

Anand, Anita. "Rethinking Women and Development." In *Women in Development: A Resource Guide for Organization and Action,* ISIS Women's International Information and Communication Service. Philadelphia: New Society Pubs., 1984, pp. 5–11.

Huston, Perdita. *Third World Women Speak Out: Interviews in Six Countries on Change, Development and Basic Needs.* New York: Praeger Pubs., 1979.

Roodkowsky, Mary. "Women and Development: A Survey of the Literature." In ISIS, *Women in Development,* pp. 13–21.

Readings for Instructors

Black, C. I. *the Dynamics of Modernization.* New York: Harper Torch Books, 1967.

Eisenstadt, S. N. "Modernization: Growth and Diversity." In *Tradition, Change and Modernity,* edited by S. N. Eisenstadt. New York: Wiley, 1973.

Elliot, Carolyn M. "Theories of Development: An Assessment." *Signs* 3, no. 1 (Autumn 1977): 1–8.

Lecture Topics

Assumptions of "Social Evolutionary" Modernization Theories.
The theory postulates that all cultures or societies can be rated on
a scale, ranging from "primitive" to "modern," based on the degree of specialization within a society.

1. So-called "simple" or "primitive" societies are those in
   which the same persons or institutions perform multiple
   functions. There is minimal differentiation between domestic and public spheres since they are merged.

2. "Modern" industrialized societies are characterized by
   complex and specialized organizational structures and a
   division of labor. Criteria for judging a society in terms
   of its state of modernization include: formal, complex
   political systems; an industrialized economy; personal
   mobility; and status based on individual achievement
   rather than ascription at birth.

3. "Social evolutionary" theory assumes that women's status
   improves with modernization. It emphasizes the replacement of physical work by intellectual labor, and often
   attributes the origins of gender inequality to differences
   in physical strength between the sexes. With Western
   education, it is argued, women will be "emancipated" by
   entry into professional, managerial, and clerical occupations. At the same time, modern legal systems will put
   men and women on the same footing (see Black).

Discussion Questions

1. Compare the experiences of Third World women, as
   expressed in Huston's book, with the predictions of modernization theory. What evidence do you find to support
   or refute the social evolutionists?

2. Is the status of women lower or higher in non-industrial
   or in industrial societies? In what respects? Can we speak
   of "a" status?

3. Is "modern" or "Western" better for women than "traditional" society? According to what value system?

4. How "modern" is the United States, measured against the social evolutionists' ideal type of modern state?

5. What assumptions do missionaries, the Peace Corps, U.S. Aid programs, and the like, share with the social evolutionists or imperialists, if any?

6. Discuss with students their understanding of the words "backward," "traditional," "primitive," "modern," and "developed," pointing out the cultural biases that underlie their usage.

7. Modernization theory often assumes that the best thing that Third World women could do is to follow in Western women's footsteps into the "modern era." Is this a legitimate assumption? Is there an ideal "modern woman"? Is there an ideal modern state? If Third World women followed the United States model, what would they gain or lose? Can one generalize? What cultural biases or values underlie your answers?

8. To what degree do the modernization theorists you have read assume a notion of individualism? Is this a cultural bias? Might modernization assume a more collectivist approach? What implications does either assumption carry for how women's equality could be implemented?

CRITICS OF MODERNIZATION THEORY

In 1970 Ester Boserup's pioneering work on women's roles in economic development challenged the assumption that women's status necessarily improved under the impact of modernization/industrialization. By utilizing examples from Asia, Latin America, and Africa in particular, she demonstrated the disruptive impact that colonial rule, urbanization, and the world market economy have had on the position of women. Colonization, for example, introduced new patterns in the sexual division of labor such that in many instances more egalitarian relationships were replaced by the marginalization of women in political decision-making spheres, in access and control over resources, and in jural rights and privileges. Urbanization placed women in economically dependent relationships with men as families moved away from agricultural regions to urban industrial employment. And the world market system imposed a plethora of changes in land tenure systems and ownership rights that significantly undermined traditional rights of access granted to women.

Subsequent scholarship has refined and expanded upon Boserup's work. Numerous case studies have substantiated her general argument. Instructors might draw upon articles in Etienne and Leacock to illustrate/document many of the destructive consequences of Western development that Boserup describes. Their text examines societies as diverse as North American Indians (Seneca, Naskapi, Algonkian), Aztecs, Tonga, and Baule, and is a useful anthropological and historical complement to Boserup's work.

Readings for Students
Boserup, Ester. *Woman's Role in Economic Development*. New York: St. Martin's Press, 1970.
Etienne, Mona, and Eleanor Leacock. *Women and Colonization: Anthropological Perspectives*. New York: Praeger Pubs, 1980.
Huston, Perdita. *Third World Women Speak Out*.
Karl, Marilee. *"Women, Land and Food Production."* In ISIS, *Women in Development*.

Readings for Instructors
Black, Naomi, and Ann Baker Cottrell, eds. *Women and World Change: Equality Issues in Development*. Beverly Hills: Sage Publications, 1981.
Buvinic, Mayra et al., eds. *Women and Poverty in the Third World*. Baltimore: Johns Hopkins University Press, 1983.
Chaney, Elsa M. *Women in International Migration*. Washington, D.C.: Agency for International Development, 1980.
Charlton, Sue Ellen M. *Women in Third World Development*, especially Chaps. 1–4.
O'Barr, Jean F., ed., "Introduction." In *Perspectives on Power: Women in Africa, Asia and Latin America*. Durham, N.C.: Duke University Center for International Studies, 1982.
Jacquette, Jane S. "Women and Modernization Theory: A Decade of Feminist Criticism." *World Politics* 34, no. 2: 267–84.
"Migrant Women." ISIS *International Bulletin* 14 (1980).
Ward, Barbara. "Women and Technology in Developing Countries." *Impact of Science on Society* 20, no. 1 (1970): 93–101.

Lecture Topics

Pre-Colonial Conditions (Boserup). By way of introduction, a brief review of horticultural and agricultural models of society may be useful, emphasizing the following points:

1. African model (horticultural). Typically, women cultivated and prepared food. The societies were characterized by low population density and slash and burn agricultural techniques. Men hunted and cleared the land, protected the society from attack, and engaged in long-distance trade.

2. Indian model (agricultural). Peasant communities in India were densely populated. They utilized the plow and large animals for farming, which was defined as men's work. Women prepared food in the home, and participated in the production of home industries.

In both models there were exceptions to the rule. For example, women in south India and in tribal societies farmed, throughout India in poorer families they participated in agricultural labor such as weeding and harvesting, and in some areas of sub-Saharan Africa women also traded.

The Colonial Experience (Boserup). To evaluate the view that colonialism adversely affected the position of women it is necessary to examine, as Boserup does, the status of women in rural and urban settings.

Rural Areas. Land holdings, where women may have had rights to land, were carefully organized and standardized for modern taxation purposes and for civil records. Women often lost their rights in this process, because Western patrilineal notions of land ownership came into existence. The Western assumption that farming is men's work meant that agricultural programs (to raise cash crops, use new techniques, tractors, collectives, etc.) were all aimed at men. The result in Africa was a shift in the productivity ratio to the male farming sector, which was geared toward the export market. Industrialization and world trade frequently destroyed home industries, like textiles and pottery manufacture, by flooding local markets with cheap manufactured goods. Family industries in which women played important economic roles were unable to compete.

Urban Areas. Colonialism brought about a shift in work patterns, with the result that women in cities often became dependent upon men for their livelihood. The problem continues today. Modern offices and factories hire far fewer women than men. In addition, women in cities are often far from the areas where gainful employment is possible. Urban migration thus often has the effect of reducing both the income-earning capacity of female family members and their in-kind contribution to family income. This is so because it is difficult for women to move directly from economically active roles in rural areas to jobs in the urban sector for a variety of reasons, some of them familiar to women in the West. These jobs characteristically require inflexible hours and a fixed location, serious barriers to women who assume, through force of custom, the duty of childrearing. Women are hampered from taking jobs outside the family home by traditional attitudes about women's sphere and women's work, especially in societies where seclusion in the family compound has been the norm. Most employers prefer male labor, and women have little access to training, especially vocational programs, that is usually designed for men.

Women and National Development (Boserup). The belief is pervasive that in a developing country with high male unemployment, especially in towns, the employment of women takes jobs away from men. Boserup has termed this belief "the unemployment scare" (see Boserup, Chap. 11). She argues that it is based on the erroneous assumption that men constitute the cutting edge of economic development. Boserup and others argue that failure to give women full access to employment actually defeats national development plans in the following ways:

1. Restricting urban jobs to males exacerbates the problem of urban migration, or the flow chiefly of men into the cities, leading to social strains in both rural and urban areas;

2. Rural areas are deprived of their most literate population, and the costly urban infrastructure (housing, transportation, etc.) is overburdened;

3. Single-income families in towns cannot amass savings; and

4. Nations fail to capitalize on the fact that women employed outside the home have fewer children, which reduces population pressures.

In a later subsequent paper, Boserup argued that including women in development plans improves income distribution because most women who work do so because they must: they are either married to poor men or they are impoverished heads of households.[2] Thus the integration of women into development plans, it is argued, is essential if the plans are to succeed for anyone.

Discussion Questions

1. How do any of the studies in Etienne and Leacock illustrate (or refute) Boserup's thesis?

2. Do the interviews in Huston's book support or refute Boserup?

3. Why don't women who have been active economically in traditional society move directly into active roles in modern society?

4. What work do women typically do when they first enter urban life in developing countries? Does that role differ from place to place? What changes take place in a woman's social role when her family moves to the city?

5. What is the "unemployment scare"? Why does Boserup say it is suspicious? Do you agree?

6. Boserup states that urban women should be encouraged to work in the lesser developed countries. Outline the economic reasoning behind her statement.

7. Judging from the interviews with women in Tunisia, Egypt, the Sudan, Kenya, Sri Lanka, and Mexico in Huston's book, how do the views of Third World women regarding their needs and rights differ from those of North American women? How do their views differ among themselves?

8. Some planners, based on an analysis of European or American economic history, assert that while the initial stages of capitalism may bring harmful effects for segments of the population (for example, a displacement of people from traditional jobs, and a decline in the status of women) the long-run effects are a rising standard of living for all, and ultimately a more just society. Evaluate this argument.

9. Discuss both the intended and unintended effects of colonialism on women's status as revealed by any of the articles in Etienne and Leacock. How did the process of

imperial control occur? What were its ideological ra-
tionalizations? What similarities or differences can be
found in imperialist, racist, and sexist ideological justifications? How were women and men induced, coerced, or
persuaded to comply with new social norms? How representative are the societies included in the volume?

EXPANSION AND CRITIQUES OF BOSERUP

Boserup's central insights into the eroding position of women
in many societies and their key role in agriculture has been confirmed, but critics argue that "although she correctly perceived
the negative effects that colonialism and the penetration of capitalism into subsistence economies often had on women, she tacitly
regarded them as anomalies that could be corrected through the
implementation of specialized programs" (Fernandez-Kelly, 269).
It is asserted that Boserup overemphasizes the cultural prejudices
responsible for women's marginalization. For example, commercial cropping, which is at the center of the decline of women's
status in west Africa, is not simply a product of patriarchy, where
men monopolize social roles and access to resources, but part of a
general process of capital accumulation and the penetration of
world capitalist markets in which many men, as well as women,
lose control over productive resources. The problem then, according to critics, is not simply one of integrating women into
development plans or into education, or of removing legal barriers to wage employment, but is intrinsic to the dynamics of
capitalism, which generates and intensifies inequalities. Education
for women as a solution ignores the high incidence of general
unemployment among the educated in the Third World. Integration of women into the economy as wage earners carries with it
the danger of wage exploitation, as is the case in multinational
microelectronic industries in southeast Asia, where employers
prefer women workers because they will accept lower wages and
are more compliant than the male workforce (Bénería and Sen,
Signs 7, no. 2 [Winter 1981]: 279–98). These critics operate within
the broad framework of "dependency theory."
    While these critics doubt whether correctives to the past ne-
glect of women in development plans will make much difference,
other feminist development theorists disagree and work on the

improvement of implementation strategies, essentially expanding the direction of Boserup's work. We will examine both the critics and the augmenters.

Student Readings

Charlton, Sue Ellen M. *Women in Third World Development*, Chaps. 1, 4–9; or Rogers, Barbara. *The Domestication of Women: Discrimination in Developing Societies*. London: Routledge & Kegan Paul, 1980.

Cottingham, Jane. "Women and Health: An Overview." In ISIS *Women in Development*, pp. 143–71.

Ehrenreich, Barbara et al. "The Charge: Gynocide, the Accused: The U.S. Government." *Mother Jones* (November 1979).

Fuentes, Annette, and Ehrenreich, Barbara. *Women in the Global Factory*. Boston: South End Press, 1983.

Karl, Marilee. "Integrating Women into Multinational Development?" and "Appropriate Technology." In ISIS, *Women in Development*, pp. 61–71, 85–94.

Safa, Helen I. "Runaway Shops and Female Employment: The Search for Cheap Labor." *Signs* 7, no. 2 (Winter 1981): 418–33.

Stoler, Ann. "Class Structure and Female Autonomy in Rural Java." *Signs* 3, no. 1 (Autumn 1977): 77–89.

Instructor Readings

Benería, Lourdes, ed. *Women and Development: The Sexual Division of Labor in Rural Societies*. New York: Praeger Pubs., 1982.

Carr, Marilyn. "Appropriate Technology for African Women." United Nations Economic Commission for Africa/African Training and Research Centre for Women. P.O. Box 3002, Addis Ababa, Ethiopia, 1978.

Dauber, Roslyn, and Melinda L. Cain. *Women and Technological Change in Developing Countries*. American Association for the Advancement of Science, Selected Symposium 53. Boulder, Colo.: Westview Press, 1980.

"International Women and Health Meeting." ISIS *International Bulletin*, no. 20, 1981.

Jain, Devaki et al. "Women's Work: Methodological Issues." In *Women and Development*, edited by Rounaq Jahan and Hanna Papanek. Dhaka: Bangladesh Institute of Law and International Affairs, 1979; distributed by South Asia Books, P.O. Box 502, Columbia, Mo. 65205.

Lewis, Barbara. "Women in Development Planning: Advocacy, Institutionalization and Implementation," Chap. 8. In O'Barr, *Perspectives on Power.*

Nash, June, and Maria Patricia Fernandez-Kelly, eds. *Women, Men and the International Division of Labor.* Albany: State University of New York, 1983.

Nash, June, and Helen Safa, eds. *Sex and Class in Latin America.* Hadley, Mass.: Bergin, 1980.

Signs 3, no. 1 (Autumn 1977). Special Issue: Women and National Development.

Signs 7, no. 2 (Winter 1981). Special Issue: Development and the Sexual Division of Labor.

Smith, Judy. *Something Old, Something New, Something Borrowed, Something Due.* Women and Technology Project, 1980. 315 S. 4 E., Missoula, Mont. 59801.

Staudt, Kathleen. *Women, Foreign Assistance and Advocacy Administration.* New York: Praeger Pubs., 1985.

Staudt, Kathleen, and Jane Jacquette, eds. *Women in Developing Countries: A Policy Focus.* New York: Haworth, 1983.

"Women and Appropriate Technology." International Women's Tribune Centre, Newsletter 9, April 1979. 777 United Nations Plaza, New York, N.Y. 10017.

Young, Kate, Carol Wolkowitz, and Roslyn McCullagh, eds. *Of Marriage and the Market: Women's Subordination Internationally and Its Lessons.* London: Routledge & Kegan Paul, 1984.

Lecture Topics

Dependency Theory (Benería, 1982; Nash and Fernandez-Kelly; Nash and Safa; Young). The last three decades have seen evidence of increasing exploitation of women in Third World countries. Dependency theorists see this trend as a consequence of the penetration of capitalist industrial interests into the periphery (Third World).[3] The marginalization of these countries began, they argue, during the colonial period when natural resources and cheap labor were extracted to service the industrialized center. Women's exploitation in the form of low salaries, poor working conditions, and inhumane work expectations is seen as a consequence of the increasing entrenchment of power of Western industrial interests in non-industrial societies. Women are but one part, yet an extreme example, of such exploitation. The "women question" in non-industrial countries will not be satisfied, therefore, with either greater inclusion of women in the process of social change à la Boserup nor with administrative and policy

attention to the needs of women in development assistance programs, like those of the World Bank or A.I.D. They argue rather
that the process so often labeled "development" is but a sequence
of establishing economic and political dependencies that satisfy
the needs of capitalism—more specifically capital accumulation.
Thus, the position of women in non-industrialized societies cannot be viewed as independent of the exploitation of Third World
peoples. The explanation for female marginalization, therefore,
lies with the structural conditions endemic to the very definition
of capitalism. For this reason any discussion of the position/status
of women in these countries must be accompanied by an examination of the political economy of gender.

There is a rich body of feminist scholarship that falls broadly
under the umbrella of dependency theory, and indeed has made
important contributions to the field. To varying degrees these
scholars have been influenced by Engels's and subsequent Marxist
analyses of the role of private property and market forces in the
subordination of women, augmented by feminist analyses of the
interaction between reproduction and production, and the sexual
division of household labor (see Chapter 4). Authors differ on the
primacy of market forces versus woman's role in the household/
reproductive sphere, but most pay attention to the interactions
between market forces/production and family structures/repro-
duction. Whatever their theoretical leanings it is fair to say that
feminist scholars recognize the differential access that men and
women have to power, including in economic and bureaucratic
state structures.

Kate Young et al. present a series of articles examining sexual
stratification in developing capitalist and post-revolutionary countries, and find both traditional Marxist and feminist analyses
inadequate. They seek to develop "a feminist theory of the sexual
division of labour within a materialist analysis." Gender subordination is defined in terms of access to and control of the mode
of production of society as well as the belief system and social
aspects of everyday life. While these scholars argue that the position of women cannot be explained deterministically in terms of a
society's economic base alone, they look at how economic relations
may underlie social relations like marriage, domestic interaction,
and inheritance practices. For example, though bearing children
may perpetuate the next generation, it also ensures reproduction of the labor force, a requisite for economic continuity in any
society. Also pertinent to Marxist-feminist analyses of women's
status in Third World countries is the issue of whether the subor-

dination of women can exist independently of material conditions where women and men have equal access to the means of production.

Lourdes Benería et al. tilt the analytic balance toward the structure of the household, the sphere of reproduction, and the "patriarchal socialization process to which women are subject," to explain women's subordination in the marketplace. Articles by Elisabeth Croll ("The Sexual Division of Labor in Rural China") and Maria Mies ("The Dynamics of The Sexual Division of Labor and Integration of Rural Women on the World Market," which includes Indian examples) show the continuing power of household structures to mold unequal outcomes for men and women in the economic sphere in two very different societies.

June Nash and Helen Safa extend the debate in another direction in discussing dependency issues in the context of Latin America. They document the crucial point that class inequality can take precedence over sexual inequality, so that different groups of women have unequal access to the distribution of wealth and income in their own countries. This underlines the reality that women do not suffer marginalization or exclusion uniformly, and that national power elites may indeed include a small but significant number of women. Essays in Nash and Fernadez-Kelly show how both Third World men and women are losers in an international division of labor that assigns them to underpaid and intermittent employment in Western companies, though many contributors see women as the most exploited sector of the workforce. A number of recent studies focus specifically on the issue of women and the impact of multinational corporations.

Multinational Corporations and Appropriate Technology (Charlton, 138–51; Dauber and Cain; Fuentes and Ehrenreich; Karl; Safa [1981]). Multinational corporations have had profound effects upon Third World men and women given their power and the ability of MNCs to utilize pools of labor across continents. Much research has focused upon how multinationals disregard local needs and undermine traditional social structures. Charlton argues that workers are "internationalized," i.e., Westernized, in the workplace through the use of cultural assumptions and values typical of Western nations but anomalous where they are implemented. This means that women placed into factory employment or at particular jobs may find themselves in conflict with prevailing cultural norms. Today, multinationals establish themselves in Third World countries, recruiting cheap, foreign labor, with women often their targeted employees. Women are attractive to employers because they are perceived to be more docile, obedient, without experience in labor organizing, a source of cheap labor, and more likely to tolerate frequent job turnover. For these reasons, in industries such as electronics, garment manufacture, and assembly work, women may constitute the majority of the labor force. Fuentes and Ehrenreich discuss the pervasiveness of discrimination and exploitation of women by MNCs from Mexico to Taiwan. Women's difficulties in the workplace are often not helped by repressive national governments that do little to encourage fair and healthy work environments. Governments sometimes even impose repression to counter worker boycotts or protests against low wages and poor working conditions. Research suggests that these women are often unaware that they are being exploited. Suggestions for rectifying these problems range from strategies that call for women workers to organize across continents to build a unified struggle, to a call for a "New International Economic Order," where power and capital would be redistributed equitably. Such changes would challenge the power of multinationals and their effects on women's lives.

Another important body of literature looks at the health and environmental impacts of the processes and products of multinational corporations on women. The issue of unsafe birth-control technologies and the dumping of these products by pharmaceutical companies in the Third World has been taken up by international feminist networks such as the International Contraception, Abortion and Sterilization Campaign, headquartered in London. Barbara Ehrenreich et al. expose the distribution of the Dalkon Shield, high-estrogen birth control pills, and Depo-Provera, sometimes with the support of U.S. aid programs, when these contraceptive technologies are banned or prescribed for limited usage at home. The pharmaceutical industry as a whole, together with high technology approaches to medical treatment, have come under increasing fire from those who argue that primary rural health needs and preventive public health measures like safe drinking water, sanitation, and nutrition are being ignored. Charlton, Cottingham, and ISIS all deal with aspects of these health issues, which bear disproportionately upon women because of poorer nutrition and/or pregnancy risks.

The issue of appropriate technology in general is also being investigated from a feminist perspective. For over two decades critics have questioned the introduction of low-labor, capital-intensive technologies into poor Third World countries with abundant, underutilized labor.[4] The environmental side-effects have also been questioned. The appropriate technology movement has had a male bias. As Judy Smith remarks: "Most of the attention on appropriate technology focuses on the traditionally male technologies of energy and transportation, rather than on traditional female technologies of food preservation and clothing production" (Karl, 91). This bias is being addressed. Feminist researchers now question whether a given technology will create more or less work for women, whose roles in agriculture and craft production are often ignored (Karl; "Women and Appropriate Technology"). Attention has also been given to simple technologies, such as hand-operated machines that can be made and repaired locally, which can assist women in food processing, food and fuel conservation, and access to safe water supplies, all vital basic needs that under the sexual division of labor are frequently women's responsibility. Carr and Charlton (Chap. 4) discuss the food cycle and appropriate technology for women, in Carr's case in the African setting.

Integrating Women into Development. Not all feminist development theorists accept the dependency critique, pointing to the continuing marginalization of women in certain socialist economies. Other, such as Barbara Lewis, find the debates "fascinating, challenging and important," but "in the absence of revolutionary transformation of unprecedented proportions, they have only limited relevance for assistance projects which are, for better or worse, constrained by political realities and elites" (103). There is a continuing body of literature that aims implicitly or explicitly to improve the performance of planners in national and international development agencies. Lewis herself has produced a useful critique of two alternative strategies of development—the "woman-to-woman" strategy and the woman's component of an integrated project.

Barbara Rogers's book documents the degree to which the sexist misperceptions of planners trained in the West distort and undermine development plans. Planners impose their own culture-bound ideology about gender and the sexual division of labor (male head of household and female domestic) upon societies where women play key economic roles, especially in subsistence agriculture. Third World women are responsible for 40 to 80 percent of all agricultural production, depending on the country (see also Charlton, Chaps. 3–4). Women, if included at all in plans, are subsumed under "special projects," a practice that continues to this day in the United Nations Development Program and the Food and Agriculture Organization. Women are channelled into nutrition or domestic science programs, and no effort is made to understand women's work in its individual cultural context.

Plans for agricultural development flounder, Rogers shows, because land is transferred into individual male title, robbing women of their resources. Development "inputs" of credit and agricultural training are directed at men, and mechanization is restricted to male labor such as plowing. This reduces male hours of work, but the new technology may increase the total hours women must work in more intensive planting and weeding. Western-trained planners assume women have ample "free time" to adapt. When women's work is mechanized (as, for example, with food processing machines), men often own the technology, putting women in a position of dependence. Plans for agricultural "development" thus may run into stiff resistance from women. Consequently a number of writers argue that hunger is a woman's issue: women are the key to increased food production in many areas, and bear a disproportionate burden of food shortages.

Some attention has focused on the study of specific development agencies and how they do or do not attend seriously to the needs of Third World women. Kathleen Staudt for example, provides an unusual insider's view of the Women and Development Office in A.I.D. by exploring the difficulties that institutional structures and value systems place upon such advocacy programs designed to assist Third World women. Her discussion shows that agencies with mandates to consider the position of women in foreign assistance may be constrained by assumptions and images of women that get in the way of serious discussion about changing gender roles. Charlton (Chap. 9) presents a brief but valuable overview of the main international, national, and private agencies operating women and development programs.

Finally Boserup's work has played a part in stimulating research on "women's work" in general. A closer analysis of rural economies and the informal urban sector shows women's labor in home industry and marketing is vastly undercounted in official statistics. Some analysts (see Jahan, *Women and Development*) question the very nature of definitions of "gainful employment." Is it only income-earning employment, or should it include goods produced for domestic consumption (clothing, home gardens)? Home production carries a value, yet it is rarely included in the GNP, and failure to do so hides some important impacts of development on women's work, and the structure of the economy.

Discussion Questions
  1. Which women "win" and which women "lose" in a free
     market system in the United States and in any other
     society that you have studied? Is there any way to effec-
     tively plan change? Must we accept social change dictated
     by market forces as inevitable?

  2. Do North American women (and workers) have any
     common interests with Third World women (and work-
     ers) in the investment and employment policies of
     multinational corporations? Where might women's self-
     interest divide along national or class lines?

  3. Barbara Rogers argues that the term "status of women" is
     erroneous because it implies that something needs to be
     done to "help" women. "A disadvantaged group does not
     see itself as the problem: it sees rather the obstacles set up
     by others as the essence of the problem." Discuss.

  4. Is the key to understanding the differential impact of
     "development" on men and women the sexual division of
     labor in the household, market capitalism, industrializa-
     tion as a technological process, the sexism of planners, or
     what?

  5. Charlton argues that hunger is a political and female
     issue. Why does she assert this? What are the implications
     for solving the food crisis, particularly in Africa?

FAMILY PLANNING AND DEVELOPMENT

The issues of family planning and the status of women are
inextricably linked and matters of international urgency. While
some argue that a redistribution of the world's economic resources could sustain present rates of population growth, most
development planners pragmatically assume that, given the present unequal distribution of wealth on the planet, population curbs
are necessary in order for nations to meet their economic targets.
Family planning programs are often incorporated into development plans. Many have failed, or have met with only partial
success.

Analyses of family planning failures, recent feminist critics claim, have often been superficial and misleading. Rural women, most often the targets of birth control programs, are often assumed to reject such programs out of ignorance and illiteracy. Such analyses fail to grasp that family planning or limiting the number of children a woman will bear, has tremendous implications for the role of women and for the economic security of poor families. Rural women throughout the Third World who do not use birth control may have compelling rational reasons for doing so, even though their behavior frustrates the "rational" planners from the modern sector.

Readings for Students
Charlton, Sue Ellen M. *Women in Third World Development,* Chap. 5.
de Lenero, Elu, and Maria del Carmen. "Women's Work and Fertility." In Nash, *Sex and Class in Latin America.*
Fullam, Maryellen. "Cries from the Hearts of Women." *People* 6, no. 1 (1979): 44.
Germain, Adrienne. "Women at Mexico: Beyond Family Planning Acceptors." *Family Planning Perspectives* 7 (September–October 1975): 235–38.
Huston, Perdita. *Third World Women Speak Out.*
Third International Meeting, Women and Health, Geneva, (6–8 June 1981). ISIS 20, 1981.

Readings for Instructors
Birdsall, Nancy. "Women and Population Studies: Review Essay." *Signs* 1, no. 3 (Spring 1976): 699–712.
Finkle, Jason L. "The Politics of Bucharest: Population and Development and the New International Economic Order." *Population and Development Review* 1 (September 1975): 87–114.
Germain, Adrienne. "Comment." *Signs* 2, no. 4 (Summer 1977): 924–27.
Greer, Germaine. *Sex and Destiny: The Politics of Human Fertility.* New York: Harper and Row, 1984.
"Health, Longevity, and Family Planning" in Chapter 6, "Women in India," this book.
Huston, Perdita. "Power and Pregnancy." *New Internationalist* (June 1977).
Newland, Kathleen. "Women and Population Growth: Choice Beyond Childrearing." *Worldwatch Papers* 16. Washington, D.C.: Worldwatch Institute, 1977.

Tangri, Sandra Schwartz. "A Feminist Perspective on Some Eth-
    ical Issues in Population Programs." *Signs* 1, no. 4 (Summer
    1976): 895–904.
Ward, Kathryn B. "Toward a New Model of Fertility: The Effects
    of the World Economic System and the Status of Women on
    Fertility Behavior." East Lansing: Michigan State University,
    Women in International Development Program, Working
    Paper 20, March 1983.

Lecture Topics

**Female Status and Family Planning ("Health, Longevity, and
Family Planning"; Ward).** Female status and control of fertility
are closely related: Restricted life options, female malnutrition,
high maternal mortality rates, and exhaustion from dual burdens
are related to constant cycles of pregnancy and childrearing in
those societies in which women bear the burden of reproduction
unaided. Women's control over their own reproductive functions
is a feminist issue that crosses many national frontiers.

Family planning experts, feminists among them, have historically argued the case that control of fertility would lead to improvements in the status of women. After several decades of
experience, and many failures in population control policies,
some analysts now argue that improvements in the status of
women may need to *precede* the acceptance of birth control.

**Women's Motives for Having Children (Newland; "Health, Lon-
gevity, and Family Planning"; Huston; Ward).** The literature on
what motivates women—and men—to limit the number of their
children is fraught with controversy. Various attempts have been
made to correlate birth control usage with national income, individual income, education, workforce participation, class, religion,
infant mortality, and other factors, with mixed results.

What is clear, however, is that women in traditional societies
have many reasons for having numerous children, reasons based
not on ignorance, as some planners assert, but on maximizing
their own security and happiness. Children may be the only resources many women control. Women's status and self-worth as
defined by their societies may depend on their fertility and their
role as mothers. Motherhood is often the most meaningful experience in their lives. Among economically marginalized women in
comparatively well-off families this may be particularly true.
Among poorer families where children enter the workforce early,

their earnings may be crucial to economic survival. Children can also ensure a ready labor pool in a labor intensive economy, and they can provide security in old age. The conclusion, Newland believes, is clear: Women need to have alternative sources of status, income, security, and emotional satisfaction for population planning, and hence development plans, to succeed.

Ward argues that systematic change in the world economic system will be necessary. Efforts to reduce fertility have been stymied, she asserts, by growing income inequalities and high infant mortality rates, which raise fertility behavior. By cross-sectional regression analyses on a sample of 105 countries she illustrates that foreign investment and trade dependency have negative effects on women's economic status.

Both theoretical perspectives would suggest that at a minimum any population control program that did not simultaneously reduce infant mortality, increase women's economic options, and increase education would be unlikely to succeed. In India, the Committee on the Status of Women has argued that this broader approach to family planning should replace purely technical or clinical educational campaigns.

Perdita Huston, a former regional director of the Peace Corps, critiques the approach of educational campaigns themselves. She argues that population planning measures must be directed at men, not just at women, as has traditionally been the case. Population issues have been seen as a "women's problem" without sufficient attention to women's lack of personal autonomy in making the decision whether or not to have children. That decision is often made by men or in-laws. Huston charges that population planning programs are conceived by male urban planners who have no idea of the reality of women's lives, particularly in rural areas.

Population Policies and the Distribution of Power (Greer). Germaine Greer raises troubling questions about the very nature of population policy framed in international and national bureaucracies. She argues that the ideologies promoting population control for men and women do not exist apart from the world distribution of power. It is the industrialized West with its limited family size and its quest for ever greater material affluence that disseminates values and norms that hold the Third World to requisite family planning programs. Is this tendency to impose reproductive controls just, she asks, if we are taking the right of making these decisions from those affected by them? Women are the reproducers in these countries and they are also often the disenfranchised.

Feminist prescriptions for improving family planning programs thus vary, mirroring positions on the issue of women and development in general. Dependency theorists see change in the international distribution of wealth as essential, others seek to improve the delivery and comprehensiveness of population programs, while Greer raises unpopular questions about the cultural imperialism of the very concept of family planning.

Discussion Questions

1. Is it fair for planners in Western or Third World agencies to persuade Third World women to accept birth control methods? What assumptions or values underlie your answer?

2. Do Western and Third World women share the same motives in bearing children? In adopting birth control?

3. Some Third World feminists have argued that Euro-American feminists neglect neocolonial issues, and are preoccupied with domestic issues. They assert, for example, that the American women's movement has concentrated too narrowly on domestic reproductive issues (such as abortion and sex education), while paying comparatively little attention to forced sterilizations in Puerto Rico or the dumping of unsafe birth control technology in the Third World, after it has been banned in the United States. Discuss.

GLOBAL DEBATES ON THE STATUS OF WOMEN

Within international forums concerned with issues of Third World economic development, most notably the United Nations, the idea of integrating women into development schemes has now gained ascendancy. The goal of integrating women into national development has in fact become part of the rhetoric of international conferences. The United Nations Decade on Women (1975–1985) opened with a remarkable international gathering in Mexico City. From numerous workshops, resolutions, and lengthy debates emerged a World Plan of Action to elevate the status of women. This was followed in July 1980 in Copenhagen by an exhaustive mid-decade review of progress and obstacles in connection with the World Plan, and by resolutions outlining methods of implementation. In 1979 the United Nations General Assembly adopted an International Convention on the Elimination of All Forms of Discrimination Against Women. The Decade ended with a review in Nairobi. It has become unfashionable for governments to admit, at least verbally, that improving the status of women is not part of their national agenda.

Media coverage of the Decade has been lamentably superficial. Most coverage has focused on the official gatherings of government representatives at Mexico City, Copenhagen, and Nairobi, and particularly on the international political tensions that surfaced (East-West and North-South disputes, and the Middle East), while failing to notice the substance of the developing international agenda on the status of women. While it is admittedly a long way from a conference resolution to actual implementation in nation-states, nevertheless the World Plan of Action has provided a valuable benchmark and lobbying tool. Far too little attention has been paid to emerging international feminist networks that the associated meetings of Non-Governmental women's organizations (NGOs) have done much to foster. These phenomena, and the World Plan, deserve further analysis.

Readings for Students

Bunch, Charlotte. "Copenhagen and Beyond: Prospects for Global Feminism." *Quest: A Feminist Quarterly* 5, no. 4 (1982): 25–33.

Charlton, Sue Ellen M. *Women in Third World Development*, Chap. 10.

Newland, Kathleen. *The Sisterhood of Man*. New York: Norton, 1979.

Quest 4, no. 2 (Winter 1978). Special Issue: International Feminism.

Stephenson, Carolyn M. "Feminism, Pacifism, Nationalism and the United Nations Decade for Women." *Women's Studies International Forum* 5, nos. 3/4 (1982): 287–300.

United Nations. Secretariat World Conference of the United Nations Decade for Women. *Final Report: Programme of Action*. Available from Secretariat, World Conference of the United Nations Decade for Women, Room A–555, 866 United Nations Plaza, New York, N.Y. 10017.

Readings for Instructors

Copenhagen and Nairobi Conference Reports. Available from International Women's Tribune Centre, 777 United Nations Plaza, New York, N.Y. 10017.

Ashworth, Georgiana, ed. *Women's Studies International Forum* 8, no. 2 (1985). Special Issue: The UN Decade for Women: An International Evaluation.

Boulding, Elise. "NGOs and World Problem-Solving: A Comparison of Religious and Secular Women's NGOs," Chap. 8; and "Female Alternatives to Hierarchical Systems, Past and Present; A Critique of Women's NGOs in the Light of History," Chap. 9. In *Women in the Twentieth Century World.* Beverly Hills, Cal.: Sage Publications, 1977.

Hevener, Elaine. *International Law and the Status of Women.* Boulder, Colo.: Westview Press, 1982.

Iglitzen, Lynne B., and Ruth Ross, eds. *Women in the World, 1975–1985: The Women's Decade.* 2nd ed. rev. Santa Barbara, Cal.: ABC-CLIO, 1985.

Tinker, Irene. "A Feminist View of Copenhagen." *Signs,* 6, no. 3 (Spring 1981): 531–35, and "Comments on Tinker's "A Feminist View of Copenhagen." *Signs* 6, no. 4. (Summer 1981): 771–80.

United Nations. Division for Economic and Social Information. Division for Public Information. *Women 1980,* Newsletter no. 4. Available from United Nations Division for Economic and Social Information/Division for Public Information, Room 1061, United Nations, New York, N.Y. 10017.

"Women's Networks." *International Women's Tribune Newsletter* 13 (1980).

Lecture Topics

The International Consensus. Governments have been urged to pay special attention both to strategies for involving women in national development and specific programs to benefit women.

Strategies. Governments are urged to:

1. Establish national machinery to ensure that women participate in and benefit from development plans. Grassroots organizations and trade unions are urged to participate in decision making and implementation.

2. Repeal all discriminatory legislation to produce a legal framework for equality.

3. Enact legislation, where it does not exist, establishing women's right to vote and to exercise all public functions, including elective and appointive office and civil service jobs, on an equal basis with men.

4. Establish independent advisory boards to monitor media policies and make recommendations on how to change the image of women in the media.

5. Promote non-governmental women's organizations such as credit co-ops and educational groups.

6. Collect data on the status of women in a systematic way.

Programs. The World Plan of Action contains over two hundred recommendations. The most important include: full and equal employment opportunities, development of accessible family planning programs, facilities to lighten women's work, introduction of appropriate technology, target dates for the elimination of male/female differentials in literacy rates, equal access to technological innovations for women in agriculture, involvement of rural women in agricultural policy making, equal rights of land ownership, special attention to women's health needs, redefinition of concepts of work to include women's unpaid labor in the GNP, removal of sex bias from educational curricula, and promotion of education for women at home. The cumulative effect of these programs would be immense.

The Convention on the Elimination of All Forms of Discrimination Against Women embodies these principles, and others, intended "to ensure the full development and advancement of women for the purpose of guaranteeing them the exercise and enjoyment of human rights and fundamental freedoms on a basis of equality with men" (the full text can be found in Charlton, 222–33). As of mid-1985 it had been signed by sixty-five nations.

Continuing Obstacles to Implementation. The United Nations official publications and events at Mexico City, Copenhagen, and Nairobi readily attest to the obstacles to improving the status of women. Women are drastically underrepresented within the structures of the United Nations itself, national delegations to the world gatherings in support of the Decade are characteristically briefed and controlled by their own governments and only minimally reflect on autonomous women's agenda, and women are underrepresented in the power structures of nation-states themselves. In Western countries women hold 5 to 11 percent of the seats in national assemblies; in developing countries the average is 6 percent; and in many instances the women elected feel no particular identification with the situation of women. Continuing problems also include the lack of political will in many countries to tackle age-old patterns of sex discrimination in any fundamental way. Where sexual stratification is embedded in the structure of the family there has been a particular reluctance to intervene. In addition, the existing structures of socioeconomic oppression are left intact while minor programs (for example, tourist handicraft production) are directed at women. Planning is rarely based on the needs of women as defined by women themselves; at best, they are made in accordance with the well-meaning benevolence of liberal-minded males.

There are also serious conceptual obstacles. Many governments fail to concede that sexism is analogous to racism. At the Copenhagen Conference, for example, delegates (primarily from the Eastern European bloc, and the Group of 77, or developing nations) initially refused to include the word "sexism" in a draft resolution analyzing the causes of women's oppression. They argued that no such word existed in their languages, and that inequality for Third World women springs solely from the unjust world economic system. At the insistence of the New Zealand delegation the word "sexism" was included in a compromise parenthetical phrase acknowledging that "in a group of countries," discrimination on the basis of sex is called "sexism." On the other hand, a number of Western governments, most notably the United States, have been resistant to participating in North-South dialogues on reforming the international economic system.

The international economic order, with its vast disparities of wealth and power, hinders all development plans, but it affects women most severely. The situation of rural women has actually worsened in comparison with rural men in the areas of employment and education during the last ten years (Buviníc). The worsening world economic picture has dictated cuts in Third World social programs, and those directed at women are often the first to go. Unrestricted transfers of technology from the West to the Third World, coupled with linkages of fragile local economies to the ups and downs of the world market system, continue to destroy family industry and subsistence agriculture. Many Third World women therefore suffer the effects of double oppression based on their sex and their nation's position in the international economic order.

The international debate on the status of women is marked by
serious conceptual flaws and political resistance. But there is a
worldwide revolution of expectations among literate, elite women
which has only begun to touch poor and rural women. It is a
revolution of distant hope, not imminent reality.

**Emerging Global Women's Networks (Ashworth, Boulding,
Charlton).** International women's networks have existed since the
latter part of the nineteenth century (Boulding), and by the late
1970s nearly fifty had gained official NGO status at the United
Nations. One cautiously optimistic note to emerge from the UN
Decade is the strengthening of some old groups and the proliferation of new ones, some with UN status and others spurning the
existing power structures. The NGO Forums, which have pre-
ceeded or paralleled the official assemblies at Mexico City,
Copenhagen, and Nairobi have assisted this process. The recent
Nairobi Forum attracted over 10,000 participants, and was described by its convenor, Dame Nita Barrow of Barbados, as "not a
meeting. . . . not a conference. It is an encounter, a happening. It
is a meeting of the minds, an exchange of ideas." Sometimes the
exchange has been acrimonious; sometimes the participants have
been uncomprehending or insensitive of cultural differences and
economic realities. Nevertheless a stimulating cross-fertilization of
ideas has occurred of which ISIS, the Women's International
Information and Communications Service, is but one measure: It
has over 10,000 contacts in 130 countries, answers questions,
publishes a news bulletin and resource guide, mobilizes international support for women persecuted on the grounds of sex, and
provides technical assistance on organizational issues.

Ultimately the fate of UN resolutions will depend on pressure
inside and outside of international and national development
agencies. As Sue Ellen Charlton points out, "women's organizations may be uniquely capable of pressuring public and private
development practitioners" (210). The Decade has also witnessed
a proliferation of regional and national women's groups and networks. Their resources may seem infinitesimal compared to the
challenge, but if ideas can be said to have any power then it is a
matter of some optimism that the knowledge base about the
condition of women has vastly expanded over the Decade, and so
have the communications links among women—and men—who
care. There are some signs that governments are taking women's
issues more seriously. Ninety percent of all nations now have
official bodies dedicated to the advancement of women, double

the number that existed at the start of the Decade. Yet many assume self-congratulatory postures or tinker with reforms. Women's consciousness worldwide, and in individual nations, of their collective self-interest has increased somewhat, yet the discouraging fact remains that over the Decade there has been no consistent increase in women's political participation. Forging links between what are still elite or middle-class networks and the vast underclass of the majority of women remains an urgent necessity.

Discussion Questions

1. Can one speak of a common "female experience" or "sisterhood of women"?

2. What concerns of the modern American feminist movement are absent from the World Plan of Action? What is included in the Plan but absent from the American feminist agenda? Why? Is either movement seriously weakened by these omissions? By what criteria are you judging?

3. What, if anything, can or should Euro-American women do to help Third World women achieve their aspirations? Would assistance constitute cultural meddling or a form of neocolonialism? Why or why not?

4. What political calculations might underlie Western nations' endorsement of the word "sexism," and some socialist and Third World nations' rejection of the same concept? How can the women's movement guard against the dangers of co-option?

5. Some Third World feminists argue that until the American feminist movement develops an economic analysis that includes issues of international trade, multinational corporations, and foreign policy, an international feminist alliance will not develop. Discuss.

6. Devaki Jain (*Quest* 4, no. 2 [Winter 1978]: 9–15) says Eastern women often reject Western feminism because it is perceived as anti-male, or as a male-mimicking quest for equality or "sameness." In societies where men and women are viewed as interdependent, complementary, and unique, such a feminist ideology is inappropriate. Discuss the accuracy of this perception of Western feminism. Discuss Jain's conclusion. How do you define

feminism? Is your definition culturally biased? Is a global definition possible?

Notes

1. United Nations, Division for Economic and Social Information, *Women 1980* (Conference booklet for the World Conference of the United Nations Decade for Women, Copenhagen, 14–30 July 1980), pp. 5–10.

2. Ester Boserup and Christian Liljencrantz, "Integration of Women in Development: Why, When, How" (New York: United Nations, Department of Public Information, Division for Economic and Social Information, 1975).

3. A summary of the voluminous literature on dependency theory can be found in Ronald H. Chilcote, *Theories of Comparative Politics: The Search for a Paradigm* (Boulder, Colo.: Westview Press, 1981), pp. 296–312. Early influential works in the field are Andre Gunder Frank, *Latin America: Underdeveloped or Revolution—Essays on the Development of Underdevelopment, and the Immediate Enemy* (New York: Monthly Review Press, 1969), especially Chaps. 1–2, and *Capitalism and Underdevelopment in Latin America* (New York: Monthly Review Press, 1968). Critiques and expansion of dependency theory include Goran Hyden, *Beyond Ujamaa in Tanzania: Underdevelopment and the Uncaptured Peasantry* (Berkeley: University of California Press, 1980); and June Nash, *We Eat the Mines and the Mines Eat Us: Dependency and Exploitation in Bolivian Tin Mines* (New York: Columbia University Press, 1979).

4. The classic work in this field is E. F. Schumacher, *Small Is Beautiful* (New York: Harper and Row, 1973).

CHAPTER FOUR

TOWARD A THEORY OF GENDER STRATIFICATION: SELECTED ISSUES

Margot I. Duley

There is as yet no comprehensive, fully articulated and agreed upon theory of the origin and perpetuation of gender inequalities, even among those who stress the importance of socioeconomic systems or culture in shaping gender stratification. Our purpose here is to expose students to some of the key issues that have emerged both historically and in recent scholarship. The theories included here are eclectic and selective. Instructors may wish to add theorists of their own choosing.

Engel's theory and subsequent scholarship on the economic bases of female subordination are presented in a lecture format with discussion questions. The complexity of the issue dictated this approach. The topics of economics and gender, women and nature, and the public versus domestic domain debate are presented as short lectures with questions for discussion. Issues surrounding lesbianism and gender stratification from a cross-cultural perspective are presented in the form of an extended interpretive narrative with headings that are easily adaptable to lecture topics. This fuller development stems from the almost total lack of secondary sources on the subject.

For instructors who wish to read general review essays on theories of gender stratification we recommend:

Reiter, Rayna R., ed. "Introduction." In *Toward an Anthropology of Women*. New York: Monthly Review Press, 1975.

Rosaldo, Michelle Zimbalist. "The Use and Abuse of Anthropology: Reflections on Feminism and Cross-Cultural Understanding." *Signs* 5, no. 3 (1980): 389–417.

Rosaldo, Michelle Zimbalist, and Louise Lamphere, eds. "Introduction." In *Woman, Culture, and Society.* Stanford: Stanford
University Press, 1974.

Schlegel, Alice, ed. "Toward a Theory of Sexual Stratification."
In *Sexual Stratification: A Cross-Cultural View.* New York:
Columbia University Press, 1977.

MARXIST CONTRIBUTIONS TO THE GENDER INEQUALITY DEBATE

Karl Marx and Frederick Engels were the first theorists to
perceive the connection between economic structures and the
status of women, and to argue that women's inferior status was
grounded in something other than biological inferiority.

The Marxist contribution to the literature on gender inequality has been fundamentally important. Much of the writing on the
subject either elaborates and refines Marx and Engels's ideas in
light of modern anthropological research (see Sacks, Gough,
Leacock, below) or seeks to refute them. Marxists argue that
women's oppressed status results from the development of private
property and the concommitant need to protect lines of inheritance. This in turn leads to the establishment of the monogamous
nuclear family with women economically dependent upon men.
In contrast, the culture and personality school, as represented
earlier in this text by Mead and Chodorow, stresses the social and
psychological origins of gender inequality to the exclusion, Marxist-feminist critics would say, of an examination of the economic
structures shaping culture and personality.

Readings for Students
Gough, Kathleen. "The Origin of the Family." In *Toward an
Anthropology of Women.*
Rowbotham, Sheila. *Women, Resistance and Revolution,* Introduc-
tion and Chaps. 3, 4, 8. New York: Pantheon Press, 1972.
Sacks, Karen. "Engels Revisited: Women, the Organization of
Production and Private Property." In *Toward an Anthropology
of Women.*

Readings for Instructors
Benería, Lourdes, ed. "Introduction." In *Women and Development:*

The Sexual Division of Labor in Rural Societies. New York: Praeger Pubs., 1982.

Engels, Frederick. *The Origin of the Family, Private Property and the State,* Chap. 2. Edited by Eleanor Burke Leacock. New York: International Pubs., 1972.

Lane, Ann J. "Women in Society: A Critique of Frederick Engels." In *Liberating Women's History,* edited by Berenice A. Carroll. Urbana: University of Illinois Press, 1976.

Sacks, Karen. *Sisters and Wives: The Past and Future of Sexual Equality,* especially Chaps. 3–7. Urbana: University of Illinois Press, 1982.

Young, Kate, Carol Wolkowitz, and Roslyn McCullagh, eds. *Of Marriage and the Market: Women's Subordination Internationally and Its Lessons.* London: Routledge & Kegan Paul, 1984.

Lecture Topics

Precapitalist Society. According to Marx and Engels, before private property and private ownership developed, men and women had separate but equal freedoms and responsibilities. Women were respected for their work, which centered on domestic duties and gathering food, and later on farming, while men hunted. When these primitive societies progressed to the point where surplus was possible, private ownership and exploitive relationships developed.

Private Property and Its Implications for Women's Status. With the development of private property came the need to defend it. Since men were physically stronger than women, they had control over war. Victory in war made it possible for men to have control over bounty, including slaves, who were a source of labor. Women continued to bring up children and to farm. Thus, men controlled socially productive labor, while women were restricted to privately productive labor in the home. It was only at this point that women became financially dependent upon men and beholden to them for security. The growth of class oppression and women's oppression went hand in hand.

Communism and the Liberation of Women. By removing the economic dependence of women upon men, a new truly human relationship would be possible under communism. Individual sexual love would be possible because the economic dependence of women on men would be eliminated. (This idea was formulated during a time when marriages were often accompanied by monetary settlements, and when women were regarded as the legal charges of their husbands.) Marxists also assumed that the physical isolation of most women in the home would disappear after the revolution as women were drawn into productive labor.

Feminist Critiques of Marx and Engels (Lane, Rowbotham). Among their criticisms are: the marginality of women in Marxist theory, and specifically the assumption that women's liberation is dependent upon the emancipation of the working class; the existence of women's oppression in precapitalist societies (however, compare this with Leacock, 18–25); and the continuation of sexist attitudes in socialist societies.

Gough's Interpretation of Engels's Theory on the Origin of the Family. Using contemporary anthropolgical evidence, Gough argues that the family arose not from a need to protect private property but rather from the combined need for prolonged child care and the necessity for hunting over extensive terrain. These factors led to a sexual division of labor which, in turn, laid the basis for later economic specialization and cooperation between the sexes. She concurs, however, that women's subordination increased with the growth of surplus wealth and a class society.

Leacock and Sacks. Both theorists agree that Engels's central points remain unchallenged: "That women's special oppression is ultimately based on the family as an economic unit" (Leacock, 57), and that in general women are worse off in class than in nonclass societies (Sacks, "Engels Revisited," 220). The Marxist analysis remains invaluable to feminist scholars of varying ideological hues because it focuses attention on the relationship between the material bases of society and the status of women.

Reproduction/Production. Increasingly, debate has focused on the relationship between the household and women's subordination. Feminist theorists, augmenting Engels, stress the importance of factors located in the household in understanding women's subordinate position in the labor market, access to which is generally seen as critical to high status. Lourdes Benería, for instance, believes a wholly economic or market interpretation of female status is incomplete and suggests that *first* we need to understand women's unequal access to power in the domestic sphere, and then to focus on the interaction between reproduction and production. Young et al. chart their course in a different direction, developing a feminist theory of the division of labor within a materialist or economic framework; household structures are not ignored, however. Young sees evidence of the subordination of women in capitalist societies and in socialist ones that have left prerevolutionary social relations intact. Though both sets of essays demonstrate the link between economics and gender, and household politics and the market—all factors originally suggested by Engels—as the debate has evolved there are important differences about whether production or reproduction should receive analytical primacy.

Discussion Questions

1. Do you find evidence of primitive communism in any of the societies you have studied? What might limit the validity of contemporary data?

2. Engels argues that the power of men to exploit women springs from the existence of surplus wealth, which permits the rise of the state, social stratification, and the control of private property by men. Does the anthropological evidence you studied earlier support or refute this contention? In particular, examine the evidence from hunting-gathering, horticultural, and agricultural societies.

3. Recalling your reading of Mead's *Sex and Temperament,* what might be the material bases of the differing social psychologies found in the societies Mead studied?

4. Are Marxist theories and the culture and personality schools incompatible?

5. Leacock and Engels claim that monogamy provides the mechanism through which private property can be privately inherited. Could there be any other reasons for monogamy? Test your beliefs against cross-cultural evidence.

6. Engels argues that "the first condition for the liberation of the wife is to bring the whole female sex back into public industry, and that this in turn demands that the characteristic of the monogamous family as the economic unit of society be abolished" (Leacock, 137–38). If Engels is correct, what changes would have to occur in United

States society to accomplish this? To what extent does the modern North American feminist movement incorporate demands for these changes? Is Engels correct?

7. If the economic dependence of women upon men were removed, would female equality result? Why or why not?

8. Do you agree with Rowbotham's contention that while a revolution against capitalism, in favor of socialism, might improve women's status, it is necessary to have an autonomous feminist movement for fundamental change to occur?

9. Gough argues that "the sexual division of labor—until recently, universal—need not, and in my opinion should not, survive in industrial society." Discuss this proposition. Is it realistic? How might the sex-role division be broken down? Is it desirable to do so, or would it defy laws of nature? Compare Gough's assertion with the findings of Bacdayan.

SEX/GENDER SYSTEMS: INTERACTIONIST ANALYSES

Readings for Students and Instructors

Callender, Charles, and Lee M. Kochems. "The North American Berdache." *Current Anthropology* 24, no. 4 (1983): 443–56.

Jacobs, Sue-Ellen. "Berdache: A Brief Review of the Literature." *Colorado Anthropologist* 1 (1968): 25–40.

Moreland-Davis, Joan A. "Women and Anthropology: A Critique of Levi-Strauss and Exchange Theory." *Atlantis* 3, part 2 (1978): 116–29.

Ortner, Sherry B., and Harriet Whitehead, eds., "Introduction: Accounting for Sexual Meanings." In *Sexual Meanings: The Cultural Construction of Gender and Sexuality.* Cambridge: Cambridge University Press, 1981.

Rubin, Gayle. "The Traffic in Women: Notes on the 'Political Economy' of Sex." In *Toward an Anthropology of Women,* 157–216.

Whitehead, Harriet. "The Bow and the Burden Strap: A New Look at Institutionalized Homosexuality in Native North America." In *Sexual Meanings.*

Lecture Topics

The Political Economy of Sex. In a provocative essay that raises as many questions as it answers, Gayle Rubin draws upon and modifies the conceptual tools of Claude Levi-Strauss and Sigmund Freud to discuss the origins of sexual oppression. She argues that the focus of research should be upon the sex/gender system present in every society. "The needs of sexuality and procreation must be satisfied as much as the need to eat" (165), Rubin points out, and she resists the temptation to see sex oppression solely as a function of capitalist economic forces. However, she sees a society's particular choices about its form of "sex/gender system" as a product of human activity, and argues that it is always tied into economic and political arrangements in any society, capitalist or precapitalist (or indeed socialist). She argues for a comprehensive and interactionist analysis of women in society that takes "everything into account," including women as commodity forms, political structures, technology, marriage forms, and sexuality. She argues for the "mutual inter-dependence of sexuality, economics and politics" (210).

Discussion Questions

1. Is Rubin's argument incompatible with that of Engels? What "causes" a sex/gender system? Is the cause economic? Cultural?

2. Using Rubin's conceptual framework, discuss the political economy of the American sex/gender system.

3. What is the political economy of the sex/gender system of any other society you have studied? Of the North American Indians as outlined by Whitehead?

4. What sanctions does our society use to enforce the notion that men and women are very different, thereby enforcing our own sex/gender system?

5. Evaluate Rubin's notion of marriage as an "exchange of women." Are women universally pawns in this exchange? What is the basis of female power in any contrary instances that can be cited?

Lecture Topics

Social Organization of Prestige and Gender. Ortner and Whitehead argue for a return to the central insights of Margaret Mead that gender, sexuality, and reproduction are symbols invested with meaning by the society in question. Gender, they argue, is only one of many prestige systems that a society may construct (other systems include caste, age ranks, occupational stratification), and indeed the concepts used to legitimize one hierarchy (say caste) may be identical to those used to differentiate between the sexes.

The prestige systems based on gender are "emergent" or "partially autonomous structures with properties not directly reducible to relations of production in the Marxist sense" (15). This autonomy is partial because even though the allocation of prestige may have originated in the past for material reasons, tradition crystalizes after conditions change.

Ortner and Whitehead suggest that the cutting analytical edge in examining a sex-gender system is "how cross-sex social relations in all their manifestations—the sexual division of labor, marriage, consanguinity—ramify upon male prestige from the point of view of the male actor." Women are defined relationally to men (wife, mother, sister), and are valued more or less highly according to how they add or subtract to male prestige as males compete with other men.

Economics, Prestige, and Gender. In a multifaceted discussion of institutionalized homosexuality among North American Indians, Whitehead shows how it was permissible for biological males to become social females. Implicit in this practice was a recognition of female prestige. In rare instances, biological females could assume male status. Those who crossed gender had a recognized and valued status in society, and are known in the anthropological literature as *berdache*.

This institutionalization of homosexuality was based on a cultural construction of gender in which sex-linked occupation and dress were seen as central to "femaleness" and "maleness." The assumption of opposite sex occupation and dress led to an individual's social reclassification; sexual object choice was of secondary importance. Whitehead is thus one of many recent anthropologists to reaffirm Mead's argument about the cross-cultural variability of constructions of gender.

Whitehead's work also throws light upon the economic basis of female prestige, which may be cross-culturally valid. The attraction of North American Indian males to female occupations, she argues, depended upon their economic importance. Women produced and controlled important trade goods such as baskets, textiles, pottery, fur, and leather. Women's occupations were a potential avenue to wealth. They were, in short, prestigious. The Indian cosmology of gender was such, however, that individuals who wished to participate in cross-sex occupations needed to assume the opposite sex role. The overall cosmology of "male" and "female" was thus never undermined. However, cases in anthropology never rest quite so definitively. Whitehead's work too has had its critics. Jacobs and Callender and Kochems take issue with her assumption that men were considered superior to women throughout North America, making a vigorous case that men's roles were simply more visible to the outside. More germane to this immediate discussion, Callender and Kochems believe female prestige went beyond the production of valued durable trade goods, for a female elite survived the destruction of these items by European traders, at least among eastern prairie tribes. Among the Iroquois, female prestige was food based.

Discussion Questions

1. What cultural stereotypes concerning women are used to legitimate the prestige system of gender in our own society? What do these stereotypes have in common with ideological justifications for stratification based on race, class, religion, ethnic origin, or sexual preference? Where do these stereotypes differ?

2. Define "prestige." What are its constituent elements? To what degree are they based on economic substructures in the Marxist sense?

3. Discuss any examples that you can find of prestige systems in which there is not a perfect correlation between status and wealth. What was that prestige system's evolutionary origin? Is the prestige system "readapting" to changed material conditions? Does it have a life of its own?

4. In what role are women valued primarily in our society? In any other society that you have studied? What is the effect of this valuation on all women?

5. How do women add to or subtract from male prestige in American society? In any other society? Are there significant differences?

6. To what degree are certain occupations associated with manhood and womanhood in Western industrial society?

Is the "gender" of those who cross these boundaries questioned?

7. What do the Rubin and Whitehead articles suggest about the nature of human sexuality?

8. Could Whitehead's article on North American Indians support an economic interpretation of female status? Was that her intent? Does the critique of Whitehead by Callender and Kochems support another variant of an economic interpretation?

9. Can one account for the berdache within Chodorow's theory of personality development? Would this be imposing an alien cultural meaning?

THE "WOMEN AND NATURE" DEBATE

Readings for Students and Instructors

MacCormack, Carol P. "Biological Events and Cultural Control." *Signs* 3, no. 1 (Autumn 1977): 93–100.

MacCormack, Carol P., and Marilyn Strathern. *Nature, Culture and Gender.* Cambridge: Cambridge University Press, 1980.

Ortner, Sherry B. "Is Female to Male as Nature Is to Culture?" In *Woman, Culture, and Society,* 67–88.

Sanday, Peggy R. *Female Power and Male Dominance: On the Origins of Sexual Inequality.* Cambridge: Cambridge University Press, 1981.

Lecture Topics

The Women and Nature Thesis. In a pioneering article, Sherry Ortner put forward a cultural rather than an economic explanation of female subordination that has stimulated much debate. Why are women—and their work—devalued? Why is the *belief* that women are inferior so common? Ortner argues that all peoples place a higher value on objects that are under human manipulation and control (culture) than they do on unregulated—and sometimes frightening—events. Women, because of childbearing and menstruation, are seen as closer to nature than to culture and, hence, are devalued.

The Counter-Argument. MacCormack, however, argues that among the Sande, a women's religious society in Sierra Leone, "rather than being uncontrolled reproduction machines, Sande women, with their secret knowledge, public laws, legitimate sanctions, and hierarchical organization, bring women's biology under the most careful cultural control" (94). Women, at least in this society, are not equated with nature, she argues.

MacCormack's position is confirmed by five studies, themselves prompted by Ortner's original article, contained in *Nature, Culture and Gender*. The dichotomy of female/male and nature/culture is apparently not valid for the Bolivian Andes and eighteenth-century France, nor for the Sherbro, Kaulong, and Gimi of New Guinea.

Discussion Questions
1. What expressions of the belief that women are closer to nature can you find in the art, literature, or philosophy of your own society?

2. Does Ortner's theory hold for any of the societies that you have studied in this course?

3. Does MacCormack's article on the Sande necessarily refute Ortner? Why might women's biology among the Sande be "under the most careful cultural control"? Might it be possible to correlate female status with the degree to which women are seen as partaking of culture?

4. What is the status of women in the five societies analyzed in the MacCormack and Strathern volume? Can it be correlated with the degree to which they partake of culture? What is women's economic role?

5. How does Sanday's work modify Ortner's?

PUBLIC VERSUS PRIVATE DOMAIN

Readings
Gamarnikow, Eva et al. *The Public and the Private.* London: Heinemann, 1983.
Rosaldo, Michelle Zimbalist. "Woman, Culture and Society: A Theoretical Overview." In *Woman, Culture, and Society.*
Sudarkasa, Niara. "Female Employment and Family Organization in West Africa." *New Research on Women and Sex Roles in the University of Michigan,* edited by Dorothy McGuigan. Ann

Arbor: University of Michigan Center for the Continuing Education of Women, 1974.

Lecture Topics

Public and Private Spheres. Another non-economic explanation of sex stratification has been put forward by Michelle Rosaldo. She argues that a woman's childrearing responsibilities inhibit her public activities at crucial times in her life cycle and limit her sphere of influence to the private domain. Because of this crucial separation, women are unable to have equal access with men to the sources of economic, political, and cultural power in the public domain.

The Counter-Arguments. Niara Sudarkasa's article points out the limitations of Rosaldo's theory, claiming that, while it may explain the situation in some societies, it does not adequately account for a number of African societies where the distinction between public and private is meaningless. Gamarnikow et al. rework Rosaldo's argument asserting that "when men act it is defined as acting within the public sphere; when women act men define it as acting within the private sphere" (26), and that male activities are more highly valued. Citing primarily Euro-American examples they argue that when women enter the public sphere they are "controlled or can only function effectively, as in the British House of Commons, when they become 'Honorary males.'"

At this point it should be made clear that cultural bias is a problem that is practically unavoidable in any attempt to study women from a cross-cultural perspective. A theoretical model that works well in one cultural context may be completely inappropriate in another. This, of course, does not disqualify all analyses from general application, but it does underscore the necessity of reading critically and testing the statements of theorists against evidence from many societies.

Discussion Questions

1. Why does Rosaldo say that biology alone does not adequately explain sex role differences? How does Rosaldo explain what she calls the "universal fact of sexual asymmetry"?

2. Why does Rosaldo say that attaining the status of women comes naturally while attaining the status of men is a feat? Do you agree? Why is it more difficult for women to

manipulate or control their public image than it is for men to control theirs?

3. According to Rosaldo, what are the distinctions between power, authority, and influence? How would you relate your own experiences to these categories? Give examples of women in your family who exercise power, authority, or influence.

4. Review the concepts Rosaldo uses when she is talking about personality, authority, achieved and ascribed status, nature and culture, women as anomalies, and production. In what sorts of societies are women most likely to have high status?

5. Why does Rosaldo say that equality of status between men and women is best achieved through male participation in the domestic sphere? Do you agree with Rosaldo's conclusion? Do you accept the plan of action suggested by Rosaldo at the conclusion of the article, or does it seem idealistic? What about the opposite plan, that women gain power outside of the domestic sphere? Does this seem more likely to succeed?

6. Sudarkasa points out an important omission from Rosaldo's data. Does this entirely disprove Rosaldo's thesis? Why or why not?

LESBIANISM AND GENDER STRATIFICATION

No discussion of gender, sexual stratification, and the status of women would be complete without considering the subject of lesbianism. Having recognized the importance of this topic, however, one is faced with a heightened version of a familiar dilemma: lack of adequate sources. This present treatment and Evelyn Blackwood's excellent M.A. thesis, "Cross-Cultural Dimensions of Lesbian Relations" (San Francisco State University, 1984), are among the few attempts at a scholarly, broad-scale, comparative analysis of non-Western data on lesbianism.[1] For the most part information on lesbianism from a cross-cultural perspective consists of stray references in diverse sources, sometimes of dubious reliability. Yet the scattered information that does exist provides some rich insights into the status of women, both homosexual and heterosexual, as well as the power of gender ideologies in shaping our very meanings of these words.

In contemporary Euro-American society the lesbian is *potentially* the woman farthest outside the male power structure. Her deepest psychological, emotional, and sexual satisfaction come from relationships with other women. Lesbianism can be deeply threatening to a patriarchal society. It can be—but it is not always. Blackwood analyzes expressions of lesbianism in egalitarian, ranked, and class societies. This present treatment attempts a different categorization, but there is agreement, to use Blackwood's words, that "lesbian behavior does not necessarily constitute an identity" (31). This approach differs from that of Judy Grahn in *Another Mother Tongue: Gay Words, Gay Worlds*. This fascinating, suggestive, mytho-poetic, intensely personal work tries to build a case for a distinctive gay culture that crosses societies and centuries. But it employs etymological and cultural leaps of faith in weaving connections. This analysis stresses cultural specificity in analyzing female or male homosexuality.

Here it is useful to consider cultural expressions of lesbianism as fitting somewhere along a spectrum, the polarities of which are dependent lesbianism and confrontive lesbianism. By dependent lesbianism we mean sexual relationships between women that are tolerated, but nevertheless controlled and proscribed within the confines of patriarchal institutions (e.g., *zenana,* harems, families, and, arguably, convents and boarding schools). By confrontive lesbianism we mean independent lesbian relations that attempt to exist on their own terms outside of the male power structure. As an ideal type, fully autonomous lesbianism has probably never existed. However, the degree to which lesbians are able to transcend patriarchal control says much about the status and options available to all women in a society, for any degree of autonomy presupposes a corresponding degree of female legal, economic, psychological, and cultural control.

In the following readings and commentary we have had to rely on and extrapolate from many works whose chief focus was male homosexuality. We have also had to rely on some Euro-American examples where none from the Third World were available. Because of the paucity of the literature, we have drawn upon the sources that do exist to provide a more fully developed narrative here than elsewhere in this curriculum guide. Much more work needs to be done in this field. We hope that in addition to providing some starting points for analysis, we may focus attention on the enormous gaps research has yet to fill.

Readings for Students

Blackwood, Evelyn. "Sexuality and Gender in Certain Native American Tribes: The Case of Cross-Gender Females." *Signs* 10, no. 1 (Autumn 1984): 27–42.

Bullough, Vern L. *Sexual Variance in Society and History,* Chaps. 2, 9, 10, 11. Chicago: University of Chicago Press, 1976.

Faderman, Lillian. "The Morbidification of Love Between Women by 19th Century Sociologists." *Journal of Homosexuality* 4, no. 1 (Fall 1978): 73–89.

Ferguson, Ann, Jacquelyn N. Zita, and Kathryn Pyne Addelson. "On 'Compulsory Heterosexuality and Lesbian Existence': Defining the Issues." *Signs* 7, no. 1 (Autumn 1981): 158–99.

Ford, Clellan S., and Frank A. Beach. *Patterns of Sexual Behavior,* Chap. 7. New York: Harper and Row, 1951.

Rich, Adrienne. "Compulsory Heterosexuality and Lesbian Existence." *Signs* 5, no. 4 (Summer 1980): 631–60.

Rubin, Gayle. "The Traffic in Women: Notes on the 'Political Economy' of Sex." In *Toward an Anthropology of Women,* 157–216.

Smith-Rosenberg, Carroll. "The Female World of Love and Ritual: Relations Between Women in Nineteenth Century America." *Signs* 1, no. 1 (Autumn 1975): 1–29.

Readings for Instructors

Ashworth, A. E., and W. M. Walker. "Social Structures and Homosexuality: A Theoretical Appraisal." *British Journal of Sociology* 23, no. 2 (June 1972): 146–58.

Baker, Susan W. "Biological Influences on Human Sex and Gender." In *Women: Sex and Sexuality,* edited by Catharine R. Stimpson and Ethel Spector Person. Chicago: Chicago University Press, 1980.

Bell, Alan P., Martin S. Weinberg, and Sue Kiefer Hammersmith. *Sexual Preference: Its Development in Men and Women.* Bloomington: Indiana University Press, 1981.

Callender, Charles, and Lee M. Kochems. "The North American Berdache." *Current Anthropology* 24, no. 4 (1983): 443–56.

Carrier, Joseph M. " 'Sex-Role Preference' as an Explanatory Variable in Homosexual Behavior." *Archives of Sexual Behavior* 6, no. 1 (1977): 53–65.

Cavin, Susan. *Lesbian Origins.* San Francisco: Ism Press, 1986.

Connexions 3 (Winter 1982). Special issue: Global Lesbianism.

Cruikshank, Margaret. ed. *Lesbian Studies: Present and Future.* New York: The Feminist Press, 1982.

Evans-Pritchard, E. E. "Sexual Inversion Among the Azande."

American Anthropologist 72 (1970): 1428–74.

Faderman, Lillian. *Surpassing the Love of Men: Romantic Friendship and Love Between Women from the Renaissance to the Present.* New York: William Morrow & Co., 1981.

Falwell, Jerry. *Listen America!* Garden City, N.Y.: Doubleday, 1980.

Fitzgerald, Thomas K. "A Critique of Anthropological Research on Homosexuality." *Journal of Homosexuality* 2, no. 4 (Summer 1977): 385–97.

Fontaine, Carolyn. "Perspectives on Lesbian Women." Available from Lesbian-Feminist Clearinghouse, Women's Studies, 1012 CI, University of Pittsburgh, PA 15260.

Gagnon, J. H., and W. Simon. *Sexual Conduct: The Social Sources of Human Sexuality.* Chicago: Aldine Publishing Co., 1973.

Gay, Judith. "Mummies and Babies and Friends and Lovers in Lesotho." *Journal of Homosexuality* 11, no. 3/4 (1985 tentative publication).

Grahn, Judy. *Another Mother Tongue: Gay Words, Gay Worlds.* Boston: Beacon Press, 1984.

Jacobs, Sue-Ellen. "The Berdache." In *Cultural Diversity and Homosexuality,* edited by Stephen Murray. New York: Irvington Press, in press. (Unexamined.)

Kelly, Ray. "Witchcraft and Sexual Relations." In *Man and Woman in the New Guinea Highlands,* edited by P. Brown and G. Buchbinder. Washington: American Anthropological Association, 1975.

Ross, Michael W., Lesley J. Rogers, and Helen McCulloch. "Stigma, Sex, and Society: A New Look at Gender Differentiation and Sexual Variation." *Journal of Homosexuality* 3, no. 4 (Summer 1978) 315–30.

Shostak, Marjorie. *Nisa: The Life and Words of a !Kung Woman.* New York: Vintage, 1983.

Ungaretti, John R. "Pederasty, Heroism, and the Family in Classical Greece." *Journal of Homosexuality* 3, no. 3 (Spring 1978): 291–300.

Weeks, Jeffrey. *Sex, Politics and Society: The Regulation of Sexuality Since 1800.* New York: Longman, 1981.

Whitehead, Harriet. "The Bow and the Burden Strap: A New Look at Institutionalized Homosexuality in Native North America." In *Sexual Meanings.*

Lecture Topics

"Causes" of Homosexuality. Given the amount of misinformation and societal prejudice surrounding the topic of homosexuality, instructors may well find it necessary to give basic information about the causes and incidence of homosexuality before proceeding with a discussion of homosexuality and its interrelationship with gender stratification.

Fontaine's excellent curriculum and source guide, which provides an interdisciplinary course focused mainly on American women, "examines the images, experiences, history, and psychology of lesbian women." It includes sections on psychological and hormonal theories of homosexuality together with criticism of those theories. Of great value too is Cruikshank's *Lesbian Studies.* In addition to extended discussions of pedagogical issues, this guide contains syllabi and bibliographies dealing mainly with the Euro-American lesbian experience.

Instructors may also wish to consult the articles by Ross, Rogers, McCulloch, and Baker. These articles review the literature on hormonal and cross-gender identity theories and find that many are deeply flawed. Ross et al. conclude that homosexuality may in many cases simply be an individual personality preference. Though this article is undoubtedly not the last word on the subject (indeed its conclusions have recently been challenged by Bell, Weinberg, and Hammersmith, researchers at the Kinsey Institute), it does provide a brief and critical overview of existing scholarship on "causation."

Sexual Preference from the Kinsey Institute is the most exhaustive and systematic study to date of a large population of homosexuals (nearly 1,000 men and women) contrasted with a control group of heterosexuals (nearly 500). Comparing the life experiences of homosexual and heterosexual respondents, the authors dismiss all of the common psychosocial explanations of homosexual development: parental influence, labelling, early seduction, poor relations with the opposite sex, etc. The only indicator of homosexual preference was a slightly greater tendency toward gender role nonconformity at an early age. Homosexual feelings manifested themselves early in life. The authors call for a reexamination of hormonal theories, even though, contrary to sensationalized press reports at the time of publication, their own research does not involve biological data.

Finally, we recommend Gagnon and Simon, and Weeks, whose works are considered the classic expositions of the theory that all sexual behavior, homosexual and heterosexual, is learned through scripts that vary cross-culturally and historically.

Cross-Cultural Survey of Homosexuality (Ford and Beach, Blackwood). An early, and still the standard, survey of homosexuality from a cross-cultural perspective was conducted by C. S. Ford and F. A. Beach and published in 1951. Drawing on data in the Human Relation Area Files, Ford and Beach found that, "In 49 [64 percent] of the 76 societies other than our own for which information is available, homosexual activities are considered normal and socially acceptable for certain members of the community" (130). However, because most anthropologists collecting this data were male and did not have, or simply neglected, data on female sexuality, the Area Files contain specific information on lesbianism in only seventeen societies. After an exhaustive survey of the ethnographic literature, Blackwood found references to lesbianism in one hundred societies, calling into question its lesser incidence.

Variables in the Cultural Expressions of Homosexuality. Although homosexuality occurs in many—and possibly all—cultures, its incidence and forms of cultural expression vary. Kinsey has argued that most people have the capacity to respond sexually to persons of the same sex. Only a comparatively small percentage of people at either end of the spectrum are exclusively heterosexual or homosexual. But it is clear that most people in fact do not act upon homosexual feelings. Social conditioning may inhibit and even totally supress such behavior (as it tends to in Western civilization), or cultural norms may permit it under certain circumstances (e.g., during male initiation rites among the Karaki of New Guinea or in female initiation rites in precolonial Lesotho in southern Africa). Society shapes the ways and structures the circumstances under which homosexuality is expressed. Further, it may shape the cultural definitions or parameters of male homosexuality and lesbianism differently, or permit one but not the other. Although lesbianism has generally been under stricter suppression than male homosexuality, there are at least two documented cases (among the North American Kaska and Kutenai peoples) where only female homosexuality was institutionalized.

We should make clear that what we are discussing here are homosexual relationships that have some form of cultural recognition (either positive or negative), and that are sufficiently widespread to have been named by the participants and by social commentators. There are doubtless countless numbers of homosexual relationships, both casual and enduring, that remain isolated and unnamed, unrecognized by society, and unadmitted by the particpants, who may believe they exist in isolation. At a sociological level, these relationships, however crucial to those involved, do not throw light upon the ways in which a society constructs its system of gender.

Whitehead draws a useful distinction, we should note, between "spontaneous" homosexuality and "institutionalized" homosexuality. Spontaneous homosexuality occurs between individuals, often despite official norms. Institutionalized homosexuality varies in its expression, and rests in each society upon a different cultural construction of gender and a different cosmology. For example, in the south-central lowlands of New Guinea, manhood is thought to be embodied in semen. Youths can be elevated to full manhood only by sexual contact with older males. Similarly, womanhood is thought to be embodied in menstrual and parturitional blood, and anthropologists think (the record is not clear) that women have parallel ways of transmitting adulthood. Among the Etoero of the southern highlands of New Guinea, homosexuality is the preferred sexual practice, and is rooted in the belief that heterosexual relations cause crops to wither and die. Clearly both homosexuality and heterosexuality are shaped by a society's cosmology, as are concepts of "male" and "female."

The cross-gender role—*berdache*—assumed by both men and women among certain Native American peoples serves as a warning not to impose rigid Euro-American sexual categories on other cultures (see Blackwood, Whitehead, and Callender and Kochems). Callender and Kochems find this cross-gender category in which members of one biological sex assumed the roles and occupations of the opposite sex among 113 groups. Most of their examples are male. Blackwood documents female berdache among 33 peoples, and provides the fullest description of the cross-gender female. Cross-gender females hunted, trapped, fought, and established households, often marrying other women. The fluidity of categories of sexuality was such that homosexual relationships could also occur between non-berdache, while the cross-gender female's sexual partner was considered a traditional female, who, if divorced might opt for a heterosexual relationship (Blackwood, *Signs*, 35–36).

Sexuality must be considered in its cultural context, and should not be assumed to mean the same thing everywhere. Beyond the common theme of same-sex sexual contact, the meaning attached to the behavior can vary. Unfortunately this cultural variety has not always been recognized by western psychoanalysts nor by some feminist writers. A survey of some of the very different ways and circumstances under which societies have encouraged, permitted, or tolerated homosexuality is instructive.

Age Groups. In some societies homosexuality is accepted among youth. This has been documented for Ngonde boys, and among !Kung girls and boys. In the latter case it seems to have been regarded as a natural period of sexual learning before heterosexuality. The literature is unfortunately silent about adult homosexuality, both male and female (Bullogh, Kelly, Shostak, Whitehead).

Intergenerational Homosexuality. In some societies pederasty (sexual relations between adult men and youths) is considered normal. To the examples drawn from New Guinea mentioned earlier, we should also add that of classical Greece (Ungaretti). In Easter Island sexual relationships between middle-aged and younger women were recognized (Blackwood, thesis, 40).

Sex-Segregated Settings. Segregation or absence of the opposite sex has sometimes been accompanied by acceptance of homosexual relationships. Among the Azande of central Africa, for example, young warriors deprived of women substituted "boy wives." Certainly the incidence of homosexual behavior rises in sex-segregated settings, as has been noted in institutions as diverse as single-sex boarding schools, harems, and prisons. Sex-segregated cultures such as Victorian England and nineteenth-century America were also characterized by all-consuming emotional relationships between women friends. Because of the general repression of female sexuality, however, these relationships did not necessarily include a sexual component, though it would be foolhardy to preclude the possibility in some instances (see for example recent feminist studies of Emily Dickinson). In polygamous societies, because older, wealthier males tended to have several wives, leaving fewer women available to younger men, there was often a tolerance for male homosexual activity, and lesbianism in large polygamous households was sometimes condoned in ancient China, among the Azande, and perhaps in harems (Ashworth, Bullough, Evans-Pritchard, Faderman, Walker, Whitehead). The references to lesbianism in harems are very unclear on the issue of social attitudes. Some writers suggest an amused toleration surrounded the practice; nineteenth-century travelers' tales in particular hint darkly at a widespread practice and toleration, but these are scarcely impeccable authorities. As Kathleen Barry has pointed out, the practice of clitoridectomy may well have been directed in part toward suppressing erotic enjoyment between women (see Chapter 11 on "Genital Mutilation" below). However, male control could ultimately be enforced. Azande wives, for instance, had to request permission of their husbands to establish lesbian relationships; unauthorized liaisons were severely punished (Blackwood thesis, 50).

Adult Life-Choices. Homosexuality as a permanent choice between two adults was recognized, as we have seen, among some native American peoples, provided one of them (the berdache) adopted the occupation of the opposite sex. Adult homosexuality is also unstigmatized in Polynesia.

Ritual Homosexuality. In some societies homosexuality was seen as "a sign of spirituality, of commerce with gods and spirits, and a source of sacred power" (Callender and Kochems, 455). These beliefs were often associated with an androgynous or bisexual conception of the divine.

Homosexuality as a Cultural Mirror of Gender Roles. We have already seen in Mead how culture shapes what are considered "male" and "female" gender roles. Homosexual social behavior often mirrors a society's sex-role ideology. Consider for example the following instances:

1. *Active-passive dichotomies.* In societies where there is a sharp dichotomy between masculine (active) and feminine (passive) sex-role behavior, homosexual behavior often copies these roles. In modern Turkey, Greece, urban Mexico, and Brazil, for example, all societies with a cult of machismo, considerably less stigma is attached to the male who plays an active, masculine "insertor" role in a homosexual relationship than to the passive partner, who plays a female role. The latter is an object of ridicule, reflecting the low status of women. Unfortunately, we do not know enough about lesbian behavior in these societies to make direct comparisons. However, in our own society, we can see the power of gender ideologies in the behavior of some lesbian couples who are unaffected by the feminist movement's critiques of traditional sex roles, and who adopt masculine (butch) and feminine (femme) roles in their relationships.

2. *The "effeminate" male and "masculine" female (Fitzgerald, Carrier).* Some cultures have made it a self-fulfilling

prophesy that "effeminate" males (or, more rarely, "masculine" females), that is, those who did not conform to cultural expectations, would be socialized to cross-gender behavior. Among some North American Indian peoples who had the category of the berdache, male children were apparently observed and tested from an early age to see if their interests conformed to same or opposite-sex occupations.

3. *Hierarchy (Ungaretti)*. Male homosexual relationships, from a cross-cultural perspective, have often reflected the unequal, hierarchical relationships between men and women. The Etoero provide one example of this, classical Greece another. In ancient Greek society, pederasty flourished. In its ideal expression pederasty provided "an adult male with the intellectual and social company of an attractive youth who, in turn, admired and hoped to learn from his adult lover." Between adult Greek males there was "a fiercely competitive ethic that made love between two men of equal age and rank practically impossible" (Ungaretti, 292–93). The practice of boy wives among Azande warriors, deprived of women, existed in a culture in which women had slave status. This hierarchical ordering was sometimes found among women: In Dahomey, female soldiers were forbidden under penalty of death to have sexual relations with men. They were provided instead with female servants (Blackwood, thesis, 52).

Contrasts in the Acceptance of Male and Female Homosexuality. It is revealing to examine the conditions under which female and male homosexuality have been accepted by societies. If we accept the thesis that a central historical fact has been the male control of women and the struggle to maintain that control, then the dynamic underlying acceptance and nonacceptance of homosexuality in different periods and in different cultures becomes clear. The dividing line is the degree to which homosexuality, male or female, upsets the prevailing patriarchal ideology, which itself can take different forms.

In ancient Greece, where male homosexuality was accepted, it was accompanied by an idealized and intensely masculine ideology. In the military society of Sparta, for example, it was said that "an army of lovers cannot fail." Furthermore, tolerance of male homosexuality went hand in hand with misogyny, rigid female sex roles, and extreme gender stratification. Male homosexuality was not perceived as threatening to the patriarchal social order; indeed it reinforced it. Lesbianism did not achieve anything like the same degree of social acceptance. The notion of female equality was totally foreign to Greek society. For example, Aspasia (470–410 B.C.), an Athenian scholar and philosopher who asserted the right of women to live as man's equal, was charged and tried for "impiety." Only the intervention of her lover, Pericles, saved her life.

In the contemporary United States, by way of contrast, opponents of gay liberation see both male and female homosexuals as deeply threatening to the prevailing patriarchal social order. The writings of Jerry Falwell, the head of the right-wing fundamentalist movement that characterizes itself as the Moral Majority, are particularly revealing of an underlying attitude: the perceived threat to patriarchal control, based on the traditional division of sex roles. Falwell's views contain many undocumented and unexamined assumptions, among them that lesbians are unfeminine and male homosexuals effeminate. The cause of the gay liberation movement, according to Falwell, is that men and women have sinfully rejected their sex roles as

> designated by God. God's plan is for men to be manly . . . In the Christian home the father is responsible to exercise spiritual control and to be the head over his wife and children . . . Women are to be feminine and manifest the "ornament of a meek and quiet spirit" . . . In the Christian home the woman is to be submissive . . . Homosexuality is Satan's diabolical attack upon the family, God's order in Creation (150–52, 184–85).

Male leadership in the family has faltered, according to Falwell, and female leadership has asserted itself out of desperation, leading to attacks upon the divine order such as the Equal Rights Amendment. "It is shocking," he says, "how many feminists are lesbians." In this world review, lesbians are a particular threat because they do not accept male authority; and male homosexuals have abrogated their responsibility to rule within a traditional family. Both attitudes undermine male authority.

It is noteworthy that in a number of the examples of the toleration or acceptance of sexual activity between women we have found, it has essentially been under male control either directly (as in the French court or harems), symbolically (among the

Mbunda and Nama), or integrated as a sexual activity concurrent with heterosexuality, which received a higher valuation (as with the Aranda). In homosexually segregated societies of New Guinea, males still maintained overall social control.

Lesbianism: A Revolt Against Patriarchy? There is a temptation in surveying the multitude of means whereby women have been oppressed and suppressed by institutions under male control to see lesbianism as a revolt against patriarchy. Adrienne Rich asserts, for instance, that "we can say there is a nascent feminist political content in the act of choosing a woman lover or life partner in the face of institutional heterosexuality" (659). At times this is undoubtedly true, but we must approach such assertions born of our own cultural experience with caution when we apply them as a universal cross-cultural or trans-historical reality.

The existence of lesbian sexual behavior in a society does not necessarily signify a revolt against patriarchy—at least not as an act that directly challenges patriarchal ideology. There are cross-cultural instances where lesbian activity is successfully integrated into patterns of male dominance and heterosexuality. Consider, for instance, the case of the Aranda women in Australia, who commonly stimulate each other's clitorises, but who simultaneously say "A man will come with a big penis and cohabit with you." The Mbundu and Nama women in Africa may furnish another example, though the evidence is less clear. They reportedly use an artificial penis while masturbating each other (Beach, 133). Admittedly the possibility of observer bias is great here; a dildo does not necessarily connote a penis to the women involved. But in the case of the Aranda, and perhaps in the latter instances as well, it seems as if heterosexuality is being affirmed either at a symbolic or real level. In the Solomon Islands, ritual lesbian activity played a part in first menstruation and marriage ceremonies (Blackwood, thesis, 43). Are these really "nascent feminist" actions, or are they simply accepted sexual behaviors in societies without our strong same-sex strictures? These are societies, we might add, in which heterosexuality is institutionalized and the women involved are or will be heterosexually married.

What of lesbianism in harems? Lesbianism in such a setting may be motivated by many reasons: by the scarcity of men, and concurrently the availability of women; by innate sexual preference (if some theorists on the origins of homosexuality are to be believed); as a form of sexual experimentation; or as a source of love and support and an act of rebellion in an oppressive situation. The difficulty for us as historical and cultural outsiders is that we are unable to gauge *intent* by listening to the words of the women themselves. Given the cross-cultural range of behaviors and cultural constructs of homosexuality, both male and female, we cannot assume from the mere presence of lesbian sexual activity that we know the underlying personal or ideological meaning.

Rich herself identifies one crucial dividing line that transforms lesbian sexual activity into a feminist political act: "For lesbian existence to realize this political content in an ultimately liberating form, the erotic choice must deepen and expand into conscious woman-identification" (659).

There are at least two historical instances where lesbianism has arisen in a community form, with a self-conscious woman-identification, and where the challenge to male dominance was central. These movements we will term confrontive lesbianism to distinguish them from the adaptive, dependent examples, which did not challenge the male power structures but whose sexual behaviors were accommodated within it. These two examples arose in sexually stratified societies, but in both instances women had gained an independent economic toehold. In the case of the Marriage Resistance Movement in Kwangtung, and especially in the modern lesbian-feminist movement of the West, male dominance has been challenged head on.

The Marriage Resistance Movement in Kwangtung, China, in the nineteenth century (see Chapter 7 on "Resistance, Alternatives, and Female Power") can be seen as the stirrings of a confrontive autonomous lesbianism in some of its expressions. Women lived apart from men, controlled their earnings, and had a religious justification for remaining unmarried. Some of the women involved remained celibate; others formed sexual relationships with other women. In current Western lesbian liberation movements, autonomy has been carried even further.

Judged against the sweep of centuries, contemporary Western lesbianism, especially its separatist wing, represents the most thoroughgoing assault to date on patriarchal control of women. Its importance lies in the degree of its self-conscious examination and rejection of the roots of patriarchy. It is multifaceted in its approach to women's liberation. Some lesbians try to build a female culture with their own unique modes of expression in the arts (in the visual arts, the work of Judy Chicago; or in music, the work of Kay Gardner). Some seek to transform the structures of male language (Mary Daly, Adrienne Rich). Others reject the patriarchal assumptions of Western religion and reclaim female spirituality as an entity apart (Zee Budapest, Mary Daly), or attempt to construct economically self-sufficient separatist communes, or mutual support systems within mainstream society. Some seek new rules of interpersonal and organizational relationships based on equality of power rather than hierarchy, while others stress the importance of women's self-defense and control of their own bodies. Full lesbian autonomy, even among separatists, however, remains qualified: patriarchal law and attitudes still exercise their power over the lesbian mother fighting for custody of her child; job and housing security for "out" lesbians remains tenuous at best; and negative social attitudes continue to take their psychic toll. Nevertheless, we may discern in the modern lesbian movement the first stirrings of what has hitherto been only a theoretical possibility: women living on their own terms, emotionally, sexually, culturally, economically, and politically bonded with other women on a permanent basis. However, this separatist solution may be culturally embedded. In relatively egalitarian societies, namely North American Indian tribes, an institutionalized cross-gender homosexual status existed in an interdependent communal framework.

Lesbianism and Female Status. A great deal more work is needed that relates the status of women in society to institutionalized and non-institutionalized lesbianism. In surveying the admittedly meager literature on the subject, one is struck by the fact that, harems aside, in most societies where lesbian sexual activity is recognized and reported, women have a relatively high status. The !Kung and Aranda are hunter-gatherers, the Mbundu are horticulturalists who are matrilineal, and the Nama are pastoralists whose women gather food and milk the herd, and brideservice is performed. In each case women have significant sources of economic power. Among native American peoples the existence of female berdache signifies that women were not regarded as so totally "other" or inferior that a transition to male status could not be made. Indeed, the existence of male berdache who assumed female roles signifies the value placed on female occupations, whereby one could amass significant wealth, and a number of scholars agree that some precolonial Native American societies were egalitarian. However, all correlations between lesbianism and status may be spurious. It may simply be that this connection is apparent because women and their sexual activities are better documented in those societies where they have high status.

We can say with certainty that lesbianism as a life choice (as distinct from a transitional activity or as an activity concurrent with heterosexuality) presupposes by its very definition that women have enough personal power to sustain themselves apart from men. In Euro-American society, the growth of a self-conscious lesbian community is linked with the rise of advanced capitalism in Western Europe and the United States (see Ferguson, 160–68). Lesbianism as a permanent life choice or possibility arose in an urban subculture in which women's education and wages permitted some degree of economic independence from the controlling influence of the patriarchal family. It also coincided with the growth of studies of human sexuality, which provided an understanding (albeit limited and oftentimes destructive) of the concept of "lesbian." Naming is a form of power.

The extreme difficulty of claiming lesbianism as a permanent "choice" (this word seems trivializing because for many concerned the drive is a deep one) without the material underpinnings can be gauged by a recent tragic report from India. Two lesbian couples, in different cities, fell in love while in school but upon graduation were unable to contend with the combined pressures of families, inadequate wages, and hostile landlords. Both couples attempted suicide, one pair successfully.[2] At school, lesbian behavior was tolerated as a phase; when the women attempted permanent bonding apart from men, it proved impossible.

Significantly, in Euro-American society the growth of women's economic independence, which made it possible for the first time for women to make permanent commitments to each other, coincided with what Lillian Faderman has called the "morbidification" of love between women. In the early nineteenth century, love between women was seen as harmless and temporary (Smith-Rosenberg, Faderman). By the end of the century feminism was on the rise and a threatened patriarchy saw same-sex love as morbid, perverted, and destructive to society. Thus we might also conclude that the more a society fulminates against women bonding with women, the greater the likelihood that profound changes are afoot in the status of all women.

Enforced Female Heterosexuality (Rubin, Rich). From the available data it seems arguable that from a cross-cultural perspective, lesbianism has been subject to more suppression than has male homosexuality. Rubin's writing on the political economy of sex provides an insight into why this is so. Rubin, drawing on Levi-Strauss, points to the fact that kinship systems depend on the exchange of women and hence involve "obligatory heterosexuality." "The suppression of the homosexual component of human sexuality, and by corollary, the oppression of homosexuals, is therefore the product of the same system whose rules and regulations oppress women" (180). However, because rights to women are held by men, obligatory heterosexuality is enforced more strongly in the case of women. Or, as we have seen, it is tolerated within strict limits. The exceptions seem to be in relatively egalitarian societies or in circumstances in which women have gained some degree of economic power.

In her provocative article, which supplements and goes beyond Rubin's notion of the political economy of enforced heterosexuality, Rich challenges the assumption that underlies even feminist scholarship, that heterosexuality is the more natural or common state for women. She argues that lesbianism is the more innate orientation for women and provides an outline of the range of "constraints and sanctions which, historically, have enforced or insured the coupling of women with men and obstructed or penalized our coupling or allying in independent groups with other women" (636). Though Rich's argument is no doubt contentious, her article nevertheless is valuable in drawing attention to the heterosexist bias in much feminist scholarship, and in its broad-reaching treatment of the many powerful forces, ranging from economic constraints to physical brutality, that compel heterosexuality.

Discussion Questions

1. If, as Rubin asserts, enforced heterosexuality is a function of a patriarchal kinship system based on the exchange of women, why are many women in those systems homophobic? What encourages homophobia in American society?

2. What might be some of the indicators (e.g., economic, political, cultural) of an autonomous lesbian relationship? Does it exist in our society? Has it or does it exist in any society?

3. Discuss Rich's assertion that women may be innately homosexual. What evidence is there to support or refute her?

4. Discuss possible reasons why homosexual relations are considered socially acceptable in some societies and not in others. Does this variation undercut Rubin's argument? Why or why not?

5. Were the romantic friendships of the nineteenth century that Faderman describes necessarily lesbian relationships?

Explore the distinction that some have drawn between "homoemotional" and "homosexual" relationships. Is there a clear distinction?

6. Discuss Rich's theory that because heterosexuality has to be so strongly enforced it is not the natural sexual orientation for women. Examine the awesome list of controls she lists. Are these directed at enforcing heterosexuality or monogamy or pure inheritance lines? Examine some of the controls in their cultural contexts. What view of female sexuality underlies them? Where do cultural views differ, and where are they the same?

7. Discuss Rich's concept of a "lesbian continuum." Who is excluded? Included?

8. What evidence of heterosexist bias can you find in any of the books that you have read thus far in the course?

9. Reflect upon how your own answers to discussion questions today may have been influenced by heterosexist or homosexist bias. How can we reduce subjectivity in scholarship? Is subjectivity always bad?

Notes

1. As we go to press, Susan Cavin, *Lesbian Origins* (San Francisco: Ism Press, 1986) has just been released. Cavin argues that the first enduring social relationships were female–female, drawing among other things upon cross-cultural origin myths and sex-ratio data in the Human Relation Area Files. Upon her own admission, she is unable to "prove" her theory, but she has mustered enough evidence to force a lively debate.

2. "Bury Us Together," *Connexions* 3 (Winter 1982): 7.

Chapter Five

WOMEN AND RELIGION

Karen Sinclair

Women's religious experiences have not been thoroughly studied and their contributions to religious life have been underestimated. Reasons for this are not very hard to find. From the available information it is clear that the religious experience of women differs from that of men. Yet all too often it is the masculine perspective that is solicited and then presented as typical and representative. More importantly, religious experiences are quite often private affairs, closed to public scrutiny. The inherently private nature of women's lives tends to reinforce the personal, confidential dimension of religious awareness.

Another difficulty, and challenge, is reflected in the nature of the data collected. On the one hand, we have anthropological analyses of non-Western, tribal cultures. On the other, we have philosophical and theological discussions of the world's major religions. Moreover, current concern in the West with the role of women in the Church has led to a strong focus on the Judeo-Christian tradition. Thus we are faced with diverse ideological systems and various modes of scholarship. Nevertheless, parallels and commonalities are clearly in evidence. Therefore, despite the emphasis on and better documentation of women in Western religion in the available literature, this module will take a cross-cultural approach. The Judeo-Christian tradition may often be a useful example to illustrate a larger point, while at the same time the experiences of women in diverse cultural contexts may illuminate the more familiar Western material.

Religious systems are ideological systems: they structure and reflect a society's perception of the cosmos and the social world. Women's position in religious systems is often a reflection, however oblique, of women's status in society. Yet religious experience frequently establishes a dimension that is absent in the more restricted secular lives of most women. Extraordinary spiritual occurrences inevitably effect a separation between religious preoccupations and daily domestic concerns. Even in less charged circumstances, religious participation often provides a means of achieving female solidarity. This can easily be overlooked when the more dramatic activities of men are the focus of study.

Many conservative scholars have argued that women's limited participation and involvement in religious life reflect their lesser social importance. For, so the argument goes, as priests and theologians, men control both information and, more importantly, salvation. But this argument is only partially true. At the very least, women participate in those rituals that concern them most— rituals that deal with birth and death. More to the point, in many societies women are religious practitioners; they are shamans, nuns, and midwives. But their true prominence and preeminence derive from their roles as religious innovators. Religious cults and movements provide a forum for the alienated and oppressed. It is no accident that women are so often foremost in these new religions. We therefore see and hear women quite clearly in the early days of Christianity, Buddhism, Islam, and, arguably, Hinduism and again in the many cults and "heresies" that have arisen in reaction to specific oppressive social structures and to the often equally oppressive ideology that supports them.

Readings for Students
Falk, Nancy Auer, and Rita Gross, eds. *Unspoken Worlds: Women's Religious Lives in Nonwestern Cultures.* New York: Harper and Row, 1980.
Plaskow, Judith, ed. *Women and Religion.* Chico, Cal.: Scholars Press, 1974.
Reuther, Rosemary. *New Woman, New Earth.* New York: Seabury Press, 1975.
Reuther, Rosemary, and Eleanor McLaughlin, eds. *Women of Spirit.* New York: Simon and Schuster, 1979.

Readings for Instructors
Carmody, Denise. *Women and World Religions.* Nashville: Parthenon Press, 1979.
Gross, Rita. *Beyond Androcentricism: New Essays on Women and Religion.* Missoula: Scholars Press, University of Montana, 1977.

Hoch-Smith, J., and Anita Spring, eds. *Women in Ritual and Symbolic Roles.* New York: Plenum Press, 1978.
O'Faolain, Julia, and Laura Martines, eds. *Not in God's Image: Women in History from the Greeks to the Victorians.* New York: Harper and Row, 1973.
Reuther, Rosemary. *Sexism and God Talk.* Boston: Beacon Press, 1983.
Reuther, Rosemary, and Rosemary Keller. *Women and Religion in America,* vol. 1 New York: Harper and Row, 1981.
Sanday, Peggy. *Female Power and Male Dominance.* Cambridge: Cambridge University Press, 1981.
Signs 2, no.2 (Winter 1976). Special issue: Women and Religion.

WOMEN AND RELIGIOUS IDEOLOGY

Religious systems both reflect and reinforce cultural values and patterns of social organization. Yet religious systems must also be viewed as symbolic systems whose "messages" may be only indirectly related to patterns of actual social relations. The mere existence of a goddess in a society's pantheon does not necessarily suggest an exalted position for women. While it might be feasible to argue that ideology (religious or otherwise) defines the position of women, it is also important to note, as Reuther does, the reciprocal claim that sexism quite often informs ideology.

Readings for Students
Bird, Phyllis. "Images of Women in the Old Testament." In *Religion and Sexism,* edited by Rosemary Reuther, 41–77. New York: Simon and Schuster, 1974.
Fiorenza, Elisabeth. "Word, Spirit, and Power: Women in Early Christian Communities." In *Women of Spirit,* 29–70.
McLaughlin, Eleanor. "Women, Power and the Pursuit of Holiness in Medieval Christianity." In *Women of Spirit,* 99–130.
Ortner, Sherry. "The Virgin and the State." *Feminist Studies* 4 (October 1978).
Reuther, Rosemary. *New Woman, New Earth.*
Reuther, Rosemary, and Eleanor McLaughlin. "Women's Leadership in the Jewish and Christian Traditions: Continuity and Change." In *Women of Spirit,* 15–28.

Readings for Instructors

Bruteau, Beatrice. "The Image of the Virgin Mother." in *Women and Religion*, 93–104.

Bullough, Vern. *The Subordinate Sex*. Chicago: University of Illinois Press, 1973.

Daly, Mary. *The Church and the Second Sex*. New York: Harper and Row Colophon Books, 1975.

Driver, Anne Barstow. "Religion." *Signs* 2 (Winter 1976): 434–42.

Falk, Nancy Auer. "An Image of Woman in Old Buddhist Literature: The Daughters of Mara." In *Women and Religion*, 105–12.

Harding, N. Esther. *Women's Mysteries: Ancient and Modern*. New York: Harper and Row Colophon Books, 1971.

Hauptman, Judith. "Images of Woman in the Talmud." In *Religion and Sexism*, 184–212.

Hoch-Smith, J., and Anita Spring. "Introduction." In *Women in Ritual and Symbolic Roles*.

McLaughlin, Eleanor. "Equality of Souls, Inequality of Sexes: Women in Medieval Theology." In *Religion and Sexism*, 213–60.

Pagels, Elaine. "What Became of God the Mother? Conflicting Images of God in Early Christianity." *Signs* 2 (Winter 1976): 293–303.

Patai, Raphael. *The Hebrew Goddess*. New York: Ictad Press, 1968.

Prusak, Bernard. "Woman: Seductive Siren and Source of Sin?" In *Religion and Sexism*, 89–107.

Reuther, Rosemary. "Misogynism and Virginal Feminism in the Fathers of the Church." In *Religion and Sexism*, 150–83.

Sakala, Carol. "Spiritual Leaders: Sarada Devi, The Mother, Anandamayi Ma and Others: [a bibliography]," 202–06. In *Women of South Asia: A Guide to Resources*. Millwood, N.Y.: Kraus International Pubs., 1980.

Scroggs, R. "Paul and the Eschatological Women." *Journal of the American Academy of Religion* 40, no. 3: 283–303.

Stone, Merlin. *When God Was a Woman*. New York: Harcourt Brace Jovanovich, 1976.

Lecture Topics

Earth Goddesses and Fertility. Many religious systems portray women preeminently as childbearers. Therefore the procreative aspects of womanhood are often idealized and deified while other aspects of feminine identity are neglected. Notions of female sexuality are at times reflected in the religious mythology of a culture. It is important to consider the variety of rationales that attempt to explain, or explain away, the existence of females in the religious pantheon. The Bullough and Reuther volumes and the Area Studies contain examinations of the views of women held by the major religions. Reuther, for example, maintains that in the Ancient Near East, goddesses enjoyed a position equal to that of the gods. With the advent of monotheism, a hierarchy developed and women were placed in a subordinate position. In the New Testament, such hierarchy takes on the form of cosmic principle.

Female Goddesses and Male Authority. As we have seen in Chapter 2, the existence of a goddess does not betoken female hegemony. Most anthropologists deny the existence of a matriarchal stage of human society but would not deny its effectiveness as mythology. Hoch-Smith and Spring suggest that if women were in charge of goddess cults, if fertility as a female principle was glorified, then at the very least, women would have thought well of themselves. In an innovative and brilliant analysis, Reuther examines the social consequences of goddess worship, and shows that the veneration of the female reproductive role in Christianity fails to grant women supremacy. On the contrary, she argues that it is precisely the worship of these feminine functions that allows and sustains a male definition of humanity. Claims of matriarchy notwithstanding, religious ideology has often been used to exclude women. The development of the early church is a history of the denigration of women and their loss of status.

Images of Women in World Religions. The position of women in the early church was transformed from one of relative equality with men to one of subordination. This change is reflected in many of the early church writings and in the decreasing range of activities acceptable for women. The cult of Mary—while representing an apparent symbolic elevation of motherhood—nevertheless firmly established the subordinate social position of women. (Marianismo, or the cult of the Virgin, may function as a source of strength for women in Latin America. It does not, however, challenge the social order.) A similar decline in the importance and status of women over time has been documented for Hinduism, Islam, and Buddhism (see Area Studies). Parallels to the cult of Mary may be found in Hinduism, where worship of various manifestations of the goddess (Devi, Durga, Kali, Lakshmi, et al.) is common, though the goddess has both compassionate and frightening characteristics. Historical women have also attained great prominence in Hindu sects, but as Holy Mothers or consorts of male religious adepts. Sarada Devi, consort of Sri Ramakrishna, and The Mother, of Sri Aurobindo's *ashram*, are modern examples. As is the case with Mary, women are venerated but their role is circumscribed.

World View and Women. There is an apparent paradox between symbolic ascendancy and social denigration of women. Quite frequently, the very aspects of womanhood glorified in a religious system are used as justification for the social and political denigration of women. Different ideological definitions and perceptions of men and women further the separation and isolation of women. Seldom does this work to women's advantage. Even when women are seen as spiritual, as in the nineteenth-century cult of true womanhood, the expression of such spirituality was believed best confined to the privacy of the domestic world.

Discussion Questions
1. Goddesses do not necessarily correlate with an exalted conception of womanhood. Why does the existence of strong masculine deities tend to support male authority in social relations while goddesses so often support female subordination?

2. Discuss the different conceptions of maleness and femaleness that typified the early years of Christianity. What were the social consequences of these ideological beliefs? How did notions of chastity demonstrate this dualism?

3. Compare Christian, Islamic, Hindu, and Confucian notions of female sexuality. Are there cross-cultural universals? How do different societies differ in their conceptions of female nature? Account for differences.

IDEOLOGY AND SOCIAL STRUCTURE

The actual position women occupy (as opposed to the conception of womanhood discussed above) may be reflected in the belief system and in the type and range of religious activity deemed suitable and appropriate for women. Women's maternal role is often reflected in reproductive rituals, which frequently exclude men. Analyses of many such rituals has led to the conclusion that women's religious experiences and perceptions may be quite different from those of men in the same society. In the case of religion, however, separate is not equal.

Readings for Students
Arnold, Marigene. "Celibes, Mothers and Church Cockroaches: Religious Participation of Women in a Mexican Village." In *Women in Ritual and Symbolic Roles.*
Betteridge, Anne. "The Controversial Vows of Urban Muslim Women in Iran." In *Unspoken Worlds,* 141–56.
Jacobson, Doranne, "Golden Handprints and the Red-Painted Feet: Hindu Childbirth Rituals in Central India." In *Unspoken Worlds,* 73–93.
Kerns, Virginia. "Black Carib Women and Rites of Death." In *Unspoken Worlds,* 127–40.
Mernissi, Fatima. "Women, Saints, and Sanctuaries." *Signs* 3 (March 1978): 101–12.

Readings for Instructors
Ardener, Edwin. "Belief and the Problem of Women." In *Perceiving Women,* edited by Shirley Ardener, 1–18. New York: Halstead Press, 1977.
Caplan, Patricia, and Janet Bujra. *Women United, Women Divided.* Bloomington: Indiana University Press, 1979.
Freeman, James. "The Ladies of Lord Krishna: Rituals of Middle Aged Women in Eastern India." In *Unspoken Worlds,* 110–26.
Gross, Rita. "Menstruation and Childbirth as Ritual and Religious Experiences Among Native Australians." In *Unspoken Worlds,* 277–92.
———. "Methodological Remarks on the Study of Women in Religion: Review, Criticism and Redefinition." In *Women and Religion,* 153–65.
Munro, Winsom C. "Patriarchy and Charismatic Community in 'Paul.'" In *Women and Religion,* 189–98.
Ortner, Sherry. "The Virgin and the State." *Michigan Discussion in Anthropology* 2 (Fall 1970). Rep. in *Feminist Studies* 4, no. 3 (October 1978).
Wadley, Susan. "Hindu Women's Family and Household Rituals in a North Indian Village." In *Unspoken Worlds,* 94–109.
Whyte, Martin King. *The Status of Women in Preindustrial Societies.* Princeton: Princeton University Press, 1978.

Lecture Topics

Social Structure and Female Participation. One of the few systematic attempts to investigate the relationship of female social subordination to religious ideology has been undertaken by Whyte. In a recent study, he links female subordination to classical religions (i.e., Christianity and Islam). He maintains that classical religious ideology tends to buttress the political and social preeminence of men. Women in these traditions have few opportunities to express social solidarity and so work their will upon the system through informal manipulations. Classical religions are associated with complex societies. In a related and useful study, Ortner links ideals of female virginity to considerations of social structure.

As we have seen, and as theologians such as Reuther have documented, female status declines as society becomes more complex. Yet the ethnographic record gives only partial support to Whyte's contention. Fatima Mernissi has demonstrated that sanctuaries for women provide an opportunity for the expression of female solidarity in the face of an Islamic system that emphasizes male dominance. This point is also made by Betteridge. The lesson is clear: women do participate, at some level, in most religious traditions, and often there are strong benefits to be derived from this activity.

Rituals of Reproduction and Domesticity. In any religious tradition the participation of women is certainly not equivalent to the participation of men. Women's religious activities are essentially reflections of concerns with fertility and domestic harmony. Nevertheless these ritual performances must not be dismissed, for they attest to the religious participation of women so often ignored or undervalued in the literature. Moreover such rituals often have consequences for the general well-being of the society. Case studies of gifted individuals illustrate the prominence that women can achieve in this arena. Women's rituals are documented in areas as diverse as India, Oceania, and Africa in the Area Studies.

Ritual and Female Solidarity. One of the advantages of such exclusively female gatherings is the opportunity to develop and to express feelings of social solidarity. The instructor should emphasize to the class, however, that such gatherings work to different ends in different types of societies.

Discussion Questions

1. Does Ortner's analysis support or detract from Whyte's findings?

2. Since women so clearly have their own perceptions and definitions of their being and of their actions, why does the masculine definition continue to prevail in most societies?

3. Women's religious participation often produces strong feelings of solidarity. Why do women stop here? Once organized, why not effect an economic and social revolution?

WOMEN AS RELIGIOUS ACTORS: SHAMANS, WITCHES, AND NUNS

Women officiants and witches might initially appear to be at odds with one another. For while one apparently supports, the other subverts the religious system. However, they have a great deal in common. Both shamans and witches often are individuals who do not fit easily into the roles of wife and mother. Women who resist such ready classification are likely candidates for exceptional, often extraordinary positions. By sheer force of personality, some women can fit quite comfortably into positions ordinarily held by men. But it is precisely these characteristics that separate them from other women. In Korea, for example, shamans are frequently recruited from those women who are least content as wives and mothers.

Readings for Students

Binford, Marsha. "Julia: An East African Diviner." In *Unspoken Worlds*, 3–21.

Harvey, Youngsook Kim. "Possession Sickness and Women Shamans in Korea." In *Unspoken Worlds*, 41–52.

Jones, David. *Sanapia: Comanche Medicine Woman*. New York: Holt, Rinehart & Winston, 1972.

Nakamura, Hyoko. "No Women's Liberation: The Heritage of a Woman Prophet in Modern Japan." In *Unspoken Worlds*, 174–90.

Nelson, Mary. "Why Witches Were Women." In *Women: A Feminist Perspective,* edited by Jo Freeman. Palo Alto: Mayfield, 1975.

Readings for Instructors

Carter, Norene, and Rosemary Reuther. "Entering the Sanctuary: The Struggle for Priesthood in Contemporary Episcopalian and Roman Catholic Experience." In *Women of Spirit,* 356–83.

Ehrenreich, Barbara, and Deirdre English. *Witches, Midwives, and Nurses: A History of Women Healers.* New York: The Feminist Press, 1973.

Ewens, Mary. "Removing the Veil: The Liberated American Nun." In *Women of Spirit,* 255–78.

Falk, Nancy Auer. "The Case of the Vanishing Nuns: The Fruits of Ambivalence in Ancient Indian Buddism." In *Unspoken Worlds,* 207–24.

Garrett, Clarke. "Women and Witches: Patterns of Analysis." *Signs* 3, no. 2 (Winter 1977): 461–70.

Harper, Edward. "Fear and the Status of Women." *Southwestern Journal of Anthropology* 25: 81–95.

Nadel, S. F. "Witchcraft in Four Societies: An Essay in Comparison." *American Anthropologist* 54: 18–29.

Reuther, Rosemary. *New Woman, New Earth.*

Shimony, Anne Marie. "Women of Influence and Prestige Among the Native American Iroquois." In *Unspoken Worlds,* 243–59.

White, Charles. "Mother Guru: Inanananda of Madras, India." In *Unspoken Worlds,* 22–38.

Williams, Drid. "The Brides of Christ." In *Perceiving Women,* 105–26.

Lecture Topics

Women as Religious Actors—New Definitions of Womanhood. Female religious practitioners are labelled extraordinary. Whether healers or witches, saints or sorcerers, such women do not accommodate themselves, or cannot be accommodated, to the society's prevailing definition of womanhood. They are indeed women apart—separated from the men of the society and from their more conventional sisters by their unwillingness and/or inability to conform to social expectations. Such women often provide examples of alternative role possibilities for women, while their activities often affect the more general assessment of feminine attributes.

Women as Officiants. Many women who wish to transcend the limiting and limited definition of womanhood prevalent in their society become religious practitioners. Frequently, public religious activity and performance entails a renunciation of womanhood, as, for example, in Buddhist and Christian nunneries. Women are rarely religious officiants as well as wives and mothers. This has significant implications, for it suggests that sanctity and womanliness are frequently antithetical attributes.

Extraordinary Women. There are several examples of exceptional women available in the literature. The Area Studies also contain examples of women who achieved religious preeminence, such as Rabi'a al-Adawiyah (712–801), a great Sufi mystic; Muktābāi (d. 1297), a Hindu "saint" from Maharashtra, in western India; and Sanghamitra, who was an early Buddhist missionary to Ceylon (ca. 200 A.D.). A description and analysis of such women, as well as more familiar Western examples, should attempt to discover similarities and differences in the women's personal, social, and religious experiences. Their preeminence should be analyzed in terms of the effect it exerts on the perception of all women. In other words, is their success attributable to an exaggeration or denial of their femininity?

Witches and Witchcraft. The view of women as witches often addresses the more general perception of women. While most societies can accommodate an individual woman of exceptional abilities, few will tolerate women who either balk at their domestic roles or who resist definition. Nadel has documented the first case quite clearly (see Chapter Nine, "Women in Sub-Saharan Africa"). In the African societies he studied, women prefer their roles as traders to the more limiting definition of themselves as wives and mothers. The price for their independence is heavy: they are seen as witches. Similarly, medieval European women who redefined their roles to exclude marriage and to include extradomestic occupations were often targets for the Inquisition. In India, Brahmin widows who can no longer be defined by their husbands' status are viewed as dangerous sorcerors (see Chapter Six, "Women in India"). Women who are labelled witches pose a social rather than a mystical threat to men. Thus, it is often women's social activities and their reluctance to accept the prevalent definition of womanhood that qualify them for extraordinary positions within religious life.

Male Reactions to Priests and Pariahs. The response of the masculine establishment to such religious adepts should be considered. Lewis notes that the same individuals who are viewed as healers by women are seen as witches by men. The social background of persecutions should be examined, noting that men are almost always the inquisitors while the objects of their searches are women who violate social rather than religious standards. In this context the male view of the ordination of women needs to be considered. Are women ministers the equivalent of shamans or witches?

Discussion Questions
1. In what ways are witches "failed" women? Whose definition of failure is operating here?
2. Does the enhanced status of one particular woman (e.g., a healer, shaman) serve to elevate the status of all women, or is she seen as an aberration? Are there behavioral and moral prerequisites to her role which will serve to set her apart?

RELIGION AND SOCIAL PROTEST

Religion as a form of social protest, usually against colonial powers, has been the subject of numerous anthropological studies. Recently, however, attention has turned to ways in which women have used participation in religious movements to express their dissatisfaction with the status quo. Women's dissatisfaction has often been expressed as an altered state of consciousness, or a mystical trance.

Readings for Students
Bass, Dorothy. "Their Prodigious Influence: Women, Religion and Reform in Antebellum America." In *Women of Spirit,* 279–300.
Ehrenreich, Barbara, and Dierdre English. *Complaints and Disorders: The Sexual Politics of Sickness.* New York: The Feminist Press, 1973.
Huber, Elaine. "A Woman Must Not Speak: Quaker Women in the English Left Wing." In *Women of Spirit,* 153–82.
Kraemer, Ross. "Ecstasy and Possession: Women of Ancient

Greece and the Cult of Dionysus." In *Unspoken Worlds*, 53–
    70.
Lewis, I. M. *Ecstatic Religion*. Baltimore: Penguin Books, 1971.
Mernissi, Fatima. "Women, Saints and Sanctuaries." *Signs* 4
    (March 1978): 101–12.
Smith, Catherine. "Jane Lead: The Feminist Mind and Art of a
    Seventeenth-Century Protestant Mystic." In *Women of Spirit*,
    183–204.

Readings for Instructors
Crapanzano, Vincent, and Vivian Garrison. *Case Studies in Spirit
    Possession*. New York: Wiley, 1977.
Douglas, Mary. *Natural Symbols*. New York: Pantheon Books,
    1970.
Finkler, Kaja. "Dissident Religious Movements in the Service of
    Women's Power." *Sex Roles* 7 (1981): 981–95.
Moore, R. L. *In Search of White Crows*. New York: Oxford
    University Press, 1977.
Pressel, Esther. "Umbanda Trance and Possession in Sao Paolo
    Brazil." In *Trance Healing and Hallucination*, edited by F.
    Goodman, J. Hennesy, and E. Pressel, 113–225. New York:
    Wiley Interscience, 1974.
Skultans, Veida. *Intimacy and Ritual*. London: Routledge & Kegan
    Paul, 1974.
Smith-Rosenberg, Carroll. "The Hysterical Women: Sex Roles in
    Nineteenth Century America." *Social Research* 39, no. 4
    (Winter 1972).

Lecture Topics

Affliction as Protest. Definitions of femininity that hinge on
frailty and incompetence can be turned to advantage by women
who succumb readily to illness; such illness is in fact a means of
protest. It is effective, therapeutic, and seldom revolutionary.
Many examples may be found in Lewis, Crapanzano and Garrison, and Hoch-Smith and Spring. Rosenberg and Ehrenreich
and English document the sexual politics of female illness in
nineteenth-century American society.
    In many parts of the world, individuals of low social standing
often discover that they are besieged by malignant spirits who
cause illness. Cults of women arise to treat these people. What is
significant about these cults is that women tend to be both the
victims and the healers. However, although they are victims in an
etiological sense, they generally emerge from treatment at least

temporarily victorious over the oppression of male dominance. The dominant ideology of male supremacy is officially intact, yet female solidarity is reinforced by shared affliction. Victims can express their dissatisfaction with the social order, but at the same time, these normally passive individuals need not accept responsibility for their actions: their angry words and subversive acts are attributed to spirits. Thus, the victims do not attack the social structure directly, and so avoid the taint of the revolutionary.

By joining these religious movements, women may consciously or unconsciously confront their own sense of powerlessness and their deprivation from lucrative and productive roles. While participation in cults may fail to bring about significant social change, Mernissi has demonstrated that such movements provide a sanctuary from a male world and must, therefore, be seen as therapeutic. A woman especially gifted in spiritual matters may be able to establish an independent source of income. Such movements, then, would appear to provide their participants with a chance to obtain and to exercise a reasonable amount of independence and autonomy.

Strategies of Mystical Attack. Illnesses take many forms depending upon the social context. Women go into trance, speak in tongues, or are possessed by intrusive spirits. In all such cases they have been transformed into an altered state of consciousness. In some instances they simply retire from social activity for weeks or months on end. All are maneuvers that permit, in a relatively safe way, expressions of discontent.

It is important to note that spiritual ascendancy is achieved through an altered state of consciousness; women are either in trance or they are possessed. The implication is that for women to assume roles that run counter to their marginal status, they must cease to be themselves. At times they are more than their passive nature would ordinarily allow, but almost always they are beings transformed. And, in this altered state they are, sometimes, able to transform their social status, overcoming some of the liabilities inherent in being a woman in that culture. In the West, women have been overrepresented in spiritist cults and in sectarian Christianity. This suggests that similar devices are effective in diverse cultural contexts.

Results and Advantages. Strategies of mystical illness often relieve feelings of neglect and powerlessness. They also provide occasions for women to express mutual support and to experiment with less constraining role definitions. In general and to a degree, men are responsive, for such activities redress the social balance temporarily while leaving intact and unthreatened the supremacy of men.

Discussion Questions
1. I. M. Lewis maintains that women are drawn to marginal cults because they themselves are marginal. Do you agree? Must this be the nature of women's participation? Does their existence augur a transformed concept of womanhood?

2. Are the mystical attacks experienced by so many women a means of changing the social order or are they an ameliorative strategy whose main goal is to help women adjust to their oppression?

WOMEN AS RELIGIOUS INNOVATORS

The women who are the focus of this section attain a degree of power and prestige from their religious training and theological erudition. As religious leaders and theologians, some women effectively enter the public domain, where their relations with men and other sources of power within the community are of critical importance. The women's cults discussed above often generate leaders who, although once victims themselves, now gain control over spirits. Men may view these women as witches who are contaminating sources of power and symbolic of the abuse of power. In other religious movements, where women move away from the periphery of society to assume prominent positions as healers and interpreters of divine wisdom, men reverse the normal flow of status relationships and follow women leaders.

Religious innovation can sometimes lead to political action in the larger social arena. There seems to be some indication that in the United States in the nineteenth century, sectarian behavior was often a starting point for subsequent political activity, as exemplified by Margaret Fuller and Lucretia Mott.

Readings for Students
Lewis, J. M. *Ecstatic Religion.*
Hardesty, Nancy, Lucille Dayton, and Donald Dayton. "Women

in the Holiness Movement: Feminism in the Evangelical
Tradition." In *Women of Spirit*, 225–54.
Umansky, Ellen. "Women in Judaism: From the Reform Move-
ment to Contemporary Jewish Religious Feminism." In
Women of Spirit, 333–55.
Zikmund, Barbara. "The Feminist Thrust of Sectarian Chris-
tianity." In *Women of Spirit*, 205–24.

Readings for Instructors
Finkler, Kaja. "Dissident Religious Movements in the Service of
Women's Power." *Sex Roles* 7 (1981): 981–95.
Goodman, F., J. Henney, and E. Pressel, eds. *Trance Healing and
Hallucination*.
Morsy, Soheir. "Sex Roles, Power and Illness in an Egyptian
Village." *American Ethnologist* (May 1978): 137–50.
Reuther, Rosemary, and Rosemary Keller. *Women and Religion in
America*, vol. 1.
Wilson, Bryan. *Religious Sects*. London: World University Library,
1970.

Lecture Topics

Women as Leaders of Possession Cults. Women often become
leaders of possession cults after several previous illnesses. However, now they are no longer victims of affliction. In a very real
sense, as cult leaders they are on the offensive. Once a woman
achieves such a position, she caters to a clientele of women. For
her efforts she receives the gratitude of her female clients and the
consternation of the male establishment, who see her activities as
subversive treachery.

Women as Healers. In many new religious movements, women
achieve preeminence because their spiritual gifts may be put to
practical use. Their status is generally high in the community and
frequently men as well as women are represented in their clientele. Since many such individuals appear in times of social up-
heaval, the socially therapeutic dimension to their work should
also be considered.

**Women as Leaders of and Participants in Dissident Religious
Movements.** Frequently dissident movements hope to substitute
equality for hierarchy in the larger society. In these instances
egalitarian impulses frequently encompass gender and women

have participated in such heterodox revolts in large numbers. Among the many cross-cultural examples that can be cited are female participation in early Buddhism, the Taiping Rebellion in nineteenth-century China, and some medieval Christian heresies. A Chinese women's revolt against marriage also had on its core an eclectic form of goddess worship. Under these conditions women are also sometimes able to assume leadership roles. Unlike healers, whose increased status may or may not affect the prevailing conception of women, women leaders tend to legitimate and in turn be legitimated by intensive female participation.

Conclusion. The instructor should review the social, economic, and cultural factors that permit women to assume innovative religious roles. The effect of the individual upon religious systems and social ideology should also be considered.

Discussion Questions

1. Compare the role of women in dissident movements to the role of women in organized religions. What are the necessary social and economic conditions for a woman's ascendance to power?

2. The existence of cults in so many areas of the world suggests not only common experiences among women but common solutions to their distress. Do similar strategies exist in our society today?

NEW APPROACHES

Many feminist theologians in the West have offered new interpretations and new visions for the future. They redefine the role of women in religious ideology by reinterpreting and investigating with a fresh perspective the history of the Judeo-Christian tradition. Their attempts are not merely to analyze and to understand; rather, they wish to transform the decidedly masculine bent of the religious ideology of the West. The provocative, often intellectually daring stance assumed by these theologians is itself a chapter in Western theology and social history.

Within the Islamic tradition there has also been no lack of articulate feminist reformers, such as Nazirah Zein Ed-Din, Nawal el Saadawi, and Azizah al-Hibri (see Chapter Eleven, "Women in the Islamic Middle East and North Africa").

Readings for Students and Instructors

Christ, Carol, and Judith Plaskow. *Womanspirit Rising.* San Francisco: Harper and Row, 1979.
Daly, Mary. *Beyond God the Father.* Boston: Beacon Press, 1973.
Harding, M. Esther. *Women's Mysteries.*
Quest (1975). Special edition: Women and Spirituality.
Reuther, Rosemary. *New Woman, New Earth.*
————. *Sexism and God Talk.*
Women's Studies International Forum 5, no. 2 (1982). Special issue: Women and Islam. Guest Editor Azizah al-Hibri.

PART TWO
AREA
STUDIES

CHAPTER SIX

WOMEN IN INDIA

Margot I. Duley

Cross-cultural contact and diffusion of knowledge between India and the West existed for centuries before the Christian era, and modern Western interest in Indian thought, ranging from eighteenth-century European romanticism to the 1960s counter-culture, follows a well-worn path. An early and still the best succinct summary of India's contributions to the West is:

Rawlinson, H. G. "Indian Influence on the West." Chap. 15 in *Modern India and the West*, edited by L. S. S. O'Malley. London: Oxford University Press, 1941.

The history of British industrialization and the rise of Britain as a preeminent world power in the nineteenth and the early twentieth centuries is also inextricably linked to the history of India and the British raj, through the exploitation of India's material and human resources.

Aside from its historic importance, India warrants greater attention because of its size: India's population of 746 million (1984) makes it the second largest nation in the world.[1]

Today India is the scene of an economic and social experiment of immense importance. Within the framework of representative institutions from the village *panchayats* to the national parliament, India is attempting to change its hierarchical structures of caste and gender, and to tackle the problem of the country's immense poverty through ambitious development schemes. The Preamble of the Constitution of the Democratic Republic of India declares that the nation shall be a welfare state committed to the pursuit of the ideal of socioeconomic justice. Article 15 prohibits discrimination on the grounds of religion, race, caste, place of birth, or sex—a constitutional statement of equality that has not yet been attained in the United States.[2]

Yet the problems that stand in the way of progress toward these ideals are formidable. Scarcities of land and food, compounded greatly by the economic legacies of imperialism, continuing disparities in the world economic order, periodic regional and religious sectarianism, increasing socioeconomic disparities linked to development in a mixed economy, and the tenacious survival of caste and gender-based hierarchies form the backdrop of Indian politics.

The question of women's roles and opportunities is crucial to the solution of India's economic problems, though in India as elsewhere this has been barely acknowledged by economic planners. Some experts contend that a reduction of the birthrate by 50 percent in the next thirty-five years is essential to provide adequate financing for industrial development.[3] Though population planning has been government policy since 1952, women have not been provided with the sort of educational and economic opportunities that appear to motivate lower birthrates. There is also strong evidence that the process of "modernization" set in motion during the British period and intensified since independence has had a negative impact on women's employment. There are also marked and increasing differentials between men and women in mortality rates and access to health care. These issues loom large on the agenda of feminist social scientists in India.[4]

India's feminist movement, whose origins may be found in social reform and nationalist groups of the nineteenth century, has a long and venerable history. Its content, priorities, and organizing strategies have differed from those in the West, and cross-cultural comparisons with American feminism may prove illuminating to American feminists. There is, as we shall see, a burgeoning women's studies movement in India, a fact that should be stressed to students whose cultural stereotypes of Indian women may well be those of meekness and seclusion. Tradition and modernity collide in India, but Western eyes may see through cultural filters that emphasize only tradition and, indeed, their view of tradition may be a narrow one.

In talking about the Indian subcontinent, there is the everpresent danger of oversimplification, for there are many traditions within India. There are differences in social structure between north and south. Although the majority of the population is Hindu, there are sizable Muslim, Jain, Sikh, Parsi, and Christian minorities. There are profound differences in the life experiences of upper and lower castes. And, of course, the world of the village and the world of the town are separated by more than miles. At the same time, there is an overall experience that can be called Indian.

For the basic facts of South Asian religions, history, culture, and geography, we recommend two excellent introductory texts:

Nehru, Jawaharlal. *The Discovery of India.* Garden City, N.Y.: Doubleday Anchor Books, 1960. An excellent introduction from a nationalist viewpoint.

Watson, Francis. *A Concise History of India.* London: Thames & Hudson, 1974. A short historical introduction with superb illustrations, though written with some Western biases.

The first three lectures focus on Indian traditions, and especially their growth within an historical framework. We examine the history of women in ancient India, and changes in the status of women over time, from a comparatively high status in the Vedic Age (2500–ca. 600 B.C.) to a subservient and restricted role by the 11th century A.D. We also examine the impact of Islam, and the traditional structures of family and caste. In short, we examine certain cultural determinants that continue to influence, to a greater or lesser extent, contemporary Indian gender relations. This historical framework is intended to facilitate the integration of Indian women into world civilization courses that treat gender issues seriously, and it draws upon some of the anthropological theories surrounding women's status that we examined in Chapters 2 and 4, above. Many theorists have noted a decline in the position of women, whether in the West or East, as social complexity increases. Indian history offers telling examples of this general process. We shall also provide some pedagogical advice in dealing with the historical background. This historical treatment also involves a discussion of women in Hinduism and other religions to facilitate cross-cultural comparisons of women and religion.

Following our discussion of tradition, we consider changes in the status of women, distinguishing whenever possible by caste or class, during the British period. Then the interrelationship between nationalism and women's rights in the twentieth century is analyzed. Finally we turn to an extended examination of women in contemporary India focusing on legal changes, political participation, educational issues, workforce participation, and health care as well as the revival of Indian feminism. The overarching theme of the latter half of this chapter is the complex and multi-dimensional impact of "development" on women.

An indispensable source for students and teachers who wish to research historical topics or modern ones up until the mid-1970s in greater depth is:

Sakala, Carol. *Women of South Asia: A Guide to Resources.* Mill-wood, N.Y.: Kraus International Pubs., 1980. This excellent annotated bibliography contains nearly 5,000 entries.

Another important reference work is:

Vaid, Jyotsna, and Barbara Miller. *South Asian Women at Home and Abroad: A Guide to Resources.* Association of Asian Studies, 1984. Includes demographic, educational, employment, fertility, and legal data; a bibliography of recent publications; a directory of periodicals and newspapers featuring articles on women's issues in South Asia; a directory of South Asian women's groups at home and abroad; information on South Asian women immigrants in the United States; a research directory; and a listing of relevant documentary and feature films.

A word about sources for some of the works referred to in this chapter: South Asia Books, a bookseller, also co-publishes works in this field. Their address is: P.O. Box 502, Columbia, Missouri 65205.

HISTORICAL CHANGE IN THE STATUS OF WOMEN IN ANCIENT INDIA

Pedagogical Strategies

The discussion of women in India begins with ancient history and the development of the classical religious tradition. The religious texts are to varying degrees deeply misogynist. To counteract ethnocentrism, we recommend that students read some broad but sympathetic treatment of Hinduism, such as that found in

Smith, Huston. *The Religions of Man,* Chap. 2. New York: Harper and Row, 1965.

We also advise that students reflect upon the misogynist elements of the Judeo-Christian tradition and their survival into modern times to disabuse themselves of any notions that Hinduism is uniquely patriarchal. Any of the following treatments can provide the comparative framework that we recommend for class discussions:

Agonito, Rosemary. *History of Ideas on Woman: A Source Book.* New York: Putnam's, 1977.

Bullough, Vern. *The Subordinate Sex.* Chicago: University of Chicago Press, 1973; New York: Penguin Books, 1974.

Daly, Mary. *The Church and the Second Sex.* New York: Harper Colophon Books, 1975.

Historiographical Issues

This historical lecture provides an interpretive framework which draws together strands from many sources. Because the history of ancient India is challenging for the non-specialist, but still nevertheless worthy of attention, we will provide a relatively complete discussion that goes beyond an outline. This is not to suggest that India is peculiarly "ancient"; rather it is a response to the limitations of the existing material that has to be selectively mined by the feminist scholar searching for information. By contrast, many more sources are available to teachers on modern India.

The standard general histories of ancient India largely neglect the role of women. On the other hand, those that make groundbreaking contributions to the field (Altekar, Indra, Upadhyaya,[5] for example) do not systematically relate changes in women's status to underlying socioeconomic trends. Our ability to do so is still limited. Two recent works by R. S. Sharma, taken together, begin to integrate the study of state formation and social stratification in ancient India with material culture. Sharma's *Perspectives in Social and Economic History of Early India* includes an examination of the role of women from a general Marxist perspective. Though many scholars writing in the field—Altekar is the preeminent example—have been sympathetic to limited social reform, their work has not been informed by feminist social theory. Mukherjee's volume of historical essays begins to address some of the issues from an Indian feminist's perspective, as she documents the deteriorating status of women from 400 B.C. to 500 A.D.

Formal religious texts and legal codes, whether from the Western or Indian tradition, pose common problems of interpretation. Both are products of a priestly, literate class commenting upon women; the voices of women are excluded from The Great Tradition of the court and temple. What texts lay down as cultural norms are not necessarily social practice. Unfortunately, women's voices as well as the voices of the lower castes are absent from the historical sources, and instructors should draw this textual limitation to students' attention.

Readings for Students
Altekar, A.S. *The Position of Women in Hindu Civilization,* Chap. 12. Delhi: Motilal Banarsidass, 1973.
Mies, Maria. "Historical, Cultural and Social Determinants of Female Roles." In *Indian Women and Patriarchy,* 36–116. New Delhi: Concept Pub. Co., 1980.
Wadley, Susan S. "Women and the Hindu Tradition." *Signs* 3, no. 1 (Autumn 1977): 113–25.

Readings for Instructors
Altekar, A. S. *The Position of Women in Hindu Civilization.*
Basham, A. L. *The Wonder That Was India,* Chap. 2. New York: Grove Press, 1959.
Buhler, G., trans. *The Laws of Manu.* Sacred Books of the East, vol. 25. Delhi: Motilal Banarsidass, 1964.
Chakraborti, Haripada. *India as Reflected in the Inscriptions of Gupta Period:* Delhi: Munshiram Manoharlal Pubs., 1978.
Misra, Shitala Prasad. *Labour Problems in Ancient and Medieval India.* Calcutta: Bookland Private, 1961.
Mukherjee, Prabhati. *Hindu Women: Normative Models.* New Delhi: Orient Longman, 1978.
Saran, K. M. *Labour in Ancient India,* Chap. 6. Bombay: Vora and Co., 1957.
Sharma, Ram Sharan. *Perspectives in Social and Economic History of Early India.* New Delhi: Munshiram Manoharlal Pubs., 1983.
————. *Material Culture and Social Formations in Ancient India.* New Delhi: Macmillan India, 1983.
Sharma, Ursula. *Women, Work and Property in North-West India.* London and New York: Tavistock, 1980.

Lecture Topics

Pre-Vedic India (2500–1500 B.C.) (Basham). To a degree, the historiography of pre-Vedic India shares the same matriarchal controversies that shape the discussion of the prehistory of the Mediterranean, Europe, Africa, and Latin America. "Matriarchal and female-dominated states existed throughout India," claims one interpreter of the "Amazon legacy."[6] However, these claims go beyond the available evidence. The Indus Valley civilization, which included towns of great sophistication, was based on river trade and alluvial agriculture. Mother goddesses were prominent in the society's religion, though the significance of this in terms of the status of women is a matter of dispute. These early goddesses were undoubtedly absorbed into the later Hindu pantheon. Though the presence of goddesses does not necessarily mean high status for women, in this case there does appear to be evidence that women's status was higher than in subsequent times.

The Vedic Age to the Mauryan Dynasty (1500–300 B.C.). Interpretations of the Vedic Age—whether the status of women was high or low—were central to the intellectual debate surrounding women's rights starting in the nineteenth century. Women's rights and nationalist leader Sarojini Naidu (1879–1949), for example, asserted that "in those beautiful days of the Vedic period of India, the glory of which still surrounds the country like a faint halo, women took part freely in the social and political life of the country. . . . It is with such a heritage as the foundation . . . that the present women's movement in India has evolved."[7] The indicators of a relatively high status in Aryan times are many. Though Basham stresses the patriarchal nature of the warring, pastoral Aryan invaders, there is evidence that women were not mere chattels. Although some women seem to have been captured in war as booty (R. S. Sharma, *Perspectives,* Chap. 3), women nonetheless played important economic roles in the society as milkers of cattle, weavers, and in the production of grain (Saran, 18; R. S. Sharma, *Material Culture,* Chap. 9; Misra, 3). There are other indications of high status.

> Women were scholars, teachers, religious sages, and composers of Vedic hymns as late as the Upanishadic writings (800–500 B.C.)— works of visionary insight and meditation, and among the most sacred texts of Hinduism (Altekar, Mukherjee).
>
> At least some women remained unmarried. The Rg Veda (ca. 1500– 1000 B.C.) refers to women growing old in their parents' house; this situation was sufficiently common to have a name *(amajur).* The Rg Veda also mentions a celibate woman student and a woman who did not marry for she did not find a man worthy to be her husband (Mukherjee).
>
> Until at least the first century A.D., some girls could study the Vedas,

and until around the third century B.C., girls could remain unmarried up to age sixteen.

The early, pastoral Vedic period was followed by technological transformations, which, as we know from cross-cultural evidence, have carried profound consequences for the status of women. Beginning around 1000 B.C. the Aryans became more sedentary, using at first wooden plowshares as well as limited dry rice production (R. S. Sharma, *Perspectives*, Chap. 9). The economic unit was probably small-scale family farming, and the Atharva-veda mentions the employment of female family members, as well as female slaves, in agriculture (Saran, 36). There is also evidence of an emerging caste of Brahmins (priests) and Kshatriyas (warriors), a process that intensified in subsequent centuries, especially after the widespread adoption of the use of iron both for plowing and clearing land, speeding population growth and the production of surplus wealth. By 600 B.C., society in the mid-Gangetic basin was transformed: numerous towns date from this period; petty kingdoms developed; the *varnas*, or four ritual orders of the caste system, were clearly differentiated; and large agricultural estates with both slave and wage labor arose in addition to smaller holdings (R. S. Sharma, *Material Culture*, Chap. 9, *Perspectives*, Chap. 6; Misra, 157–66).

A number of anthropologists have asserted that the growth of surplus wealth and private property and the concomitant concern to protect inheritance lines in the patriarchal family led to increased restrictions on the position of women. Others have argued that the process of state formation, removing the locus of political power from local or kinship groups, led to a deterioration in women's status. The earliest textual references to women as property with a status akin to Sudras (the lowest varna) are found in texts (the Brahmanas) contemporaneous with this period (800–500 B.C.).

The Mauryan Dynasty (322–200 B.C.) (Misra; Mukherjee; Saran; R. S. Sharma, *Perspectives*, Chap. 10). The Mauryan Dynasty was economically centralized with a vast bureaucracy and a huge army estimated at from 400,000 to 600,000 men. The economic roles and legal position of women are relatively well documented thanks to *The Arthasastra*, a practical manual of statesmanship akin to Machiavelli's *The Prince*. It was written by "Kautilya," probably Chanakya (ca. 345–300 B.C.), a chief minister of the kingdom, and it is thought to reflect reality.

Peggy Sanday, among others, has argued that prolonged warfare and consequent male absence or shortage of labor in the subsistence sphere can provide the precondition for the development of female public status. While women—and most men—in Mauryan times certainly did not participate equally in the public sphere, they did play important economic roles, and the legal code contained rights that were lost in later time. Women were employed as wage laborers in the state-owned textile factories where they spun, wove, dyed, and embroidered; women were also employed as basket makers and wine distillers in addition to court attendants, courtesans, and temple dancers (Saran, Chap. 6). The kingdom also made provision for "displaced women," perhaps reflecting its need for productive labor, though this is more commonly interpreted as a reflection of Buddhist humanism. Kautilya directed that widows, female ascetics, dismissed temple dancers, and "defective girls" be given work spinning (Misra, 79). Kautilya also laid down conditions of work for men and women, including the punishment of men "found guilty of looking at the face of a female worker or of talking to her" (Saran, 66).

This latter provision probably reflects a notion of women as male property subject to protective seclusion, but it is clear that women retained important personal rights in the Mauryan legal code. *The Arthasastra* invests women with property rights, most notably the *stridhana* (means of subsistence and/or jewelry received from her family upon marriage or subsequently as a gift from her husband). The wife retained certain absolute rights to this property, which were subsequently lost in the Laws of Manu, and then restored in part in medieval times. Widow remarriage was also permitted, though widows lost lifetime rights to their husband's property if they remarried. *The Arthasastra* also contained one form of marriage *(asura vihara)* in which brideprice was paid, signifying woman's economic value, though its practice was probably limited to the lower castes. (The complicated details of property rights and marriage can be found in Mukherjee, Chaps. 6 and 8, and Sharma, *Material Culture,* Chap. 6.) It was probably women of lower castes who formed the labor pool for the textile factories. This point illustrates a more general one: strictures contained in religious and legal texts were products of the upper varnas, whose doctrines, while prestigious, did not always correspond with the needs or realities of the lower castes.

Post-Mauryan and Gupta Periods (200 B.C.–528 A.D.). During this period (R. S. Sharma argues around the third century A.D., while

other historians place it earlier) Indian society apparently underwent a deep economic crisis whose precise causes and nature
remain obscure. There is agreement, however, that during these
centuries Indian states decentralized their authority: there was
widespread use of land grants to functionaries, instead of salary
payments in cash, somewhat akin to the process of feudalization in
Europe. In this process Brahmans and Kshatriyas acquired taxation and legal rights over peasants and aboriginal peoples (R. S.
Sharma, *Perspectives*, 32–33, 147–50, 229–34). R. S. Sharma's view
that feudalism arose in this period is disputed by other historians.
Much of the disagreement hinges on whether the term should
only be applied to the European model of reciprocal obligations
between king and noble, donor and donee, and the presence or
absence of military obligations. However, Sharma's central contention that a landed class with coercive power over peasants and
subleasing to tenants existed by Guptan times is confirmed by
inscriptions cited by Chakraborti, 63–70.

Associated with this process are demonstrable changes in the
Smritis, or laws, governing castes and women articulated by
Brahmin scholars. The Laws of Manu (ca. 200 A.D.), a reference
point for much subsequent legal authority, indicate the extent to
which women's position was deteriorating. "Manu" is a mythological name. Portions probably date as early as 200 B.C., and the later
parts to 400 A.D., pointing to the necessity of further unraveling
literary strands. Manu defines a position of total legal dependence
of the female upon the male, similar to that found in Confucian
thought, Roman Law, and the English Common Law's Doctrine of
Coverture, echoes of which are to be found in American law to
this day. Manu (see Buhler) entrenches the patriarchal family:

> A wife, a son and a slave, these three are ever ordained destitute of
> property; whatever they acquire becomes his property whose they
> are (Manu I, 147).

> In childhood a female must be subject to her father, in youth to her
> husband, and when her lord is dead, to her sons; a woman must
> never be independent (Manu I, 149).

Manu also forbade the remarriage of widows; a widow was to
live a celibate life, practicing austerities. She was threatened with a
terrible fate in her next life if she remarried. Manu's tirades
against widow remarriage are so extreme that Mukherjee suspects
that it was practiced, at least in some castes (Chap. 7). Control of
females was further insured by instituting child marriage. Later
medieval law reinforced these trends: By 1000 A.D., *sati* (widow
burning) was held out as an ideal for Kshatriyas, the practice

gradually spreading to the Brahmins as well (Altekar, 356–57). All these practices, and their restriction to or stricter enforcement among higher than lower castes, suggest underlying economic motives in retaining property within the patriarchal family.

A modern anthropologist, Ursula Sharma, asserts that "it is the distribution of property rights (especially rights in land) which we ought to look at first of all if we wish to understand the position of rural women" (9). "The poor have little property to protect; the norms governing female roles while permitting them to participate freely in labor, nevertheless, limit the ways in which women can actually use whatever economic power they may derive from their role in production" (201). Sharma also sees a custom such as *purdah* (seclusion) as a practice that reinforces male control of property. Thus, Sharma's conclusion about the interrelationships between the status of women and property is consistent with the historical record in which caste and gender stratification, and expansion of land grants to upper castes, apparently coincided. Concerns with female chastity at the time of Manu verged upon an obsession: "It is the nature of women to seduce men in this world . . ." (Manu II, 213) and may have stemmed from a desire for pure inheritance lines, nervous male asceticism, and an anxiety that uncontrolled women might undermine caste distinctions. The parallel between the rise of asceticism in Christianity and in Hinduism and misogynous statements about women's sexual nature is striking.

The spread of the emerging doctrines of women's place from the literate elite to the illiterate masses was facilitated by two Epic poems, the *Mahabharata* and the *Ramayana*. Both are believed to be loosely related to historical events that took place between 1000 and 700 B.C. But their present forms were recorded during the first four Christian centuries. Their didactic portions are almost certainly post-Mauryan and Guptan and reflect Brahminical values. The *Mahabharata*, which consists of 90,000 couplets, is the longest poem in the world. In their final forms the poems are amazing works of cultural integration: All of the tribes and agricultural peoples of the subcontinent, with their own myths and totems, gods and goddesses, are represented in some way. The Epics are also moral documents or moral tales: the characters depict cultural ideals, and form the basis of popular religion. The Epics are central to Indian culture—to song, theater, dance, painting, sculpture, and cinema.

Mahabharata. This Epic depicts the struggle between two related families, the Kauravas and Pandavas, over land rights in the fertile region north of Delhi. The Epic is important in depicting the doctrine of *dharma*—the disinterested performance of one's duty, however painful—which is central to the formal ideology of caste (see particularly Arjuna in the Bhagavad Gita).

The Epic also comments on the ideals of female marital duty. Madri, for example, ascends the funeral pyre of her husband, Pandu, and is burned to death. This is an early example of the practice of sati—in this case "voluntary." It is a wife's dharma to serve her husband.

The *Mahabharata* also contains the courageous and polyandrous Draupadi, queen and wife of the five Pandava brothers, a literary strand which may reflect earlier times or disappearing tribal or non-Aryan customs. But it was not the ideal of a strongwilled woman that was to gain ascendancy as a cultural norm; instead, it was the long-suffering, uncomplaining Sita of the *Ramayana* who was to provide the cultural role model for the Indian wife.

Ramayana. The doctrine of wifely loyalty, long-suffering, and submission *(pativrityam)* is fully articulated in this Epic, which also depicts Aryan political and cultural penetration into southern India. Sita, the heroine, is married at age six to prince Rama, who is subsequently wrongfully banished from the kingdom into a dark forest. Sita begs to accompany him, saying: "Thou art my king, my guide, my only refuge, my divinity." She is subsequently abducted by the evil King Ravana and carried away to Ceylon. She resists all Ravana's advances, but when Rama finally recovers her after a battle, he doubts her purity. Sita successfully undergoes an ordeal by fire to prove her innocence. Rama eventually regains his throne, but to placate a restive public who continue to believe Sita has been unchaste, he abandons her in a forest. She bravely carries on, and gives birth to twins, continuing to believe that her husband is all-wise and that her suffering will bring ultimate good to the kingdom. Rama, seeing the twins years later, relents and calls Sita back, but he is once again stricken with jealousy and asks for proof of her chastity while in the forest. Sita in agony cries to the mother earth to swallow her up. The earth gapes open, and Sita disappears into it.

The central ideology associated with Sita—chastity, obedience, and loyalty to the husband—remain powerful forces within Indian culture to this day. Both Manisha Roy (Chap. 2) and Rama Mehta (152–53) have described its survival in less extreme forms among educated women of the upper castes; Hemalata Dandekar documents the pervasiveness of Sita-like qualities as an ideal in the countryside, facilitated in modern times by the news media and the cinema which have reached the village.[8] However, the legend of Sita is sometimes considered to be a dual one. It contains another idealization of femininity aside from submission, namely endurance and bravery. Thus women's rights leaders like Sarojini Naidu could emphasize this aspect of tradition in urging women to courageously involve themselves in the struggle against British rule.

Discussion Questions

1. How do the aspects of womanhood idealized in the Laws of Manu and the Epics justify the social and political control of women? In what roles are women revered? Despised?

2. What parallel doctrines governing female behavior (submission/fear/reverence) can you find in Christianity, Islam, and any of the major world religions? Do these beliefs stem from common sources (economic, psychological, etc.)?

3. The ideology of women's place that evolved in ancient India was originally the product of the upper castes. Do men as a "class" have a stake in maintaining it? Does ideology once articulated have an autonomy of its own, or does it respond solely to socioeconomic changes? Can it shape socioeconomic change itself? What relevance do these theoretical considerations have for changing the status of women in India or elsewhere today?

4. The Laws of Manu (II, 213–15) contain various expressions of fear of women's uncontrolled sexuality. Are there Western parallels to this fear? What controls might one expect to be imposed on female behavior in such a belief system?

5. What religious mythologies of woman's place and nature contained in the Judeo-Christian tradition continue to shape cultural attitudes toward women in the West today? Compare them with those in Hinduism.

6. Discuss the relative explanatory force of workforce participation, development of private property, state formation, and religious asceticism in the changing status of women in ancient India.

THE SOCIAL STRUCTURES OF TRADITIONAL
HINDUISM: CASTE, FAMILY, AND SOCIAL MOBILITY

The caste system was and is a fundamental part of the Indian social order, though it has undergone many changes over time. In the previous lecture we examined the historical development of the formal ideology, or Great Tradition, of Hinduism, in which the ideals of female behavior and place are outlined. It is important to emphasize, however, that the degree to which these ideals were and are normative vary from upper to lower castes. There are also tribal peoples, or *Adivasis* (original inhabitants), who were and are to varying degrees outside Hindu orthodoxy. It is essential then to sketch out the structure and functions of the traditional Indian caste system and to examine the variations of women's place in the system. We will also examine the traditional Indian joint family and women's role within it. Our treatment will dwell on tradition as a method of setting the background for subsequent discussions of continuity and change in modern times. Where historical materials are lacking, we shall refer to modern studies as a method of rough extrapolation.

For many years, scholarship on caste, much of it by Westerners, depicted Indian society as static. This reflected in part the cultural biases of scholars and officials writing during the colonial period; it also stemmed from an overreliance on Brahminical accounts of ideal systems. Older accounts, which still find their way into modern textbooks, describe a largely static society mired in a fatalistic acceptance of a religiously defined status quo. The view of caste as divinely ordained; the belief that one's *dharma* (duty) is to obey its strictures; and the doctrine of *karma*, in which one's present position is dictated by past lives, do indeed permeate religious texts. However, the degree to which this belief structure, promulgated by Brahmins, actually led to a fatalistic acceptance of one's lot has undergone serious challenge.[9]

More recent work, and especially the proliferating field studies done by Indian scholars since independence, presents a more dynamic view of caste. As in any other stratified society, the Indian response to oppression has included "individual escape or artful manipulation of the situation" as well as "organized, overt challenge and revolt" (Berreman, *Caste and Other Inequities*, 220). Caste and individual mobility have been documented for historical times as well as in the present. Of interest to us here is the question of how the situation of a woman changes as her kin or caste rises (or falls) in the hierarchy.

Readings for Students
Chaki-Sirkar, Manjusri. *Feminism in a Traditional Society: Women of the Manipur Valley.* Delhi: Shakti Books, Vikas Pub. Co., 1984.

Falk, Nancy Auer. "The Case of the Vanishing Nuns: The Fruits of Ambivalence in Ancient Indian Buddhism." In *Unspoken Worlds: Women's Religious Lives in Non-Western Cultures,* edited by Nancy Auer Falk and Rita Gross, 207–24. New York: Harper and Row, 1980.

Jacobson, Doranne. "The Women of North and Central India: Goddesses and Wives." In *Women in India: Two Perspectives,* 17–111. New Delhi: Manohar Book Service; Columbia, Mo.: South Asia Books, 1977.

Kinsley, David. "Devotion as an Alternative to Marriage in the Lives of Some Hindu Women Devotees." In *Tradition and Modernity in Bhakti Movements,* edited by Jayant Lele, 83–93. Leiden: E. J. Brill, 1981.

Status of Women in India: A Synopsis of the Report of the National Committee on the Status of Women (1971–74), Chap. 3, "The Socio-Cultural Setting." New Delhi: Indian Council of Social Science Research, 1975.

Wadley, Susan S. "Women and the Hindu Tradition." In Jacobson, *Women in India,* 113–39.

Readings for Instructors
Berreman, Gerald D. *Caste and Other Inequities.* Meerut: Folklore Institute, Kirpa Dai Series in Folklore and Anthropology, 1979.

Barber, Bernard. "Social Mobility in Hindu India." In *Social Mobility in the Caste System of India,* edited by James Silverberg. The Hague: Mouton, 1968.

Bose, Devabrata. *The Problems of Indian Society.* Bombay: Popular Prakashan, 1968.

Choudhury, N. C. "Womanhood in Tribal India." In *Tribal Women in India,* edited by Committee, Tribal Women in India, 9–20. Calcutta: Indian Anthropological Society, 1978.

Desai, Neera, ed. "Impact of Bhakti Movements on the Status of Women in India." In *Women in Modern India,* 34–47. Bombay: Vora and Co., 1957.

Dube, S. C. *Indian Village.* London: Routledge & Kegan Paul, 1955.

Karve, Irawati. *Hindu Society—An Interpretation.* 2d ed. Poona: Deshmukh Prakashan, 1968.

Mann, R. S. *Social Structure, Social Change and Future Trends: Indian Village Perspective,* Chap. 2. Jaipur: Ravat Pubs., 1979.

Mehta, Hansa. "Literary Achievements of Indian Women." In *Women in Modern India,* edited by Evelyn Gedge, 78–102. Bombay, 1929. Repr. Westport, Conn.: Hyperion Press, 1976.

Mies, Maria. *Indian Women and Patriarchy.*

Ray, Reginald A. "Accomplished Women in Tantric Buddhism of Medieval India and Tibet." In *Unspoken Worlds,* 227–42.

Sen, Jyotsi. "Status of Women Among Tribes." In *Tribal Women in India,* 20–31.

Sharma, Ursula. *Women, Work and Property,* Chap. 3.

Srinivas, M. N. *Caste in Modern India and Other Essays.* Bombay: Asia Pub. House, 1962.

Stein, Burton. "Social Mobility and Medieval South Indian Hindu Sects." In *Social Mobility in the Caste System,* 78–94.

Talim, Meena. *Women in Early Buddhist Literature.* Bombay: University of Bombay, 1972.

Ulrich, Helen. "Caste Differences between Brahmin and Non-Brahmin Women in a South Indian Village." In *Sexual Stratification: A Cross-Cultural View,* edited by Alice Schlegel, 41–66. New York: Columbia University Press, 1977.

Verma, H. N., and Amrit Verma. *Indian Women through the Ages.* New Delhi: Great Indian Pubs., 1976.

Wadley, Susan S., ed. *The Power of Tamil Women.* Syracuse, N.Y.: Foreign and Comparative Studies, South Asian Series, No. 6, Maxwell School of Citizenship and Public Affairs, Syracuse University, 1980.

Lecture Topics

Definitions of Caste. Castes (or *jatis*) are endogamous groups in which membership is by birth. Castes claim a real or mythological common ancestor and occupation. The essentials of the caste system emerged by 600 B.C. and were fully articulated by about 200 A.D. Castes can be arranged into four orders *(varnas),* but precise measurement of rank and criteria of ranking have defied easy explanation (see Berreman, Chap. 5). The system can be conceptualized along two dimensions: religious/ritual and secular.

Ritual Dimensions of Caste. The ritual rankings of castes are those reflected in Brahminical texts. The classical orders, together with their historical occupations, are Brahmins (priests),

Kshatriyas (warriors and rulers), Vaishyas (merchants), and Shudras (or Sudras) (cultivators). Outside the caste system are the Untouchables, service workers (sweepers, butchers, potters, etc.) who historically were landless or displaced from their land. Recently militant Untouchable leaders have begun to use the word "Dalits" or "downtrodden ones" to refer to their community, which forms about 12 percent of the population. Gandhi popularized the name "Harijan," or "Children of God." Also outside the pale of ritual respectability are the tribal peoples (adivasis), who are divided into numerous ethnic, linguistic, and cultural groups. The tribes have survived in rugged terrain, and many of them (at least until recent times) have been largely unabsorbed into Hindu culture. The adivasis were characteristically hunter-gatherers or horticulturalists without the occupational stratification typical of the caste system. Underlying the structural distance between castes was and is the ideological notion of pollution and purity.

Pollution may be invested in certain occupations dealing with the destruction of life or involving contact with human emissions (butchers, street sweepers, leather workers, etc.), and in diet (higher castes traditionally are vegetarians and abstain from alcohol). A number of anthropologists have stressed a connection between pollution beliefs and attitudes toward women: for example, a woman is supposed to be isolated from other household members during her menses (Srinivas, 120), and she is also to be considered polluting for a period after childbirth (a notion present in traditional Catholic practice as well). Harsh prohibitions against liaisons between a high-caste woman and a low-caste man, but not the reverse, have also been attributed to pollution beliefs, as have the practices of female monogamy, child marriage, and restrictions on widows.[10] The failure of lower castes to follow these practices makes them polluting, according to this line of interpretation. As we shall see, some feminist anthropologists, such as Ursula Sharma, locate these practices in property relationships. Further, Hanna Papanek, a feminist sociologist, believes "feminist scholars should actually look at what has been written on pollution and at pollution beliefs themselves to examine them as didactic practices to demean women."[11] Certainly the Laws of Manu had precisely this demeaning intent, saying:

A Candala (Untouchable), a domestic pig, a cock, a dog, a menstruating woman and a eunuch must not look at Brahmans while they are eating (Manu, III, 239).

For our immediate purposes, however, it is sufficient to note that whatever the causation, upper castes were generally more stringent in controlling female behavior.

Secular Dimensions of Caste (Srinivas, Barber). Ritual considerations are only one aspect of caste. "Dominant caste" is a term coined by M. N. Srinivas for what is a universal feature of Indian villages: the existence of one or more castes that dominate the political and economic structures through possession of land or, increasingly, through modern electioneering, by numbers. This political and economic dominance does not always correspond with the classical varnas. Landowners are generally of higher castes but it is their access to strategic resources, rather than their ritual prestige, that gives them secular dominance. If religious and secular dimensions of caste are not roughly correlated, a caste (or an individual) may rise (or fall) until a position consistent with wealth and power is achieved. This process of mobility has been documented for both historical and modern times. It is, however, a form of mobility that accepts the essentials of the caste structure: the principle of hierarchy remains.

Social Mobility and Women. Upwardly mobile castes have sought ritual acceptance in a variety of ways, and the path chosen may have a differential impact on men and women. This issue has not been studied with the care it deserves, but we can note several vehicles for social protest historically and their implications for women.

Sanskritization (Chaki-Sircar, Srinivas). M. N. Srinivas has documented in detail a process that he terms "Sanskritization" whereby a lower caste (or individual) changes occupations and adopts the behavioral norms of an upper caste. Over time, the adopting caste or member rises in ritual status. Because there are variations in the restrictions placed on women by individual castes, this has obvious consequences for women. Upper castes have generally been more likely to seclude women (a practice discussed in "Muslim Rule and Islamic Influences," above), prohibit widow remarriage, and to practice child marriage, though this last practice became generally widespread. Lower-caste women have also generally been more active in agricultural and service occupations. Some anthropologists have seen workforce participation, particularly where women control the production of a valued good, as leading to a high status, or at least to a greater egalitarianism between husband and wife. Modern studies of low-caste women workers have not always confirmed this picture, depicting instead a woman's "double day" of outside and household labor, exploitative wages, and a general inegalitarianism among low-caste women and men.[12] Other studies, however, do depict a greater egalitarianism and sharing.[13] However, it is hazardous to extrapolate an historical conclusion from these data because the forces of modern urbanization and market capitalism may have profoundly altered low-caste relationships. It seems likely that a low-caste woman traded greater physical freedom, less restrictive marriage practices, and poverty for comparative comfort, seclusion, and marriage restrictions as her caste or kin Sanskritized in the pre-modern era. A tribal woman experienced an equally complex process of social change as her people were drawn within the fold of Hindu orthodoxy.

It is not easy to generalize about the effects of Sanskritization upon those tribes who have undergone it because at the point where reliable studies begin they ranged from hunting-gatherers, pastoralists, and horticulturalists to settled agriculturalists, most of whom were patrilineal but some of whom were matrilineal. Nevertheless, anthropologists beginning in the nineteenth century have remarked upon the comparative freedom of tribal women, the relatively low degree of regulation of premarital activity, the availability of divorce, and the lack of a marked preference for male over female births among many tribes. However, as with modern studies of low castes, current tribal studies generally do not depict relatively egalitarian relationships between men and women (see particularly Sen, 19). Here we should recall Eleanor Leacock's warnings about male bias, the ahistorical nature of anthropological studies, and the degree to which so-called primitive people have been affected by outside forces as a caution against assuming that the current inegalitarian picture is historically accurate (see Chapter 2, "Male Dominance: Myth or Reality?" above).

However, a recent important work by Manjusri Chaki-Sircar on the Metei women of the Manipur Valley of northeastern India begins to restore the history of tribal women. Looking at Metei society with a refocused and feminist eye she finds a society in which women held and still hold crucial positions in social, religious, and political life. Because of women's economic importance in agricultural subsistence as well as their exclusive control of trade and weaving, they have warded off many aspects of Sanskritized marriage customs and behavior despite over two centuries of Brahminical cultural imperialism. Women's power was also entrenched by reason of male depopulation in early nineteenth-century warfare. Manjusri Chaki-Sircar suggests that Sanskritization "will not be successful unless the entire caste-group [or tribe] achieves considerable economic gain which would then enable the system to exclude women from the economic sphere" (188). Sanskritization failed in Metei culture because women were too valuable to be replaced, and they protected their interests by collective action, including "Nupi-lan" or "Women's War" against adverse colonial policies. Clearly much more research is needed on the conditions under which Sanskritization succeeded or failed among both upper- and lower-caste groups. Where it did succeed the consequences were often drastic for women. Other routes to ritual respectability may not have had such clearcut consequences.

Buddhism (Falk, Ray, Talim). Buddhism is one of many sects or religions in India that contains elements of social protest and mobility. Jainism, Sikhism, Islam, Christianity, and such modern Hindu reform movements as the Brahmo Samaj and the Arya Samaj have all drawn part of their popularity from those seeking reform and emancipation. For the pre-Islamic period the issue of gender and Buddhism is the best documented, and serves to illustrate some of the points made in Chapter 5 ("Women and Religion"), namely, that women have been drawn to sects that offer more positive images of themselves and greater opportunities for participation.

Buddhism arose in part as a casteless protest against Hindu orthodoxy in the sixth century B.C. Many of its adherents were from the lower castes and from states on the periphery of the Aryan advance. Although Buddhism virtually died out in India by the tenth century, it is undergoing a current revival among Dalits. There have been some mass conversions. Thus it continues to be a religion of social protest. For women, Buddhism also offered an alternative:

> *Buddha's view of women.* Although Buddha shared some of the harsh views of women's nature current at the time, he did repudiate the idea that a husband was virtually a woman's god, and instead recognized her as an individual with functions other than wife and mother. With reluctance, he allowed women to join Buddhist orders.
>
> *Buddhist nuns.* In a nunnery women could receive an education and perform careers of some importance as

theologians, nurses, and care givers to the poor. These tasks of teaching and compassion were extensions of women's traditional roles. There were nuns of great distinction in the history of early Buddhism, including Sanghamitra, a daughter of the Indian king Asoka and one of the first Buddhist missionaries to Ceylon (ca. 200 B.C.), where she is venerated to this day.

Bhakti Movements (Desai, Kinsley, Mehta, Wadley). Bhakti movements arose in the eleventh century A.D. as an anti-Brahminical revolt, and they have continued to modern times. They centered upon the ecstatic spiritual union between the adherent and a particular god or goddess. The goddess, worshipped under many names and guises (Kali, Durga, Radha), embodies power or *shakti,* the dynamic and often destructive as well as regenerative forces of the universe.[14] Susan Wadley believes the status of women in South India is related to beliefs in shakti. Women, like the goddess, possess shakti and their powers for good or evil must be kept under male control. Although the attitude of male bhakti saints towards women was often ambivalent, nevertheless, the use of vernacular languages and the unmediated approach to worship was attractive to women. Women have been recognized as bhakti poets and saints in both medieval and modern India. Though bhakti movements were vehicles of both caste and gender revolt, they had little apparent overall impact on the status of women.

The lives of individual mystics do show signs of female rebellion expressed within the cultural avenues provided by bhakti cults. Mahadeviyakka, an eleventh-century devotee of Siva, renounced an unhappy marriage to a king; Lallesvari, a fourteenth-century religious singer, left a harsh domestic life to become a wandering religious singer; Mirabai (1498–1546), a Rajput princess who was abused by her in-laws after her husband's death, became an ascetic who wrote devotional poems to Lord Krishna that are still cherished in North India (see Kinsley). Stretching the boundaries even further was Muktabai, a thirteenth-century Marathi saint, who preached the equality of men and women. The bhakti cults were important as vehicles for female literary achievement. Hansa Mehta identifies over fifteen female bhakti poets who made significant contributions to vernacular languages from the twelfth to nineteenth centuries.

Women's Place in the Traditional Family (Dube, Chap. 5; Karve; Mies, 41–116; Sharma, Chaps. 3, 8; Ulrich). The traditional

Indian joint family shares common features with those of other
societies built on plow agricultural systems (China, the Middle
East): it is patriarchal and patrilineal, and brothers, uncles, cousins, and nephews often live under one roof. The father is head of
the house and administrator of the joint property. (A short discussion of variations in this generalized pattern, and especially of
matrilineal and matrilocal elements in southern India may be
found in Mies, *Indian Women and Patriarchy,* 89–90). The family,
rather than the individual, is the main unit of the Indian social
system, and women—who are "outsiders" in the family into which
they marry—are a potentially disruptive element. Anthropologists
and sociologists have recently questioned how widespread the
joint family actually was. Srinivas suggests that it never encompassed more than 20 percent of the population, and was a feature
only of upper castes and those who were Sanskritizing. Studies of
lower-caste families are comparatively rare.

Within the joint family in a traditional marriage, women are
deferential not only to their husbands but to all adult males.
Romantic love between husband and wife is frequently suppressed in these circumstances (the Laws of Manu denounce it),
deference to elders is inculcated, and parents often arrange marriages at an early age, when a wife's character is more pliant.
Mothers-in-law have great power in the domestic sphere and
tension is often high between her and her daughters-in-law. A
woman's status thus could increase with age, especially if she had
sons. Tension is also common between fathers and sons. Highly
ritualized behavior between family members, and clear rules of
deference, are methods of channeling and controlling these rivalries and preventing family breakups.

Traditionally, upper-caste women had no grounds for divorce, though a few lower castes permitted it. This, together with
widow remarriage, was one of the customs that kept them in low
ritual rank. In the past, men could divorce on grounds of a
woman's adultery, failure to bear sons, bad behavior, or disease. A
divorced woman was dependent upon the charity of her parents
or brothers; if they were unwilling or unable to assist, the most
common options were begging or prostitution.

Widowhood was (and often still is) a dreaded condition in
Indian society. The widow had no rights to property; she was
despised and often blamed for her husband's death. Her
usefulness was over, and *sati* was a cultural ideal among upper
castes until reformers campaigned against it in the nineteenth
century. If she lived, she was often given the hardest jobs, unless

her sons protected her; her head was shaven; she was forbidden to attend ceremonies; she was considered polluting to pregnant women; and she was spoken to contemptuously.

Sources that speak directly from women's experiences of their lives in the traditional family in historical times are sparse. An accessible autobiography covering Indian family life in the early twentieth century is:

Mazumdar, Shudha. *A Pattern of Life: The Memoirs of an Indian Woman*, edited by Geraldine Forbes. New Delhi: Manohar Book Service, 1977. The memoir covers the author's life from 1900 to 1930, and includes an account of her abandonment of many purdah restrictions and her involvement in social work with women.

For modern studies comparing women's lives, see:

Hobson, Sarah. *Family Web: A Story of India*. Chicago: Academy Chicago, 1982.

Jacobson, Doranne. "The Women of North and Central India: Goddesses and Wives." In *Women in India.*

Ideal and Actual Behavior (Altekar, Verma). In any society there are discrepancies between cultural ideals and actual behavior, regardless of class (or caste). Indian history even before the modern era is full of colorful, forceful, and accomplished women who defied patriarchal norms, or who turned them to their own advantage.

In the arts, among those who might be mentioned are Mollati, the sixteenth-century author of a popular Telegu version of the *Ramayana;* and Akka Mahadevi, a mystic poet of twelfth-century Karnataka. Though literate women were frequently from royal or upper-caste households, this was not always the case. The fifteenth-century lyric poet, Sursari, was a sweeper before she became a disciple of Nabha. Dancing girls could also sometimes achieve fame and fortune: Achala founded a school of classical dance in the tenth century. Defying all simple stereotypes of Indian women is Hariyakka, who achieved fame as a wrestler in the fifteenth-century kingdom of Vijayanagar.

There is also a long tradition of Hindu women rulers, though the vast majority reigned as regents or dowagers. Even in the Gupta period when reactionary religious texts were being articulated, dowager queens used to administer the kingdom when the heir was a minor. One queen, Kumaradevi, may have ruled in her own right. Perhaps the most famous ruler was Lakshmibai, Rani of Jhansi, who, though a nineteenth-century figure, represented an older dying order. She led the fight against British annexation of her Mahratta state, and died on the battlefield in 1857. These and other examples allow the avoidance of a monochromatic picture of Indian women in the Hindu tradition in historical times.

Discussion Questions

1. What variations in acceptable female behavior exist in the United States or other Western countries that can be related to race or class? What are the reasons for these variations? Are there Western parallels to "Sanskritization?"

2. What "pollution" beliefs exist in Western folk tales or practices?

3. If you were an Untouchable woman, would you want to undergo Sanskritization? What values underlie your answer?

4. What are the differential family controls and socialization processes North American nuclear families place on girls and boys? Why are they imposed? What are the parallels and differences with the traditional Indian joint family?

5. Discuss any similarities or differences in areas of female achievement in the public domain in pre-modern India and Europe. Did these accomplishments defy or reinforce prevailing attitudes of womanhood?

6. Compare and contrast the role of some religions as a mode of social protest or achievement in India and the United States.

7. Is it accurate to see bhakti movements, Buddhism, etc. as avenues of female rebellion, or is this imposing a modern, Western feminist meaning?

MUSLIM RULE AND ISLAMIC INFLUENCES

Anti-Islamic biases are pervasive in Western culture, and the assumption that Muslim women are particularly degraded is unfortunately virtually automatic in Europe and North America. Harems of a Hollywood variety, the veil, and Islamic fundamentalists are likely to be the cultural windows through which women in Islam, whether in India or elsewhere, are viewed. A broader, contextualized vision is essential in order to understand the complex ways in which Islam affected women's status. Islam should also be distinguished from the culture of the peoples who absorbed and adapted its message.

The chief bearers of Islam to India were the invading Turks who established the Delhi Sultanate (1175–1526) and subsequently the fabled Mughal Empire (1526–ca. 1761), whose riches and splendor attracted Europeans to the Indian coasts first to trade and subsequently to conquer. Throughout this period, areas of India, particularly in the south, remained independent of Muslim rule, and relatively insulated from outside cultural influences. However, by multiple processes of conquest, migration, and conversion (especially of ruling houses anxious to come to terms with their new overlords and lower castes escaping the strictures of Hinduism), eventually about one-quarter of the subcontinent's population became Muslim.

The original thrust of Islam regarding the status of women was reformist, as is discussed in Chapter Eleven ("Women in the Islamic Middle East and North Africa," above), which should be read in conjunction with this section. By the time Muslim influence was felt on a large scale in India in the twelfth-century incursions, the reformist message had been diluted by interaction with the indigenous practices of the Turks and Afghan troops who formed the main cohorts of the invaders. Nevertheless, one should guard against the automatic assumption that the incoming cultural practices were uniformly negative. An analysis of the Muslim impact is complicated by the fact that during the five centuries of Muslim political domination of the subcontinent, many Hindus converted to Islam, retaining elements of past caste practices, and even the descendents of the invaders were influenced by the culture of the subcontinent. At the same time Islamic cultural influences affected Hindu culture: Vijnaneshvara, the writer of the reform Mitakshara Digest (eleventh-twelfth century A.D.) vested Hindu wives with the right to sue in court for certain inheritance rights, thus breaking with an important precept of the Laws of Manu. He did so under the influence of Islamic law (Mies, 58–59).

The ways in which Muslim rule and these reciprocal crosscurrents affected women in India have not been studied with great historical specificity. The historiography of the period moreover is marred by a number of biases. Hindu historians, especially those writing under the influence of the nationalist period, tend to assume the Muslim impact was negative (Altekar, Misra): Hindu women get hidden in seclusion from lusty Turks. Most historians, however, have simply neglected the topic in preference for the "real" history of political, administrative, or military affairs. Unless a woman entered the public realm, she was of little interest.[15] For feminist historians of Muslim India there is a particular challenge in reconstructing women's historical experience. Many women lived in seclusion, invisible to the European travelers and the Persian and Hindi court chroniclers who are the chief primary sources. In writing this section we have drawn upon the sparse but best historical treatments to date, supplemented by the work of feminist researchers on purdah practices. We will survey three interrelated topics: women's roles in the life of the court, Islamic law, and purdah practices. As with the section on Hinduism, we recommend that instructors assign a sympathetic treatment of the overall values of Islam before dealing with issues of gender. Huston Smith offers one such explication.

Readings for Students
Ahmed, Leila. "Western Ethnocentrism and Perceptions of the Harem." *Feminist Studies* 8, no. 3 (Fall 1982): 521–34.
Levy, Reuben. *The Social Structure of Islam.* Cambridge: Cambridge University Press, 1965.
Misra, Rekha. *Women in Mughal India: 1526–1748*, Chap. 1, "Position of Women Before the Advent of the Mughals." Delhi: Munshiram Manoharlal, 1967.
Mukerjee, Ila. *Social Status of North Indian Women, 1526–1707 A.D.* Agra: Shiva Lal Agarwala Co., 1972.
Papanek, Hanna. "Purdah: Separate Worlds and Symbolic Shelter." Chap. 1 in *Separate Worlds: Studies of Purdah in South Asia,* edited by Hanna Papanek and Gail Minault. Delhi: Chanakya Pubs., 1982; Columbia, Mo.: South Asia Books, 1982.
Smith, Huston. *The Religions of Man,* Chap. 6.

Readings for Instructors
Chapter 11, "Women in the Islamic Middle East and North Africa," below.
Jacobson, Doranne. "Purdah and the Hindu Family in Central India." Chap. 3 in *Separate Worlds.*
Misra, Rekha. *Women in Mughal India.*

Mujeeb, M. *The Indian Muslims.* London: Allen and Unwin, 1967.
Sharma, Ursula. *Women, Work and Property,* especially Chaps. 1, 3, 8.
Papanek, Hanna. "Purdah: Separate Worlds and Symbolic Shelter." Chap. 1 in *Separate Worlds.*
Vatuk, Sylvia. "Purdah Revisited: A Comparison of Hindu and Muslim Interpretations of the Cultural Meaning of Purdah in South Asia." Chap. 2 in *Separate Worlds.*

Lecture Topics

The Status of Women in Islamic Law (Levy; Chapter 11 this volume). Islamic law may well have improved the status of women when it was first articulated in sixth century Arabia. Similarly, in the context of the growing doctrines of submission indigenous to India, the formal rights given to women under Islamic law may have been progressive in some respects, even though in other instances the effect was negative. For example, Islamic law gave a woman rights of inheritance (one-half that of a man), a provision that influenced the reformist Mitakshara law code in Hinduism. A woman's dower *(mehr),* property or money received from her husband upon marriage, was her own; a woman could testify in court (though her word was worth half that of a man); and widows could also remarry. These latter rights were generally absent in Hindu law. However, these progressive impulses were diluted over time on the subcontinent (Mujeeb). In other aspects Hindu and Muslim laws were similar: a man could easily obtain a divorce but a woman could not under any circumstances. The Muslim male's right of instant divorce by repudiation *(talaq)* provided a loophole through which the spirit of the laws of inheritance could be evaded. Deathbed divorce of wives could result in their disinheritance. Islamic laws also sanctioned polygyny.

Both legal codes, however, were fundamentally patriarchal: women were under male control. Both reflect central concerns with property arrangements within a male kinship group. The comparative liberalism in Islamic law regarding women's inheritance rights was counterbalanced by a preference for cross-cousin marriages within the kin group to maintain property intact. Property concerns also underlie part of the cultural matrix of purdah practices, of which female seclusion is one expression. Seclusion was practiced by the Muslim invaders.

Purdah (Jacobson, Papanek, Sharma, Vatuk). The seclusion of women has multiple roots and its practice has not been limited to the Muslim world. Pre-Islamic India, China, Mediterranean Europe, and parts of northwestern Europe have all experienced the same phenomenon at some period. It is important to note that seclusion has many characteristics in common with other systems governing woman's sphere; it is a reflection in a heightened form of modesty codes pervasive throughout many cultures (Vatuk, 59–60). Indeed the desirability of female seclusion was debated among the Puritan fathers of sixteenth-century New England.[16] This broader context should be borne in mind when approaching Muslim—or Hindu—seclusion practices.

Purdah (literally curtain) refers to a range of behaviors having as their purpose the "limitation on interaction between women and males outside certain well-defined categories which differ among Muslims and Hindus" (Papanek, 3). The limits on interaction are set in a variety of ways, with a multitude of degrees of observance. Seclusion in the home can be one aspect of purdah. Among Muslim women, wearing a *burqa,* a tent-like garment functioning as a kind of "portable seclusion" is another aspect of purdah (Papanek, 10). A parallel practice among Hindu (and some Muslim) women is the concealment of the head and face by the draped end of a sari. However, in other instances, purdah may still be practiced without overt physical concealment through gestures and speech. Essentially purdah is a principle that can be adapted to a wide variety of circumstances.

Papanek, Jacobson, and Sharma argue that two different systems of purdah, Muslim and Hindu, operate in India. Among Muslims, restrictions on female behavior do not apply within the immediate kin group, but only to the outside world, which is seen as potentially threatening. Among Hindus, purdah practices order relationships of respect and submission especially to in-laws within the affinal family (Papanek). Vatuk, however, questions whether so clear-cut a distinction exists, citing certain instances of avoidance of kin among Muslims (though not necessarily through seclusion or use of the burqa), and of dispensing with veiling when a woman is among total strangers (64–68). She suggests that "one observes purdah with reference to the social approval of persons whose opinions about one's respectability matter" (68; see also Sharma, 45). Vatuk stresses the similarity between Hindu and Muslim purdah practices such as common concern with "protecting the sexual modesty of women" (69). All authors stress the physical and social separation of men and women into different spheres of activity.

Papanek provides a very useful conceptualization of these

spheres as "separate worlds and symbolic shelter" (see her article). The "separate worlds" involve a sharp sexual division of labor, and at the same time a high degree of interdependence between women and men, who are mutually reliant on each other. "Symbolic shelter" involves a cluster of related values: women are seen as vulnerable in and to the outside world. Among Muslims, women are thought to need protection especially against sexual desire and sexual aggression, for both sexes are regarded as having strong sexual drives. Among Hindus, women are more likely to be seen as temptresses, and avoidance rules protect men (36). *Izzat* (honor or family pride) is vested in the female's respectability, and men struggle to control female behavior and in some instances to avenge infractions. However, veiling and seclusion are observed not merely to control sexuality. Purdah is also related to considerations of prestige and to the desire to maintain high rank, much like the Victorian cult of domesticity (Jacobson, 96–97).

The question of the causes and origins of purdah is a difficult one. Ursula Sharma suggests that norms such as seclusion or family honor should be viewed "not so much as antidotes to misalliance (though they certainly perform this function) so much as a system of practices which reinforce male control of productive resources" (201). There is, as we saw, historical evidence for the parallel growth of doctrines of female subordination and restrictions on behavior with the development of intense class stratification in India. Purdah, in the strict sense of seclusion, seems to have arisen first in the upper strata of society (Mies, 66–68). This is entirely consistent with the conclusion that its function is male control of productive resources or property. But, whatever its origins, the practice has now spread to lower-income groups (Papanek, 42–43; Sharma, 118–26). So powerful are considerations of prestige and the desire to emulate the behavior of one's social betters that some poor families restrict female participation in the workforce at the cost of considerable economic hardship.

Royal Women and Seclusion. If social prestige has been of importance in furthering the practice of seclusion, then the harems of the Delhi Sultans and Mughal Emperors should be considered as important vehicles for its promotion and legitimization historically. The Imperial harems contained thousands of women (wives, concubines, female relatives, and their household staffs) housed in architectural splendor and complete seclusion. Lesser Muslim nobles and Hindu rajas followed similar practices on a less lavish scale. (Descriptions of the royal harems may be found in Misra, Chap. 5 and Mukerjee, 33–41.)

Descriptions of the royal harems, whether by contemporary chroniclers or later historians, often have a breathless quality, stressing their pomp and conspicuous consumption; the very word "harem" conjures up visions of captive and indolent women kept for purposes of sexual debauchery on a grand scale. It would be unwise to entirely discount the element of male egotism in constructing harems and in procuring their many inhabitants. It is also undeniable that some of the Delhi Sultans and Mughal Emperors led dissolute lives: royal succession on the subcontinent as elsewhere did not always produce competent heirs. However, such analyses fail to highlight the strategic value of marriage alliances in an age of state-building that relied on personal bonds to help solidify loyalty to the dynasty. Some proportion of the "ladies of the harem" were sent to court to cement or create bonds of kinship, though of course on male terms.

The Mughal harem was elaborately organized with a chief female administrator (or *Mahaldar*), superintendents of sections, writers, treasurers, personal attendants, and the like; in short, it was staffed by ranked female civil servants. The principle of sexual seclusion also dictated that the internal guards were women, skilled in archery and other arms, while eunuchs guarded the outer perimeter (Misra, 79). There was also an educational system for young girls and boys, who seem to have been taught together until primary age, then separated. The education of girls continued into their youth either privately or in court-sponsored schools, the teachers being women or old men (Misra, 12–13; 87–92). Then as now the logic of seclusion carried with it avenues of sex-segregated female employment (Papanek, Chap. 7). Some noble women were accomplished poets and painters as well as important patrons of the arts (Misra, Chap. 6).

Women in harems were not mere ciphers. Within the very real limits on their access to power, and the physical limitations of seclusion, a number of loyal wives and mothers played important political roles, as Rekha Misra outlines. Misra cites dozens of examples of political maneuvering from "behind the curtain": Shah Turkan (1236 A.D.) attempted to put her indolent son on the throne and concentrate power in her own hands, but was put to death by harem rivals (6–7). Two Emperors of the Lodi period (fifteenth century) whose fathers died when they were minors, owed their succession to the vigorous championing of their claims by their mothers (10–11). Babur, the founder of the Mughal

Dynasty, relied upon his grandmother's advice, and one of his wives, Bibi Mubarika, the daughter of an Afghan tribal chief, helped to strengthen the Emperor's power in Afghanistan (17–19). When the Emperor Jahangir (1605–1627) was captured by a political rival, Empress Nurjahan tried to rescue him herself by force; a frontal assault proving unsuccessful, she undermined the usurper's power by organizing a conspiracy (35–40).

Though instances of female influence in the courts of the period are fairly well documented, analyses of these power struggles from the perspective of the women involved are incomplete, superficial, and oftentimes sexist. The *Oxford History of India*, for example, dismisses two years (1560–62) in the reign of the young Emperor Akbar in which he took little interest in the affairs of state as an era of "petticoat government" in which the kingdom was "mismanaged by unscrupulous women."[17] Even Misra's characterization of motivation in harem politics rarely goes beyond the depiction of a partisan as an "ambitious lady" (10). What is needed is a more contextualized treatment in which the terms (mother, wife, etc.) and channels (kinship links, regional affiliations) by which women could exert influence are made plainer, and those maneuverings related to broader court factions. Internal harem politics are also an unexplored area, though there are hints of intense rivalries (Misra, 28, 34).

What is clear, however, is that while women at court could attempt to advance the claims of sons or relatives, their power was that of indirect influence severely circumscribed. This is best illutrated in the career of the extraordinary Sultan Razia (1236–1240), who was nominated by her father to succeed to the throne in preference to his incompetent sons. She led military expeditions unveiled. She was quickly overthrown and killed. The *Tabaqat-i-Nasiri*, the contemporary authority for her reign, declared she "was endowed with all the admirable attributes and qualifications necessary for kings; but as she did not attain the destiny in her creation of being computed among men, of what advantage were all these qualifications unto her?"[18]

If purdah practices shaped the limits of and political methods used by women in the courts of the Delhi Sultanate and Mughal Empire, they had an equally profound effect upon the ideology and methods of the women's rights movement, both Hindu and Muslim, which arose during the British period. Sex segregation encouraged the formation of single-sex schools as well as social and political associations. Demands for improvements in the status of women tended to be based on the ideological grounds of improving women's performance of their separate, traditional female roles rather than in more recent Western terms of achieving identical rights and roles for women and men. Purdah practices also have a continuing influence upon women's roles and workforce participation to this day, as we shall subsequently examine.

Discussion Questions

1. Discuss the assertion in this text that "seclusion has many characteristics in common with other systems of governing woman's sphere; it is a reflection in a heightened form of modesty codes pervasive throughout many cultures."

2. Discuss the methodologies and sources that might be employed to reconstruct the history of "the common woman" in Mughal India.

3. What limitations on interaction between males and females exist(ed) in American society, historically and currently? Compare these with traditional India. Are American women "symbolically sheltered?"

4. Discuss the relative explanatory power of "prestige" and "economics" as the basis for purdah practices.

5. Leila Ahmed argues that "the harem can be defined as a system that permits males sexual access to more than one female. It can also be defined, and with as much accuracy, as a system whereby the female relatives of a man—wives, sisters, mothers, aunts, daughters—share much of their time and their living space, and further, which enables women to have frequent and easy access to other women in their community, vertically, across class lines, as well as horizontally" (524). Discuss the accuracy of both descriptions, and the origin and perpetuation of Western stereotypes of Muslim women.

THE BRITISH PERIOD: NINETEENTH-CENTURY REFORM MOVEMENTS

Scholarly criticism of the effects of British rule is of longstanding duration beginning with nationalists like Dadabhai Naoroji (1825–1917) and Romesh Chunder Dutt (1848–1909), who were early, forceful exponents of the "drain theory," an explication of colonial economic dependency that proved influential not only in India but among nationalists throughout the British Empire.[19]

It is relatively easy to enumerate the technologies, institutions, and ideas the British imported directly and indirectly, wittingly and unwittingly into India: industrial processes, including textile manufacturing; the beginnings of agricultural modernization through irrigation schemes and cash cropping, partly for export; modern communications such as railways, the telegraph, and printing press; the foundations of a modern nation-state with an elaborate, centralized bureaucracy, chosen at least in part by educational achievement, backed by systematic taxation settlements, systematic legal codifications, and military power; and Western schools and colleges, and with these the prevailing nineteenth-century Western notions of scientific and human progress, individualism, equality before the law, and liberal democracy. It is far more difficult, however, to assess precisely how and to what extent Indian society was altered, the scope and direction of change, and who benefitted and who was harmed. All of the areas of British impact can potentially be examined with gender differentiations in mind.[20]

Unfortunately, the study of Indian economic history from the perspective of gender is largely neglected. We need to know much more about the role of women in the traditional Indian economy, and then to examine the effects of India's integration into the world market system, under the aegis of imperialism, upon women's work. The transition from subsistence to market village economies, and the introduction of cash crops, modern agricultural methods, and new land revenue systems all need examination with gender issues in mind. Yet the little that is known suggests that lower-caste women's economic position eroded. Women, for example, were important in the production of handicrafts; spinning on the *charkha* was damaged badly by competition from machine-made goods; the *chikan* (embroidery) industry which flourished during the Mughal period, languished in the nineteenth and twentieth centuries, until it was revived again after independence; and weaving, which in tribal areas was a woman's job, was undermined by the power loom. Women (and children) were hired in large numbers in the early stages of industrialization, though they were subsequently displaced, possibly through the effects of Factory Acts enacted between 1881 and 1911 which limited women's hours of work and forbade the employment of children. Most of the historiography of the Indian textile industry, however, ignores gender issues and concentrates instead on the issue of the economic effects of enforced free trade.

We also know little about women's customary land rights before the British raj, and the combined effects of new land settlements and uniform legal codes. Among tribal peoples with communal property rights, women were undeniably negatively affected, as Manjusri Chaki-Sircar has documented for Manipur (see *Feminism in a Traditional Society*). In matrilineal areas of South India female claims to maintenance under joint-family ownership were undermined by new revenue settlements and laws enshrining absolute ownership of private property, and by investing male heads of households with property rights, as K. Saradamoni has shown in a groundbreaking study.[21] But even in solidly patrilineal and patriarchal areas, British administration and legal codification may have introduced a new rigidity. In 1772 Warren Hastings, the Governor General, designated Hindu texts as the exclusive source of Hindu law, thus imposing Brahminical conceptions on lower castes who had previously not been governed by them, though the degree to which customary law continued is not well understood (see Everett, 144). British administrators also did not comprehend—or did not care about—the nature of customary law in Muslim areas, as David Gilmartin's study of the effects of codification on women's inheritance rights in the Punjab illustrates. British administrators built the basis of their rule on the tribal and kinship structures of rural elites, presumed women had no inheritance rights in customary usage, and bypassed the Muslim law. Restoration of Islamic law was to become a nationalist issue among urban Muslims.[22] Much more work needs to be done combing district land records, travelers' accounts, early village studies, district officers' memoirs, court records, and census records to document what may prove to have been a social revolution in gender relations among middle and lower castes/classes.

The otherwise excellent literature on the social mobility of castes and tribes during the British period also largely fails to include gender as a category of analysis.[23] This omission is serious, for as M. N. Srinivas has noted, the era is marked by "the rise everywhere of caste *Sabhas* [associations] who tried to introduce reforms by Sanskritizing the way of life of their respective castes."[24] Detailed studies of Sanskritization and variations in its impact on women, as well as comparative studies of other avenues of mobility such as Christianity (differentiating by sect) and

Hindu reform movements such as the Arya Samaj are all needed to evaluate the complex and multidirectional nature of change.[25]

Analysis of gender must also be sensitive to the fact that "Westernization gave birth to forces which are mutually at cross-purposes."[26] The printing press, for example, was just as easily used to disseminate traditionalist as reform viewpoints. Western ideas aided nationalism and social reform, but British cultural and racial arrogance, missionary intolerance, enforced deposition of ruling houses, new land revenue systems, and interference with social customs also led to a backlash that diminished the effectiveness of Indian reformers of caste, class, and gender. Recent Indian scholarship has noted the limitations imposed on social reformers by reason of the colonial context.[27]

Finally, in analyzing the British period from the perspective of gender it is crucially important to bear class/caste distinctions in mind. The social reform movements, as we shall see, led to a broadening of options for elite women, even while complex and insufficiently researched countercurrents affected lower-caste women negatively. Upper-class women were in a different relationship to the forces of modernization, such as access to schools and the time to avail of them, than women living on the margins of subsistence. Significant numbers of poor women were displaced from the workforce, mirroring a global "development" process (see Chapter 3, "Women, Colonialism, and Development," above), while elite women began slowly in the nineteenth century and then more dramatically in the twentieth to enter the professions. Job displacement has been documented from census data for the twentieth century; the trend as we have suggested may well have begun earlier.[28]

Having noted these differential impacts and broader trends, we nevertheless shall focus our subsequent discussion on women and social reform, reflecting the scope of most existing historical studies. The social reform movements were part of a larger and vigorous debate about appropriate responses to the British conquest. They were closely linked with the history of the nationalist movement. If students know nothing about the British conquest of India and the Indian nationalist movement, as is unfortunately likely to be the case, a few key events (the Battle of Plassey, the Indian Mutiny, the founding of the Indian National Congress in 1885 and the Muslim League in 1905) and names (Clive, Bentinck, Curzon, Ranade, Tilak, Gokhale, Gandhi, Nehru, and Jinnah) might be reviewed to give them a passing knowledge of the context in which the nationalist and the social reform movements

occurred. In addition to the surveys of Indian history mentioned
in the introduction to this chapter, we recommend the following
treatments of the British period and the Indian response.

General Background
Sarkar, Sumit. *Modern India, 1885–1947.* Delhi: Macmillan India,
    1983.
Spear, Percival. *India.* Ann Arbor: University of Michigan Press,
    1961.
Wolpert, Stanley. *A New History of India.* 2d ed. London: Oxford
    University Press, 1982.

The social reform movements in the early nineteenth century
were local in character, but by the latter part of the century they
operated at an all-India level. The reform groups were characterized by male leadership, and were upper caste or class. Reformers often had British allies, who, in addition to a genuine
concern for Indian social conditions, saw reform as a justification
for British rule.

The social reform movements and the nationalist movements
had some overlap of leadership (such as Dadabhai Naoroji and
G. K. Gokhale), though in other instances reformers believed
customs needed to be changed as a prelude to self-rule along
liberal, democratic lines (K. T. Telang and B. M. Malabari). This
cautious, Westernized emphasis was increasingly discredited by
the end of the century as the original, modest demands of the
Indian National Congress, established in 1885, met with a slow
and reluctant response from Britain.

During the nineteenth century, reforms centered chiefly on
abolishing sati, permitting widows to remarry, raising the age of
marriage, modifying purdah, expanding educational and health
facilities for women, and suppressing temple prostitution. The
pressure group activities of the various reform groups and the
ideology and lives of the male leadership are relatively well documented in English. Less accessible in secondary literature in English (and indeed in Indian languages) are the voices of Indian
women, whether as activists, leaders, or masses. While scholars
have studied Jyotiba Govinda Phule (1827–1890), a vehement
critic of caste and champion of widows' rights, his wife, Savitribai
Phule (b. 1831), a pioneer with him in the fight for *dalit* and
widows' rights and female education, has been virtually neglected.[29] Similarly, Mahadev Govind Ranade (1842–1901),
founder of the Indian Social Conference and a reformer who

helped shape modern Maharashtra, justifiably has his biographers.[30] The activities of his wife Ramabai Ranade (1862–1924) on behalf of the economic advancement of widows and village women's uplift have not received the attention they deserve, though they can be traced in volumes now out of print:

Cousins, Margaret E. *The Awakening of Asian Womanhood.* Madras, 1922. Includes a discussion of Ramabai Ranade.

Ranade, Ramabai. *Himself: The Autobiography of a Hindu Lady.* Translated from Marathi and adapted by Katherine Van Akin Gates. New York, 1938. Also published as *Ranade: His Wife's Reminiscences.* Translated from Marathi by Kusumavati Deshpande. Faridabad: Publications Division, Ministry of Information and Broadcasting, Government of India, 1963.

Another nineteenth-century Indian woman activist whose work can be recovered by English readers with some digging is Pandita Ramabai (1888–1922). Despite the early publishing dates, many of these volumes may be available in older American colleges, reflecting an American missionary and suffragist interest in India. This literature often has strong Western and Christian biases and hence must be read in context.

Dongre, Rajas Krishnarao, and Josephine Patterson. *Pandita Ramabai: A Life of Faith and Prayer.* Madras: Christian Literature Society, 1963. More difficult to locate than the other works cited, but important in that it includes a reprint of Ramabai's autobiography, "A Testimony" (ca. 1907).

Dyer, Helen S. *Pandita Ramabai: The Story of Her Life.* New York, 1900. The life story of an Indian widow who coverted to Christianity and worked to establish widows' homes and educational facilities, and against child-marriage.

Fuller, Mary. *The Triumph of an Indian Widow: The Life of Pandita Ramabai.* New York, 1928. The author spent several years at the Ramabai Mukti Mission and knew the Pandita.

Ramabai Sarasvati, Pandita. *The High-Caste Hindu Woman.* Philadelphia, 1887. Pandita Ramabai's appeal to the British and American public for funds in support of her work, together with her analysis of Indian social customs.

Noticeably absent are the voices of ordinary women, and especially lower-caste women. Recent works by Ghulam Murshid and Meredith Borthwick start to expand the chorus. Both deal with the female relatives of the *bhadralok,* the respectable upper castes of Bengal who made up the professional "middle class." Despite their regional and class limitations both works begin the process of reconstructing how women conceived of their own situation and reacted to largely male-initiated reforms.

Readings for Students
Agnew, Vijay. *Elite Women in Indian Politics,* Chaps. 1–2. New Delhi: Vikas Pub. House, 1979.
Borthwick, Meredith. *The Changing Role of Women in Bengal, 1849–1905.* Princeton: Princeton University Press, 1984.
Everett, Jana Matson. Chap. 1 in *Women and Social Change in India.* New York: St. Martin's Press, 1979.
Felton, Monica. *A Child Widow's Story.* New York: Harcourt, Brace and World, 1965.
Jahan, Roushan, ed. and trans. *Inside Seclusion: The Avarodhbasini of Rokeya Sakhawat Hossain.* Dacca; Women for Women, 1981. Available from Women for Women, Road No. 4, House No. 67, Dhanmondi R.A., Dacca, Bangladesh.
Mazumdar, Vina. "Comment on Suttee." *Signs* 4, no. 2 (Winter 1978): 269–73.
Minault, Gail. "Shaikh Abdullah, Begum Abdullah, and Sharif Education for Girls at Aligarh." In *Modernization and Social Change Among Muslims in India,* edited by Imtiaz Ahmad, 207–36. New Delhi: Manohar Pubs., 1983.
Mirza, Sarfaraz Hussain. *Muslim Women's Role in the Pakistan Movement,* Chap. 1. Lahore: Research Society of Pakistan, University of the Punjab, 1964.
Murshid, Ghulam. *Reluctant Debutante: Response of Bengali Women to Modernization, 1849–1905.* Rajshahi, Bangladesh: Shitya Samsad, Rajshahi University, 1983.
Stein, Dorothy K. "Women to Burn: Suttee as a Normative Institution." *Signs* 4, no. 2 (Winter 1978): 253–68.

Readings for Instructors
Ahmad, Aziz. *Islamic Modernism in India and Pakistan, 1857–1964,* Chap. 2. London: Oxford University Press, 1967.
Ashraf, Mujeeb. *Muslim Attitudes Towards British Rule and Western Culture in India in the First Half of the Nineteenth Century,* particularly Chaps. 8 and 9. Delhi: Idarah-I-Adabiyat-I Delli, 1982.
Heimsath, Charles. *Indian Nationalism and Hindu Social Reform,*

particularly Chaps. 1, 2, 6, 7, 8, 12. Princeton: Princeton University Press, 1964.

Ingham, Kenneth. *Reformers in India, 1792–1833: An Account of the Work of Christian Missionaries on Behalf of Social Reform.* Cambridge: Cambridge University Press, 1956.

Mazumdar, Vina. "The Social Reform Movement in India— From Ranade to Nehru." In *Indian Women from Purdah to Modernity,* edited by B. R. Nanda, 41–66. New Delhi: Vikas Pub. House, 1976.

Mies, Maria. *Indian Women and Patriarchy.*

Nandy, Ashis. "Sati: A Nineteenth Century Tale of Women, Violence and Protest." In *Rammohan Roy and the Process of Modernization in India,* edited by V.C. Joshi, 168–94. New Delhi: Vikas Pub. House, 1975.

Oddie, G. A. *Social Protest in India: British Protestant Missionaries and Social Reforms, 1850–1900,* Chaps. 1, 3. New Delhi: Manohar Pubs., 1979.

Ramesh, Asha, and Philomena H. P. "The Devadasi Problem." In *International Feminism: Networking Against Female Sexual Slavery,* edited by Kathleen Barry, 82–88. New York: International Women's Tribune Center, n.d.

Sarkar, Sumit. "Rammohan Roy and the Break with the Past." In *Rammohan Roy,* 46–68.

Sharma, Ram Sharan. *Perspectives in Social and Economic History,* Chap. 2, "Historiography of the Ancient Indian Social Order."

Lecture Topics

Issues in the Interpretation of the Social Reform Movement (Heimsath, Mazumdar [1976], Oddie, Sarkar). Many accounts, including the early and still influential work of Charles Heimsath and the more recent work of G. A. Oddie on missionaries and social reform, stress the role of Western ideas in stimulating debate over Indian social customs. This approach is shared by a number of Indian scholars as well. Indeed the early reformers themselves often acknowledged an intellectual debt to such nineteenth-century European thinkers as Jeremy Bentham, John Stuart Mill, Georg Friedrich Hegel, and Herbert Spencer. Authors who accept implicitly or explicitly the argument that English education had a liberalizing effect on Indian society include Heimsath, Oddie, Vijay Agnew, Ghulam Murshid, and Radha Krishna Sharma (see "Twentieth Century Political Activities," above). However, others (see Mazumdar) have argued that the role of English education has been exaggerated, for it affected only a minority of India's population. The relationship between a Western education and social reform was not necessarily a direct one. Opponents of reform, such as B. G. Tilak, were sometimes educated in British schools and proponents, such as Jyotiba Phule (1827–1890) and Iswar Chandra Vidyasagar (1820–1891), who led the campaign for the Widow Remarriage Act of 1856, had little or no direct connection with English education. Vidyasagar, in fact, was principal of Sanskrit College, Calcutta (Mazumdar, 46–48).

The actual impact of the social reformers is also difficult to disentangle from the effects of urbanization and economic pressures upon middle-class families. The effect of ideas is never unidirectional. As Gail Minault's study of education for Muslim girls at Aligarh documents, "in the process of gaining social acceptance for women's education, such schools may have strengthened certain traditions," such as purdah (Minault, 208).

Social reform also stimulated a cultural backlash, especially as the legislative changes it characteristically involved, dictated an appeal to British rulers. Revivalists condemned this as mendicancy. Some modern critics also question the priorities pursued by the social reformers (widow remarriage and sati), which affected primarily the upper castes, as well as their style of activity (editorials, petitions), seeing in these choices the distorting effects of working in a colonial context and a "false consciousness."[31]

The Intellectual Context of the 19th-Century Debates (Sharma, Oddie). Whatever one's conclusions about the degree of influence of Western education upon the social reformers, it seems undeniable that new ideas entering India through many filters encouraged the intelligentsia to reexamine Indian customs. The nineteenth century saw an explosion of scholarship about ancient India, as reformers and their opponents selectively mined texts to justify or condemn social reform (R.S. Sharma). Though stimulated by outside ideas and critics, especially Christian missionaries (Oddie), the degree to which reformers sought to justify change by appeals to an idealized ancient tradition is striking. Ram Mohan Roy (1772–1833), sometimes called the "Father of Modern India," tried to show that sati was not in accordance with the *Sastras*, while his opponent, Raja Radhakanta Dev, marshalled *pandits* to prove the opposite. Iswar Chandra Vidyasagar in the *Marriage of Hindu Widows* (1855) scrutinized the *Smriti* literature to argue widows could marry in ancient times. Swami Dayanand, the founder of the Arya Samaj, called for a purified Hinduism based on the Vedas. He united Hindu revivalist pride with social reform, and brought out a collection of Sanskrit texts to support modifications of caste and widow remarriage and in support of female education. Thus many social reformers attempted to argue for reforms within tradition, and a return to a purified Vedic Hinduism, rather than a mechanical imitation of the West. They were reformers, not transformers, though their opponents argued otherwise.

Campaign to Abolish Sati (1829) (Ingham; Mazumdar [1978]; Murshid; Nandy; Stein). The first social reform campaign sought to abolish sati. As we have seen, the practice of sati, or the self-immolation of widows, was the ultimate in the wifely ideal of self-sacrifice among upper castes. In theory the practice was voluntary, and meritorious widows went willingly to their deaths, the subjects of highest veneration. The degree to which upper-caste Indian women had internalized the ideal of self-submission is tellingly illustrated in such cases. In practice a number of widows were physically coerced into performing sati; others feared a life of poverty and social ostracism. The practice of sati may have actually become more widespread in India in the initial period of British rule, reflecting status anxieties and worsened economic conditions among some upper-caste families (Nandy, 171–75).

Sati was abolished in 1829 by governmental fiat. Credit belongs to Governor-General Lord William Bentinck and to Ram Mohan Roy. Bentinck was a utilitarian, or Benthamite, who believed the custom to be contrary to universal moral law. He and the British government were also under pressure from a vigorous missionary campaign against sati. Orthodox Indian opinion protested the abolition of sati. However, Bentinck was backed by Ram Mohan Roy, who both typified and enormously influenced the first generation of Indian social reformers. Ram Mohan Roy was the first Indian to found and edit a newspaper; he started several secondary schools on the Western model; and he founded the Brahmo Samaj, an influential religious movement that incorporated aspects of Christian humanism with Hinduism. He drew on Hindu scriptures to justify reform. Sati was gradually suppressed.

Widow Remarriage Movement (1856) (Heimsath; Oddie; Mazumdar [1978]; Murshid). By 1850, one of the surest signs of being a reformer, or a liberal, was to advocate that widows be allowed to remarry. Many of the reformers were male members of the Brahmo Samaj, which published Vidyasagar's *Marriage of Hindu Widows*. Petitions were circulated among the upper classes encouraging support, and in 1856—one year before the Indian Mutiny made British rulers much more cautious about supporting social reform—the Imperial Council passed legislation permitting widow remarriage. A few prominent Hindus publicly married widows. The papers and news magazines created a great furor, and some of the men involved were denied access to Hindu rituals.

The widow remarriage movement had little mass impact since the legislation preceded a change in the beliefs and sentiments of the high-caste population. The legislation also damaged the inheritance rights of some lower-caste widows whose communities permitted them to inherit property given to them by their husbands, even after remarriage. The new legislation, which superseded local custom, removed this right (Mazumdar [1978], 271).

Somewhat greater success was achieved in promoting education among widows. A number, among them Subalakshmi Subramaniam of Madras (see Felton) and Pandita Ramabai, became social reformers in their own right. Educated widows were in demand as teachers in the new schools for Hindu girls. Ghulam Murshid also argues that the widow remarriage debate, though it did not drastically alter marriage practices, nevertheless altered society's attitudes toward widows in a more positive direction (178–79).

The Age of Consent Debate (1891) (Heimsath, Oddie, Murshid). According to the 1881 census, about one-fifth of the women of India were listed as widows, and a significant proportion had been widows since childhood.

When in 1889 the British Indian government considered passing a bill against child marriage, a stormy all-India debate resulted. Indian nationalists were not united on the issue. B. G. Tilak, the leader of the extremist wing of the Indian National Congress, which wanted a swift devolution of British power, agitated against the legislation. Although his own daughters were not married until they were sixteen and had been educated, he believed it was humiliating to have the imperial overlord legislate on Hindu law and religion. Tilak's technique of political mobilization was to appeal to religious and cultural tradition. This linkage of traditional norms for women with an anti-imperialist appeal occurred in other nationalist movements as well (compare Algeria in Chapter 11, "Women in the Islamic Middle East and North Africa," below).

On the other hand, many Indian moderates—those content with a slower pace of political reform—backed the notion of raising the age of marriage. They appealed to the British public through petitions to the parliament and Queen Victoria. Despite nervousness within the British Indian government about a backlash, the "Age of Consent" bill passed in 1891. The age was set at twelve for the entire population. The act was a product of elite politics, and its provisions were largely ignored.

The Origins of Modern Female Education (Agnew, Chap. 1; Mazumdar [1976]; Murshid). Schools for girls, along Western lines, were established in the early nineteenth century by missionaries and philanthropists. The first was established in Calcutta in 1820 by David Hare, a watchmaker, much influenced by European rationalist philosophy. The missionaries had an explicitly evangelical mission and at first attracted only students from the lower castes. The Brahmo Samaj, the Arya Samaj, and others, suspicious of missionary motives, responded by opening schools for girls to stem conversions as well as to respond to a need. The first school to attract high-caste women was established in Calcutta by Vidyasagar, with the help of J. E. D. Bethune, the Law Member of the Governor General's Council. Named Bethune School (later College), it opened in 1849. Starting in 1854 the Indian Government began modest grants-in-aid for girls' schools, supplementing the work of individuals, reform societies, and the missionaries.

By 1882, when the Indian Educational Commission issued its report, there were 2,697 educational institutions for women in the country, most at the primary level; 82 secondary schools; 15 teacher training institutes; and 1 college, enrolling a total of 127,066 female students (Mies, 131). Though only a minute fraction of India's female population, the graduates of these schools provided crucial leadership in the second generation of social reform.

As was the case with schools established for women in the early national period in the United States, the motive behind female education was not egalitarian. The curriculum was limited, geared toward women's traditional vocation of mother and homemaker with an "emphasis on home science and simpler liberal arts—rather than the 'manly' subjects like mathematics, sciences, or professional courses like law, engineering" (Mazumdar, 53).

Schools observed strict sex segregation, and they rarely challenged purdah restrictions, though the boundaries were stretched. At first schools (and medical facilities for women) were staffed with European women, widows, and Christian converts, but gradually an acceptable, female-oriented, avenue of employment opened for middle-class women.

Male reformers, many of whom worked in Westernized professions and an urban environment were acutely aware of the cultural gap between the workplace and home, and wanted educated wives and daughters. However, despite some new opportunities female education did not keep pace with male education, even among the elite. By 1907, for example, 3.6 percent of school-age females were enrolled in school compared with 23.1 percent of school-age males.[32] Vina Mazumdar states that "modern education and urbanization introduced a new barrier between men and women" in many families (49).

The Campaign to Suppress *Devadasis* **(Mies, 70–73; Oddie, 102– 109; Ramesh).** The suppression of ritual temple dancers and prostitutes *(devadasis)* and the accompanying anti-*nautch* movement (movement seeking to ban employment of female dancers at public and private festivities) did not directly affect large numbers of women, though the campaign had wider symbolic importance. Devadasis were most numerous in South India where there were around 11,500 in 1881 (Oddie, 103).

The practice of ritual temple prostitution has been traced back to Tantricism, a sixth-century A.D. anti-Brahminical and anti-Buddhist revolt that incorporated non-Vedic fertility beliefs. In Tantricism the goddess embodies power, or shakti, the dynamic force of the universe. Throughout South India the goddess was thought to be incarnated in the temple by the devadasis, dancers and ritual prostitutes. The use of the term "prostitute" in connection with this practice in itself poses interpretive problems, for the devadasis in fact were invested with high prestige by the believer. On the other hand, non-believers, modern feminists among them, see ritual prostitution as inherently demeaning and exploitive, flourishing when women are provided with no other skills or alternatives.

Traditionally devadasis formed a caste of their own, had equal inheritance rights with their brothers, could perform funeral rites for ancestors, sometimes supported their own natal families, married no human male (married as they were to the temple god), and generally enjoyed more freedom than conventionally wedded women. They horrified missionaries, Victorian British administrators, and Indian social reformers alike. Devadasis were suppressed but not eliminated during the late nineteenth and early twentieth centuries. Deprived of their religious prestige many became common prostitutes in urban slums. The practice still exists in an attenuated form in adjoining districts of Karnataka and Maharashtra, and a study by the Joint Women's Programme, Northern Karnataka, condemns it as "prostitution practiced under the garb of religion" (Ramesh, 86).

Muslim Social Reform Movement (Ahmad; Ashraf, 232–41; Roushan Jahan; Minault; Mirza). The Muslim community also vigorously debated women's issues. In general, however, the impact of Westernization occurred at a slower pace as the defeated rulers (the Mughals) turned inward and the Hindu upper castes sought new opportunities with new rulers. The downfall of the Mughal Empire precipitated a divisive debate (see Ahmad). Reformists argued that Islamic rule had ended because of traditionalism. Conservatives countered that military defeat was a sign of divine punishment for laxity.

Central to any discussion of reform within the Muslim community in the subcontinent is Sir Sayyid Ahmad Khan (1817–1898), who believed English education, weapons, and system of justice had aided in the establishment and maintenance of British rule in India (Ahmad, Ashraf). He admired British technology and sought to selectively diffuse Western ideas, especially science, into Muslim intellectual life. He also defended the Islamic social system from Western attack, and laid the foundations for reform exegetical studies of the *Qur'ān* and *hadiths*. His enduring monument was the Aligarh College (later University), founded in 1875, which taught Western science within a Muslim atmosphere.

Sayyid Ahmad Khan was only modestly reformist when it came to women (Mirza). Although he argued that purdah was not sanctioned by Islam, nor was the denial of female education, it was his view that men should be educated first, especially in Western subjects; women's education was to emphasize moral and spiritual values. He opposed higher education for women along Western lines and acted as a brake on more radical reformers in the Mohammadan Educational Conference, established in 1886. It was not until the first decade of the twentieth century that schools for Muslim girls, with some Western content, opened in a number of cities. Purdah was strictly upheld, and as Minault's study of girls' education at Aligarh shows, educators stressed "a continuation of family traditions and observances, obedience and authority" (216), while a short distance away at Aligarh College young men were encouraged to reinterpret tradition.

The struggle to modify upper-class purdah practices is vividly depicted in the recently republished writing of Rokeya Sakhawat Hossain (1880–1932), described by her biographer, Roushan Jahan, as "the first and foremost feminist" of Muslim society in Bengal. "Avarodhbasini" links forty-seven contemporary incidents of purdah excesses into a denunciation of the oppression of women. The account includes the death of the author's aunt who fell on train tracks but could not be rescued because of prohibitions on letting strange men lift her. Born into the household of a wealthy, conservative Bengali *zamindar* (landlord), Begum Rokeya was secretly taught to read and write by her elder brother, and was also fortunate in marrying a supportive husband. In 1911 she started the first Muslim girls' school in Calcutta, initiated adult literacy programs for both Hindu and Muslim women, and founded Anjuman-e Khawatin-e Islam (The Association of Muslim Women). When "Avarodhbasini" was first published in 1929, Begum Rokeya was vigorously attacked and the incidents condemned as fictitious. However, a younger generation of modernizers, who were influenced by reforms in Turkey under Ataturk, rallied to her side. This republished work with a lengthy introduction by Roushan Jahan, setting the biographical and historical context, is recommended as a Student Reading.

Women's Modified Roles (Borthwick, Murshid). The nineteenth century saw the growth, at least among elite women, of an awareness of the outside world, and modification of traditional roles to allow public participation but without a radical redefinition of the female sphere. Though the vast majority of social reformers were male, "women did have some influence in accelerating reform—directly, through active encouragement, and marginally through acquiescence" (Borthwick, 42).

Purdah practices underwent considerable change: elite women received a basic education, and appeared in mixed social gatherings. Borthwick also believes a different style of marital relations arose "assimilating new qualities of romantic love and companionship," though "in the absence of other structural changes, the balance of power and authority . . . remained with the husband" (109). However, it became increasingly acceptable for women to function publicly in social and philanthropic women's organizations (Borthwick, Chaps. 7–8). A minuscule number of women—725—held professional employment by 1901, but this was a highly significant social trend. There were, however, countercurrents: lower-caste women still adopted purdah restrictions as part of the process of Sanskritization, even as these restrictions lessened among elite women. There was also evidence of male backlash even within the reform movement. In the few instances where literate women began to challenge the authority of men over women, male reformers became alarmed (Murshid, "Conclusion"; Borthwick, 332–33).

The nineteenth-century social reform movements were important in stimulating debate about the condition of women. Arguably, the educational institutions established by a generation of male reformers were their most important legacy. The aims of the reformers were limited: They attempted to soften the more inhumane aspects of social customs without questioning the position of women within the patriarchal family. The legislation that was passed in this era affected relatively few women, and the issues raised generally did not address the circumstances of lower-caste women. Nevertheless, despite the limited terms of the debate and the evidence of backlash as the century progressed, the issue of women's status had been broached. Elite women had undergone subtle but real changes in self-perception, relationships with husbands and in-laws underwent modification, and purdah boundaries were stretched. Tradition had not given way drastically but it had been somewhat altered.

Discussion Questions

1. Discuss the advantages, disadvantages, limitations, and dangers of inducing change in the status of women from the outside. Who were the most effective reformers in nineteenth-century India? Why were they successful?

2. The political designations of wings of the Indian nationalist movement as moderate and radical, based on their attitudes towards British rule, illustrate a larger problem in women's history; namely, that the common categories of analysis do not always fit. What other designations of historical periods or movements need modification when women are brought into the picture?

3. Attempt to argue for reforms in the status of women with a Hindu traditionalist and a Muslim traditionalist within the framework of each tradition.

4. Maria Mies argues that the paternalistic attitude of male social reformers in the nineteenth (and twentieth) centuries "made sure that the women's movement did not go beyond the basic structure of a patriarchal society: the patriarchal family and the caste system. Nowhere have the leading women of this epoch tried to transcend the area of political and theoretical activity which has been carved out for them by men" (120–21). Is she correct? Is this transcendence a reasonable expectation in the nineteenth century?

5. Devadasis saw themselves as freer than respectable married women. Reformers saw them as degraded. Some feminist commentators condemn the institution as sexual slavery existing for the sexual gratification of men. What value system lies behind each viewpoint?

6. Meredith Borthwick argues that it cannot be automatically assumed that purdah "was repressive and unbearable for those who lived under it. It is not particularly meaningful to use a standard of judgment based on the concept of individual freedom to analyze the social structure of nineteenth-century Bengal, in which group identification was preeminent" (Chap. 1). Discuss.

7. Are there, or are there not, absolute standards of human rights upon which we should stand? What values lie behind your answer? Can you justify them?

TWENTIETH-CENTURY POLITICAL ACTIVITIES: THE GANDHIAN ERA

The conflicting analyses of the Indian women's movement in the Gandhian era depend upon the nature of the event the historian believes she has been covering. And it depends upon the analyst's sense of the final objective. As Geraldine Forbes remarks, "the different interpretations . . . come from people holding different views of the essential goals of a woman's rights movement" ("Indian Women's Movement," 53).

To contemporaries involved in the closely associated social reform and nationalist movements in the Gandhian era, the new assertiveness and prominence of elite women in the public domain was indeed remarkable. "If a person who died a hundred years ago came to life today, the first and foremost important change that would strike him is the revolution in the position of women," declared K. Natarajan in the *Indian Social Reformer*.[33]

The percentage of literate women grew from 0.9 percent in 1901 to 3.4 percent in 1941. By 1936 over three million Indian girls and women were enrolled in 38,262 schools, contrasting with the handful who bravely entered the first elite school, Bethune College, nearly a century earlier.[34] Elite women had taken over leadership of the social reform movement, forming their own associations. The leaders of the nationalist movement, Mahatma Gandhi and Jawaharlal Nehru, of the Indian National Congress, and Mohammed Ali Jinnah, President of the Muslim League, were receptive to the idea of an enlarged sphere of female activity. Gandhi saw female emancipation as an essential component of India's nationalist regeneration: "We must be incapable of defending ourselves or healthily competing with the other nations, if we allow the better half of ourselves to become paralyzed."[35] Indian women by the tens of thousands involved themselves in nationalist causes, earning themselves considerable influence in nationalist circles. Yet historians of the period differ in their analyses of what was finally accomplished. We have included this diversity of viewpoints in the Readings for Students and Instructors.

Radha Sharma's admiring account of Gandhi and women's rights activists depicts the change in the condition of women as "vast and varied" and "immediate and effective" (ix). She sees Gandhi as a "radical social reformer" (38). Similarly Pratima Asthana believes the women's movement "revolutionized the position of women" (vi). Both generally support the ideology that framed the Indian women's movement's approach to "the woman question," namely that women and men play complementary but different roles in society. While activists of the era demanded equal rights to education and the vote, and before the law, Indian feminists, as Asthana understands it, "unlike in the west did not take the form of a craving to acquire man's outlook, man's ambitions, man's freedom and man's power" but "kept in mind the ancient ideals and values of an Indian culture, the high spirituality and the spirit of service and devotion that women symbolize" (160; see Asthana's entire "Conclusion"; also Radha Sharma, 155). Neither Sharma nor Asthana probes very deeply into the social class of the leaders of the women's movement, nor whether changes in the status of women permeated beyond the elite.

Other commentators, with different theoretical presuppositions about the causes and nature of women's oppression, reach diametrically opposed conclusions about the era. Maria Mies interprets the paternalistic support of nationalist leaders for limited women's rights as an exercise in cooptation that "made sure that the women's movement did not go beyond the basic structure of a patriarchal society: the patriarchal family and the caste system" (120). Jana Everett is also skeptical of the Gandhian legacy, arguing that the emphasis on complementary sex roles and a sexual division of labor made it more difficult for women who wished to enter new fields; she believes that while the absence of an attack on many traditional values lessened opposition, the result was relatively little change ("Women and Political Leadership," 215). Both Mies and Everett point to the elite class basis of the women's movement. Geraldine Forbes argues for a more contextualized analysis (see particularly her comments on Mies and Gail Omvedt's approaches to the period in "Indian Women's Movement," 52–53). Noting that most of the women had grown up in purdah or at least in very sheltered environments, Forbes believes that "looking back at the times in which they worked for social change I think we should marvel that they dared as much and that they accomplished so much" ("Caged Tigers," 534).

The growing literature on the Indian women's movement in the twentieth-century nationalist era is rich in both content and controversy which can enliven class presentations and discussions. The controversy stems in part from interpretations of historical events, personalities, and organizational aims whose influences are still felt in contemporary India. Controversial too in the minds of Western feminists (and to a small number of contemporary Indian feminists as well) is the ideological content of this wave of Indian feminism. Indian feminists were careful to distance themselves from what they perceived to be the acerbic, sexual antagonism fostered by the Western movement, reflecting perhaps the prevailing and generally hostile press coverage of the militant Pankhurst and Alice Paul wings of the suffrage movements in Great Britain and the United States. While Indian leaders argued for a uniquely Indian approach, readers familiar with the influential social feminist ideology that permeated the British and American women's movements in the late nineteenth and early twentieth centuries will be struck by important parallels. While

Indian feminism clearly responded to the constraints, challenges, contexts, and traditions of India's rich culture, there is also a logical and appealing avenue of argument that can be pursued by women living in a sexually segregated society, common in varying degrees to upper-middle-class feminists both in Victorian America and India during this era. In either instance the separate but equal appeal, based on woman's unique reproductive nature, challenges the assumptions of those today who frame a feminist case based on minimal, if any, essential sex differences, and who argue for an interchangeability of sex roles. Indeed the alert reader will remind us that we have tilted towards these assumptions ourselves. Nevertheless the Indian feminist case, both in theory and in historical practice, can be used to debate these assumptions. Related Discussion Questions draw on the theoretical materials in Chapters 2 and 4, above, to probe the complex issue of definitions of egalitarianism between men and women.

The activities of Muslim women are not nearly as well documented as those of Hindus. Once again, the focus is primarily upon elite political activity and social reform, though we have attempted to include references to some broader consequences of these activities. Certain trends are noteworthy: throughout the twentieth century, women's workforce participation declined, and men's life expectancy rose more quickly than that of women. While the sphere of activity for elite women broadened, the process of industrial development, agricultural modernization, and population growth carried negative consequences for some women, especially the poor. Until the publication of *Towards Equality*, the Report of the Committee on the Status of Women in India in 1974, these deleterious forces were overshadowed in analyses by the accomplishments of the era.

Readings for Students
Agnew, Vijay. *Elite Women in Indian Politics*, Chaps. 3–6. New
    Delhi: Vikas Pub. House, 1979; or
Everett, Jana Matson. *Women and Social Change in India.*
Asthana, Pratima. *Women's Movement in India*, Chap. 6. New
    Delhi: Vikas Pub. House, 1974.
Forbes, Geraldine H. "Votes for Women: The Demand for
    Women's Franchise in India, 1917–1937." In *Symbols of
    Power: Studies on the Political Status of Women in India*, edited
    by Vina Mazumdar. Bombay: Allied Pubs., 1979.
———. "Caged Tigers: 'First Wave' Feminists in India." *Women's
    Studies International Forum* 5, no. 6 (1982): 525–36, or

————. "From Purdah to Politics: The Social Feminism of the
All-India Women's Organizations." In *Separate Worlds.*
Gandhi, Mahatma. *To the Women.* Edited and published by
Anand T. Hingorani (Karachi, 1941). See especially excerpts
titled "The Hindu Wife," "Regeneration of Women," "What
is Woman's Role?" "Mrs. Sanger and Birth-Control," "An
Appeal to the Indian Women," and "Tear Down the Pur-
dah."
Mies, Maria. *Indian Women and Patriarchy,* 122–30.

Readings for Instructors
Bondurant, Joan V. *Conquest of Violence: The Gandhian Philosophy
of Conflict.* Rev. ed. Berkeley: University of California Press,
1971.
Brown, Judith. *Gandhi's Rise to Power: Indian Politics 1915–1922.*
Cambridge: Cambridge University Press, 1971.
Everett, Jana Matson. "Women and Political Leadership." In
Women and Work in India: Continuity and Change, edited by
Joyce Lebra, Joy Paulson, and Jana Everett, Chap. 10. New
Delhi: Promilla and Co. Pubs., 1984.
Forbes, Geraldine H. "The Ideals of Indian Womanhood: Six
Bengali Women During the Independence Movement." In
Bengal in the Nineteenth and Twentieth Centuries, edited by John
R. McLane, 59–74. East Lansing: Asian Studies Center,
Michigan State University, 1975.
————. "Indian Women's Movement: A Struggle for Women's
Rights or National Liberation?" In *The Extended Family:
Women and Political Participation in India and Pakistan,* edited
by Gail Minault. Delhi: Chanakya; Columbia, Mo.: South
Asia Books, 1981.
Low, D. A., ed. *Congress and the Raj: Facets of the Indian Struggle,
1917–47.* Columbia, Mo: South Asia Books, 1977.
Mazumdar, Vina. "The Social Reform Movement in India—
From Ranade to Nehru." In *Indian Women from Purdah to
Modernity.*
Minault, Gail. "Introduction: The Extended Family as Metaphor
and the Expansion of Women's Realm." In *The Extended
Family,* Chap. 1.
————. "Sisterhood or Separation? The All-India Muslim Ladies
Conference and the Nationalist Movement." In *The Extended
Family,* Chap. 4.
————. "Purdah Politics: The Role of Muslim Women in Indian
Nationalism, 1911–1924." In *Separate Worlds.*

Mirza, Sarfaraz Hussain. *Muslim Women's Role in the Pakistan Movement.* Lahore: Research Society of Pakistan, University of the Punjab, 1969.

Misra, Lakshmi. *Education of Women in India, 1921–1966.* Bombay and London: Macmillan, 1966.

Naravane, Vishwanath S. *Sarojini Naidu: An Introduction to Her Life, Work and Poetry.* New Delhi: Orient Longman, 1980.

Sharma, Radha Krishna. *Nationalism, Social Reform and Indian Women.* Patna and New Delhi: Janaki Prakashan, 1981.

Lecture Topics

Development of Women's Organizations (Agnew, Chaps. 5–6; Everett, Chaps. 4–5; Forbes, "Caged Tigers" and "Purdah to Politics"; Minault, "Introduction: The Extended Family"; Sharma, Chap. 4). With the formation of the All-India Muslim Ladies Conference (1914), the Women's Indian Association (1917), the National Council of Women in India (1925), and the All-India Women's Conference (1927), leadership of the women's social reform movement passed into the hands of elite women themselves. The title that the Women's Indian Association chose for itself is revealing of the general tendency of this generation of reformers, linking women's causes to the broader issue of the regeneration of India, rather than focusing on the more narrowly defined sphere of women's self-interest that might be implied by the alternative title that was debated, namely, the "Indian Women's Association."

The Women's Indian Association drew its strength from the south and took the initiative in pressing for women's suffrage in 1917. The National Council of Women in India sponsored a variety of women's uplift projects at the local level (orphanages, hostels for working girls, rescue homes for prostitutes, educational facilities, and the like), had a predominantly wealthy membership, and attempted to stay away from partisan politics. The All-India Women's Conference was the largest, most diverse, and most politicized of these groups, and many of its leaders had strong pro-Congress Party ties. (An extended discussion of these groups' approaches, formation, and differences can be found in Everett, *Women and Social Change,* Chaps. 4–5; Forbes, "Purdah to Politics" and "Indian Women's Movement"; and Sharma, Chap. 4).

Jana Everett sees a shift in the ideology of the women's rights movement over time (1920s–1940s) from a "woman's uplift" to a "women's rights" orientation (Chap. 5). The former approach stressed reform of social practices and the elevation and extension of traditional ideals into the public realm, while the latter concentrated on the extension of male civil rights to women to enable them to achieve their full capacities. "Whether these capacities were distinct or similar [to men's] was ambiguous," according to Everett (*Women and Social Change*, 83). She sees Sarojini Naidu (1879–1949), President of the Indian National Congress in 1925 and an important lieutenant of Mahatma Gandhi, as representative of the uplift school; and she sees presidents of the All-India Women's Conference after the 1930s as representative of the equal rights school familiar to Western liberals.

Forbes, however, stresses other themes which she believes permeated the entire period, namely, a "social feminism" that accepted the traditional roles of women, the psychobiological uniqueness of the sexes, and the existence of "separate spheres." The upper-middle-caste/class women in the movement appealed to a nationalist pride in India's culture by holding up a Vedic Golden Age in which women participated centrally in religious and public life. They urged that a free India return to the genius of its past. Avoiding direct confrontation with men, activists believed customs such as purdah resulted from subsequent "wars and imperialism." The progress of the nation now depended upon the progress of women, and on the application of women's spiritual and nurturing "inner nature" to the social and economic problems of the day. Like those turn-of-the-century American feminists who argued for the vote as necessary for the domestic housekeeping they wished to bring to an impure and insensitive political order, Indian activists expanded the definition of woman's role to include the nation as a sort of extended family (Minault). However, as Forbes points out, "Indian women did not share all the assumptions of western feminists." Many indeed rejected the term, though their entire lives were spent in improving the condition of women. They adapted powerful imagery within the Hindu tradition to embolden their claims. Sita, for all of her submission to her husband's authority, was also a woman of courage and superhuman endurance; and Draupadi was a symbol of strength. Women's active power in the form of shakti, the regenerative and destructive force of the universe, provided another concept that could legitimize action. Forbes suggests that Indian women "were reluctant to abandon these images for the western feminist image of woman as powerless. They developed an ideology which emphasized women's strengths . . ." ("Caged Tigers," 534; also Minault, "Purdah Politics," 253–54). This ideology stretched the boundaries of purdah and fostered the acceptance of change among elite women, but within the boundaries of woman's sphere.

Women in Gandhian Politics (Agnew, Chap. 3; Everett, *Women and Social Change*, Chaps. 5–7; Forbes, "Indian Women's Movement"; Mazumdar; Sharma, Chaps. 2–3. While Gandhi's exact legacy to the women's rights movement is a matter of dispute, undeniably, improvements in the status of women were central to Gandhi's nationalist agenda. He vigorously attacked the practices of dowry, child marriage, and polygamy; deplored the high level of female illiteracy; attacked seclusion on the grounds that chastity is an inner quality that cannot be imposed by external forms; and urged that child widows remarry, though he admired the voluntary withdrawal from remarriage of the mature woman. He settled the controversy about whether social reform or political emancipation should receive precedent by arguing that both must proceed simultaneously. His definition of the "regeneration of women" was cast in terms of complementary but separate sex roles. "Man is supreme in the outward activities of a married pair, and, therefore, it is in the fitness of things that he should have a greater knowledge thereof. On the other hand, home life is entirely the sphere of woman, and, therefore, in domestic affairs, in the upbringing and education of children, women ought to have more knowledge" (21). However, he also believed that "domestic work ought not to take the whole of a woman's time," that "Hindu culture had erred on the side of excessive subordination of the wife to the husband," and that woman is "gifted with equal moral capacities. She has the right to participate in the minutest detail in the activities of man, and she has an equal right of freedom and liberty with him" (225, 2, 18). This equal right was tempered by his skepticism about women working outside the home for a living, or "undertaking commercial enterprises." Gandhi also opposed artificial forms of birth control, urging both men and women to achieve "self-realization through self control," an outlook that permeated his entire philosophy of life (55–63). The All-India Women's Conference did not share his outlook on birth control and passed a resolution in its favor in 1935. This incident illustrates a larger point: while activists in the women's movement supported nationalist aims, there were at times tensions between the two goals (see Forbes, "Indian Women's Movement").

Gandhi formulated a special role for women in the nationalist movement. He did not believe that woman will "make her contribution to the world by mimicing [sic] or running a race with men," which he saw as the American woman's approach (27). She could make a unique contribution based upon, in Gandhi's view, a greater moral and spiritual strength than man's and a greater capacity for disinterested suffering in the service of others (223–24). *Satyagraha,* or passive resistance and non-violent protest, he thought, was especially suited for women to utilize, and he urged women to join the nationalist cause. Women responded with alacrity.

The success of the Noncooperation Movement of 1920–1922 depended heavily on women to boycott foreign goods and to spin *khadi* or homespun. In "An Appeal to the Indian Woman," which he presented as a religious duty, or *dharma,* Gandhi asserted that "the economic and the moral salvation of India . . . rests mainly with you" (168–71), legitimizing and ennobling the political importance of the domestic sphere. In all the subsequent major actions leading to independence women were at the forefront, including collecting subscriptions and resisting police charges during the Bardoli tax strike in 1928; and marching by the thousands in the Salt March of 1930, in which Sarojini Naidu led the raid on the Dharsana salt field (Sharma, Chap. 3). Many nationalist women displayed bravery and heroism in the three-decade struggle, enduring arrest, detention, verbal abuse, and violence from the authorities. Under the strenuous circumstances of the nationalist movement a number of elite women moved into new and prominent public roles, extending the definitions of the possible.

How much the social changes wrought in this era extended beyond the elite, whether for women or peasants, has been a matter of dispute. The predominant interpretation of the Congress Party under Gandhi has been to emphasize its mass base, and to focus upon the immense achievement in forcing a British withdrawal. Recently some critics have questioned the vertical linkages of the party, arguing that power was "subcontracted" to existing local leaders, dominant peasants in the countryside, and business and professional leaders in cities, which weakened the reformist thrust of Gandhi's program and blunted real change in the condition of the dispossessed.[36]

Terrorist Women (Agnew, Chap. 4; Forbes, "Ideals of Indian Womanhood"). An entirely different form of political participation—with restricted results—was engaged in by some elite women; namely, terrorist activities. The female terrorists were mainly from Bengal, and, like their reformist counterparts, many were the sisters or wives of male activists.

The women who took part in these protests, which involved robbery and assassination, did not feel they were in the mainstream of Indian society, and, unlike the women who participated in Gandhi's campaigns, they did not have the approval of the larger Indian society, neither at the time of their acts nor in the eyes of history. Even terrorist women were influenced by traditional notions of self-sacrifice. They were, however, deeply conscious of the degree to which they were violating norms. As a group they were elite, articulate, unique, and few in number.

Reforms During the Nationalist Era. The successes and limitations of the women's movement in the Gandhian era can be gauged by an examination of its chief struggles, briefly outlined here. The details are well documented in the sources indicated.

Political Representation (1917–1939) (Everett, Women and Social Change, Chap. 6; Agnew, Chap. 6; Forbes, "Votes"). Throughout the twentieth century there was a progressive acceptance of the principle of female suffrage both by the Indian National Congress and the Muslim League. Women's participation in nationalist agitation gained them powerful allies. Women's suffrage became a symbol of modernity and was pointed to by nationalists as a sign of India's "fitness" for self-government. It was not seen as a vehicle for profound alterations of relations between the sexes.

The fight for women's suffrage in India was short compared to the British or American experience, but Geraldine Forbes suggests it was not the "easy victory" some have pictured it to be: "The right to vote was not 'granted' without pressure from organized women" (3). The campaign was conducted at multiple levels: before British Parliamentary Committees and Indian constitutional conferences, and at the provincial and all-India level.

An important suffrage argument was the unique perspective and qualities women would bring to politics, but most women's rights activists rejected the notion of special women's seats. A "communal award" of guaranteed minority representation had been proposed by the British in the Round Table Conferences of 1930–31 against a background of demands from various groups, including the emerging Muslim League. Reserved seats for women were an extension of this concept. The Congress Party, which claimed to speak for all Indians, condemned the communal award as a British device to divide and rule. Women's organizations backed the Congress in demanding adult franchise, without designated seats, a position that some Muslim women in the All-India Women's Conference found objectionable (Forbes, 15). Everett also argues that the "women's uplift" proponents tended to back special women's seats, and that the "equal rights" group aligned with the Congress rejected them (116–19). There were also important internal debates about holding out for adult suffrage versus accepting and extending various educational and property qualifications.

The suffrage campaign was one of vigorous elite representation before appropriate committees, conferences, commissions, and legislatures. It was not one of mass mobilization. The principle of female suffrage was incorporated in the Government of India Acts of 1919 and 1935, which gave a limited form of franchise. Upon independence, in 1947, India instituted universal adult suffrage.

Child Marriage Reform (Forbes, "Caged Tigers" and "Indian Women's Movement"; Sharma, Chap. 6). The campaign against child marriage continued in the tradition of nineteenth-century social reform. The Age of Consent Act of 1891 had proven ineffective, and improved legislation was attempted. The campaign against child marriage was closely linked with concerns about female education and health. The Women's Indian Association and the All-India Women's Conference lobbied intensively for the Child Marriage Restraint Act (or Sarda Bill, named after its legislative sponsor) and Congress politicians backed the proposal. The chief opponents were Muslim traditionalists who claimed (erroneously) that child marriage was not a problem in their community and that the Act set a dangerous precedent for state interference in the *shariah*, or religiously-based law.

The Report of the Joshi Committee, which documented marriage abuses and reported that 42 percent of Indian girls married before age fifteen, helped to create a favorable legislative climate and stiffen the resolve of nervous British officials. The Sarda Bill of 1929 raised the age of marriage to eighteen for boys and fourteen for girls, and was an improvement over the 1891 measure in that it attempted to set penalties (one month's imprisonment and/or a fine of 1000 rupees) for those convicted under its provisions. However, it contained numerous flaws: police could only intervene in the unlikely event of a complaint, and marriages performed in defiance of the age limits were not declared void. Birth dates were also hard to document in rural areas. The Act was in advance of public opinion, and authorities were very reluctant to enforce it especially as they feared political unrest, illustrating the difficulty of inducing reform in a colonial setting.

Reform of Family Law (Everett, Women and Social Change, Chap. 7; Forbes, "Caged Tigers" and "Indian Women's Movement"; Sharma, 236–39). By the 1930s, reform of various aspects of Hindu personal law governing marriage practices and inheritance were important issues for the National Council of Women in India and the All-India Women's Conference. The controversy these issues engendered was far greater than that surrounding the franchise, or even child marriage, and continued into the early years of independence. Vital property issues as well as drastically differing conceptions of the nature of the family appeared to be at stake.

Women's rights activists supported various proposals to equalize divorce, outlaw polygamy, permit intercaste and interfaith marriage, grant equal rights of guardianship, require the consent of both parties to a marriage, and invest women with equal rights to inheritance. Some attempts were made to pass piecemeal legislation during the 1930s, one of which resulted in the Hindu Women's Right to Property Act of 1937 (the Deshmukh Act) which gave widows under the Mitakshara Code a limited estate during their lifetimes. Measures to permit the dissolution of marriage were introduced by Liberal members of the Central Assembly but were withdrawn after stiff opposition.

By the 1940s support emerged in progressive legal circles and among Congress leaders for a comprehensive reform of the Hindu Code. The issue stalled because of the outbreak of World War II and the Civil Disobedience Campaign. Members of the male elite were themselves divided on the issues, especially on divorce, despite the Congress Party's endorsement. These issues continued to be debated in the Constituent Assembly (1947–51), charged with drawing up the constitution for an independent India.

Labor Regulations (Asthana, Chap. 6; Sharma, 249–50). The women's movement had considerably more success in pressing for protective labor regulations. In 1929 a bill was enacted, with the backing of the All-India Women's Conference, eliminating women from underground work in mines. This was followed in 1934 by an act reducing the maximum number of hours a woman could work in a factory to eight hours per day. In 1943 the Maternity Benefit Act required that factory employers pay benefits of eight annas per day (raised to twelve annas in 1945) up to a maximum of eight weeks to women employees who gave birth. An act in 1945 also began to require industrial concerns to provide crèches.

Purdah (Forbes, "Caged Tigers," "Purdah to Politics," "Indian Women's Movement"). The women's movement did not seek such legislative solutions as the abolition of veiling. They preferred to involve women who observe purdah in their organizations, thus extending permissible limits of the female sphere. Many believed purdah was not wrong in principle, but only in degree, and accepted separate institutions and the concept of separate male/female functions. The schools, orphanages, industrial training centers, and medical facilities that this generation of women sponsored, "for females, run by females, and staffed by females," provided respectable, segregated employment for middle-class women (Forbes, "Purdah to Politics," 229).

Among the women's groups only the All-India Women's Conference sponsored anti-purdah days. Gandhi, Nehru, and Jinnah all denounced the practice of purdah. Forbes suggests that Hindu women activists were able to avoid antagonizing men of their community by blaming the practice on Islam rather than on male oppression, an argument that contributed to tensions between Hindus and Muslims (Forbes, "Indian Women's Movement," 66–71).

Muslim Women's Political Activities (Minault, "Purdah Politics," "Introduction: Extended Family," "Sisterhood or Separation?"; Mirza, 32ff). Like their Hindu counterparts, Muslim women adhered to tradition while seeking change. They too stretched the definitions of purdah, justifying their actions as extensions of household roles, a point that is well illustrated in the political career of Abadi Banu Begum (1852–1924) who achieved prominence during the campaign to save the Ottoman Khalifat, a symbol of Muslim unity, from destruction by the British government. When her sons, the Ali brothers, were arrested, she toured the country as a mother protective of her children and the Islamic religion, urging Muslims to follow in her sons' footsteps. Brought up in strict purdah, she first spoke briefly in public from behind the veil, with a picture of one of her sons beside her. By 1921 in the joint Hindu-Muslim non-cooperation campaign she appeared before a mass meeting in the Punjab, lifted her veil, and declared all present her children in the nationalist cause. She drew on traditions involving women's ethical duties and the fictive family to extend her role (Minault, "Introduction: Extended Family," 11–13; Mirza, 31–33).

The first Muslim women's organization with an explicit reform focus was the All-India Muslim Ladies Conference (Anjuman-e-Khawatin-e-Islam) founded in 1914 (see Forbes, "Sisterhood or Separatism?"). It consisted of upper-class literate wives and relatives of important professionals and educators, many connected with the Aligarh College or the Mohammadan Educational Conference. Its focus was primarily educational, but it also passed related resolutions on raising the age of marriage and lessening purdah restrictions. In 1918 it passed a resolution condemning polygamy as being against the true spirit of Islam, arguing that it was impossible to practice the Prophet Mohammad's injunction that each wife was to be treated equally. This caused an uproar in part of the Muslim press.

Like their Hindu counterparts, Muslim women's rights leaders had access to and support from elite male politicians, most notably Mohammad Ali Jinnah, President of the Muslim League.[37] A secularist by temperament, a barrister by training, Jinnah paradoxically led the demand for a separate Islamic state to protect Muslim interests that he believed were being trampled upon by Congress politicians. In 1940 the Muslim League adopted the goal of a separate state. Like Gandhi, Jinnah appealed to women for support, and promoted women's uplift as essential to the national cause: "No nation can make any progress without the cooperation of its women. If Muslim women support their men as they did in the days of the Prophet of Islam, we should soon realize our goal" (Mirza, 63). Women were encouraged to march and picket, and were organized by the Women's Central Sub-Committee of the All-India Muslim League. In the 1945 elections, which were critical to the League's claim to speak for all Muslims, Muslim women ran for seats and played an important organizational role in registering and canvassing Muslim women voters, and in fundraising. Many were subsequently jailed when they picketed and protested against the Punjab government. In the violence and immense suffering that accompanied Partition, Muslim women volunteered for dangerous service, provided medical relief for the wounded, and conducted blood, food, and clothing drives. In February 1949 the All-Pakistan Women's Association was founded by elite women vet-

erans of the freedom struggle. Like their Hindu counterparts
they had earned, and expected, substantive reforms upon independence.

The Indian women's movement demanded equal political
and legal rights, extended woman's sphere to include public participation and the performance of certain categories of professional employment, often of a sex-segregated nature. The issues
they stressed—inheritance rights, right to divorce, the franchise,
and modifications of purdah—were those of importance to the
upper castes/class but of limited relevance to the majority of
women. (Similar critiques have of course been made of first-wave
feminism in the United States).

Discussion Questions

1. "On the whole, Indian women's movement leaders appeared more skillful than their Western counterparts in
   appealing to popular values to legitimize women's movement demands" (Everett, *Women and Social Change,* 194).
   Discuss.

2. Based on the Indian experience, how would you establish
   priorities among the importance of legal, economic, or
   religious/attitudinal change in improving the status of
   women? How would you rank these issues in importance
   within the United States? Are the priorities different?
   Why or why not? Do they differ by class or race?

3. Discuss Forbes's theory that Western feminists of the
   period saw women as powerless, while leaders of the
   Indian women's movement saw women as powerful.

4. Were Indian women's rights leaders feminists even if, as
   was the case with Sarojini Naidu, some rejected the label?
   How do you define feminism?

5. Drawing on the anthropological theorists such as Sanday,
   Leacock, and Rubin discussed in Chapters 2 and 4, can
   separate be equal as some Indian feminists argued? In
   societies in which anthropologists assert egalitarianism
   exists, on what has its basis purportedly rested? How are
   you defining egalitarianism? Is your definition culture-
   bound? Was theirs?

6. Nationalists have tackled the issue of women's status in
   diametrically opposed ways. Some (Tilak) have defended
   tradition and condemned "Westernization" and "outside

meddling." Others (Gandhi, Jinnah) saw reform in varying degrees as essential to "national regeneration." What might account for these differences in India, and in any other nationalist movement (such as Kenya, Algeria, China) with which you are familiar?

WOMEN IN COMTEMPORARY INDIA

The Preamble of the new Indian Constitution promised to secure to all citizens "equality of status." Among the guarantees of Fundamental Rights that applied to women were equal protection of the laws (Article 14–1) and equal opportunity in employment (Article 16–1), albeit with the proviso that "rational" and "reasonable" gender-based distinctions could be drawn for the purpose of benefitting women. Women's groups accepted this formulation. By 1956, the last outstanding items on the agenda of the women's movement—reform of the Marriage and Property Laws—had been completed.

The most visible symbol of change, however, was the prominence of elite Indian women on the national and international scene. The late Prime Minister Indira Gandhi is simply the best-known of an able and well-connected series of women who have achieved prominence in Indian political life, among whom might also be mentioned Nehru's sister, Vijayalakshmi Pandit, former Ambassador to Washington and Moscow, and High Commissioner to the United Kingdom; Rajkumari Amrit Kaur, President of the International Red Cross; and Lakshmi Menon, Deputy Minister of External Affairs and later Chief of the United Nations Section on the Status of Women, among many others.

Because of the elite focus of the earlier women's movement and its apparent victories, there was a lapse into premature complacency on the part of established women's groups in the 1950s. Real legal equality has remained a distant reality for most Indian women. Many are either unaware of or unable to secure the enforcement of their theoretical rights. Further, the law contains gaps and inequities that stand in the way of legal equality even for those comparatively few women who are in a position to appeal to the judicial system.

The laws on which the movement concentrated were also largely irrelevant to the vast majority of impoverished Indian women—and men—for whom the day-to-day struggle to exist is the overwhelming priority. While widened horizons opened to elite women, the processes of economic development originating in the nineteenth century, continuing in the nationalist era, and accelerating greatly since independence, have exacerbated socio-economic strains. The increased opportunities open to educated women in the middle and upper classes obscured the deterioration in the condition of disadvantaged women.

The subject of women and development is a central thrust of women's studies scholarship in India. We will examine some of it in the context of particular topics such as women and employment and women and education. Two valuable volumes which give overviews of the South Asian context should be mentioned at the outset:

Jahan, Rounaq, and Hanna Papanek, eds. *Women and Development: Perspectives from South and Southeast Asia.* Dacca: Bangladesh Institute of Law and International Affairs, 1979. (Distributed by South Asia Books.) A compilation of twenty-two papers by researchers, public policy experts, and activists in the field originally presented to a 1977 conference, the Regional South and Southeast Asian Seminar on Women and Development. It contains a summary report and recommendations; papers on public policy, including law; methodological issues in measuring women's work and integrating it into development plans; research issues; and the aims and implementation of actual women's programs in non-formal education and for the self-employed. It is best suited for instructor reading.

Nelson, Nici. *Why Has Development Neglected Rural Women? A Review of the South Asian Literature.* Oxford: Pergamon Press, 1979. A pungent critique of conceptual biases in development literature that renders rural women's work "invisible," springing from, in Nelson's view, the tendency of male social scientists to see women as marginal, coupled with an elite, urban bias. The book has four sections: the meaning of development and women's role; a literature survey covering Bangladesh, India, Pakistan, and Sri Lanka; an analysis of what has been learned thus far; and suggestions for future theoretical and action-oriented research. Sometimes Nelson's primary expertise as an Africanist leads to hasty judgments on South Asia, but this does not detract from the overall usefulness of her identification and survey of over 300 works.

The Indian situation broadly confirms the insights of Ester Boserup that development does not necessarily produce improvement in the status of women, but rather that it may deteriorate. Concepts developed in Chapter 3 of this volume, "Women, Colonialism, and Development," might usefully be reviewed with students as a prelude to the discussion of modern India.

The deterioration of the condition of many women—and the simultaneous benefits derived by elite women—is ultimately linked with structural changes in India's economy. There is considerable variation in the weight assigned to particular factors by various researchers, feminists included.

One profound change is the development of a commercial, market economy with capital-intensive production. In the agricultural sector India's "Green Revolution" of high-yield seeds, and utilization of new capital-intensive technologies of irrigation, fertilizer, pesticides, and farm machinery, have led to recent self-sufficiency in basic foodstuffs. The increasing concentration of land ownership has caused the displacement of marginal farmers, tenant farmers, and agricultural laborers, and has increased rural poverty leading to migration, both rural and urban. Women cultivators and agricultural workers have been displaced in large numbers, as have men to a lesser extent.

At the same time the low technology, labor-intensive craft sectors where women workers predominate, such as pottery or spinning, have been undermined by new industrial processes. Women in service industries, such as market sellers, are also in increasing competition with organized, mass-marketing structures.

The results for many women have been dire. The Committee on the Status of Women stated, "We received reports of increasing destitution among women from various quarters" (*Report,* 64). Displacement of workers, coupled with rising population pressures, have resulted in an extremely exploitable labor force of men and women, though women have suffered disproportionately.

Much of the literature on women and development focuses on the failure on the part of planners to acknowledge the importance of women's work, both paid and unpaid, and their failure to recognize the impact of industry, new technologies, and commercial market forces upon women. While "modernization" may displace women, there is a growing recognition that it also may hold them in place, or leave them behind, as men primarily reap the benefits of education, political participation, health facilities, and new employment opportunities. This unequal access is embedded in patriarchal family structures.

There are, however, important class differences in the impact of development on women. At the village level, prosperous farmers withdraw their womenfolk from the labor force even while other women are in an increasingly desperate search for work. In the cities, educated middle-class women's employment opportunities expand as the increasing cost of living weakens taboos about women working outside the home, while sweeper women may be abused and work for exploitive wages for members of this same class. Some women's studies scholars in India criticize Western feminist scholarship for failing to acknowledge sufficiently class differences and for "minimis(ing) the fact that women exploit other women—and men—in every society."[38]

The overall deterioration in women's status, albeit with important class differences, remained largely ignored and unremarked until the publication in 1974 of the report of the National Committee on the Status of Women. The *Report* is a rarity of its kind among officially appointed bodies of any nation, combining remarkable candor, impeccable research, and real eloquence. The full report is nearly five hundred pages long, and might usefully be acquired for instructors' and library reference.

Government of India. Ministry of Education and Social
    Welfare. *Towards Equality: Report of the Committee on the
    Status of Women.* New Delhi, 1974.

The *Report* is also available in an abbreviated (188-page) form:

*Status of Women in India: A Synopis of the Report of the National
    Committee on the Status of Women (1971–74).* New Delhi:
    Indian Council of Social Science Research, 1975.

In the wake of the Committee's findings, which were given added impetus by the United Nations Decade on Women, and the general social unrest in India in the mid-1970s, there has been an explosion of scholarship on contemporary Indian women. It is beyond our scope to attempt a comprehensive overview. However, many such works published in English up to the late 1970s may be found in Carol Sakala's *Women of South Asia.* An important new reference work is:

Vaid, Jyotsna, Barbara D. Miller, and Janice Hyde, eds. *South
    Asian Women at Home and Abroad: A Guide to Resources.* Ann

Arbor: University of Michigan, 1 Lane Hall, Ann Arbor, Mich. 48109, Committee on Women in Asian Studies of the Association for Asian Studies, 1984. This volume contains a bibliography of many of the recent books, articles, and working papers on women in India, Pakistan, Bangladesh, Nepal, and Sri Lanka, as well as on South Asian women immigrants. It also contains a useful list of films, periodicals, and organizations.

Two helpful overviews of current research in modern South Asian women's studies are:

Papanek, Hanna. "False Specialization and the Purdah of Scholarship—A Review Article." *Journal of Asian Studies* 44, no. 1 (November 1984): 127–48.

Singh, Andrea Menefee. "The Study of Women in South Asia: Some Current Methodological and Research Issues." Chap. 2 in *Women in Contemporary India and South Asia*. 2nd ed. Edited by Alfred de Souza. New Delhi: Manohar, 1980.

To keep abreast of the rapidly evolving field of women's studies in India, instructors might request membership in or inclusion upon the mailing lists of the following organizations:

Indian Association for Women's Studies, c/o Centre for Women's Development Studies, B–43 Panchsheel Enclave, New Delhi 110017, India. The Center publishes a bulletin and a journal of women's studies, *Samya Shakti*. *Samya Shakti* is available for $10 per annual issue from The Feminist Press at The City University of New York, 311 East 94 Street, New York, N.Y. 10128.

Committee on South Asian Women (COSAW), c/o Jyotsna Vaid, Department of Psychology, C–009, University of California, San Diego, La Jolla, CA 92093. The quarterly COSAW Bulletin is available for $12 for individuals and $20 for institutions.

It is difficult to keep informed about the activities of the revived but decentralized women's movement in India. One indispensable source, however, is:

Manushi: A Journal About Women and Society, published by the *Manushi* collective in New Delhi. The United States distributor is c/o Esther Jantzen, *Manushi* Distributors, 5008 Erringer Place, Philadelphia, PA 19144. Others may write *Manushi* Trust, C1/202 Lajpat Nagar, New Delhi, India 110024.

Also of interest are:

Newsletter of the Asian Women's Research and Action Network (AWRAN), which publishes listings of women's organizations in Asia, as well as bibliographical materials. C/o Irene Santiago, editor, Pilipina, c/o Kahayug Foundation, P.O. Box 208, Davao City, Philippines.

Women's International Network News, Frank Hoskens, editor, 187 Grant Street, Lexington, MA. 02173. *WIN News* abstracts news reports and government documents worldwide, and regularly includes South Asian information.

Scholarship on women in earlier periods suffered as we have seen from a focus only on the experience of elite women, reflecting in many instances the available evidence, for it is the literate and powerful who leave records of themselves. In the post-independence era, more attention has been paid to the condition of lower-caste/class women in both villages and towns, as well as to regional and religious differences. Topics addressed in this section include Law and Social Change; Women and Politics; Women and Education; Women and Employment; Health, Longevity, and Family Planning; Muslim Women; and the Modern Indian Women's Movement. Space considerations preclude an examination of women in Pakistan and Bangladesh. Bibliographies on both countries are contained in the works by Nelson, Sakala, and Vaid mentioned above. Another useful source is:

Ayub, Nighat. *Women in Pakistan and Other Islamic Countries: A Selected Bibliography with Annotations.* Karachi: Women's Resource Centre/Shirkat Gah, 1978.

Law and Social Change

Legislative enactments have had only a very limited impact as a method of social engineering in India, a point that may be illustrated by examining the provisions and actual effects of the Special Marriage Act, the Hindu Marriage Act, the Hindu Succession Act, and the Dowry Act.

Readings for Students
Everett, Jana M. *Women and Social Change in India,* Chap. 7.
Sharma, Ursula. "Dowry in North India: Its Consequences for
     Women." In *Women and Property—Women as Property,* edited
     by Renee Hirschon, 62–74. London: Croon Helm; New
     York: St. Martin's Press, 1984.
*Status of Women in India: A Synposis of the Report of the National
     Committee on the Status of Women (1971–74),* Chap. 4. New
     Delhi: Indian Council of Social Science Research, 1975.
     (Cited as *Report*).

Readings for Instructors
Blumberg, Rhoda Lois, and Leela Dwaraki. *India's Educated
     Women: Options and Constraints,* Chap. 4. Delhi: Hindustan
     Pub. Corp., 1980.
Derrett, J. Duncan M. *The Death of a Marriage Law: Epitaph for
     The Rishis.* Durham, N.C.: Carolina Academic Press, 1978.
     Written with a nostalgic backward glance but invaluable for
     its index of case law.
Kumar, Manju. *Social Equality: The Constitutional Experiment in
     India.* New Delhi: S. Chand & Co., 1982.
Lebra, Joyce, Joy Paulson, and Jana Everett, eds. *Women and Work
     in India: Continuity and Change,* Chap. 1, Introduction, and
     Chap. 2, "Housewives."
Minattur, Joseph. "Women and the Law." Chap. 6 in *Women in
     Contemporary India and South Asia,* edited by Alfred de Souza.
     2nd ed. New Delhi: Manohar, 1980.
Murickan, J. "Women in Kerala: Changing Socio-Economic Sta-
     tus and Self-Image." In *Women in Contemporary India.*
Sharma, Ursula. *Women, Work and Property in North-West India,*
     47–59.
Srinivas, M. N. *The Changing Position of Indian Women.* Delhi:
     Oxford University Press, 1978.
Towards Equality, Chap. 4.

Lecture Topics

**Reform of Marriage and Property Laws: Historical Background
(*Report*, Everett).** No uniform legal code governs marriage and
inheritance laws in India: Hindus, Muslims, Christians, Parsis,
Sikhs, and even residents of former Portuguese Goa and French
Pondicherry are governed by different personal laws, the details
of which are outlined in the *Report* (Chap. 4). This lack of uni-

formity was criticized by the Committee, but vocal minority groups, led by men, have resisted change. The Committee reported that minority women, and specifically Muslim women, were much more receptive to the idea of reform.

The Hindu Code itself was passed against considerable opposition. Proponents argued that political equality was meaningless without social equality in family law; opponents argued that men's and women's roles and obligations differed, and hence that it was unfair for women to have the same marriage or property rights. Everett believes that the real issues for opponents of the Code were female inheritance rights and a conception of women as dependent not equal (176–86).

By 1952 Nehru alone of the top leaders supported these legal reforms, and he used his own immense prestige to force changes through Parliament. What was originally conceived of as a comprehensive act was divided into different parts to minimize overall opposition.

The Special Marriage Act (*Report*, Derrett, Kumar, Minattur). The Special Marriage Act (1954) tackled the longstanding issue of child marriage, setting the marriageable age at twenty-one for males and eighteen for females. However, as with earlier acts, offenses are not cognizable (subject to judicial hearing and decision), and marriages in contravention of the law remain valid. Thus, the law has had only limited impact. The age of marriage rose during the century from an average of 13.3 years for females and 20.2 for males in the 1911 census to 17.2 years for females and 22.2 years for males in the census of 1971. The Committee on the Status of Women reported in 1974 that in one third of the total districts in India (mostly in rural Madhya Pradesh, Bihar, Rajasthan, and Uttar Pradesh), the average age at marriage for females was below fifteen. The strong emphasis on purity and chastity of women continues to encourage early marriage, particularly in rural areas, where the overall age at which girls marry (16.7 years) is significantly lower than in urban areas (19.2 years). The Committee recommended massive public education coupled with the compulsory registration of marriages, the declaration of early marriages as invalid, and the appointment of Special Officers with powers to prosecute and enforce the act. Many are still aware of the law, or, if aware, can easily evade it. In response to the *Report*, the Child Marriage Restraint Act (1978) made marriage violations a cognizable offense.

The Hindu Marriage Act (*Report;* Derrett; Lebra, Chap. 1; Minattur). The Hindu Marriage Act (1955) has had a similarly limited impact. Its main provisions were to outlaw Hindu polygamy and to permit a variety of "at fault" divorces after a three-year waiting period, including among the grounds adultery, venereal disease, and conversion to another religion. This latter provision was sometimes used to evade the restrictiveness of the act. Women could additionally divorce polygamous husbands or ones convicted of rape, sodomy, or bestiality. Divorces were not permitted on the broader grounds of the breakdown of a marriage or cruelty. In 1976 the law was liberalized to permit divorce by mutual consent after a one-year separation.

Formal divorces remain comparatively rare in India; it is estimated that only one-half of one percent have availed themselves of the law, though lower castes have long permitted customary divorce and these continue outside formal channels. For most women even knowledgable of the law, there are the problems of social opprobrium and economic survival.

Despite the 1955 ban on polygamy, it is estimated that 5 to 8 percent of Hindu marriages are polygamous—roughly the same percentage can be found among Muslims among whom it is legally permitted. The Committee on the Status of Women called for a ban on polygamy in all communities, and "found widespread resentment among Muslim women against legal sanction of this practice" (*Report* 23, 40).

The Hindu Succession Act (*Report;* Everett; Kumar; Sharma, Women, Work and Property, 47–59). The Hindu Succession Act (1956) was perhaps the most revolutionary of the acts passed in this decade. If a man died intestate, equal and absolute inheritance rights were to be vested in his widow, mother, sons, daughters, and their immediate heirs. From the beginning, however, the law was weakened in a number of respects. Women could be excluded in formal wills. State laws governing the devolution of agricultural tenancy holdings were excluded from the scope of the act, and in some states "dominant conservative groups" have "successfully excluded widows and daughters" from inheriting agricultural tenancies (*Report,* 54).

Nevertheless, the principle of the inheritance by a woman of property, and especially the absolute inheritance of land, represents in theory a breach in the historic pattern of female economic dependency upon males in the propertied classes. It has proven extremely difficult to enforce this principle in reality, as Ursula Sharma (47–59) among others has shown. In extreme cases a widow claiming her rights may be beaten; in other cases, in conservative communities, the widow may have difficulty conducting her affairs (hiring labor, selling produce) without violating the rules of purdah, and may still be dependent upon males.

The Committee on the Status of Women concluded that, for some widows from propertied families, the legal reforms may have helped. However, in the absence of property or the ability to enforce claims, "the remarriage and condition of widows still constitutes a problem which cannot be described as insignificant." There are over twenty million widows.

Dowry Prohibition Act (*Report;* Lebra, Chap. 2; Murickan; Sharma, *Women, Work and Property,* 137–43 and "Dowry"; Srinivas). Social custom has rendered the Dowry Prohibition Act (1961) totally ineffective. In fact, the practice of giving dowry has spread in recent years, from upper castes to lower castes. Instances have even been reported among Calcutta sweepers. Brideprice, once prevalent throughout South India (except Kerala) and among lower castes, seems to be declining in favor of dowry, though with considerable regional, caste, and class variation (Srinivas 26–26; Sharma, "Dowry").

The provisions of the Act are weak and poorly publicized. J. Murickan reports that 44 percent of a relatively well-educated sample of women in Kerala were not aware that dowry was illegal. Dowry-giving is not a cognizable offense, and for those who are bothered by the law a deed can be sworn certifying that "dowry" is really a gift to the bride in lieu of her share of family property. Though the view that dowry is a form of *pre mortem* inheritance is popular in India, Ursula Sharma ("Dowry") argues that dowry property is not in fact women's wealth. It does not represent a fixed share of family assets nor does the bride control it, for it is paid to her husband's family (70).

Aside from the aura of a market transaction surrounding the marriageability of a woman, critics of dowry have attempted to mobilize against instances of dowry abuse, and especially against extortionary demands that continue after marriage leading in some instances to the mysterious death of the new bride, through suicide or murder. The Home Ministry reported that 2,670 women died of burns in 1976, and 2,917 from the same cause in 1977, and women's rights groups suspect most were dowry deaths.[39]

The reasons for the spread of dowry geographically and vertically through lower socioeconomic groups are complex and controversial. The usual explanation for dowry historically among higher castes has rested on what Ursula Sharma terms a "cost-benefit" analysis,[40] in which "dowry compensates the groom's family for the addition of a dependent non-productive member, whilst bridewealth compensates the bride's family for the loss of an active productive member" (67).

The paradox surrounding its current spread in India, however, is that according to some reports "neither education nor employment of the bride reduces the incidence of dowry" (Murickan, 83). Yet other data suggest that education and employment may actually increase dowry demands. A study of housewives showed that roughly half the respondents believed that if girls were educated to a modest level (beyond six grades but not beyond high school) and employed, husbands could be found with little or no dowry expense (Lebra, 42), but if women received education beyond that level it would be difficult to find husbands (see also Murickan, 85). M. N. Srinivas, in contrast, suggests that the mounting cost of dowry has contributed to the rise in the age of marriage for girls and assisted in the spread of female education rather than damaging it (26). More studies of dowry in particular socioeconomic groups are clearly necessary before easy generalizations can be drawn.

Dowry practices have prompted the mobilization of women's groups in a number of urban areas. Actions have ranged from pickets outside households suspected of dowry atrocities, to a major conference culminating in the demand for legal reforms and greater police enforcement of existing laws, such as compulsory post mortems after suspected dowry deaths, limitations on dowry payments, enforcement of inheritance rights, and establishment of abandoned women shelters. The Committee on the Status of Women recommended "multi-pronged" remedies including "re-assessing the value of housework and homemaking as socially and economically productive," increasing employment opportunities for women, banning the display of dowry gifts, making offenses under the Dowry Act cognizable, and entrusting enforcement to a social work agency (*Report,* 26/44).

Though feminists have worked hard to forge a sense of female solidarity on the issue of dowry, they are hampered as Ursula Sharma points out by differing self-interests among the women themselves. It is often "the bride's mother-in-law who has the greatest say in how these items (of dowry) are distributed" in a joint family. It is "the senior women's responsibility to maintain correct relations of reciprocity within and outside the household," with the mother-in-law generally controlling the distribution of goods, and her husband any sums of cash ("Dowry" 65–66). Dowry strengthens the power of the mother-in-law, and even the bride's mother may derive satisfaction from "a public and honourable display of generosity" ("Dowry," 73). Thus women within the patriarchal family are divided among themselves.

A number of studies of dowry report the practice is deplored but considered inevitable because of the overwhelming pressure on girls to marry. Ninety-nine percent of all women in the age group of twenty-five to forty-four are or have been married. Blumberg and Dwaraki report what is a very small but perhaps significant shift in the attitudes of female graduates of Bangalore University: a tiny fraction were in rebellion against the practice of dowry, and were viewing instead the possibility of lifetime careers (62). For the vast majority, however, this remains an inconceivable option.

Political Participation

Women's political participation, either as political candidates or voters, is a neglected field of study. Until the publication in 1979 of *Symbols of Power*, edited by Vina Mazumdar, no full-length study had been devoted to the subject. This important and groundbreaking collection has inevitably raised as many questions as it answers.

The Committee on the Status of Women in India challenged a number of the prevailing assumptions about women's political awareness. Female voters had been generally characterized as more conservative than men, more susceptible to religious appeals, and heavily influenced by their husbands' views (see Chitnis, 14). It has also been often assumed that greater literacy, education, urbanization, and exposure to mass media leads to greater political participation (*Report*, 107–8). All of this was questioned by the Committee, and subsequent scholarship has attempted more precise empirical verification of the determinants of female voting behavior with results that largely confirm the Committee's skepticism. If any one generalization can be made about the proliferating data it is, in the words of the Committee, "that there is no single homogeneous pattern. Levels of political awareness vary from region to region, from class to class and from community to community, and are conditioned greatly by the political culture of the area, the approach of political parties to the women and quality of local leadership" (*Towards Equality,* 7.39).

Women's suffrage and the right to run and be elected to local, state, and national legislative bodies was one of the great achievements of the women's movement in the nationalist era. Yet the franchise remains an unexploited tool for the furtherance of women's self-interest, a very serious deficiency, given the deteriorating status of many women under the impact of development.

Finally, Indian politics present an enormous paradox, which has often been noted by political commentators: India, where women remain unorganized as a voting block and where the belief in separate spheres is still strong, has had a powerful woman prime minister, as well as women cabinet ministers, ambassadors, and governors and chief ministers of states. How is this paradox to be explained?

Readings for Students
Khan, Mumtaz Ali, and Noor Ayesha. *Status of Rural Women in India: A Study of Karnataka,* Chap. 4, "Participation in Social Organisations." New Delhi: Uppal Pub. House, 1982.

Katzenstein, Mary Fainsod. "Towards Equality? Cause and Consequence of the Political Prominence of Women in India." In *The Extended Family,* edited by Gail Minault, Chap. 11.

Omvedt, Gail. *We Will Smash This Prison: Indian Women in Struggle.* London: Zed Press, 1980.

Report, Chap. 7.

Usha Rao, N.J. In *Women in a Developing Society,* Chap. 8, "Political Awareness Among Rural Women of Chickmaglur." New Delhi: Asia Pub. House, 1983.

Readings for Instructors
Banerjee, Nirmala. "Politicization of Women in West Bengal." In *Symbols of Power: Studies on the Political Status of Women in India,* edited by Vina Mazumdar, 140–70. New Delhi: Allied Pubs./S.N.D.T. Women's University, 1979.

Chitnis, Suma. "International Women's Year: Its Significance for Women in India." In *Women in Contemporary India.*

D'Lima, Hazel. *Women in Local Government: A Study in Maharashtra.* New Delhi: Concept Pub. Co., 1983.

Dubey, B. R. "Rajasthan." In *Symbols of Power,* 291–304.

Everett, Jana. "Women and Political Leadership." Chap. 10 in *Women and Work in India.*

Jacob, Lucy. "Kerala." In *Symbols of Power,* 226–45.

Limaye, P. N. "Politicization of Women in Maharashtra." In
    Symbols of Power, 119–39.
Mazumdar, Vina, ed. *Symbols of Power,* Editor's Note, ix–xxiii.
Muni, S. D. "Women in the Electoral Process." In *Symbols of
    Power,* 24–50.
Rajput, P. "Punjab." In *Symbols of Power,* 265–90.
Sheth, Pravin. "Gujarat." In *Symbols of Power,* 200–20.
Shukla, Dinesh M. "Politicization of Women in Gujarat." In
    Symbols of Power, 85–118.
Sirsikar, V. M. "Politicization of Women in India: an Overview."
    In *Symbols of Power,* 81–84.
Tawale, S. N. "Maharashtra." In *Symbols of Power,* 246–64.
Towards Equality, Chap. 7.
Upretti, Nandini, and D. B. Mathur. "Women Voters and the
    Mid-Term Poll (1971)." In *Symbols of Power,* 51–66.

Lecture Topics

Women and Political Representation: National and State Legislatures. Despite the prominence of Indira Gandhi, the level of direct political involvement of elite women has not been sustained since independence. The number of women candidates running and the percentage who have been successful has declined steadily at the national and state levels. Only a small percentage of women in the Indian Parliament is elected by adult suffrage. It should be noted, however, that the percentage of female national legislators in the mid-1970s (4.2 percent) compares favorably with the United States (3.0 percent). In the state assemblies women constituted 3.9 percent of the legislators in the late 1970s (Everett, 218–23).

Various explanations are given for the erosion in representation (*Report;* Everett). Prestigious members of the nationalist generation have died, retired, or transferred their focus into social reform groups or elsewhere, and have not been replaced. The Gandhian legacy of women's political involvement has become diluted in the Congress Party which has never met its stated aim of 15 percent women candidates (Muni, 35). The expense of conducting an election is also reported as a serious barrier. Women interested in becoming politically active complain about the decline of idealism and the rise of corruption in politics, the social disapproval toward women in politics, and the character assassination that women candidates have to endure (Tawale, 247; Everett, 226). A number of states report a decline in interest in politics among upper-middle-class women (Tawale, 249), and it was from precisely this group that most women legislators had been drawn.

Thus far women candidates have rarely entered legislatures from a personal power base. They have, in S.D. Muni's words, "heavily depended upon either the party machine or a band of loyal men workers in conducting their respective election campaigns" (39). They have also depended heavily on prestigious family backgrounds and kinship connections in securing nominations. Hence the paradox of Indira Gandhi's success is easily resolved: she inherited a great deal of power from her father, Jawaharlal Nehru, and she is from a wealthy family of Kashmiri Brahmins with a long and distinguished history of political involvement. Overall the socioeconomic background of women legislators is more elitist than that of male legislators.

The Committee on the Status of Women was very critical of female legislators for taking little interest in women's issues (*Report,* 109). Drawn from political and economic elites, legislators believed women's problems had been solved, and assumed no personal responsibility to women. Vina Mazumdar, Member-Secretary of the Committee and current Director of the Center for Women's Development Studies, believes that the complacency of women's organizations, and their non-partisan, social-work orientation have also played a role in the general neglect of women in the legislative arena (Everett, 226).

The legacy of Indira Gandhi herself in the furtherance of women's status is a mixed one. She said repeatedly that she did not think of herself as a woman in politics. There were more women in her father's Cabinet in 1951 than in any subsequent ones; in 1980 Mrs. Gandhi appointed no woman to a Cabinet-level position. Balanced against this is the fact that she may have been a role model, legitimizing the idea of women's political activity.

Panchayats. A vital component of social and economic development in India are village *panchayats,* or representative congresses, grouped into progressively larger units called Panchayat Samities and Zila Parishads. Panchayats are elected by adult suffrage, typically on a ward basis, with several seats guaranteed for the Scheduled Castes and Tribes. Most states have also provided for the nomination of one or two women members, if none are elected through the normal process. Because the panchayats are involved in critical ways with rural development programs, and may also initiate or institute projects themselves, they are important sources of power and influence at the local level. Despite the nomination of women members, the participation of women has been low, and the panchayats have not functioned as instruments for social progress for women. Officials at the village level and development officers often hold women themselves responsible, and attribute it to "backwardness."

Women members say that they are burdened by domestic commitments, that the meetings are often held too far away, that when they speak they are not listened to, and that the programs suggested by development officers are unhelpful to women. The pattern in urban municipal elections is also similar.

The Committee on the Status of Women described the reservation of women's seats as "tokenism" and recommended the formation of statutory women's panchayats with resources of their own as a method of integrating women into local political structures. This was seen as a "transitional measure, to break through the attitudes that inhibit most women from articulating their problems and participating actively in local bodies" (*Report*, 114).

Women's Voting Behavior (Everett, Muni, Usha Rao, Upretti and Mathur). The study of women's political behavior in India (as in the United States) is comparatively new and there are many geographical and socioeconomic gaps in the available data. All of this makes attempts at valid generalizations a perilous exercise. Perhaps the most that can be said is that virtually every assumption about women's voting behavior is open to question or modification.

One point is unambiguously clear: the gap between male and female turnout declined from 15.4 percent to 11.8 percent between 1961 and 1971, with roughly half of the eligible women voters casting their ballots. State participation rates vary vastly from a 13.2 percent turnout of women voters in Orissa to 67 percent in Kerala in the 1961 election, to cite one example (Everett, 219).

State or Union Territories with lower female voting participation (Orissa, Bihar, Rajasthan, Uttar Pradesh, Madhya Pradesh, and Himachal Pradesh) are noted for their social, political, and economic backwardness, and in some instances "feudal" land relationships; those with comparatively high turnouts are more prosperous, many are clustered in the south (Kerala, Tamil Nadu, Andhra Pradesh) and/or are highly urbanized (Delhi) and industrialized (Gujarat), but it is difficult to draw easy correlations with these factors.

Literacy and education are often assumed to have a positive

influence on voting. The Committee found literacy to be "an important determinant for both awareness and participation," and while education correlated with awareness, this did not necessarily translate into voting (*Towards Equality*, 7.41). Some investigators have reported a generational difference in educated women's voting participation, with the older, pre-independence generation outstripping younger women (Banerjee, 164). A number of studies report a growing apathy toward politics among educated, middle-class women (Jacob, 243–44; Limaye, 131, 138). The Committee found more generally that there was "no positive relationship between higher socio-economic status and degree of awareness" (*Towards Equality*, 7.43).

Rural women are sometimes characterized as voting blindly as their husbands do. With regard to voting participation, the Committee found no overall differences between urban and rural women. Usha Rao's electoral study of the women of rural Chickmaglur, Karnataka, also undermines assumptions made about rural and illiterate women voters. The candidates in Chickmaglur were Indira Gandhi and a respected leader, Sri Veerendra Patil of the Janata Party. Rural women walked miles to campaign meetings, and showed a high discernment of overall class issues and on particular points at issue. Usha Rao found that Chickmaglur women showed caution in airing their views to strange pollsters, and showed a surface deference to their husband's wishes. They, nevertheless, showed private independence and a knowledge of why ballots were secret. This should prompt further probing of women's political behavior.

The Committee also cast doubt on assumptions about women's conservatism. In the 1971 midterm poll women were asked "whether India needs revolution for real progress and not the ritual of elections," and 42 percent of the respondents supported revolution (*Report*, 108; Upretti and Mathur, 57–58). Banerjee's study of West Bengal, among others, reveals a growing disillusionment with electoral politics among women: about 27 percent said having a vote made no difference to women or men (162).

The general political disillusionment in India in the 1970s has been attributed to rising unemployment, exacerbated tensions between social classes, rising prices, corruption, and periodic breakdowns in law and order, coupled with a feeling that the political system had failed to deal effectively with these issues (*Towards Equality*, 7.47). There is ample evidence, however, that where women perceive there is definite hope for a solution they will respond vigorously. Women are concerned with practical survival issues: "They have shown themselves ready to protest against rising prices, adulteration of food, unemployment, and poverty" (*Report*, 108). These protests have often taken the form of direct action. Brief accounts of this mobilization may be found in the Mazumdar volume (see especially Jacob, 240–42; Sheth, 209–13; and Tawale, 254–56). The classic account of attempts to mobilize and politicize women around class and gender issues is Gail Omvedt's, *We Will Smash This Prison*. Omvedt, an American socialist and feminist, spent two years assisting the Lal Nishan (Red Flag) Party's organization of a women's movement with a mass base in the famine-stricken Ahmednagar district of Maharashtra. The book illustrates simultaneously the depth of women's oppression and their growing awareness of it. It deals with the enormous practical difficulties of forging a self-generating grassroots women's movement that bridges caste and class differences and controls its own agenda, which may differ from that of male Marxists who insist that class oppression is primary and that oppression based on sex is secondary and can wait.

Education

If the electoral process has thus far failed as a method of equalizing gender stratification, so too has the educational system failed to make a difference to the vast majority of women. Education was, of course, one of the chief vehicles of social change promoted by the earlier generation of social reformers. The Indian Constitution contains a directive to provide free and compulsory education to all children up to age fourteen. This goal has not been met. The female literacy rate was a minuscule 0.69 percent in 1901; by 1951, shortly after independence, it was 8 percent, and by 1981 it had risen to around 25 percent. Female literacy rates are less than half that of males.

In formal school enrollment there are even greater discrepancies. Statistics on school attendance from the mid-1970s show 99 percent of males and 68 percent of females enrolled in primary school, but progressively higher attrition among females widens the gap to 33 percent male and 13 percent female enrollment by high school (Trembour, 110–11; *Report*, 93–94). At the college level, however, the popularity of female higher education among the middle and upper-middle classes has meant that the gap between men and women is declining more rapidly than at the grade school level. In education, as elsewhere, the benefits of development have been unevenly distributed.

The Committee on the Status of Women saw the expansion and upgrading of female education as an urgent necessity. We will examine material and attitudinal obstacles to this goal, as well as the issues of coeducation and the content of women's education.

Readings for Students

Blumberg, Rhoda Lois, and Leela Dwaraki. *India's Educated Women*, especially Chap. 3, "Students in Saris: The Meaning of Education."

Kapur, Promilla. *Changing Status of the Working Women in India*. Delhi: Vikas Pub. House, 1974.

Khan, Mumtaz Ali, and Noor Ayesha. *Status of Rural Women in India*, Chap. 2, "Educational Status."

Omvedt, Gail. *We Will Smash This Prison*, Chap. 3.

Mehta, Rama. *The Western Educated Hindu Woman*. London: Asia Pub. House, 1970.

Mies, Maria. "Role Conflicts of Studying and Working Women." In *Indian Women and Patriarchy*, 163–294.

Report, Chap. 6.

Readings for Instructors

Aggarwal, J. C. *Indian Women: Education and Status*. New Delhi: Arya Book Depot, 1976. An uneven compilation of documents from various government commissions, but somewhat useful as a reference.

Karlekar, Malavika. *Poverty and Women's Work: A Study of Sweeper Women in Delhi*, Chap. 3. New Delhi: Vikas Pub. House, 1982.

Misra, Lakshmi. *Education of Women in India, 1921–1966*.

Roy, Manisha. *Bengali Women*. Chicago: University of Chicago Press, 1972.

Towards Equality, Chap. 6.

Trembour, Mary. "Women in Education." In *Women and Work in India*, edited by Joyce Lebra et al., Chap. 5.

Lecture Topics

Unequal Access to Education. Women's unequal access to education is closely linked with the sexual division of labor within the Indian family and cultural attitudes towards women. Education is not seen to be as useful or as appropriate for girls compared with boys because formal schooling is often not considered necessary preparation for housewives and mothers. Moreover, most families cannot afford to educate children to the high school or university level required for employment in modern sector jobs. "Wastage" or attrition among girls who do go to school is very high: roughly 60 percent of school dropouts are girls.

As with political participation and representation, there are significant regional differences in female literacy. The highest literacy rate (around 60 percent) is found in Kerala, where a matrilineal tradition and a large Christian population are seen as important influences. The lowest female literacy rates (ranging from 10 to 15 percent) are found in Rajasthan, Uttar Pradesh, Orissa, Bihar, and Madhya Pradesh (Aggarwal, 87). The highest female literacy rates are found among Christians, and the lowest among Muslims and Scheduled Castes and Tribes.

In some states, such as Rajasthan and Bihar, strict purdah practices affect female school enrollment, especially in the absence of sufficient numbers of single-sex schools. There is also a lack of female teachers, especially in rural areas, where a one-room school with a male teacher is common. There are also too few schools, especially at the intermediate and secondary levels, which means girls may have to travel unacceptably far distances from home. The Committee found more acceptance of coeducation among Muslims in areas where they were in a majority than in a minority. Overall, there was greater acceptance of coeducation in the primary grades than at the secondary level (*Towards Equality*, Chap. 6).

The issue of coeducation is a serious one not only because, in Gandhi's words, it promotes "healthy and harmonious relationship(s)" but also because of India's budget constraints. There are widespread complaints about the poorer facilities, poorer standards, and narrower curriculum in girls' schools, and coeducation is seen as one method of raising girls' educational levels. The Committee supported coeducation as a long-term goal on the grounds of "efficiency, economy and equal opportunities," but in view of divergent opinion recommended a compromise interim solution of coeducation at the primary level and the university level, and single-sex schools at the middle and secondary levels "where there is great demand for them" (*Report*, 97–98).

The female literacy rate in rural areas is less than one third that in urban areas (Aggarwal, 87). There are also enormous caste/class differences within these geographical sectors. "Free education" as mandated constitutionally has hardly any meaning for the poor in villages, for aside from tuition, education involves expenses for materials and clothing. It also means a loss of family income with children withdrawn from the workforce or from domestic responsibilities that help the mother perform dual roles.

Poverty and the sexual division of labor emerge as the chief impediments to girls' education among the urban poor. Historically, lower-caste women enjoyed relationships of greater egalitarianism within the family than did upper-caste women. Under the impact of development, gender stratification is increasing, at least in some sectors, as is made clear in Malavika Karlekar's study of sweeper women in Delhi. Differential male/female access to education is part of this complex process of social change. Karlekar's sample of eighty women worked either as private domestic sweepers or as cleaners for the Delhi Corporation. Though more girls were in school than in their parents' generation, it was primarily boys for whom education was a vehicle of social mobility. Lower-caste men were "increasingly involved in 'passing' in society aided by education, changes in name, learning a trade and dressing in the latest style" (129). Girls were needed to assume domestic responsibilities to relieve their mothers of their exhausting double duty of child care and low-paying jobs. In other studies of the urban poor, children as early as age five have been found working in cigarette factories.

Because of the unequal access and curricular irrelevancy of the formal educational system to the mass of poor women, the Committee on the Status of Women declared that the greatest problem in women's education was to expand informal basic education (*Report*, 100–101). Karlekar's study, for instance, shows that sweeper women were interested in skill training with practical implications, and basic literacy (17). The Committee on the Status of Women proposed that the organization and management of non-formal education for women be entrusted to Women's Panchayats, elected by women (*Report*, 101).

Middle-class women have had significantly better access to the educational system, though scarcely equal opportunities with men of their class. The number of women per one hundred men attending universities, for example, doubled from 10.9 in 1950–51 to 21.9 in 1970–71, but there still is clearly a considerable imbalance.

A great deal of literature has been devoted to the educated Hindu woman (Blumberg and Dwaraki, Kapur, Mehta, Mies, and Roy among others). Blumberg and Dwaraki are of particular interest because they show change over time (from 1967 to 1977), as does Promilla Kapur's study with a slightly earlier cutoff date.

Because these studies are based on survey research they may not always convey the immediacy and complexity of individual women's lives. Consequently, either Mies's interviews with women in Pune and Bombay in 1966–67 and 1970, or Rama Mehta's sensitively drawn portrait of fifty Western-educated North Indian women are indispensable supplements. Manisha Roy's study of upper-class Bengali women has been criticized by some as being overdrawn.

Common themes emerge in this literature: with a few exceptions (see particularly Mies, "Women Who Study and Work Out of Opposition," 216–29; and Blumberg and Dwaraki, 69–73, 61–62), the priority of marriage over education (and work), and the necessity of male approval for permission to study are almost universal. But significant change is evident. In the Blumberg and Dwaraki sample the median age of marriage was twenty-four, and a Bachelor's degree was "becoming increasingly acceptable and functional for urban middle class women," (53), though a postgraduate degree was considered a hindrance to marriageability. It is important to note, however, that in a study of the middle class done fifteen years earlier, the "acceptable" line was drawn at matriculation (or high school).[41] Further, though their numbers are small in comparison with the total population, there is a new phenomenon of the unmarried woman. For many such women, according to Mies, this is not so much a sign of "liberation" as a sign of "too much" education, financial responsibilities to parents or siblings, or an inability to meet dowry demands (Mies, 234). Some, nevertheless, simply do not wish to marry (134 out of one sample of 541 unmarried women) and their high education, and consequent employment opportunities, may enable them to do so, though the unmarried woman is still regarded with suspicion and finds her life difficult without male chaperones (Blumberg and Dwaraki, 68–70).

Whether the broader horizons of middle-class women are trendsetters is a controversial point. On the one hand less than 3 percent of Indian women have a university education, and their life experiences are far removed from those of the mass of women living at near-subsistence levels. On the other hand, M. N. Srinivas comments that the educated middle class is "minuscule in size but its life-style is envied and admired by others" (Blumberg and Dwaraki, 13).

Sexism in Education (*Towards Equality*, Misra). India's educational system has reflected a deep ambivalence about the appropriate nature of female education. Two separate educational commissions that reported on curricula shortly after independence reflect the poles of the debate. The University Education System (1950) argued for "equality of opportunity, but not necessarily identity of opportunity" and stressed the importance of fine arts, nursing, teaching, and home economics as appropriate subjects for women. The Report of the Secondary Education Commission (1953) countered with a recommendation to admit women into all areas of study (Misra, 134–36).

This continuing ambivalence about the purpose of female education and women's roles in society is reflected in the slow process of education among girls. The Committee on the Status of Women was highly critical of the existing educational system's reinforcement of the traditional socialization process of boys and girls, which serves to perpetuate sexual inequality (*Towards Equality*, 6.108). The committee recommended that education prepare women for multiple roles as "citizens, housewives, mothers, contributors to the family income and builders of the new society."

The Committee also recommended the opening of a common course of general education for both sexes, and with needlecraft, music, and dancing taught to all children at the primary level. In secondary school, girls should have "full opportunity to choose vocational and technical courses" geared to the local job market (*Towards Equality*, 6.81).

Employment

Most women work in agriculture. Most women workers are low-caste poor women or members of scheduled castes. Highly educated women have had professional jobs for decades, but they are few, relative to the total female workforce. The recent expansion of female employment in the last decade—a result of development planning—does not offset the decline in employment of unskilled women. In general, the total figures for the employment of women show a marked decline throughout the twentieth century. Between 1961 and 1971, while male employment increased by 15 percent, the percentage of female workers declined by 41 percent. The majority of women workers are to be found in the "unorganized sector," the vast majority as landless agricultural laborers, others as street vendors, day laborers, and workers in traditional village and cottage industries.

Readings for Students
Everett, Jana. "Women in Law and Administration." In *Women and Work in India.*
Ghosh, Chitra. "Sweepers." In *Women and Work in India.*

Gulati, Leela. "Agricultural Laborers." In *Women and Work in India.*
————. *Profiles in Female Poverty: A Study of Five Poor Working Women in Kerala.* Delhi: Hindustan Pub. Corp. (India), 1981.
Kapur, Promilla. *Changing Status of the Working Women in India.*
Karlekar, Malavika. *Poverty and Women's Work.*
————. "Sweepers." In *Women and Work in India.*
Kishwar, Madhu, and Ruth Vanita, eds. *In Search of Answers: Indian Women's Voices from Manushi,* "Introduction"; Part 1, "Women's Lives." London: Zed Press, 1984.
Lebra, Joyce. "Women in Medicine." In *Women and Work in India.*
Mies, Maria. *Indian Women and Patriarchy,* 163–288.
————. *The Lace Makers of Narsapur.*
Trembour, Mary. "Women in Education." In *Women and Work in India.*

Readings for Instructors
Blumberg, Rhoda Lois, and Leela Dwaraki. *India's Educated Woman,* especially Chap. 4.
Devi, U. Lalitha. *Status and Employment of Women in India.* Delhi: B.R. Pub. Corp., 1982.
Jahan, Rounaq, and Hanna Papanek. *Women and Development: Perspectives from South and Southeast Asia.* Dhaka: Bangladesh Institute of Law and International Affairs, 1979, distributed by South Asia Books.
Jain, Devaki et al. "Women's Work: Methodological Issues." In *Women and Development,* 128–65.
Khan, Mumtaz Ali, and Noor Ayesha. *Status of Rural Women in India,* Chap. 3.
Manohar, K. Murali, ed. *Socio-Economic Status of Indian Women.* Delhi: Seema Pubs., 1983.
Mazumdar, Vina. "Women, Development and Public Policy." In *Women and Development,* 39–54.
Mehra, Rekha, and K. Saradamoni. *Women and Rural Transformation: Two Studies.* New Delhi: Concept Pub. Co./Indian Council of Social Science Research, Centre for Women's Development Studies, 1983.
Mehta, Rama. *The Western Educated Hindu Woman.*
Mehta, Sushila. *Revolution and the Status of Women in India.* New Delhi: Metropolitan Book Co., 1982.
Sawant, S. D., and Rita Dewar. "Rural Female Labour and Economic Development." *Economic and Political Weekly* 14, no. 26 (30 June 1979): 1091–99.

Sharma, Ursula. *Women, Work and Property in North-West India*. *Towards Equality*, Chap. 5.
Trivedi, Harshad R. *Scheduled Caste Women: Studies in Exploitation with Reference to Superstition, Ignorance and Poverty*. Delhi: Concept Pub. Co., 1977.
Usha Rao, N. J. *Women in a Developing Society*.

Lecture Topics

The Unorganized Sector. A rich and growing body of fieldwork captures the grinding struggles and remarkable resilience of women in the unorganized sector. These studies balance immediacy, reflective analysis, and commitment in a way that makes them particularly appropriate for undergraduate students. Leela Gulati's *Profiles in Female Poverty* describes the life histories of an agricultural laborer, a brickworker, a fish vendor, a construction worker, and a coir worker. Joyce Lebra et al., *Women and Work in India*, consists of a collection of interpretive essays, often based on field research, of middle-class (housewives, lawyers, doctors) and poor women workers (sweepers, construction workers, agricultural laborers, among others). Specialized studies of particular occupations include Maria Mies's study of *The Lace Makers of Narsapur*, women in an exploited cottage industry who produce for the world market; and Malavika Kalekar's study of Delhi sweepers, *Poverty and Women's Work*.

Women agricultural workers are the largest single category of Indian working women, consisting of 80 percent of all women who work for wages, and about one-third of the total agricultural labor force. Studying this sector is therefore crucial to an understanding of Indian working women in general. They have been severely damaged by development; the richest villages have the lowest labor force participation of women (Sawant and Dewar), and while there has been a small amount of upward mobility, the general pattern of change has been downward (*Report*, 65–67). The unemployment rate is twice as high among women agricultural laborers, and their number of days worked lower than men's (138 versus 193 days). About 95 percent of women agricultural laborers are illiterate compared with 80 percent of the men (Gulati, *Women and Work in India*, 63–66). The all-India process documented by Leela Gulati is mirrored in Khan and Ayesha's village-level studies. Their micro-level analysis of three generations of women workers showed 8 percent of grandmothers had been "self-employed" (basket makers, clothes washers, pottery workers, cottage industry) and 92 percent worked for wages (most in agriculture). By their grandchildren's generation 32 percent were "self-employed" in increasingly marginal occupations, and 67 percent worked for wages (only half of which were in agriculture, the rest having been absorbed into an exploited labor pool of coolies, stone cutters, and road and building construction workers).

Women's traditional familial roles, especially in a highly sex-segregated society like India's, put them at an obvious disadvantage in gaining access to new technologies. This was reinforced by the biased approach of agricultural extension workers, influenced in part by Western "experts" who emphasized home science training, a process documented for India by Rekha Misra, just as it has been elsewhere (see Chapter 3 above).

Women's lack of access to land ownership, and inability to enforce their inheritance rights, are also part of this process of deterioration (Sharma). In all land redistribution measures since independence, tenancy rights have been given to male heads of household. Wives are treated as dependent, while needy females without male support, such as widows, are totally bypassed.

This neglect prompted seven women's organizations, including the All-India Women's Conference and the Centre for Women's Development Studies, to present a joint Memorandum to the Indian Government in 1980 requesting that in all cases of government land transfer, women should get joint title with their husbands. This concept was subsequently incorporated into the Sixth Five Year Plan, India's national economic planning document.

The agricultural displacement of women in the countryside has been accompanied by an influx of women migrating to the city in search of employment as maids, sanitary workers, cigarette rollers, construction workers, petty traders and the like. Their handicaps include illiteracy, ignorance of the laws that exist to protect unorganized workers, and often a helpless dependence on intermediaries (*jamadars*) to obtain employment. Infant mortality is high, and life expectancy low.

Women in cottage industries, such as cigarette rollers and lacemakers, work in "the most sweated industries in the country" (*Report*, 69). Maria Mies's study of the lacemakers of Narsapur shows a dual process of exploitive labor plus increasing polarization between men and women, similar to Karlekar's findings among sweeper families in Delhi. Women produce the lace, working on it six to eight hours per day, in addition to doing seven hours of housework; men do not share in household work or production; and it is some men, and no women, who become the agents, traders, and exporters of women's products onto the world market. The lacemakers are from families of pauperized peasants with small and medium land holdings who became marginalized during the Green Revolution.

Legislation to control the conditions of work in the unorganized sector has been totally ineffective. It includes Equal Pay Acts, Minimum Wages Acts, Abolition of Contract Labour Acts, and provision of welfare benefits such as crèches, housing, and sanitary services on the part of government contractors (Ghosh, *Women and Work in India*). But the enforcement machinery is weak and not all states have complied with national directives. The Committee on the Status of Women agreed that "the basic solution for the exploitation of agricultural workers lies in redistribution of land, but legislation for that purpose has been grossly ineffective so far." As an additional solution it recommended unionization of agricultural and other unorganized workers, coupled with vigilant enforcement machinery (*Report*, 66–68). Local attempts to organize these vulnerable women workers are one of the hallmarks of feminist activism in India.

Organized Sector. About 6 percent of all employed women work in the organized sector, which, like the unorganized one, contains a diverse group of industrial, professional, and service workers in the government and in private industry where ten or more persons are employed. It is more highly regulated than the unorganized sector. Women's proportion of jobs in this sector has remained constant, though employment in industry and mines has declined. A number of authors (Mehta, 172–79; Kishwar and Vanita, 63–68) attribute this decline to protective labor legislation, which is permitted under India's constitution. The state is permitted to make gender-based distinctions in law if it is for the "benefit" of women. Distinctions based on sex, and upheld by the courts, have included single-sex educational institutions, provisions to protect female modesty (such as separate train cars), reservation of women's seats on panchayats, and a series of protective labor regulations.

The Factories Act of 1948, for example, empowers state governments to prohibit employment of women in dangerous occupations; it also requires employers of fifty or more women to provide crèches. Modest maternity benefits are in theory provided through the Employer's State Insurance Act (1948), and various state enactments. Critics of protective legislation argue that it negatively affects female employment by instituting inflexible work rules and increased cost. They also criticize such legislation because serious work hazards remain for male workers, while women are supposedly protected.

The Committee on the Status of Women rejected the theory that protective legislation had, by and large, affected women negatively. In practice the ban on night work only applied to a few industries with multiple shifts; crèches and maternity benefits were "negligible" expenditures, and in some areas were now borne by the state, not employers; and as for mines, the decline began before laws were enacted. The Committee concluded that the decline in women's mining and industrial employment was due to the introduction of capital-intensive, new technologies that displaced women, who were not subsequently retrained, as well as to women's comparatively restricted mobility. The Committee called for quotas for women in industrial training programs, and an extension of the Maternity Benefit Act to cover all industries including agricultural laborers and women in home industry, to be financed jointly by the state and employers (*Report* 72/85).

The Committee also called for the extension and enforcement of the Equal Pay Act, which had been so widely evaded, in its opinion, as to have no effect. Devaki Jain reports of a subsequent case from Maharashtra where women construction workers resisted the enforcement of the Equal Remuneration Act (1976). Contractors had permitted them time off for child care, intermittent hours, and smaller loads. With equal pay legislation, women who could not meet identical employment conditions with men were being replaced (Jain, 160). On the other hand many women now perform identical jobs and get less pay (Kishwar and Vanita, 64–65; Gulati, *Profiles*, 165).

Though the debate has not reached the proportions it assumed in the history of American feminism, particularly in the interwar years, the issue of equal rights versus special benefits is under discussion in India.

The Services and Professions. It is in parts of this sector that some women have gained the benefits of development, though employment patterns are uneven. Low prestige jobs in the clerical services are now seen as suited to women; among women professionals, teaching and medicine are the largest categories of employment. Constitutional guarantees of non-discrimination have assisted in this process, as has women's education, changing values among the urban middle class, and expansion of parts of India's economy (see *Report*, 75–79). About 17 percent of all professional, technical, and related workers in India are women.

Not that this group of professionals is without problems. Women teachers are the largest group (three-quarters of all female professionals) but they are disproportionately clustered at the low prestige, primary school level (Trembour). Women doctors are in a high prestige occupation, their advance assisted by seclusion norms. Many women (and their families) prefer female doctors for female patients to satisfy the norms of female modesty. Many women doctors, like other professionals, are reported to feel there is comparatively little discrimination against women in Indian salary and promotion, compared with the United States. However, many women doctors do not practice their profession (Lebra). Other important areas of professional employment are nurses (Lebra), lawyers (Everett), and social workers, 30 percent of whom are women. As in the United States, women professionals are disproportionately concentrated in the nurturing fields.

Though middle-class families under economic pressures and with rising aspirations have broadened their attitudes toward married women's employment, many investigators still report a "big gap between the changes in attitudes and behaviour patterns of the educated urban middle class women and those of their husbands and inlaws" (Kapur, 29). The Committee on the Status of Women reported a continuing deep ambivalence about the gainful employment of women, and a widespread belief that working women are bad mothers and housewives. Women as a consequence suffer guilt over the supposed neglect of their children. Some reports continue to suggest that husbands and in-laws fail to assist the working wife, and that she is sometimes withdrawn from the workforce when economic circumstances permit it (*Report*, 31–33; Kapur, 27–28; Mies, passim; Blumberg and Dwaraki, passim).

Health, Longevity, and Family Planning

While overall statistics show a general decline in women's health and longevity, chances are that there are sharp differences between the poor majority and women in the better-off social groups. The negative impact of change is not uniform. In 1921–23 the life expectancy for both sexes was 26 years. By 1981 it was 47.1 years for men and 45.6 years for women. More telling perhaps is the comparative sex ratio. In 1901 there were 972 women for every 1,000 men; in 1981 the ratio was 935 per 1,000. In most parts of the world, the sex ratio is tilted in women's favor. In the United States, for example, it is 950 males for every 1,000 females. We shall examine explanations for what is literally a life and death issue, an issue that Indian feminists see as one of their highest priorities.

Readings for Students
Hobson, Sarah. *Family Web,* Chaps. 10, 11, 14, 15.
Horowitz, Berny, and Madhu Kishwar. "Family Life: The Unequal Deal." In *In Search of Answers,* 69–103.
Khan, Mumtaz Ali, and Noor Ayesha, *Status of Rural Women in India,* Chap. 4, "Participation in Social Organisations."
Report, 118–26.

Readings for Instructors
Mazumdar, Vina. "Women, Development and Public Policy." In *Women and Development,* 39–54.
McCarthy, Florence E. et al. "Program Assessment and Development of Women's Programs: The Views of Action Workers." In *Women and Development,* 355–78.
Miller, Barbara D. *The Endangered Sex: Neglect of Female Children in Rural North India.* Ithaca, N.Y.: Cornell University Press, 1981.
Singh, K.P. *Status of Women and Population Growth in India.* New Delhi: Munshiram Manoharlal Pubs., 1979.
Towards Equality, Chap. 8.

Lecture Topics

Health and Longevity (*Towards Equality;* Khan and Ayesha). Inadequate access to health care is a general problem for the urban poor and in many rural areas in India. Shortages of medical supplies and equipment, overcrowding, and distance and inaccessibility of facilities are major problems. The distribution of resources favors urban areas, which have 90 percent of the hospital beds and two-thirds of the doctors and nurses. Yet 80 percent of the population is rural. Within this context of poverty and shortage, women's secondary status in the family determines their access to medical care. Women's relative powerlessness in the family and in the broader culture is reflected in data on utilization of medical facilities. Overall, twice as many hospital beds are provided for men than women. Despite an extremely high maternal mortality rate there is a chronic shortage of maternal (and child) health care services (*Towards Equality*, 8.38–8.49).

Yet if objective need were the determining factor, women would have claim to the majority of medical resources, for they have higher rates of physical and mental illness, "the result of malnutrition, frequent pregnancies and anemia." It is customary in Indian households "for the women to serve the family first and then to eat whatever is left." In poorer families this often results in greater malnutrition for women than men (*Towards Equality*, 8.27–8.35). A high fertility rate, resulting from a low age of marriage and underutilization of family planning, puts an additional burden on poor women, affecting both mental and physical health. "Pregancy wastage" (stillbirths and abortions) are reported as high as 30 percent among low-income groups, a reflection of maternal malnutrition (*Towards Equality*, 8.3).

Despite this desperate need for medical attention and improved nutrition, the percentage of males getting medical treatment is higher than women. Rules of modesty also inhibit women from seeking medical advice when it is available, and there is a shortage of women doctors in rural areas. The Primary Health Centre, the lowest unit in the rural arm of the Health Service, serves on average a population of sixty to seventy thousand with only one female doctor and four Auxiliary Nurse-Midwives (ANMs). As a result women tend not to seek medical attention until the point of collapse (*Towards Equality*, 8.27, 8.38).

While few texts offer a sustained coverage on the subject of health care, the issues appear in several broader studies. Khan and Ayesha include a good village survey of the low participation rates of women in the local Primary Health Centre. Only 42 percent of women overall used it; this declined to 25 percent among Muslim women. Women perceived the mostly male staff as arrogant and indifferent. Horowitz and Kishwar document how resources are distributed and decisions made in the families of small farmers and agricultural laborers in a Punjabi village. They include a detailed analysis of food distribution in the family, document arduous work during malnourished pregnancies, and a high rate of neglected serious illnesses within a general analysis of discrimination within the household. Finally, Sarah Hobson's description of family life in a remote village in Karnataka includes several chapters on health and reproductive crises.

Family Planning (*Towards Equality*, Mazumdar, McCarthy, Singh). *Towards Equality* asserts that childbearing, for the majority of Indian women, is "more a health hazard than a natural function" (315). Both for the interests of individual women and for national economic development in general, the Committee recommends that the fertility rate be lowered. (India's total fertility rate from 1975–80 was 5.3 compared with 1.8 for the United States.[42] Total fertility rate refers to the average number of children that would be born to each woman in a nation if she were to live through her childbearing years (15–49) bearing children at the current rate.) Yet family planning has foundered, and *Towards Equality* (8.56–8.88) and Vina Mazumdar suggest why.

Fertility behavior is very complex, and may well differ in different cultures and among different socioeconomic groups, though this has only recently become apparent to researchers. Attempts have been made to correlate fertility (and use of family planning) with socioeconomic group, women's education, women's workforce participation, infant mortality, and ability to control fertility decisions, among other factors. The data have often been contradictory, and the causal interrelationships obscure. However, within the context of India's experience with family planning, certain conclusions are emerging.

Family planning advocates, including feminist groups, have often argued their cause in terms of raising woman's status by releasing her from reproductive bondage. The causal relationship, however, may well be the reverse, that is, once woman's status is improved through a higher age of marriage, increased education, and better waged employment, then family planning is more likely to be adopted (*Towards Equality*, 8.56–8.57).

Vina Mazumdar suggests that there are important class variables in the adoption of family planning. It has been highly successful in the educated urban middle class. In poorer families, where children join the workforce early and are regarded as an economic asset, there is resistance to family planning especially when infant mortality is high and children's life expectancies low. A reduction of the infant mortality rate and improved child care is thus crucial to any overall family planning program. In the more affluent lower middle class, however, where women have often been newly withdrawn from the workforce, high fertility may be a result not of infant mortality but a compensatory strategy to maintain women's value through a socially acceptable channel: childbearing.

Mazumdar's argument receives indirect substantiation from K.P. Singh's attempts to correlate education and employment with fertility. He found less-educated homemakers and women in the paid labor force all had roughly the same mean fertility rates (4.5–4.6 children). Singh believes that the prestige of education and work affect fertility, but he concedes that there are many other variables.

Family planning has had only modest success in India despite a government commitment since 1952. Initially the focus was on education about contraception; then in the 1970s there was a "clinical approach" involving massive propaganda, mass sterilization camps, paid "motivators," and financial incentives to acceptors. There was considerable public backlash, especially in the wake of abuses. *Towards Equality* and Mazumdar suggest deep-rooted causes for the failure of family planning in India. Schemes have neglected maternal and child health services, and it is this, rather than traditional values or ignorance, that is the primary stumbling block. *Towards Equality* advocates an integrated approach of providing health care, upgrading nutrition, and increased literacy. Florence McCarthy et al. suggest an additional necessity—the provision of safe birth control devices with adequate follow-up. In a report from Bangladesh, these authors found that resistance to family planning was not born of ignorance or lack of motivation: "Village women openly discuss family planning" (McCarthy, 363). But severe health problems among women who had received intrauterine devices had naturally made women very wary, a problem that is also discussed in *Towards Equality* (8.69).

Female Infant Mortality (Miller). Maternal mortality, generally poorer health, and malnutrition account in part for India's lower sex ratio of women to men. A high female infant mortality rate also plays a part. Barbara Miller has documented female child neglect in northwest India, showing that it occurs more in the upper classes than the lower ones. Poorer nutrition and health care are given to daughters, and less love and nurturance. Miller attributes this to burdensome dowry expenses, and to the economic marginality of women in the rural upper classes. Though some reviewers have questioned Miller's emphasis on labor force participation, few have disputed her overall findings about infant and child mortality.

Muslim Women in Modern India

The almost overwhelming focus of studies of women in modern India is on the Hindu community. Yet about 11 percent of the population of independent India is Muslim, amounting to over 70 million people. Much of the material on women and development that we have examined is of relevance to the study of Muslim women, many of whom have suffered the effects of "negative development" in an even more intense form when literacy rates, workforce participation, and political participation are considered. Muslim women have remained even more isolated from the benefits of development than Hindu women. We have made occasional references to Muslim women in the preceding discussion. The following is a short supplementary treatment. The reading list is intended to augment earlier titles and contains additional works without repeating earlier relevant references.

Readings for Students and Instructors
Ahmad, Imtiaz. *Family, Kinship and Marriage Among Muslims in India*. Delhi: Manohar Pubs., 1976.
Bhatty, Zarina. "Muslim Women in Uttar Pradesh: Social Mobility and Direction of Change." Chap. 8 in *Women in Contemporary India*.
Brijbhushan, Jamila. *Muslim Women: In Purdah and Out of It*. New Delhi: Vikas Pub. House, 1980.
Haniff, Niesha Z. "Muslim Women and the Minority Mentality." Chap. 7 in *Modernization and Social Change Among Muslims in India,* edited by Imtiaz Ahmad. New Delhi: Manohar Pubs., 1983.
Jeffery, Patricia. *Frogs in a Well: Indian Women in Purdah*. London: Zed Press, 1979.
Lateef, Shahida. "Modernization in India and the Status of Muslim Women." Chap. 6 in *Modernization and Social Change Among Muslims*.
A'La Maududi, Abdul. *Purdah and the Status of Women in Islam*. Translated and edited by Al-Ash'ari. Lahore: Islamic Pubs., 1972.
Menon, M. Indu. *Status of Muslim Women in India: A Case Study of Kerala*. New Delhi: Uppal Pub. House, 1981.
Rahman, Fazlur. "The Status of Women in Islam: A Modernist Interpretation." Chap. 11 in *Separate Worlds*.
Towards Equality, Appendix II, "Report of the Survey on Status of Women in a Minority Community."

Lecture Topics

Class Differences in the Muslim Community (Bhatty, Lateef). As with Hindu women there are fundamental class differences among Muslim women which must be borne in mind in assessing the impact of development. The Muslim community in South Asia is divided into the Ashraf, or upper social strata, which claim foreign origin and the Ajlaf (commoners), mostly converts who, contrary to the spirit of Islam, are regarded as social inferiors. Non-Ashraf women have greater freedom of movement, and may work in the fields or in craft industries alongside their husbands. Some act as petty traders selling items to upper-class women in purdah. Like lower-caste women, this comparative freedom makes them not as "respectable." In a process analogous to that in the Hindu community, women in the urban, Westernized element of the Ashraf have entered colleges and professions, while some upwardly mobile Ajlaf are becoming more conservative in gender relations, copying traditional Ashraf norms. Workforce participation among upper-class women has been affected by purdah both in rates of entry into employment and the sort of jobs considered suitable. Working-class Muslim women, like their Hindu counterparts, have experienced job displacement in the development process.

Resistance to Social Change? Commentators are agreed that Muslim women's educational participation rates have lagged behind Hindu women's. They have also not been as active politically: there have only been seven Muslim women in parliament since 1952, and three were nominated rather than elected. Workforce participation rates are also lower for Muslim women. Purdah practices have played an important role in shaping these responses throughout the Islamic world. However, there are also factors unique to India.

A common explanation is the uneasy minority position of Muslims in India after the trauma of the subcontinent's partition into India and Pakistan in 1947. Lateef argues, for example, that a disproportionate number of the urban immigrants to Pakistan were young, educated professionals leaving a preponderance of poorer Muslims behind. The gap between the elite and the poor is enormous, and Muslim political parties play on minority fears of engulfment by traditionalist religious and social appeals in order to protect the survival of the Muslim community (Lateef, 163–65; see also Brijbhushan). A statement of the fundamentalist position may be found in Maududi's work, which has had a highly retrograde impact on the position of women in Pakistan, thanks to General Zia al Haq's backing of Maududi's views on the "Islamic" basis of purdah, his opposition to "promiscuous mingling" of men and women in coeducation, and his rigid interpretations of family law. Maududi's views are less influential among Indian Muslims, though there is an Indian branch of the movement, Jamaat-i-Islami-i-Hind. The reformist counterattack can be found in Fazlur Rahman's essay. More on the fundamentalist–reformist debate can also be found in Chapter 11, "Women in the Islamic Middle East and North Africa," below.

Reform of Muslim family law in India has been hampered by the fear of successive governments of being accused of "Hindu majority meddling," with an accompanying fundamentalist backlash. Reform of Muslim personal law in India has consequently lagged behind that of many majority Islamic states, despite a constitutional commitment to the equality of all citizens. Polygamy remains legal in India as does divorce by repudiation, and unequal inheritance laws remain in effect (*Towards Equality*, Chap. 4). The slow pace of change is reinforced by the fact that Muslim jurists are bitterly divided among varying legal schools (Shafi, Hanafi, Ismaili, and Ithna Ashari). The "onus of change" has been placed on the community itself (Lateef, 181; and Brijbhushan, Chap. 10).

Yet Muslim women in India should not be viewed in a one-dimensional way. The diversity of Muslim women's lives and outlooks may be gauged through three sets of readings. Jamila Brijbhushan, a Western-educated writer from a Syed family presents a critical indictment of traditionalism from a feminist perspective. (Syeds claim to be directly descended from the Prophet Muhammad through his daughter Fatima. They are the most prestigious of the Ashrafs.) Patricia Jeffery's study of women in strict purdah, self-described as "frogs in a well" because their horizons are literally circumscribed by the sky above, presents the other end of the spectrum. Jeffery describes the women of a community of custodians of a religious shrine in Old Delhi. Niesha Haniff's study is from the same city, but in this instance of poor Muslim working women. She shows them to be self-confident, observing only minimal aspects of purdah, and devoid of any defensive "minority mentality." Haniff, Lateef, and the Committee on the Status of Women all see evidence of Muslim women poised for change. Whether such a movement will develop political force remains to be seen.

Modern Indian Women's Movement

Let us re-examine the whole question, all the questions. Let us take nothing for granted. Let us not only redefine ourselves, our role, our image—but also the kind of society we want to live in.
Inaugural Issue, *Manushi*, January 1979

The 1970s were an era of social protest in India. Drought, famine, dislocations caused by the increasing commercialization of agriculture, rising unemployment, rising food and energy prices, rising violence, and shortages of fuel for cooking, led many people to question the existing sociopolitical order. In the midst of this decade came the publication of the *Report* of the Committee on the Status of Women with its devastating detailing of the eroding conditions of life for the majority of Indian women. The publication coincided with the opening of the United Nations Decade on Women. It is in this context that the Indian women's movement was reborn. We have refrained from using the word "feminist" as an overall description of the objectives of what is a diffuse and multifaceted movement. Some urban-based groups of Western-educated women do use this term. Others, and Madhu Kishwar, editor of *Manushi* ("Woman"), is one, no longer use the term, feeling it imposes a set of Western definitions (and ideological cleavages among women) that stand in the way of perceiving Indian realities. Terms like Stree Shakti ("women's power") and Stree Sangathana ("women's organization") are commonly used. Many of the groups working on women's issues (left-wing activists, church groups, civil libertarians) have a broad agenda. In some cases the initiative on women's issues has been taken by left-wing men. As Madhu Kishwar describes it, unlike in the United States, "The split of women's movements from left movements has not taken place. The struggle goes on internally" ("Woman-power," 17–18).

Readings for Students

Jain, Devaki. *Women's Quest for Power: Five Indian Case Studies.* Sahidabad, U. P: Vikas Pub. House, 1980.

Kishwar, Madhu, and Ruth Vanita, eds. *In Search of Answers: Indian Women's Voices from Manushi.*

Lateef, Shahida. "The Indian Women's Movement and National Development: An Overview." Chap. 8 in *The Extended Family.*

Omvedt, Gail, *We Will Smash This Prison.*

Readings for Instructors

Bald, Suresht Renjen. "From Satyartha Prakash to *Manushi:* An Overview of the 'Women's Movement' in India." East Lansing: Women in International Development, Michigan State University, Working Paper #23, April 1983.

Basu, Amrita. "Two Faces of Protest: Alternative Forms of Social Mobilization in West Bengal and Maharashtra." Chap. 9 in *The Extended Family.*

Bhatt, Ela R. "Organising Self-Employed Women Workers." In
   Women and Development, 425–33.
Butalia, Urvashi. "Indian Women and the New Movement."
   Women's Studies International Forum 8, no. 2 (1985): 131–33.
   Special issue: The UN Decade for Women: An International
   Evaluation, edited by Georgiana Ashworth.
Desai, Neera et al. "Women's Studies and the Social Sciences: A
   Report from India." *Women's Studies International: A Supplement to the Women's Studies Quarterly* 3 (April 1984): 2–6.
   Special issue: Focus on India.
Everett, Jana. "Women and Political Leadership." Chap. 10 in
   Women and Work in India.
Report.
Sebstad, Jennefer. "Struggle and Success: Building a Strong,
   Independent Union for Poor Women Workers in India."
   Women's Studies International 3 (April 1984): 7–11.
Shah, Kalpana. *Women's Liberation and Voluntary Action*. Delhi:
   Ajanta Pubs., 1984.
"Urvashi Interviewed." *Spare Rib* 146 (September 1984): 53–55.
"Womanpower in India (Interview with Madhu Kishwar)." *Trouble and Strife* 4 (Winter 1984): 17–21.

Lecture Topics

General Overview (Bald, Everett, Shah, Lateef). Though an all-India lobbying organization with a common agenda has yet to emerge, there has been a proliferation of local groups, research units on women, "self-help" and single-issue groups, and among those women—and men—who care about such things, a ferment of ideas that call into question many of the presuppositions of the earlier social reform era. Some Indian feminists are reconceptualizing the terms of the debate on women in ways that might prove to have relevance to women in other nations.

Some of the women's organizations from the nationalist era, most notably the National Council of Women in India and the All-India Women's Conference continue to exist, chiefly as deliberative and social welfare bodies. Kalpana Shah's study of the AIWC's Surat branch shows it as having little fire. Its social welfare activities (hostels, craft training, child welfare, and the like) are routinized and professionalized, and it has lost lobbying force. Its members are upper class with little understanding of the circumstances or worldview of the disadvantaged. More recently, however, the AIWC has spoken out nationally on development issues and dowry deaths among other things.

The newer movement rejects a top-down, welfare-oriented approach. Shahida Lateef writes that "there has been an instinctive realization on the part of new women leaders that the Indian women's movement cannot advance, and women become a pressure group, without the involvement of women at all economic and social levels" (199). The urgent issues are preeminently issues of survival—workforce participation (including credit and child care), health, basic education, and violence against women. This practicality is reflected in the academic wing of the movement: It is significant that the preeminent centers of women's studies in India have focused on women in economic development issues, both theoretical and applied. The new generation of researchers, while rigorous in their academic standards, are also often advocates. They are, in Hanna Papanek's words, "convinced that women face injustice and that something must be done about it," and there is a commitment to studies of the economically disadvantaged.[43]

Organizational Modes and Ideologies. Suresht Bald sees women's groups in India falling into several different clusters: autonomous, affiliated, and self-help groups. They operate from a wide variety of ideological frameworks, from humanitarian to explicitly feminist, and from Gandhian to Marxist. There is no sustained, in-depth overall analysis of the contemporary Indian women's movement, but aspects of it have been studied more carefully.

"Self-Help" Groups (Bald, Jain, Bhatt). Many of the new women's groups in India have an intensely practical orientation. Unlike the earlier top-down social welfare efforts, these groups seek to link disadvantaged women together horizontally to achieve common goals. Devaki Jain has analyzed five such groups, which operate with varying degrees of success: cooperative milk producers in Gujarat, the Madhubani folk painters, Bombay housewives marketing a dried snack, women of Manipur who patrol the streets for alcoholics, and the Self-Employed Women's Association (SEWA) of Ahmedabad.

The best known and one of the most successful of these

groups is SEWA, and organization of women vendors and casual wage-earners, working in the unorganized sector. Heavily influenced by the Gandhian philosophy of self-reliance and self-help, it offers members financial credit and social welfare services (legal aid, maternity and widows' benefits), and provides generally supportive linkages with other women. Devaki Jain's study led her to conclude that simply earning income did not necessarily guarantee these women an improved status in their families, or in society's perception of them, but that "one of the levers to this emancipation is the strength women gain through participation in non-family association" (4). SEWA is able to add collective strength to women's needs as women—help with crèches, help in cases of wife beating—as well as deal with more general issues like access to credit and stopping police harrassment. While SEWA provides the practical help poor women need,and draws women from the community into leadership roles, Ela Bhatt, its General Secretary, also stresses that separate organizations alone are not enough: "The poor women and men should be effectively united in one organisation to be able to combat with and resist the tremendous powers of the vested interests" (432). This desire to bridge both class and gender differences to build a more just society is characteristic of many Indian feminists today. It can be a difficult goal: SEWA's success through non-traditional union organizing and dynamic female leaders so threatened its parent body, the male-dominated Textile Labor Association, that it was recently ousted (Sebstad).

Autonomous Women's Groups (Bald, Omvedt, Kishwar and Vanita, "Womanpower"). Local groups, mobilizing around specific issues such as dowry deaths, rape, and media sexploitation of women, have sprung up in many cities, towns, and campuses in recent years. They are an urban phenomenon. In Hyderabad, for example, the Progressive Organisation of Women (see Omvedt and Bald), primarily a group of well-educated young women, was galvanized into action by dowry deaths and "Eve-teasing" (street harassment of women). Police violence, including police rape, has also been an important organizing issue (see Kishwar and Vanita, 186–202). Whether coordination among these groups will emerge on an all-India basis is uncertain. There has also been some criticism of the urban groups for class bias in focusing on dowry violence while ignoring the oppression of poverty and neglect in the countryside (see "Womanpower" and Butalia, 132).

Affiliated Women's Groups (Everett, Bald, Kishwar and Vanita, Basu, Omvedt, Report). This heterogeneous collection of women's caucuses—informal and formal—includes women's wings of political parties, trade union women, civil liberties groups, church organizations, and left-oriented social action groups. Many of these groups have also been active in anti-dowry agitation.

The best studied of the affiliated women's groups are those sponsored by the left. Amrita Basu provides a critical look at how the Communist Party of India (Marxist) in Bengal has mobilized, or failed to mobilize, women. Despite a high level of women's political activism in Bengal in the 1940s she sees a degeneration of the party's women's branch into a centralized, political support service that sponsors vote drives and general social and recreational activities, while failing to articulate women's interests and demands. Indeed, all the political parties in India have women's wings and have been criticized for a similar failure (*Report*, 110–12).

Where left-wing groups have mobilized women around specific economic grievances—as with the self-help groups, what seems to work is a practical economic survival orientation—the response has been impressive. In Maharashtra, for example, two women activists from the Socialist Party and the CPI(M) organized women into resistance against price rises in 1973, though the political momentum declined during the Emergency (Basu).

Rural women's struggles among tribal groups, low castes, and the landless poor are captured in some of the available literature. The communist and socialist left have been most active in these sectors. Omvedt's studies in rural Maharashtra have already been mentioned (see "Political Participation" above). The magazine *Manushi* makes a conscientious effort to cover the struggles of poor women, recognizing that the gains Indian women have made have been restricted to the middle and upper classes. Madhu Kishwar characterizes these rural struggles as having a common theme: "scarcity and restrictions of use of fuel, water, forest rights, and demands for minimum wages and implementation of food for work programmes, especially during times of distress, have been the starting point of many rural struggles. Once women are galvanised in large numbers during the course of these struggles, they inevitably raise specific issues concerning their own oppression and powerlessness" (36).

The Search for an Indian "Feminist" Ideology. The Indian women's movement is characterized by wide ideological diversity.

Some groups, such as SEWA, operate at least in part from a Gandhian framework, and others from varying socialist and Marxist positions. Conservatives, such as the All-India Women's Conference, may still argue their case in the traditional terms of improving motherhood. Others, for example the women in the Amul dairy project studied by Devaki Jain, may simply seek a practical solution to the problem at hand with no particular ideological framework beyond the need to "co-operate." Still others, like the Committee on the Status of Women, argue their case as one of equity, linking it with national goals of economic growth.

Among those who have or do embrace the term "feminist" there is a strong desire to follow an Indian path. Some commentators have tried to pigeonhole *Manushi* as "radical feminist" or "socialist feminist," and in some respects it would fall within either Western feminist category. In its drive to "examine everything" it has published probing critiques of the Indian family, asserting that "for too many women in India, their own fathers, brothers, and husbands act like virtual prison guards." It questions role socialization, and any aspect of internalized submission to male authority. It questions the earlier espousal of women's rights by men for it "often leads to overmuch dependence on male approval, with a consequent raising of issues within parameters defined and found acceptable by male political leaders." At the same time *Manushi* questions the fundamental socioeconomic structure in which 80 percent of India's resources are controlled by 20 percent of the population (Kishwar and Vanita, 230, 258, 27, 273), thus considering gender and class issues simultaneously.

Yet *Manushi* and others do not argue for a transformation in gender relations in Western modernist terms. As Madhu Kishwar says, "We must learn to begin with more respect for traditions which people hold dear," following in this respect the path trodden earlier by Sarojini Naidu. While condemning excessive self-denial, there is also a recognition of what is positive in this aspect of women's culture: "(The) urge to submerge one's narrow interests . . . is not, in itself, to be condemned" (Kishwar and Vanita, 46). There is a desire to avoid the perils of excessive Western individualism and to recognize that the family, for example, can be supportive as well as oppressive. There is also a conscious effort to draw on Indian symbolism. Urvashi Butalia, the founder of India's first feminist book publishing company, has chosen "Kali" as its name: "She is the only Goddess in Hinduism who is Black . . . she is very powerful, very dynamic, and very sexual as well . . . she is seen usually in the destructive aspect but . . . she destroys in order to recreate the world" ("Urvashi," 55).

Thus far the resurgent movement has avoided the more acerbic sexual politics that marked at least some aspects of the U.S. scene in the late 1960s. Parts of the press and media have been supportive and have covered the women's movement sympathetically. Butalia attributes this to the relative liberalism of the male elite, and the legitimizing presence of some older women who have taken part in nationalist struggles. She also suggests this may have "influenced the 'middle of the road' path the movement was to take" (131). The size and communications difficulties within India present an enormous challenge, as do vast caste/class differences. The newly formed Indian Association for Women's Studies attempts to bring together teachers, students, activists, voluntary workers, and government officials to increase awareness of the socioeconomic, political, as well as attitudinal obstacles to improving the status of women. All are signs of a rebirth of a women's movement. The challenge, however, is as vast as the subcontinent itself. What India does not lack is an imaginative, articulate, and committed new generation of women's leaders who are conceptualizing issues and responses in new ways.

Discussion Questions

1. Discuss the role of law in securing social change in the status of women. Is it useless or useful? Would your answer vary from the Indian to the U.S. context? Why or why not?

2. Karlekar in *Poverty and Women's Work* (11) accuses Western feminists of minimizing the fact that women exploit other women—and men—in every society. Is this an accurate view of Western feminism? What examples of exploitation by women are to be found in India? The United States?

3. In arguing for separate legislative seats for women, Lotika Sarkar and Vina Mazumdar argued that "The application of theoretical principles of equality in the context of unequal situations only intensifies inequalities, because equality in such situations merely means privileges for those who have them already and not for those who need them." Discuss the accuracy and implications of this in terms of political and economic structures.

4. The following exerpt from the *Report of the Conference on the Role of Women in Development of Non-Aligned and Other*

Developing Countries, Baghdad, 6–13 May 1979 is quoted approvingly by Indian women's studies scholars in a recent article (see Neera Desai et al., 6): "The roots of women's oppressive and unequal position lie deep, within poverty, inequitous utilisation and distribution of resources and power that characterise the present world order, as well as within oppressive social structures, and obsolete, irrational attitudes, that thrive on inequalities of all types." Debate the completeness and accuracy of this analysis in the Indian context, and in the context of the United States.

5. Where, and to what degree, does tradition survive in the lives of Western-educated Indian women? What has changed?

6. In what ways does your life seem similar to or different from that of Western-educated Indian women? Consider this question in terms of the theoretical issues discussed earlier—male dominance, power in domestic versus public domains, role socialization.

7. Discuss the problems of Indian female college students as compared to those in the United States. How do concerns differ or appear similar?

8. In any of the studies you have read, are village women the passive, obedient creatures that religious orthodoxy presents as ideal?

9. What problems, if any, do upper-caste/class Indian women share with lower-caste/class women? Do either have problems similar to those experienced by American women, distinguishing by race and class? Is there a common "sisterhood," or not?

10. Are village women more oppressed by sex, caste, or class? Urban women working in the unorganized sector? Women from the Dalit caste? College students? How are you measuring "oppression"? Can it be measured?

11. Should Indian planners—or foreign development consultants—induce changes in the Indian village? What have been the results of development projects? How can mistakes be avoided? Are women's panchayats the answer?

12. Many development experts from the West place great

hope in the democratic vote as a method of changing the lives of the destitute over time. What is your conclusion about the vote's efficacy, and why? What are the obstacles to democracy? Are there any signs of success?

13. Why do women in Patricia Jeffery's study remain in purdah? What benefits do they derive? What are their support systems? What are the disadvantages of their lives, as they see them? As you see them? Are there any differences in their responses and yours?

14. Evaluate Maududi's argument that purdah honors and protects women, who by nature are physically disadvantaged, and that requiring women to do men's work, far from being liberating, is a hardship; and that by nature women are best suited to motherhood and domesticity. What parallel arguments can be found among Christian fundamentalists? Sociobiologists?

15. Compare and contrast the Indian women's movement in the nationalist era and today in terms of its analysis of the root of women's oppression, its goals, its prescriptions, and its rhetorical style.

16. The Lal Nishan and other leftist and communist efforts at organizing a women's movement represent a break with the earlier nineteenth- and twentieth-century elite reform efforts. Discuss their contention that "without social revolution there can be no women's liberation; without women's liberation social revolution is incomplete" (Omvedt, *Prison*, 57). Is this true for India? The United States?

17. Read the POW Manifesto reprinted by Omvedt. How does its analysis differ or agree with that of NOW in the United States in terms of priorities and its analysis of the sources of women's oppression?

18. What are the difficulties, as Omvedt sees them, of building a self-generating mass movement of women? Why, if you have studied China, was the Communist Party in China successful in its mobilizing and organizing techniques, whereas such efforts in India have largely failed in the long run?

19. Is a moderate or a confrontive form of feminism more likely to induce change in the Indian context?

Notes

1. 1984 World Population Data Sheet, Population Reference Bureau (Washington, D.C., April 1984).

2. For a discussion of India's constitutional experiments to ensure social equality for women, scheduled tribes, and untouchables, see Manju Kumar, *Social Equality* (New Delhi: S. Chand, 1982).

3. K. P. Singh, *Status of Women and Economic Growth in India* (New Delhi: Munshiram Manoharlal Pubs., 1979).

4. Indian Council of Social Science Research, Advisory Committee on Women's Studies, *Critical Issues on the Status of Women: Employment, Health, Education: Suggested Priorities for Action* (1977).

5. M. A. Indra, *The Story of Women in Ancient India* (Benares: Motilal Banarsidass, 1955); Bhagwat Saran Upadhyaya, *Women in Rg Veda*, 3rd ed. rev. (New Delhi: S. Chand, 1974).

6. Phyllis Chesler, "The Amazon Legacy," in *The Politics of Women's Spirituality*, ed. Charlene Spretnak (Garden City, N.Y.: Doubleday Anchor Press, 1982), p. 111.

7. Sarojini Naidu, "The Status of Women in India," in *Women in Modern India: Fifteen Papers by Indian Women Writers*, ed. Evelyn C. Gedge (Bombay, 1929; reprint ed., Westport, Conn.: Hyperion Press, 1976), p. 4.

8. Manisha Roy, *Bengali Women* (Chicago: University of Chicago Press, 1975), Chap. 2; Rama Mehta, *The Western Educated Hindu Woman* (Bombay: Asia Pub. House, 1970), pp. 152–53; and Hemalata Dandekar, "Women Left Behind: Rural Women's Responses to Development in the Deccan Maharashtra, India, 1942–82" (unpublished manuscript, April 1984).

9. Devabrata Bose surveyed modern male villagers on the subject of "karma" and found that only fourteen out of twenty-five gave any credence to it (*Problems of Indian Society*, p. 174). M. N. Srinivas, however, believes these beliefs did strengthen hierarchy (Bose, pp. 10–11). A recent volume edited by Charles E. Keyes and E. Valentine Daniel, *Karma: An Anthropological Inquiry* (Berkeley: University of California Press, 1983) supports the view that "karma" as a notion has practical influence at the village level, while showing techniques villagers use to overrule it (see Susan S. Wadley, "Vrats: Transformers of Destiny").

10. See, for example, Nur Yalman, "The Flexibility of Caste Principles in a Kandyan Community," in *Aspects of Caste in South Asia, Ceylon and North-West Pakistan*, ed. E. R. Leach (Cambridge: Cambridge University Press, 1971), pp. 78–112; and J. H. Hutton, *Caste in India*, 4th ed. (Oxford: Oxford University Press, 1963), Chap. 6.

11. Personal communication, 6 February 1985.

12. Malavika Karlekar, *Poverty and Women's Work: A Study of Sweeper Women in Delhi* (New Delhi: Vikas Pub. House, 1982); Leela Gulati, *Profiles in Female Poverty: A Study of Five Poor Working Women in Kerala* (Delhi: Hindustan Pub. Corp., India, 1981); K. Murali Manohar, *Socio-Economic Status of Indian Women* (Delhi: Seema Pubs., 1983); and Maria Mies, *The Lace Makers of Narsapur: Indian Housewives Produce for the World Market* (London: Zed Press, 1982).

13. Mary Searle-Chatterjee, *Reversible Sex Roles: The Special Case of Benares Sweepers* (Oxford: Pergamon Press, 1981); and Helen Ulrich, "Caste Differences between Brahmin and Non-Brahmin Women in a South Indian Village," in *Sexual Stratification: A Cross-Cultural View*, ed. Alice Schlegel (New York: Columbia University Press, 1977), pp. 41–66.

14. A number of excellent studies of gender and divinity in Hinduism have recently been written. Among them are Stratton Hawley and Donna Marie

Wulff, eds., *The Divine Consort: Radha and the Goddesses of India* (Berkeley: Graduate Theological Union, 1982); Wendy O'Flaherty, *Women, Androgynes and Other Mythical Beasts* (Chicago: University of Chicago Press, 1980); and David Shulman, *Tamil Temple Myths: Sacrifice and Divine Marriage in South Indian Saiva Traditions* (Princeton: Princeton University Press, 1980).

15. A characteristic treatment can be found in Vincent A. Smith, *The Oxford History of India*, ed. Percival Spear, 3rd ed. (Oxford: Clarendon Press, 1964). A more recent example is an important article by Stephen P. Blake, "The Patrimonial-Bureaucratic Empire of the Mughals," *Journal of Asian Studies* 34, no. 1 (November 1979): 77–94, in which the Empire is described as a "patrimonial state" where the ruler "governs on the basis of a personal, traditional authority whose model is the patriarchal family. Patrimonial domination originates in the patriarch's authority over his household . . ." Despite this, the political function of the harem is entirely ignored.

16. B. R. Burg, "Should Christian Women Be Veiled? The Controversy in the Massachusetts Bay Colony 1630–1638," *Pakistan Journal of American Studies* 2, no. 2 (September 1984).

17. Spear, *Oxford History of India*, pp. 339–40; cf. Rekha Misra, *Women in Mughal India: 1526–1748* (Delhi: Munshiram Manoharlal, 1967), pp. 25–29.

18. Quoted in Spear, *Oxford History of India*, p. 240.

19. The literature on this controversial issue is voluminous. For a short explication see Tapan Mukherjee, "Theory of Economic Drain," in *Economic Imperialism*, ed. Kenneth E. Boulding and Tapan Mukherjee (Ann Arbor: University of Michigan Press, 1972).

20. The most recent scholarship on the British impact can be found in N. R. Ray, ed., *Western Colonial Policy* (Calcutta: Institute of Historical Studies, 1981).

21. K. Saradamoni, "Changing Land Relations and Women: A Case Study of Palghat District, Kerala," in *Women and Rural Transformation*, ed. Rekha Mehra and K. Saradamoni (New Delhi: Concept Pub. Co., 1983).

22. David Gilmartin, "Kinship, Women and Politics in Twentieth Century Punjab," Chap. 6 in *The Extended Family: Women and Political Participation in India and Pakistan*, ed. Gail Minault (Delhi: Chanakya; Columbia, Mo.: South Asia Books, 1981).

23. M. S. A. Rao, *Social Movements and Social Transformation: A Study of Two Backward Class Movements in India* (Delhi: Macmillan, 1979); and K. S. Singh, ed., *Tribal Movements in India* (New Delhi: Manohar Pubs., 1982), are two good examples.

24. M. N. Srinivas, *Social Change in Modern India* (Berkeley: University of California Press, 1966), p. 6.

25. One partial exception to the general neglect of gender is Karen I. Leonard, *Social History of an Indian Caste: The Kayasthas of Hyderabad* (Berkeley: University of California Press, 1978), which does note alterations in marriage boundaries and new occupational choices for women.

26. Srinivas, *Social Change in Modern India*, p. 55.

27. See essays in V. C. Joshi, ed., *Rammohan Roy and the Process of Modernisation in India* (New Delhi: Vikas, 1975), and especially that by Sumit Sarkar.

28. In 1911 women constituted 34 percent of the labor force; in 1936 this had declined to 17 percent. *Status of Women in India: Synopsis of the Report of the National Committee on the Status of Women (1971–74)* (New Delhi: The Indian Council of Social Science Research, 1975), p. 61.

29. *Manushi* 7 (1981): 37 has a brief article on Savitribai Phule as part of its

236   AREA STUDIES

admirable effort to expand awareness of early women's rights leaders.

30. The best is T. V. Parvarte, *Mahadev Govind Ranade: A Biography* (Bombay: Asia Pub. House, 1963). Chap. 18 gives a brief account of Ramabai Ranade.

31. Sumit Sarkar, *Bibliographical Survey of Social Reform Movement in the Eighteenth and Nineteenth Centuries* (New Delhi: Indian Council of Historical Research, 1975), p. 54; also see article by Sarkar in Readings for Instructors.

32. Suresht Renjen Bald, "From Satyartha Prakash to *Manushi:* An Overview of the 'Women's Movement' in India" (East Lansing: Michigan State University, Working Papers on Women in International Development, no. 23, April 1983), p. 4.

33. 25 September 1937.

34. Statistics from Lakshmi Misra, *Education of Women in India, 1921–1966* (Bombay and London: Macmillan, 1966), pp. 5, 57, 58.

35. *Young India*, 3 February 1927.

36. Extended treatment of those themes can be found in Judith Brown, *Gandhi's Rise to Power: Indian Politics 1915–1922* (Cambridge: Cambridge University Press, 1972); and D. A. Low, ed., *Congress and the Raj: Facets of the Indian Struggle, 1917–37* (Columbia, Mo.: South Asia Books, 1977), especially articles by Gyanendra Pandey, James Manor, and Robin Jeffrey.

37. The best English biography of Jinnah continues to be Hector Bolitho, *Jinnah: Creator of Pakistan* (London, 1954).

38. Karlekar, *Poverty and Women's Work*, p. 11.

39. Statistics from Manohar, *Socio-Economic Status of Indian Women*, p. 22.

40. See also J. Comaroff, ed., *The Meaning of Marriage Payments* (London: Academic Press, 1980).

41. Margaret Cormack, *The Hindu Woman* (Bombay: Asia Pub. House, 1961).

42. Jyotsna Vaid et al., *South Asian Women at Home and Abroad*, p. 6.

43. Papanek, "False Specialization and the Purdah of Scholarship," *Journal of Asian Studies* 44, no. 1 (November 1984): 131.

CHAPTER SEVEN

WOMEN IN CHINA

Margot I. Duley

In any study of the status of women cross-culturally, Chinese women occupy an important place. Today the Chinese constitute one quarter of humanity; for this reason alone, any course that fails to include China could be accused of imbalance and ethnocentricity. Sheer numbers apart, the example of China is fascinating for other reasons. Classical Chinese civilization, built largely on plow agriculture, illuminates in detail the status of women who are economically marginal to society, and this is an important case study of the anthropological and economic theories examined in the first part of this text. Further, a study of the degree to which the status of women has been altered by the Chinese Communist Revolution provides important insights into the enduring role of cultural attitudes, even when the material basis of a society is transformed.

A helpful bibliographical tool has been published recently, with 1100 annotated entries arranged under 14 topic headings—Bibliographies; Biography; Autobiography and Memoirs; Economics and Employment; Education; Family Planning, Fertility and Health; Female Roles, Social Status and Customs; Feminism and the Women's Movement; General Works and History; Legal Status, Laws, Etc.; Literature and the Arts; Marriage and the Family; Philosophy and Religion; Politics and Government; and Special Issues of Journals:

Wei, Karen T. *Women in China: A Selected and Annotated Bibliography.* Westport, Conn.: Greenwood Press, 1984.

Scholarship on women in China suffers from an imbalance in that far more attention has been paid to women since the Communist revolution than to women in the many centuries of Chinese civilization preceding it. We have attempted to give references to the literature on earlier times that does exist, but the instructor will nevertheless discern that in comparison with, say, India, the historical treatment of women is regrettably sketchy. Two recent volumes that focus on neglected historical perspectives are:

Guisso, Richard W., and Stanley Johansen, eds. *Women in China: Current Directions in Historical Scholarship.* Youngstown, N.Y.: Philo Press, 1981.

Yao, Esther S. Lee. *Chinese Women Past and Present.* Mesquite, Tex.: Ide House, 1983.

For those who want a short introduction to early Chinese history as a whole, we recommend:

Hucker, Charles O. *China to 1850: A Short Introduction.* Stanford: Stanford University Press, 1975.

This chapter is divided into six lectures. The first four examine the status of women in traditional China, relying heavily on anthropological and religious studies. The final two sections survey both change and continuity in the modern period, for which there is far better documentation.

THE CHINESE FAMILY:
SOCIAL AND ECONOMIC FACTORS

In China the family was considered the keystone of civilization. A series of interacting and reinforcing pressures—economic, legal, social, and religious—made the Chinese family the distinguishing feature of traditional Chinese culture. The position of women in China is inextricably linked to the structure of the family.

The Chinese family was recognized as the basic unit of governance in the state, and lineages (related families) frequently controlled entire villages. In the south, clans (lineages with common surnames, who in theory descended from a common ancestor) often controlled a broader geographical area.

Though the Chinese family is in some respects unique in the degree to which it was reinforced by law, custom, religion, and economic necessity, it nevertheless shares similarities with the forms found in other peasant societies. A review of the theoretical literature on agricultural societies (see Chapter 2, above) should therefore be integrated into the lecture.

Readings for Students
Wolf, Margery. *The House of Lim: A Study of a Chinese Farm Family.* New York: Appleton-Century-Crofts, 1968.

Yang, C. L. "Religion in the Integration of the Family." Chap. 2 in *Religion in Chinese Society.* Berkeley: University of California Press, 1967.

Readings for Instructors
Baker, Hugh D. R. *Chinese Family and Kinship.* London: Macmillan, 1979.

Boserup, Ester. *Woman's Role in Economic Development.* New York: St. Martin's Press, 1970.

Thompson, Lawrence G. *Chinese Religion: An Introduction.* Belmont, Cal.: Dickerson Pub. Co., 1969.

Wolf, Margery. *Women and the Family in Rural Taiwan.* Stanford: Stanford University Press, 1972.

Yang, C. L. *The Chinese Family in Rural Taiwan.* Cambridge: Massachusetts Institute of Technology, 1959.

Lecture Topics

The Ideal Chinese Family (Yang, Chap. 8; Baker, Chap. 1). The ideal Chinese family, or *fang,* encompassed five generations of male descendents living in one household. Although this ideal was rarely achieved because of death, family conflicts, poverty, or married sons' separation into households of their own, filial bonds and obligations remained strong. So too did kinship ties along the paternal lineage for three generations (i.e., between brothers' great grandchildren).

Patriarchal Control (Baker, Chap. 1). The Chinese family had a strong authoritarian character and was stratified according to sex and age. It was patriarchal, patrilineal, and patrilocal, and the subordination of women, who were in essence outsiders in their affinal family, was essential for its smooth functioning. Inheritance followed the male line: all sons received equal shares, while daughters normally did not inherit. Women were perpetual legal minors, passing from the control of their fathers to their husbands, and upon widowhood to their sons.

The Family as a Unit of Governance (Baker, Chaps. 5, 6). The Confucian state regarded the family as a "mutual responsibility group" in which all were held responsible for the behavior of the individual. This legal underpinning was a powerful force of social control.

The authority of male patriarchs was enshrined in law. A son who struck a parent was subject to decapitation. The father, however, could freely beat his son for a wide variety of offenses (gambling, laziness, impiety). A wife was subject to flogging if she beat her husband; a husband was punished only if injury resulted. Parents-in-law were not liable for wife beating if they could show cause. A wife who ran away could be beaten or sold if caught. In short, there was strong legal support for hierarchy based on sex and age.

Ancestor Worship and Social Control (Baker, Chap. 4; Thompson, Chap. 3). Ancestor worship provided another powerful reinforcement of family authority. The Chinese saw individual lives imbedded in a matrix of past and future. The individual existed only by virtue of ancestors, and in turn descendents existed through the current generation. Ancestors lived on in the spirit world, and required earthly belongings for their maintenance. Goods such as houses, horses, and clothes were transferred by burning paper replicas; and ancestors were thought to be able to extract the essence of food offerings. Ancestors bestowed blessings on those who pleased them and punishments on those who brought shame or displeasure. Those who died heirless, or whose line became extinct, were destined to wander as "hungry ghosts" and eventually be extinguished.

Women could only achieve ancestral status through their husbands and male children. In death, the fate of a woman's spirit rested upon its succor by male descendents. The lifelong spinster faced a dismal afterlife. Nuns duplicated family ancestral rites by claiming an ancestral line of former nuns. For most women, however, rebellion from male control, even if it could have been conceived of, imperiled existence both in this life and the next.

The Economic Basis of the Chinese Family and the Status of Women (Boserup, Chaps. 1, 4). The bases of Chinese agriculture were plow agriculture in the north and rice cultivation in the south. Female participation in productive labor was low, particularly in the north, though the labor intensive demands of rice cultivation meant the labor value of women in the south was higher, and practices such as footbinding were less prevalent. There were, however, important class distinctions in women's labor participation: among poor families women worked in the fields, even in the north, and textile production in the home was part of the sexual division of labor. Population density was high; fragmentation of land into uneconomic units needed to be avoided. An extended family with male kinship ties both ensured adequate labor and discouraged fragmentation.

The status of women paralleled that of women in other agricultural societies. The subordination of women was a necessity for the system to succeed, for women were a threat to male kinship ties. If the bond between wife and husband were too strong, or if a woman retained ties with her own family, the patrilineal extended family might fragment.

Discussion Questions

1. Compare the sources of patriarchal control in the traditional family of China, India, the Middle East, and the West.

2. Discuss the reasons why women accepted their status within the traditional Chinese family.

3. To what degree was male individualism or individual achievement possible or desired in traditional Chinese society? How does your answer to this question shape your conceptualization of women's status in traditional China?

4. In India the ideological and social sanctions for caste and sex hierarchies are similar. Is this true for age and sex hierarchies in China? Is it true for race and sex hierarchies in the West?

PHILOSOPHICAL AND RELIGIOUS SANCTIONS FOR FEMALE SUBORDINATION

Three philosophical traditions interacted in China to produce complex views of women's nature: Confucianism, Taoism, and Buddhism. As with India, though the historical evidence for

China is less well documented, there is evidence that the prevailing attitudes toward woman's nature hardened over time, roughly paralleling the growth of a bureaucratic and stratified state system with an agricultural economic base. H. G. Creel's important study of Chinese state formation in the Western Chou period (twelfth and thirteenth centuries B.C.) contains many references to the political roles of women. From the sixth century, however, Confucian theory permeated both Chinese political theory and the way in which all social relationships (including ruler and subject, father and son, husband and wife) were conceptualized. It formed the philosophical basis of the state. Taoism and Buddhism were the religions of private, individual inspiration tolerated by the Confucian state. At times they formed the ideological basis for political rebellion. All three traditions had views on the nature and place of women which formed a syncretic whole.

Readings for Students
Bullough, Vern L. *The Subordinate Sex,* Chap. 10. Chicago: University of Illinois Press, 1973.

Ortner, Sherry B. "Is Female to Male as Nature Is to Culture?" In *Woman, Culture, and Society,* edited by Michelle Zimbalist Rosaldo and Louise Lamphere. Stanford: Stanford University Press, 1974.

Smith, Huston. *The Religions of Man,* Chaps. 3, 4, 5. New York: Harper and Row, 1959.

Readings for Instructors
Ames, Roger T. "Taoism and the Androgynous Idea." In *Women in China,* 21–45.
Creel, H. G. *The Origins of Statecraft in China.* (Chicago: University of Chicago Press, 1970.
Guisso, Richard W. "Thunder Over the Lake: The Five Classics and the Perception of Women in Early China." In *Women in China,* 46–61.
Sangrem, P. Steven. "Female Gender in Chinese Religious Symbols: Kuan Yin, Ma Tsu, and the 'Eternal Mother.'" *Signs* 9, no. 1 (August 1983): 4–25.
Thompson, Lawrence G. *Chinese Religion: An Introduction.*
Yang, C. K. *Religion in Chinese Society: A Study of Contemporary Social Functions of Religion and Some of Their Historical Factors.* Berkeley: University of California Press, 1961.

Lecture Topics

Confucian Theory of Social Harmony (Bullough; Guisso, 46–61; Smith, Chap. 4; Thompson, Chap. 3). Confucius (551–479 B.C.), whose political and ethical theories formed the philosophical basis of Chinese society, wrote at a time of civil war. His central concern was the basis of social harmony, that is, how to order a just and peaceful state. Confucius believed there was a fixed code of conduct—a system of etiquette—that was in harmony with Tao, the natural order of the universe. If an individual disobeyed these rules, he or she threatened the very basis of the social order.

Two Confucian concepts that had important implications for women should be particularly noted. First is the concept of Three Dependencies: 1) a woman's dependency upon her father when young; 2) dependency upon her husband after marriage; and 3) dependency upon her son when widowed. She could never act autonomously. Second is the concept of Filial Piety. To serve and revere one's parents (and after marriage, one's in-laws) was a woman's first duty. Filial piety was a basic ethical principle, and it took precedence over bonds between husbands and wives.

The Confucian Classics also stress the ideals of female behavior: women should be kind, docile, pure, gentle, decorous, modest, diligent, dutiful, and quiet. A woman's unrestrained nature—that is, uncontrolled by men—is pictured harshly; such a woman is sexually promiscuous, has an "evil tongue," and cannot be taught (Guisso, 54–55).

Taoist Attitudes Toward Woman's Nature (Ames, 21–45; Smith, Chap. 5). Confucianism provided part of the ideological justification for female submissiveness. Taoism, another formative influence on Chinese philosophy, also reinforced ideas about female inferiority. Although Taoism is sometimes interpreted as presenting an androgynous ideal, female qualities in fact tended to be evaluated negatively. The context of Taoist beliefs and their implications for the status of women can be usefully discussed in light of Ortner's theory of women and nature, developed in Chapter 4, "Interactionist Analysis: Economics and Gender," above.

According to Taoist theory, the universe is powered or sustained by the interaction of opposites, yin (the female or negative principle) and yang (the male or positive principle). Although superficially separate but equal, the female principle is evaluated in a negative way. It is passive, dark, and evil, while the polar opposite male principle is active, light, and good. Female inferiority is therefore inherent. It was believed that sexual relations could sap the male of his yang, or vital force, unless rigorously controlled. Both Confucian and Taoist concepts were used to justify women's subordination.

Buddhism and Women. Although Buddha apparently had a skeptical view of women's nature, he did recognize them as individuals and reluctantly allowed them to join the Buddhist order as nuns. (See also Chapter 6, above).

Buddhism appealed to a wide cross-section of women. The nunnery was a place of refuge for women who did not wish to marry, widows, abandoned concubines, and prostitutes. Some nunneries offered an education. As a nun a woman could undertake a career of service (nursing, visiting the poor, teaching) that fit into her traditional role, yet offered a degree of independence. Thus, in China as elsewhere, a heterodox religious movement was embraced by some women as a means of escape (see Chapter 5, "Women as Religious Actors," above).

Discussion Questions
  1. Do Taoist views of women, men, and nature confirm or refute Ortner's theory of women and nature and culture?

  2. Discuss parallels in Western thought to the Confucian notion that there is a natural order with appropriate roles, the defiance of which imperils humanity. What are the implications for women in both cases?

  3. Even a century or two ago, Western society showed reverence for the old, and stressed the concept of obedience to parents to a greater extent than is done currently. What socioeconomic forces reinforced traditional notions, and what has led to their decline? Are there similarities with the Chinese experience?

  4. Compare Chinese, Indian, Middle Eastern, and Western notions of "woman's nature," as well as the cultures' ideals of female behavior. How is a woman who rebels against accepted norms characterized? Why do many women accept these traditional views?

FROM BIRTH TO DEATH: THE LIFE CYCLE
OF THE TRADITIONAL CHINESE WOMAN

Because of space limitations and the paucity of sources, it is impossible to capture here the full complexity of life for traditional Chinese women. The life of the literate wife of a Ch'ing court official was obviously different from that of the wife of a poor peasant in Fukien. And aside from class differences, there were differences in lifestyles between the north and south.

As was the case in India, the degree to which submissive ideals were normative varied by class and region. In the south and among the poorer classes, women were less restricted and less secluded. For all women, however, life was defined to a greater or lesser degree by a culture whose ideal was that women should be respectful, courteous, and subordinate. How the submissive female personality was produced from infancy, and the many reinforcing messages of inferiority that she received, will form the substance of this section. We will also examine the variations in status and power that accrued to women according to age.

Readings for Students
Dworkin, Andrea. *Woman Hating*, Chap. 6. New York: E. P. Dutton, 1974.
Mace, David, and Vera Mace. *Marriage East and West*. Garden City, N.Y.: Doubleday, 1959.
Spence, Jonathan D. *The Death of Woman Wang*. New York: Viking Press, 1978.
Wolf, Margery. *The House of Lim*.

Readings for Instructors
Drucker, Alison R. "The Influence of Western Women on the Anti-Footbinding Movement 1840–1911." In *Women in China*, 179–99.
Lee, Bernice J. "Female Infanticide in China." In *Women in China*. 163–77.
Levy, Howard S. *Chinese Footbinding: The History of a Curious Erotic Custom*. New York: W. Rawls, 1966.
Wolf, Margery. "Chinese Women: Old Skills in a New Context." In *Woman, Culture, and Society*, 157–72.
———. *The House of Lim*.
———. *Women and the Family*.
Yang, C. L. *The Chinese Family in Rural Taiwan*.

Lecture Topics

Birth (Lee, 163–77; Wolf, *Women and the Family*, Chaps. 5, 6).
From the moment of birth, a girl was at risk; the valuation of females was such that female infanticide was widespread. For the mother too, giving birth had mixed cultural valuations. Birth was considered contaminating, and the mother was often blamed for the birth of a daughter. On the other hand, the birth of a son was a source of honor and potential power.

Childhood Role Socialization (Wolf, *Women and the Family*, Chaps. 5, 6). Childhood role socialization prepared boys and girls early and well for their adult destinies. Boys were indulged, while girls were disciplined early. Girls were taught to defer to males, even those younger than themselves.

A mother's indulgent relationship to her sons reflected her own self-interest (girls would leave; boys would stay and support her).

Marriage (Wolf, *Women and the Family*, Chaps. 7, 8, 11; Yang, Chap. 2). As in most peasant societies, marriage was an agreement between families, not individuals. The following points should be especially stressed:

1. The wishes of individuals were irrelevant:

2. The bride went to her in-laws' house, not her husband's; thus they had control over her;

3. Love matches were rare and public displays of affection between husband and wife were strongly discouraged because of their implied threat to the cohesiveness of the extended family;

4. The marriage ceremony symbolized a woman's place in patriarchal society;

5. The bride entered a strange household in which she was regarded as an outsider;

6. The bride's relationship with her mother-in-law was crucial;

7. There were strong pressures for early marriage to ensure dutiful brides (i.e., Sim-pua marriages; early betrothals).

Mothers-In-Law (Wolf, "Chinese Women"). There were crucial differences in the status of Chinese women according to their position in the life cycle. If a woman had sons who remained at home with their brides, she occupied a key role in the extended family, influencing many household decisions. A harrassed bride might with the passage of time become a domineering mother-in-law.

Divorce (Yang, Chap. 4; Mace, Chap. 11). The unequal divorce laws were a sword of Damocles hanging over the heads of rebellious wives, or those who failed to procreate. There were no legal grounds upon which a wife could divorce her husband. If her husband agreed, a wife might leave but she had no rights to property or children, and she was censured by the community. Husbands, however, could divorce wives on a number of grounds, including childlessness, negligence in serving his parents, stealing, adultery, disease, or loquaciousness.

Widows (Yang, Chap. 3; Mace, Chap. 11). The lot of a Chinese widow, especially if she did not have sons, was often not a happy one. Although there were no legal or religious prohibitions against widow remarriage, there were strong economic and social ones.

A widow retained obligations to her husband's family. Furthermore, widows were considered "damaged goods" and hence undesirable wives. A sonless widow had no natural allies in the family and might be regarded as useless.

There was one comparatively rare, but certainly not unknown circumstance when a widow exercised power, namely, when she was the most senior surviving member of a family. A number of empress dowagers actually reigned over the Chinese state in these circumstances, and in lesser families such widows controlled the family estate.

Old Age (Wolf, *Women and the Family*, Chap. 14; Yang, Chap. 5). The Chinese venerated the elderly, and women with sufficient age and character commanded respect. Old people symbolized wisdom in a largely illiterate society in which the accumulated experience of years counted for much. Thus, for some Chinese women at least, age had its rewards.

Concubines (Yang, Chap. 3; Mace, Chap. 9). Concubinage was a form of polygamy restricted to the upper classes. It existed for several reasons: to obtain a male heir, as an outlet for male romantic love, and as a status symbol. A concubine had an inferior status in the family and was generally purchased from a poor family. Her existence was precarious.

Footbinding (Mace, Chap. 3; Dworkin, Chap. 6; Drucker). The most compelling symbol—and physically painful expression—of female subordination in China was footbinding. The first unequivocal reference to the practice dates to 1130 A.D., and it seems to have first been practiced upon court dancers. It gained acceptance for a number of reasons: it was an upper-class status symbol; bound feet acquired erotic overtones; and it made women's movement physically difficult, thus ensuring their passivity and controllability. Eventually footbinding became a prerequisite for marriage among the upper classes, and was widespread in the north. Where women were needed for rice planting in the south, and among the minorities living in the Chinese empire, women's feet remained unbound. Nevertheless, millions of women suffered excruciating pain and physical immobility through this practice.

Chinese Feminists and Marriage Reform. As we shall see in the discussions on "Early Efforts to Emancipate Women" and "Women and the Communist Revolution," below, a demand for free choice marriages, equal treatment before the law (including equal divorce and inheritance rights), the abolition of concubinage and footbinding, and widow remarriage became crucial issues in the Chinese feminist movement in the late nineteenth and twentieth centuries.

Discussion Questions

1. Compare Chinese and Western marriage ceremonies. What are the symbolic similarities and differences?

2. Are marriages based on love more natural than arranged marriages? What values underlie your answer?

3. Compare traditional Chinese and traditional Western role socialization. What are the similarities and differences?

4. What historical instances can you find in Western society of arranged marriages between families? What socioeconomic factors entered into these?

5. What historical similarities and differences were there between Western and the traditional Chinese attitudes toward divorce? Widows? Infanticide?

6. What similarities exist between the life cycles of Chinese and Indian women? What accounts for them?

7. Dworkin interprets footbinding as a symptom of woman hating. Is she correct?

8. Are there parallels in Western culture to Chinese males' eroticization of a practice that is physically damaging to women?

9. What evidence, if any, do you find in Chinese childrearing practices to support or refute Nancy Chodorow's theory of male-female personality development and attitudes toward women?

10. In what ways do the lives of women in *The Death of Woman Wang* and *The House of Lim* illustrate or vary from the generalized picture drawn in the lectures? Account for any differences.

RESISTANCE, ALTERNATIVES, AND FEMALE POWER

Though the picture of women in China presented thus far has been harshly negative, it should not be supposed that women were always entirely powerless or submissive. Indeed, one future trend in scholarship on women in China, as is currently the case in Middle Eastern and North African studies, will likely be the articulation of areas of female power, modes of resistance, and individual achievements. Several recent studies listed here signify the beginning of a reexamination. This material can be easily dealt with either by lecture or discussion.

Despite the sanctions placed by society on "deviant" women, some unusually determined and gifted individuals overcame their lot. Such was the case with Cheng I's wife (see Murray), whose career spanned prostitution in a Canton brothel and the position of co-commander of a confederacy, which she constructed, of 70,000 pirates who controlled the coast of Kwantung Province in the late eighteenth century. The Marriage Resistance Movement of rural Kwantung provides another spectacular example of defiance. Less dramatically, women's networks carried on ameliorating activities, and the growing literature on women rulers in Chinese history analyzes conditions and circumstances under which elite women were able to achieve political power.

Readings for Students

Chung, Priscilla Ching. "Power and Prestige: Palace Women in the Northern Sung (960–1126)." In *Women in China,* 99–112.
Fitzgerald, Charles Patrick. *The Express Wu.* Melbourne: F. W. Cheshire, 1968.
Murray, Dian. "One Woman's Rise to Power: Cheng I's Wife and the Pirates." In *Women in China,* 147-61.
Topley, Marjorie. "Marriage Resistance in Rural Kwangtung." In *Women in Chinese Society,* edited by Margery Wolf and Roxane Witke, 67–68. Stanford: Stanford University Press, 1975.

Readings for Instructors

de Crespigny, Rafe. "The Harem of Emperor Huan: A Study of Court Politics in Later Han." *Papers on Far Eastern History* 12 (September 1975): 1–42.
Hibbert, Eloise Talcott. *Embroidered Gauze: Portraits of Famous Chinese Ladies.* New York: E.P. Dutton, 1941. Repr. Freeport, N.Y.: Books for Libraries, 1969.
Levy, Howard S. *Harem Favorites of an Illustrious Celestial.* Taipei, Taiwan: Chung-t'ai Printing, 1958.
Warner, Marina. *The Dragon Empress: The Life and Times of Tz'u-hsi, Empress Dowager of China, 1835–1908.* New York: Macmillan, 1972.
Wolf, Margery. *Women and the Family,* Chaps. 3, 4.
———. "Women and Suicide in China." In *Women in Chinese Society,* 111–42.
Yang, Lien-sheng. "Female Rulers in Imperial China." In *Excursions in Sinology,* 27–41. Cambridge: Harvard University Press, 1969.

Lecture Topics

Women's Community (Wolf, *Women and the Family,* Chaps. 3, 4). Peasant women, who were not secluded in the family compounds, met one another at the well, washing areas, market, and so forth. Here a network of friendships and informal alliances was forged. By gossip and conversation they could sometimes ameliorate the condition of someone whom they believed had been wronged.

Suicide (Wolf, "Women and Suicide"). Though a drastic and unhappy solution, suicide or the threat of suicide was one means of revenge against tormentors.

A Marriage Resistance Movement (Topley). A dramatic example of women's resistance to their traditional fate occurred in Kwangtung province in the Canton delta, from the early nineteenth to early twentieth centuries. Women took vows not to wed, or, after betrothals, refused to join their husbands' families. They lived in "sisterhoods" or women's residence halls. Some practiced celibacy, others entered into lesbian relationships. It is important to note the economic and ideological bases of this resistance:

1. The economy of the area was based on highly labor intensive silk production, and women's labor was valued.

2. An eclectic cult (Hsien-t'ien sect) flourished, whose highest deity was a mother goddess and whose beliefs stressed sexual equality. This cult also advocated chastity, for it regarded childbirth as a sin, and believed that women would be reborn as men if they remained celibate. The religion thus was explicitly anti-marriage. These were highly unusual conjunctions of circumstances, but the popularity and historical length of the resistance movement is indicative of the tensions generally felt by women in traditional society.

Women of the Imperial Court (Yang, Chung). Informal women's networks, suicide, and the Marriage Resistance Movement involved varying degrees of resistance to male authority. Women rulers in China did not so much resist traditional norms as they turned them to their own advantage. Confucian principles required that sons venerate both parents. A widowed mother who was the eldest family member was uniquely positioned to exploit mother-son bonds, and while sons were young, to wield power.

There are a number of instances of empress dowagers ruling as regents, and even one instance during the T'ang dynasty when an empress, Wu Chao (reigned 690–705), founded her own dynasty, the Chou (Fitzgerald, Hibbert). These women ruled despite stern warnings against such regencies in the *Five Classics*. Not all empress dowagers actually served as regents. The favorable circumstances an empress dowager could exploit included an emperor's minority or an emperor's illness. An emergency during a dethronement provided another opportunity, as did the sanction of a posthumous edict naming the empress dowager as regent (see Yang, 50–53). While nothing like a systematic analysis of women at court, or harem politics, has yet been written, the best of the scattered studies are included here (de Crespigny, Levy, Yang), though they sometimes need feminist "decoding." The best known, and most notorious female ruler is undoubtedly Tz'u-hsi, who presided over the downfall of the Manchu Dynasty. Marina Warner's study is one of the most reliable and balanced accounts.

Discussion Questions
1. Guisso asserts that "traditional China has been notable among the major civilizations for its lack of feminist protest and of overt sexual conflict" (60). Do you agree with this evaluation? If it is true, what might the causes be?

2. To what degree did China's female rulers and court officials defy norms or accommodate them?

3. Is suicide an act of taking control or of helplessness?

4. What instances of women's networks analogous to those of peasant China do you know of in other cultures? What functions do they perform?

5. Do you agree with the assertion that Chinese women were subordinate because they cooperated and consented to this status? What of Western women? Whose "fault" is it? Justify your answers.

6. Contrast the skills and attitudes necessary for the success of Cheng I's wife as leader of a pirate confederacy with those required for upward mobility in the imperial court.

EARLY EFFORTS TO EMANCIPATE WOMEN

The early history of Chinese feminism is inextricably linked with the other broad currents of reform and revolution set in motion in Chinese society as a reaction against Western and Japanese imperialism. If students have no prior knowledge of modern Chinese history, it would be well to briefly survey the weakening of the Ch'ing (Manchu) dynasty, the economic dislocation caused by the Western powers, and the collapse of Confucian orthodoxy.

For those with little knowledge of Chinese history in the nineteenth and early twentieth centuries, we recommend the following surveys:

Sheridan, James. *China in Disintegration: The Republican Era in Chinese History 1912–1949.* New York: The Free Press, 1975.

Wakeman, Frederick. *The Fall of Imperial China.* New York: The Free Press, 1975.

The economic collapse of China is an important historical theme for this period, and much has been written about damage to Chinese craft industries and agriculture. Virtually all of the economic histories have omitted any discussion of gender issues. Bobby Siu's groundbreaking study of women's roles in cotton textiles and agriculture is therefore a must (Chaps. 2, 3).

The early women's movement is best seen as one of many movements that aimed to reform and strengthen Chinese society in the face of a depredatory onslaught from the West. The first revolutionary movement to address the status of women was the peasant-based Taiping Rebellion. After its defeat the impetus passed to liberal male reformers and to literate urban women. Later, as we shall see, the Chinese Communist Party mobilized this discontent and carried the struggle back to the countryside.

With the steady encroachment of the West and the imposition of a series of bankrupting "Unequal Treaties" upon the faltering Ch'ing dynasty, Chinese intellectuals put forward various reform schemes to save China. Nationalism (often directed against the Manchus as well as the West) and social reform went hand in hand. Reformers argued that China would have to borrow and adapt aspects of the West in order to save itself from the West. The first generation of reformers, including Wei Yuan and Lin Tse-hsü, believed that the importation of Western technology alone held the key to Chinese regeneration. Later reformers, such as Kang Yu-wei, realized that in order to successfully utilize industrial technology, a whole interrelated series of social and cultural reforms were crucial, including the modification of Confucian orthodoxy in the educational system, civil service, and imperial court; sweeping reforms of the military; and in general a relaxation of the hardened class divisions of Chinese society with the ultimate goal of a constitutional monarchy. Further to the left, when these reforms failed, were Sun Yat-sen and his comrades, who believed China's only hope lay in a republican form of government and the total abolition of the Chinese dynastic system.

Readings for Students
Croll, Elisabeth. *Feminism and Socialism in China,* Chaps. 1–6. New York: Schocken Books, 1980.
Curtin, Katie. *Women in China,* 9–33. New York: Pathfinder Press, 1975.
Pruitt, Ida. *A Daughter of Han: The Autobiography of a Chinese*

Working Woman. Stanford: Stanford University Press, 1967.

Siu, Bobby. *Women of China: Imperialism and Women's Resistance, 1900–1949.* London: Zed Press, 1981.

Readings for Instructors

Beahan, Charlotte L. "In the Public Eye: Women in Early Twentieth Century China." In *Women in China,* 215–38.

Drucker, Alison R. "The Influence of Western Women on the Anti-Footbinding Movement 1840–1911." In *Women in China,* 179–99.

Levy, Howard. *Chinese Footbinding.*

Lin, Siu-Tsung. "Chinese Women on the Road to Complete Emancipation." In *Women in the World: A Comparative Study,* edited by Lynne B. Iglitzin and Ruth Ross, 345–62. Santa Barbara, Cal.: Clio Press, 1975.

McElderry, Andrea. "Historical Background on Chinese Women." In *Lives: Chinese Working Women,* edited by Mary Sheridan and Janet W. Salaff, Chap. 2. Bloomington: Indiana University Press, 1984.

Rankin, Mary Backus. "The Emergence of Women at the End of the Ch'ing: The Base of Ch'iu Chin." In *Women in Chinese Society,* 39–66.

Ropp, Paul S. "The Seeds of Change: Reflections on the Condition of Women in the Early and Mid Ch'ing." *Signs* 2, no. 1 (Autumn 1976): 5–23.

Rowbotham, Sheila. *Women, Resistance and Revolution,* Chap. 7. New York: Vintage, 1972.

Shih, Vincent Y. C. *The Taiping Ideology.* Seattle: University of Washington Press, 1967. See especially Chap. 3.

Tse-tung, Chow. *The May 4th Movement: The Intellectual Revolution in Modern China.* Cambridge: Harvard University Press, 1960.

Revolution from Below: Women and the Taiping Rebellion (Shih). The revolutionary potential among women may be gauged from the dynamics of the Taiping Rebellion, which raged in south China. From 1853 to 1864 peasant rebels established an independent state covering most of Hupeh, Anhwei, Kiangsi, Kiangsu, and Chekiang. Though this rebellion ultimately failed, large numbers of women were drawn into it partly because of its doctrine, however flawed, of equality between the sexes. The social strains fueling the Taipings—landlord exploitation, poverty, and oppression of women—would later be drawn upon with far greater effectiveness by the Chinese Communist Party. The Taiping Rebellion is considered a watershed in the history of Chinese rebellions, which hitherto were characterized by gentry leadership and resulted in periodic dynastic overthrows in which the structure of society remained largely untouched. The Taiping leaders were mostly peasant nationalists, influenced in part by Western ideas, and they attempted not merely to overturn the ruling dynasty but to remake the basis of society itself.

The Taiping leader, Hung Hsui-Chuan (1814–64), proclaimed a new anti-Confucian religion in which he assumed the title of Heavenly King, and claimed Jesus Christ as his brother. His social philosophy was radically egalitarian: private land was abolished in areas under Taiping control, and sexual equality was proclaimed. Women were permitted to compete in the Taiping civil service exams, and served in the Taiping army. Footbinding was abolished.

The theory of sexual equality, compromised from the start by injunctions that women should be obedient to their husbands, degenerated with the increasing corruption of the Rebellion itself. Internal power struggles weakened the armies, and the male elite misused women as concubines.

Reform and Revolution in Last Days of Ch'ing Dynasty. In the waning days of the Dynasty, several reforms in the status of women began to make headway, especially the abolition of footbinding and the establishment of schools for women. Women's rights groups also began to form.

Anti-footbinding Movement (Drucker, Levy). Western public opinion—shaped in part by Protestant missionaries—encouraged the formation of an indigenous anti-footbinding movement. Chinese diplomats, students, and other travelers to the West were disturbed that they were viewed as barbaric because of the practice. Within China, Western influence was also important. Though only 1 percent of the Chinese ever converted to Christianity, Western pamphlets on footbinding, Christian schools, and lobbying of the Ch'ing court played a part in changing elite opinion. Anti-footbinding literature stressed pragmatic and nationalist arguments, rather than feminist ones: abolition of footbinding would lead to better health and more efficient labor. In 1902 the empress dowager issued a mild edict against footbinding. Though compliance was voluntary, it made the cause respectable. In 1911 the Republican government banned footbinding. Its incidence markedly declined throughout the next decades.

Women's Rights Organizations (Beahan, Rankin, Siu). By the turn of the century a number of women's rights groups had been founded in China. They involved primarily urban, Western-educated women, often from the gentry. Chang Chu-chun, a Cantonese feminist, was characteristic of this pathbreaking generation. Chang graduated from the Hackett Medical School for Women in 1900, and opened a charity clinic. She lectured on women's rights and held up Harriet Beecher Stowe (because of her role in the American abolitionist movement) and Florence Nightingale as examples for Chinese women to emulate. She established the Women's Educational Protection Association to promote women's education. She remained single.

The efforts to emancipate women were greatly aided by the intense nationalist currents in China. The earliest examples of women making public speeches were at nationalist rallies protesting the Boxer treaties in 1901. Women's patriotic societies formed to help pay off the national debt and to boycott foreign goods. A group of prostitutes even organized to buy railway stock to reduce China's dependence on foreign loans. These groups gave women opportunities to develop speaking, organizing, and leadership skills.

Reform from Above: The One Hundred Days Reform Movement (1898) (Rankin, Siu, Curtin). In the wake of the humiliating Sino-Japanese war (1894–95), in which China was decisively beaten by the newly westernizing Japan, whom China had hitherto dominated for centuries, an ill-fated Hundred Days Reform Movement gained the upper hand in the imperial court. Sponsored by the young Emperor Kuang Hsü, and inspired and aided by the radical monarchist Kang Yu-wei, who was known for his reformist interpretation of the Confucian classics, the reformers ran into stiff opposition from the Empress Dowager Tz'u-hsi, who had nominally given up the reigns of power to her adopted son when he reached manhood.

Among the edicts promulgated were decrees to change the syllabus for future state examinations; simplify administrative rules; establish a Bureau of Agriculture, Commerce, and Industry; institute westernized training for the army; direct selected members of the imperial clan to study overseas; convert existing schools with traditional curricula into westernized schools; and encourage the education of women, in the hope of strengthening the nation.

The shattering of the reform movement in the conservative backlash encouraged by the empress dowager destroyed any remaining illusions that the dynasty could or would reform itself. Revolutionary alternatives soon followed.

"Revolutionary Women" (Jiu Jin) Ch'iu Chin: A Feminist Revolutionary (1875–1907) (Rankin, Siu, Beahan). The life of Ch'iu Chin encapsulated the passionate dedication to nationalism and feminism felt by her generation of revolutionary feminists. Ch'iu Chin broke drastically with tradition. Tired of what seemed to be a meaningless, unproductive married life at a time of national crisis, she left her husband in 1903 and joined radical expatriates in Japan. Ch'iu dramatized her protest against female restrictions by adopting male dress, and she prepared herself for revolutionary activities by practicing bomb making and marksmanship. Ch'iu believed that freedom for women would only come if the existing Confucian order were destroyed and if women proved themselves by participating in revolutionary work. She died leading an insurrection against the government of Anhwei and has become a folk heroine to all Chinese regardless of their political perspective.

The Republican Era (1911) (Beahan, Lin, Siu). Chinese feminists participated actively in the movement to overthrow the Manchu dynasty and replace it with a new republican form of government with an elected president. The T'ung-meng Hui (Chinese United League), founded by Sun Yat-sen, promised not only to restore China to the Chinese, but also promised a vaguely defined socialist redistribution of land and equal rights between women and men. When the National Assembly met to draft a new constitution, however, it rejected the idea of female suffrage. Outraged feminists stormed the parliament building, but to no avail. Chinese suffragists were severely disillusioned; some sought individual solutions through marriage to male revolutionaries, some returned home unhappily, a few committed suicide or joined Buddhist convents. By 1912 the Kuomintang (the organizational successor of the T'ung-meng Hui) had entirely dropped the notion of male and female equality from its platform.

The Republic itself was never more than a shell. Real power was in the hands of Yuan Shih-kai, the commander in chief of the Manchu Imperial Army, who had engineered the dynasty's abdication after the revolutionaries seized Nanking in the south. He, not Sun Yat-sen, became president, and he quickly moved to consolidate his power by packing the parliament and having himself voted the new monarch. Yuan died in 1916 leaving a legacy of chaos, as his actions precipitated a prolonged civil war and the breakup of China into a system of separate regions controlled by warlords. The Kuomintang, first under Sun Yat-sen (who died in 1925), and then under his successor Chiang Kai-shek, established a new revolutionary government in Canton. Their dream was to launch an expedition north to bring the warlords under control, and to consolidate China under one government.

The May 4th Movement (Beahan; Chow; Lin; Siu; Curtin; Rowbotham, 173–84). Though the Kuomintang backtracked on its commitment to female emancipation, the issue did not die, as is evident from the ideology of the May 4th Movement, a series of mass demonstrations touched off in virtually every Chinese city by the news that the Versailles Treaty of 1919 had transferred Germany's rights in Shantung to the Japanese, despite the fact that China had been an ally of the victorious powers during World War I. The May 4th Movement was as much cultural as it was political. Further Japanese encroachment stimulated widespread doubt about traditional values among the young of both sexes, and prompted new proposals for national regeneration. Inspired by the writings of two Peking professors, Hu Shih and Chen Tu-hsiu (who later joined the Communist Party), the New Culture Movement attacked the Confucian code of obedience to the family and to elders, and argued for the liberation of the individual. Tens of thousands of young people eagerly endorsed these ideas and fought for the right to select their own mates and decide on their own careers. This breakdown in reverence for the old ethical system was a fertile ground in which both the Kuomintang and the newly formed Chinese Communist Party recruited political followers.

In the excitement of the May 4th Movement and its aftermath, a number of women's political action groups sprang up in urban areas, linking women's rights with nationalism. Their demands included women's access to education; changes in the civil law regulating marriage, inheritance, and property; equal pay; the prohibition of concubinage, prostitution, footbinding and the sale of children; and equal constitutional rights. As with Ch'iu Chin and Sun Yat-sen, the intellectual influences on these groups were primarily Western. And, like earlier movements, these women's groups failed to mobilize peasant and working-class women. Further, as Beahan points out, these groups were concerned not only with women's rights but with national rights as well. As the already desperate conditions in China worsened throughout the twenties and thirties, women's groups came to view their demands as a goal that could be achieved only after Chinese sovereignty had been restored. Feminists attracted to the Communist or Kuomintang party saw the victory of one of these causes as a necessary precondition to tackling the full range of women's grievances. Their sense of autonomy declined.

The Kuomintang Under Chiang Kai-shek (Croll, Curtin, Siu, Rowbotham, Lin). Although the Kuomintang and the Chinese Communist Party briefly formed an alliance under the leadership of Sun Yat-sen, during which time women's rights and the mobilization of women were crucially important, this alliance and its approach to women's liberation were repudiated by the right wing of the Kuomintang led by Chiang Kai-shek. Chiang consolidated his military power in a way that had eluded Sun Yat-sen. In 1926 he defeated the three strongest warlords, made alliances with the rest, and united China, at least nominally, under his control. In 1927 Communists were purged from the party and army with great brutality. Thousands of Chinese women who had bobbed their hair were shot on the assumption that they were Communists or sympathizers. With the support of the urban merchants, commercial and industrial elite, and the rural landlord class, Chiang articulated a new, mildly reformist political philosophy in which real political change as well as cultural reform were subverted. The new Civil Code promulgated in 1930 laid down legal reforms that satisfied many middle-class feminists: women could choose their own husbands and had equal rights to divorce, inheritance, and ownership of property. In 1931 a new Factory Law required equal pay for equal work, though as a "protective" measure it barred women from some jobs. A number of femininsts, characteristically college-educated, Christian lawyers, educators, and doctors, hailed the new laws as signifying the full emancipation of the Chinese woman. Others saw the partial and class-bound nature of the reforms but they were driven underground. The Kuomintang also embarked upon a nationwide campaign called the "New Life Movement" as a counter to radical notions. It called for a revival of Confucian rules of deference, and the Women's Department under Madame Chiang exorted women to be virtuous, obedient, helpful, clean and frugal. The Department taught women reading and writing, hygiene, and household skills and railed against the "free love amazons," as it characterized the more radical women of the Communist Party, whom the Kuomintang had failed to annihilate.

Discussion Questions

1. What reforms necessary to bring about equality of the sexes were left untouched by the Kuomintang legal reforms of 1930 and 1931?

2. Critics of the early Chinese feminists have condemned them as bourgeois and narrowly class-bound in their demand for the vote. Were they? Justify your answer.

3. The Kuomintang attempted to renew reverence for traditional values instead of seeking fundamental changes in the power structures of Chinese society as a method of stabilizing China. What other political movements have attempted a similar appeal to tradition, and why?

4. Did Western missionaries play a helpful or hindering role in the various movements to reform the status of Chinese women? Be specific in your answers.

5. In what other Third World feminist movements have there been alliances between nationalism and reform in the status of women? Were the paths of development the same or different? Account for any differences.

6. Third World feminists sometimes accuse Western feminists of cultural and political blindness for failing to perceive that the emancipation of Third World women must come in partnership with men as part of a broader nationalist and anti-imperialist struggle. Does the Chinese experience confirm or refute that viewpoint? What of other Third World feminist movements you have studied?

WOMEN AND THE COMMUNIST REVOLUTION

The role of women and women's issues in the Chinese revolution has been insufficiently appreciated by mainstream scholarship on modern Chinese history. There are voluminous books and articles on peasant mobilization and the techniques of guerilla warfare (both implicitly or explicitly depicted as male activities), but relatively few studies recognize the centrality of women's participation to the Chinese Communist cause. Recent feminist scholarship has begun to make Western audiences aware of how the Chinese Communist Party (CCP) mobilized women's discontent, its motives in doing so, the resistance it encountered, the changes it induced in female status, and the continuing dialogue between feminism and socialism in China. This feminist scholarship, together with the selective mining of more general works, permits the instructor and student to examine the impact of the revolution on women in some depth.

One trend in the historiography of women in Communist China should be noted. Earlier works (Croll, *Feminism and Socialism*) are very optimistic about the degree to which traditional attitudes toward women have changed. Later writing, while not disparaging the very real strides that have been taken, is marked by a greater note of caution (Andors, *The Unfinished Liberation of Chinese Women;* Croll, *The Politics of Marriage;* Stacey, *Patriarchy and Socialist Revolution;* Johnson, *Women, the Family and Peasant Revolution;* and Parish and Whyte, *Village and Family*).

In pointing to the importance of women of all classes to the Communist cause, we do not mean to minimize the role of peasants of both sexes. Grievances of class and sex were both powerful revolutionary motivators. By the 1930s the condition of the Chinese peasant was desperate. The countryside was racked by natural disasters and famine; warlords plundered freely; the central and provincial governments were corrupt, indifferent, and lacked real authority; and landlords and tax collectors exacted outrageous payments. Some 80 percent of the cultivated land was held by a little over 10 percent of the population, and 65 percent of the peasantry was estimated to be landless or "land-hungry." China's economy was in ruins: a flood of cheap Western manufactured goods damaged domestic production, and governments were deeply in debt to Western powers. Millions fled from the countryside to swell the ranks of the unemployed in cities or formed marauding bands in warlord areas. Many Chinese men and women were sold into indentured service; poor women were sold to rich families as concubines, or into prostitution (Isaacs, 25–31; Siu, Chaps. 2, 3).

In the midst of such human despair and misery, the CCP offered hope and a concrete program of land redistribution, swift if harsh justice to the oppressive landlord class, the relatively exemplary conduct of its own troops and officials, and a strong anti-Western and anti-Japanese nationalism. It also stood for a world of sexual equality.

For those who wish to do background reading on the Chinese Revolution and its aftermath we recommend:

Harrison, James P. *The Long March to Power: A History of the Chinese Communist Party, 1921–1972.* New York: Praeger Pubs., 1973.

Lee, Hong Yung. *The Politics of the Chinese Cultural Revolution.* Berkeley: University of California Press, 1978.

Meisner, Maurice. *Mao's China: A History of the People's Republic.* New York: The Free Press, 1979.

Schurmann, Franz. *Ideology and Organization in Communist China.* 2d ed. Berkeley: University of California Press, 1971.

Townsend, James R. *Political Participation in Communist China.* Berkeley: University of California Press, 1967.

A more recent book that surveys China after the Cultural Revolution is:

Garside, Roger. *Coming Alive: China after Mao.* New York: Mentor/New American Library. 1981.

Study of China since 1949 provides valuable theoretical insights into the relative roles of economics, law, and social attitudes in dictating the status of women. The question of whether all culture has a materialistic base (or, to use the Marxist terminology, whether culture including sexism is the superstructure of an economic substructure) can be usefully debated in light of the Chinese experience.

Readings for Students

Andors, Phyllis. "'The Four Modernizations' and the Chinese Policy on Women." *Bulletin of Concerned Asian Scholars* 13, no. 2 (April–June 1981): 44–56.

Croll, Elisabeth. Chaps. 7–11 in *Feminism and Socialism in China.*

Hinton, William. *Fanshen: A Documentary of Revolution in a Chinese Village,* Chaps. 16, 18, 44, 51. New York: Random House, 1966.

Sidel, Ruth. *Women and Child Care in China.* Baltimore: Penguin Books, 1973.

Smedley, Agnes, *Portraits of Chinese Women in Revolution*. New York: The Feminist Press, 1976.

Readings for Instructors

Andors, Phyllis. *The Unfinished Liberation of Chinese Women, 1949–1980*. Bloomington: Indiana University Press, 1983.

Belden, Jack. *China Shakes the World*. New York: Monthly Review Press, 1949.

Croll, Elisabeth. *China's One-Child Family Policy*. New York: St. Martin's Press, 1985.

———. *The Family Rice Bowl: Food and the Domestic Economy of China*, Chap. 6. London: Zed Press, 1983.

———. *Chinese Women Since Mao*. London: Zed Books, 1983.

———. *The Politics of Marriage in Contemporary China*. Cambridge: Cambridge University Press, 1981.

———. *The Women's Movement in China: A Selection of Readings, 1949–1973*. London: Anglo-Chinese Educational Institute, 1974.

Davin, Delia. *Woman-Work: Women and the Party in Revolutionary China*. Oxford Clarendon Press, 1976.

Galston, Arthur. *Daily Life in People's China*. New York: Crowell, 1975.

Hemmel, Vibeke, and Pia Sindbjerg. *Women in Rural China: Policy Towards Women Before and After the Cultural Revolution*. Scandanavian Institute of Asian Studies Paper #7. Atlantic Highlands, N.J.: Humanities Press, 1984.

Isaacs, H. R. *The Tragedy of the Chinese Revolution*. Stanford: Stanford University Press, 1961.

Johnson, Kay. *Women, the Family and Peasant Revolution in China*. Chicago: University of Chicago Press, 1983.

New Women in New China. Peking: Foreign Language Press, 1972.

Parish, William L., and Martin K. Whyte. *Village and Family in Contemporary China*. Chicago: University of Chicago Press, 1978.

Schram, Stuart R. *The Political Thought of Mao Tse-Tung*. 2d rev. ed. Baltimore: Penguin Books, 1969.

Stacey, Judith. *Patriarchy and Socialist Revolution in China*. Berkeley and Los Angeles: University of California Press, 1983.

WIN News 9, no. 1 (Winter 1983).

Lecture Topics

The Importance of Women's Liberation in Chinese Communist Ideology (Schram, 250–59; Croll, *Feminism and Socialism*, 185–

89). As we discussed in the theoretical section of this syllabus (see Chapter 4 on "Marxist Contributions to the Gender Inequality Debate"), European Marxists argued that women's oppressed condition was a result of the development of private property, women's financial dependence on men, and the necessity to protect lines of inheritance. Precapitalist communal societies, so they argued, were egalitarian both in regard to class and sex. The status of women, therefore, was an ideological benchmark against which Communist parties would in theory measure their success in transforming feudal or capitalist societies into Communist ones. Further, the structure of the family, in Marxist theory, stood in the way of both women's equality and communalism.

The CCP was far more successful than its Russian counterpart in drawing upon these theoretical insights to make women an integral part of revolutionary ideology and strategy. Mao Tse-tung's earliest writings on the revolutionary potential of the Chinese peasantry, which represented a departure from traditional Marxist reliance on the industrial worker as the keystone of the revolution, also recognized the interrelationship of the subordination of women and landlord power (see Schram, 250–59). Women, according to Mao, were controlled by political, clan, and religious authority as well as the power of their husbands. But "the political authority of the landlord is the backbone of all other systems of authority. Once this has been overthrown, so clan authority, religious authority, and the authority of the husband all begin to totter" (Schram, 258).

Central, too, to the thought of Mao Tse-tung was the notion that "China's women are a vast reserve of labor power. This reserve should be tapped and used in the struggle to build a mighty socialist country" (Schram, 338–39). The CCP faced a prolonged internal civil war as well as external enemies who greatly outnumbered the Red Army and were vastly better equipped. After the revolution, the Chinese people were at a severe technological disadvantage in competing in world markets and producing goods for home consumption. Mao Tse-tung stressed the "power of the people"—that is, of the aroused masses—who could, with sufficient motivation and by guerilla warfare and labor intensive production techniques ("voluntarism"), triumph over the technologically superior Kuomintang, Japanese, and the West. Thus Mao Tse-tung sought to turn China's vast population from a disadvantage into an advantage. The full integration of women into productive roles was essential.

Techniques of Mobilizing Women (Croll, *Feminism and Socialism*, Chap. 7; Hinton, Chaps. 16, 44; Belden, 275–307). As Croll discusses extensively, mobilizing women's discontent into a revolutionary force carried the danger of backlash from men, and there were and are periods of tension with the CCP regarding the demands of feminism and socialism, the former usually succumbing to the latter. Nevertheless, the CCP throughout its rise to power drew women into military roles, sometimes directly as soldiers but more often in support services, and into agricultural and industrial labor supporting the war effort. Appeals to patriotism, class grievances, and women's liberation were successfully intertwined. The mobilization techniques included the formation of women's associations to represent women's interests; "speak bitterness" meetings (public consciousness-raising sessions at which women were encouraged to ventilate their grievances and discuss solutions), and "pin-point" coercion, in which key figures in the patriarchal-land lord power structure were dealt with by force and killed or driven from the area. The attempt to transform public attitudes about women and undo centuries of internalization of submissive norms were accompanied by intense propaganda through plays, songs, and study meetings. The CCP's new vision of social relationships was embodied in new legal codes instituted first in liberated areas and then in China as a whole.

Transformation of the Legal System (Yang, Chaps. 2–4; Croll, *Women's Movement*, Appendix; Croll, *Feminism and Socialism*, 223–38; Johnson, Chaps. 9–10). The New Marriage Law (1950) represented a complete break with Confucian law, which had regarded the patriarchal family as the cornerstone of social order. (The complete text of the 1950 law is reprinted in Croll, *Women's Movement*, Appendix.) The general principles, as stated in Article 1, were that

> the feudal marriage system based on arbitrary and compulsory arrangements and the supremacy of man over woman, and in disregard of the interests of the children, is abolished. The New Democratic marriage system, which is based on the free choice of partners, on monogamy, on equal rights for both sexes, and on the protection of the lawful interests of women and children, is put into effect.

Specific provisions of the code include the prohibition of concubinage, child betrothal, interference in widow remarriage, and the exaction of dowry; and equal rights of husband and wife in the possession and management of family property, in inheritance, in the use of their family names, in divorce, and in free choice of occupation.

The New Marriage Law also idealistically enjoins couples to "love, respect, assist and look after each other, to live in harmony, to engage in productive work, to care for their children and to strive jointly for the welfare of the family and for the building up of the new society" (Article 8).

Thus, by this law, one of the traditional underpinnings of female inferiority—the Confucian legal code—was formally removed.

Transformation of the Economic System (Yang, Chap. 8; Croll, *Feminism and Socialism*, 238–59, and Chap. 9; Galston; Sidel, (Chaps. 3–7). Land reform has been central to attempts to transform both class and sex hierarchies in China. The first stage involved the redistribution of land to male and female peasants and was completed by 1953. This was followed in 1958 by communal ownership of all but an estimated 5 percent of the land. This small fraction remains in private, that is, family, hands. Workers are assigned work-points for productive labor on the communes and in factories, and the principle of equal work-points (or equal pay) for equal work is part of Chinese law.

Communal child care, and household services such as communal cafeterias, have also been established to alleviate the double burden of women workers with family responsibilities in order to free more of their time for wage labor. These alterations in the material bases of society—the liberation of women from exclusive financial dependence upon the families into which they marry and the elimination of private property and the landlord class—might reasonably be expected to lead to a profound transformation in the status of Chinese women, if Marxist or more general economic interpretations of female status are indeed correct.

Indicators of Resistance and Change (Croll, *Politics of Marriage;* Johnson, Part 4; Parish and Whyte, Part 3; *WIN News* 9, no. 1). The Chinese experience throws light upon how far and how fast changes in the status of women can be implemented, and on the degree to which economic factors are a sufficient explanation of sexual hierarchies. The emphasis of earlier scholarly accounts on the element of change has given way to a note of caution, a note that is mirrored in press reports from China itself. Croll's most recent volume, *The Politics of Marriage*, is based on data from the 1960s. Parish and Whyte's work is based on intensive interviews of former residents of sixty-three different villages in Kwantung, who had left China for Hong Kong, and covers conditions in China from 1969 to 1974. Johnson's book is based on a wide variety of written primary and secondary sources, as well as extensive fieldwork conducted in China during the late 1970s and 1980. Their findings are consistent and complementary, with Johnson providing the most pessimistic account.

Effects of the New Marriage Law. Croll argues that despite the New Marriage Law and intense public education about its provisions, marriage in rural areas still falls considerably short of the egalitarian, free choice socialist ideal. Young peoples' initiatives to choose a partner are seen by parents as expressions of disobedience, and cause a loss of dignity and face among kin and neighbors (33). Still, a pattern of joint consultation is gaining ground. Betrothal gifts to the bride's family and sedan chairs to carry the bride, vestiges of the notion of women as property exchange and marriage as a contract between kin groups, are still in evidence, though some see these as harmless customs, especially as the value of the gifts has declined, and marriage ceremonies have been generally simplified and secularized. The legal age of marriage is twenty for men and eighteen for women, but despite government pressure to marry later, in rural areas most marry as soon as possible after the legal age has been reached. Virilocal marriage patterns persist. Parish and Whyte assert that in divorce cases women usually lose the children, and retain only clothes and personal property (245) despite legal guidelines that emphasize joint property.

Though marriage patterns have changed to a greater extent in urban areas, Croll argues that in rural areas where villages are close-knit, there is no chance of anonymity and local mores still tenaciously hold that it is indecent and immoral for young men and women to talk with one another. The power of gossip remains strong, and both the spirit and letter of the New Marriage Law have been deflected.

Economic Policy and the Status of Women. Current economic policies have hampered change (Croll, *Politics of Marriage*, esp. Chap. 8). In rural areas the family is still a unit of production and consumption. Important sideline income is derived from private land plots. Community services, such as day care and cafeterias,

are unevenly distributed and mainly found on the more prosperous communes; hence, women work less than men outside the
home. Within the home, unpaid domestic labor (performed by
women, usually the elderly) reduces the cost of household maintenance, but produces a dependent class of women. But perhaps of
most importance is the fact that the household budget is still
reckoned collectively. Whyte and Parish reveal that commune
work-point accounting is by household, and payments are made
to the male head of household. Monies cannot be disposed of
individually without permission. Thus women do not have that
crucial power—control of earnings. The structure of patriarchy
has been left intact. In towns, however, households are often
nuclear, wages are paid directly to the worker, and day care,
cafeterias, and other household services are more widespread.
Here traditional attitudes have changed to a greater extent.

Rural conservatism may also be related to the continuing
pattern of women being integrated into their husband's family,
often in another village. This, according to Parish and Whyte,
puts them at a political disadvantage; they are outsiders with less
time, because of household chores, to build up the contacts and
mutual trust necessary to assume leadership positions. Parish and
Whyte also point out that educational campaigns have virtually
neglected the idea of involving men in household tasks in order to
free women's time (201). The proportion of women members in
the Communist Party is probably less than one-quarter (239). At
the village level the Chinese Women's Federation, which in earlier
periods took a fairly vigorous stand in implementing the New
Marriage Law, emerges in the Parish and Whyte account as little
involved in advocacy, and is chiefly in evidence as a means of
organizing women behind general national goals, such as increased production and birth control (239–40).

There is also ample evidence that women's work continues to
receive a lower cultural valuation than men's. A number of visitors
to communes and factories have pointed to a continuing pattern
of sex-role differentiation in jobs. Women's work receives lower
work-points than men's work (see, for example, Galston's account
of field labor in a commune), even where it is difficult to find a
rational reason based on such factors as skill or strength.

Female Infanticide. Most serious of all, girls' lives are still more
expendable than boys'. The Chinese press has recently high-
lighted the continuing problem of female infanticide by abandonment, exposure, or drowning. In some communes just 200 girls

survive out of every 500 children born, though the birth rate of girls is only slightly lower than that of boys. Women are still sometimes cursed and beaten by their husbands and mothers-in-law for bearing girls. Males constitute 51.8 percent of the Chinese population; females 48.5 percent.

The pressure to prefer male babies is said to have intensified because of the current government campaign to curb China's enormous population (now estimated at 1.03 billion) by instituting a "one-child family" drive. Communities have been assigned a quota of new babies, and couples must receive authorization before trying to have a child. Compliance is rewarded economically through such means as a monthly stipend, priority admission to schools, and free medical care for the child. Faced with a one-child choice, couples may choose to sacrifice a baby girl. Sons are still more valuable economically, and according to an official report, many Chinese still believe that without a son, there can be no descendents. (see *International Dateline,* December 1982, and *Observer,* December 12, 1982, reprinted in *WIN News* 9, no. 1 p. 51).

Thus, although there has been a considerable advance in the status of women in China, especially if one compares present conditions with the prerevolutionary norm, the picture remains one of incomplete equality.

Discussion Questions

1. Engels argued that "participation in social labour by all women is a prerequisite to their emancipation. To attain that aim, it will be necessary to eliminate the family as an economic unit of society." (Croll, *Feminism and Socialism,* 276). To what degree has the Chinese family been altered as an economic unit? Are the remaining elements of the family as an economic unit sufficient to explain the secondary status of women?

2. Compare the roles of ideology and economics in altering the status of women in the Kwantung Marriage Resistance Movement and the Chinese Communist Revolution.

3. In light of the politics of women's liberation in the Chinese Communist Revolution to date, evaluate whether an independent women's movement is necessary to liberate Chinese women or whether liberation can occur only as part of a total revolutionary movement.

4. Discuss the relative importance of legal, political, ideological, and economic reforms in upgrading the status of women in light of the Chinese experience.

5. Is the remaining discrimination against women in China based on the economic system, vestiges of "feudal thought," women's biological functions, male chauvinism, or is there no single cause for its perpetuation?

6. Compare the techniques of the CCP with those of the Marxist groups in western India described by Gail Omvedt (see Chapter 6 on "Women in Contemporary India," above). Account for the success of one and the failure of the other in moblizing women.

7. Mao Tse-tung argued that freeing women from household labor was crucial to their equality. The solution, he said, did not lie in household gadgetry but in the socialization of individual household chores into collective paid endeavors (Croll, *Feminism and Socialism*, 267–68). Discuss his assumptions and his solutions.

CHAPTER EIGHT

WOMEN IN OCEANIA

Karen Sinclair

As an ethnographic area, Oceania encompasses Polynesia, Melanesia, Micronesia, and Australia. Such striking cultural diversity makes generalizations about the lives and experiences of women in the area difficult if not impossible. The information available is by no means uniform throughout the Pacific; women have been studied extensively in some areas, ignored in others, and in most, treated as a by-product of more interesting masculine machinations. For example, widespread sexual antagonism in Melanesia was reported quite early in this century but it is only recently that a woman's perspective has been available (in Marilyn Strathern's *Women in Between* and in Diane Bell's *Daughters of the Dreaming*).

In many parts of the Pacific, recognition of the male bias typical of early ethnography has prompted new research as well as some reexaminations and reanalyses of the data. Nevertheless, notions of sexual polarity, gender inequality, and male dominance will not disappear or diminish in significance with a new analysis. By examining the perspectives of women, we may be better able to understand the complex social and cultural processes that are found in Oceania. Recent work by Herdt, O'Brien and Tiffany, Ortner, and Poole has increased our awareness of the complexity of the issues.

The first lectures describe the aboriginal conditions of the Pacific, concentrating on the role women played in the complex stratified systems of Polynesia and comparing these to the roles assumed by women in Melanesia and Australia. The next section focuses on gender ideology and its effects on social and ceremonial life. The final section is concerned with modernization and social change in the Pacific.

The following bibliography is suggested as an overview of the
status of women in the different culture areas of Oceania. There is
no text for Micronesia.

General Bibliography

Readings for Students
Brown, Paula, and Georgida Buchbinder, eds. *Man and Woman in
the New Guinea Highlands.* Special publication of the Amer-
ican Anthropological Association, no. 8, 1976.
Mead, Margaret. *Coming of Age in Samoa.* New York: William
Morrow & Co., 1973.
————. *Sex and Temperament in Three Primitive Societies.* 3d ed.
New York: William Morrow & Co., 1960.
Rohrlich-Leavitt, Ruby, Barbara Sykes, and Elizabeth Weather-
ford. "Aboriginal Woman: Male and Female Anthropological
Perspectives." In *Toward an Anthropology of Women,* edited by
Rayna R. Reiter, 110–126. New York: Monthly Review Press,
1975.
Salmond, Anne, and Amiria Stirling. *Amiria: The Life History of a
Maori Woman.* Wellington, New Zealand: A. H. & A. W.
Reed, 1976.
Strathern, Marilyn. *Women in Between.* London: Seminar Press,
1972.
Weiner, Annette B. *Women of Value, Men of Reknown: New Perspec-
tives in Trobriand Exchange.* Austin: University of Texas Press,
1976.

Readings for Instructors
Bell, Diane. *Daughters of the Dreaming.* Sydney: Allen & Unwin,
1984.
Gale, Fay, ed. *Women's Role in Aboriginal Society.* Australian Ab-
original Studies, no. 36. Canberra: Australian National
Institute of Aboriginal Studies, 1970.
Goodale, Jane. *Tiwi Wives.* Seattle: University of Washington
Press, 1971.
Herdt, Gilbert. *Guardians of the Flutes: Idioms of Masculinity.* New
York: McGraw-Hill, 1981.
Herdt, Gilbert, ed. *Ritualized Homosexuality in Melanesia.* Berkeley:
University of California Press, 1984.
————. *Rituals of Manhood.* Berkeley: University of California
Press, 1982.

Heuer, Berys. *Maori Women.* Wellington, New Zealand: A. H. & A. W. Reed, 1972.

Kaberry, Phyllis. *Aboriginal Woman: Sacred and Profane.* London: Routledge & Kegan Paul, 1939.

O'Brien, Denise, and Sharon Tiffany. *Rethinking Women's Roles: Perspectives from the Pacific.* Berkeley: University of California Press, 1984.

Ortner, Sherry, and Harriet Whitehead, eds. *Sexual Meanings: The Cultural Construction of Gender and Sexuality.* Cambridge: Cambridge University Press, 1981.

THE ROLE AND STATUS OF WOMEN IN TRADITIONAL PACIFIC SOCIETIES

The diversity of Oceania must be acknowledged as the instructor begins this set of lectures. Although Polynesia was contacted by adventurers early in the eighteenth century, parts of New Guinea remained unexplored until fairly recently. The nature of contact was different in the many island societies and produced significantly different results. Furthermore, traditional social structures were quite diverse. In Polynesia, the nature of chieftainships varied; in Melanesia, political and economic arrangements were far from consistent across the culture area. Nevertheless, several patterns tended to typify the indigenous cultures. In Polynesia, rank as well as gender was a factor in status differentiation. There were institutionalized roles for high-ranking women such as the *taupo* of Samoa, the *puhi* in New Zealand, and the *mayakitanga* in the Cook Islands. In Hawaii, women often exerted considerable political influence. Even in kinship systems in which the male line was supreme (such as Tonga), women were accorded some prestige in recognition of the often awesome powers of fathers' sisters.

The position of women throughout Polynesia was intertwined with the religious system; while women were seldom priests, they could participate as family mediums. This differential participation in religious ritual reflected the general opposition of men and women in the ideological system. Such notions were greatly elaborated in New Zealand, where women were viewed as potential pollutants and so were restricted in their activities. However, these beliefs were not so consistently developed in other areas of Polynesia. Perhaps because of this variability, some anthropologists have argued that Polynesians have complementary role relations, while others have seen opposition.

In Melanesia, the activities of women have been obscured by the more dramatic rituals and events that attend masculine endeavors. As a general rule, the perception of women is negative, especially regarding the biological functions that mark them as antithetical and therefore dangerous to men and masculinity. It is in this context that notions of pollution are most often expressed. Although menstruating women are often segregated and viewed as contaminating pollutants, men often seek to appropriate and to imitate the reproductive capacity of women. Homosexuality, nose bleeding, and genital operations assert male dominance in the face of the dangerous and threatening fertility of women. Moreover, men seem to recognize, at least implicitly, the importance of women's contribution; their economic production (of pigs and garden produce) and reproduction have been essential to the perpetuation of indigenous political and economic systems. In New Guinea, these capacities have been controlled by senior men, who negotiate and finance marital exchanges and alliances. In the Trobriands, women have considerably more autonomy. In Australia, research by Goodale and Kaberry indicates that aboriginal women are active in all spheres of life. Contrary to earlier views, they are far from mere pawns in masculine games of prestige and power. Similarly, Bell asserts that the traditional independence and productivity of Australian women made them indispensable to the group. Moreover, Bell discovered and demonstrates in her book that women too possess ritual access to esoteric knowledge that complements the ritual expertise of men.

Readings for Students
Langness, L. L. "Sexual Antagonism in the New Guinea Highlands: A Bena Bena Example." *Oceania* 37 (1967): 161–77.
Mead, Margaret. *Coming of Age in Samoa.*
———. *Sex and Temperament.*
Rohrlich-Leavitt, Ruby, Barbara Sykes, and Elizabeth Weatherford. "Aboriginal Woman." In *Toward an Anthropology of Women.*
Weiner, Annette. *Women of Value, Men of Reknown.*

Readings for Instructors
Bell, Diane. *Daughters of the Dreaming.*
Blackwood, B. *Both Sides of Buka Passage: An Ethnographic Study of*

Social, Sexual, and Economic Positions in the Northwestern Solomon Islands. Oxford: Clarendon Press, 1935.

Goldman, Irving. *Ancient Polynesian Society.* Chicago: University of Chicago Press, 1970.

Goodale, Jane. *Tiwi Wives.*

Gunson, Neil. "Great Women and Friendship Contract Rites in Pre-Christian Tahiti." *Journal of the Polynesian Society* 73 (1964): 53–69.

Hanson, F. Allan. "Female Pollution in Polynesia?" *Journal of the Polynesian Society* 91 (1982): 335–82.

Hecht, Julia. "The Culture of Gender in Puka Puka: Male, Female and the Mayakitanga 'Sacred Maid.'" *Journal of the Polynesian Society* 86 (1977): 183–206.

Herdt, Gilbert. *Guardians of the Flutes.*

Hogbin, Ian. *Wogeo: The Isle of Menstruating Men.* New York: Chandler Pub. Co., 1970.

Kaberry, Phyllis. *Aboriginal Woman.*

Keesing, F. "The Taupo System of Samoa: A Study of Institutional Change." *Oceania* 8 (1937): 1–14.

Keesing, Roger. "Kwaio Women Speak: The Micropolitics of Autobiography in a Solomon Island Society." *American Anthropologist* 87 (1985): 27–39.

Langness, L. L. "Discussion." In *Man and Woman in the New Guinea Highlands.*

Lutkehaus, Nancy. "Ambivalence, Ambiguity and the Reproduction of Gender Hierarchy in Manam Society, 1933–79." *Social Analysis* 12 (1982): 36–51.

Mead, Margaret. "Weaver of the Border." In *In the Company of Men,* edited by Joseph Casagrande. New York: Harper and Row, 1964.

Meigs, Anna. "Male Pregnancy and the Reduction of Sexual Opposition in a New Guinea Highlands Society." *Ethnology* 25 (1976): 393–407.

O'Brien, Denise. "Women Never Hunt: The Portrayal of Women in Melanesian Ethnography." In *Rethinking Women's Roles.*

O'Brien, Denise and Sharon Tiffany. *Rethinking Women's Roles.*

Ortner, Sherry. "Gender and Sexuality in Hierarchical Societies: The Case of Polynesia and Some Comparative Implications." In *Sexual Meanings,* 359–409.

Rogers, Garth. "The Father's Sister Is Black: A Consideration of Rank and Power in Tonga." *Journal of the Polynesian Society* 86 (1977): 157–82.

Sebbelov, G. "The Social Position of Men and Women Among the
    Natives of East Malekula, New Hebrides." *American An-
    thropologist* (1913).
Thurnwald, Hilde. "Women's Status in Buin Society." *Oceania* 5
    (1934).
Wedgwood, C. H. "Women in Manam." *Oceania* 7 (1936): 401–
    29; *Oceania* 8 (1937): 170–93.
————. "The Nature and Functions of Secret Societies." *Oceania* 1
    (1930): 129–45.

Lecture Topics

Pacific Women and Male Bias. Many of the societies in the Pacific
appear to celebrate male dominance. In some cases, this appearance has been promoted as a result of research efforts in
which male anthropologists conveyed, often inadvertently, at
times deliberately, only a masculine perspective in their descriptions of Oceanic societies. By talking to women, female anthropologists are now able to provide an alternative, or counter-
ideology. For example, Weiner, Goodale, Strathern, and Bell have
been important in demonstrating the limitations of a male perspective and in establishing the autonomy of women's lives and
work. There is also the problem of interpretation. As early as
1937, Wedgwood cautioned against interpreting Melanesian
cultures against a background of European values. She wrote:
"Women are junior partners rather than employees, cooperators
rather than dependents" (but see a more recent interpretation of
Manam culture by Lutkehaus).

Yet religious systems throughout the area have tended to
stress masculine preeminence and feminine exclusion. The instructor should discuss with the class to what degree this is a result
of a male bias in Western academic interpretations and to what
extent men actually do dominate the cultural concerns of the
Pacific.

Gender, Status, and Social Structure. Aboriginal Polynesian societies were stratified chieftainships. The degree of stratification
varied, and the complexity of the society in turn affected the
position of women. In general, the more highly stratified the
society—that is, the greater the degree of status differentiation—
the better the position of women was likely to be, for considerations of descent and rank often complicated explicit notions of
gender. In the more simple Polynesian chieftainships (e.g., the

Maori of New Zealand), descent, rank, and gender reinforced women's subservient position. However, in the more highly elaborated societies, high rank and chiefly descent countered the liabilities of feminine gender. In Polynesia generally, and in western Polynesia especially, power was given to the male line while honor was ascribed to the female line. In the Cook Islands, such notions gave substance to women's participation in social life. In Tonga, a father's sister (an institutionalized status) ostensibly had considerable powers to utter maledictions, thus calling down curses upon the heads of her opponents. Although clearly not formal authority, such informal, negative control was not to be underestimated.

Honorific Status Positions. In many cases, the prestige of high-ranking women was institutionalized, as among the *taupo* in Samoa, the *tapairu* of the New Zealand Maori, and the *mayakitanga* among the Cook Islanders. It is not clear that the existence of sacred maidens enhanced the position of all women, although Ortner maintains that virginity "thus appears in its cultural context to be an expression and cultivation of the overall higher value of women in such systems."

Women as Wives, Mothers, and Sisters. Women's roles were substantially different, and they received different ritual and social recognition as sisters and as wives. In Polynesia a woman lost status when she married, for a wife had neither the power nor the influence of a sister in a kinship group. Similarly, in Highland New Guinea, sisters were powerful while wives were polluting. In unilineal, unilocal kinship groups with endemic warfare, female affines could not help but be threatening. Although in many Melanesian and Australian societies men still control marriage transactions and hence the movement of women, it is quite clear that women are more than pawns in marital exchanges. Goodale writes: "Both male and female Tiwi view their culture's rules governing choice of mates as providing them with considerable freedom and variety throughout their life . . ." Nevertheless, marriage is viewed differently by men and women. Men have more opportunities to express their individuality while women are expected to participate but not to innovate.

In all Pacific societies, women made substantial economic contributions. Recent studies, as well as some of the early work by Margaret Mead and Gregory Bateson, indicate that women's roles were complex; as helpmeets or antagonists they aided or subverted their husbands' ambitions. Similarly, as socializers of children they exercised important influence.

Women and Religion. In general, the religious system reinforced the expected and predictable male hegemony. In extreme cases (e.g., the Maori in Polynesia and many Highland New Guinea societies in Melanesia) women were viewed as common and were prohibited from any contact with the sacred. Men operated the religious machinery while women were active only at the lowest levels, usually as family mediums. Yet in other societies, women were given somewhat greater opportunity to participate in religious affairs. In Melanesia and Australia, women had their own secret societies and their own exclusive ceremonial activities. Prohibitions that restricted female activity were generally relaxed as women aged; elderly women were not uncommonly in positions of authority, and were permitted access to spheres that were off limits to the younger members of their sex. The ascendance of elderly women has been reported for Australia, Melanesia, and Polynesia.

Women of Influence and Prestige. At least one lecture should be devoted to the presence and effect of prominent and successful Polynesian women like Queen Charlotte of Tonga, Kaahumanu of the Hawaiian Islands, and Phebe Parkinson, whom Mead portrayed in "Weaver of the Border." Their examples demonstrate that despite religious and cultural notions of female inferiority, women were able to understand and manipulate the complex rules that governed their lives.

Discussion Questions
1. In what ways were the sacred maidens of Polynesia considered different from other young women? What obligations and responsibilities went along with sacred office? Is there an analogue in contemporary American society?

2. Through what loopholes in Polynesian social organization could women gain power and prestige?

3. What do Tongans mean when they say "the father's sister is black"?

4. What factors have complicated our understanding of women in the Pacific?

GENDER IDEOLOGY

The relationship between the sexes is very complex in Pacific societies. In some societies men and women complement one another, while in others they are viewed as mutually dangerous. Nevertheless, men and women operate within a single sociopolitical system, even if their roles are somewhat distinct and they occupy separate spheres. Research in Polynesia suggests that a domestic/public dichotomy is not really applicable. Moreover, there is ample evidence to suggest that women become formidable political figures in Polynesia once they pass childbearing age. Antagonistic gender relations are not common. But in some Polynesian societies there are clear concerns with the defiling aspects of womanhood; menstruation and childbirth receive considerable ritual attention. By contrast, in Melanesia, gender ideology permeates the social and cultural landscape. Maleness and femaleness are antithetical principles whose separation is essential for the well-being of the society. Women occupy a peculiar, anomalous position: while viewed as a source of pollution and danger, they are nonetheless responsible for the perpetuation of the society.

In many Melanesian societies, maculinity and femininity are central issues that require a great deal of ritual consideration. Despite the diversity of Melanesian cultures, certain patterns do emerge: political organizations revolve about "big men" and warfare; male initiation ceremonies; male cults; and the widespread emphasis on male solidarity and superiority. Thus male/female relations can only be considered within the context of complicated ideological and social structures that emphasize the social differences between men and women as well as the spiritual antipathy between masculinity and femininity. Women's perspectives have been presented by Strathern, Weiner, and Miranda.

Readings for Students

Faithorn, Elizabeth. "The Concept of Pollution Among the Kafe of the Papua New Guinea Highlands." In *Toward an Anthropology of Women*.

Goodale, Jane, *Tiwi Wives*.

Heuer, Berys. *Maori Women*.

Langness, L. L. "Ritual Power and Male Dominance in the New Guinea Highlands." In *The Anthropology of Power*, edited by Raymond Fogelson and Richard Adams. New York: Academic Books, 1977.

Mead, Margaret. *Male and Female*. New York: William Morrow &
    Co., 1949.
————. *Sex and Temperament*.
Miranda, Elli. "Lau Malaita: A Woman Is an Alien Spirit." In
    Many Sisters: Women in Cross-Cultural Perspective, edited by
    Carolyn J. Matthiasson. New York: The Free Press, 1974.
Strathern, Marilyn. *Women in Between*.

Readings for Instructors
Allen, M. R. *Male Cults and Secret Initiations in Melanesia*.
    Melbourne: Melbourne University Pres, 1967.
Bateson, Gregory. *Naven*. Stanford: Stanford University Press,
    1936.
Bell, Diane. *Daughters of the Dreaming*.
Brown, Paula, and Georgida Buchbinder, eds. *Man and Woman in
    the New Guinea Highlands*.
Faithorn, Elizabeth. "Women as Persons: Aspects of Female Life
    and Male-Female Relations Among the Kafe." In *Man and
    Woman in the New Guinea Highlands*.
Feil, D. K. "Women and Men in the Enga Tee." *American Eth-
    nologist* 5 (1978): 263–79.
Goldman, Irving. *Ancient Polynesian Society*.
Herdt, Gilbert. *Guardians of the Flutes*.
Herdt, Gilbert, ed. *Ritualized Homosexuality in Melanesia*.
————. *Rituals of Manhood*.
Hogbin, Ian. *Wogeo: The Isle of Menstruating Men*.
Hooper, Antony, and Judith Huntsman. "Male and Female in
    Tokelau Culture." *Journal of the Polynesian Society* 84 (1975):
    415–30.
Kaberry, Phyllis. *Aboriginal Woman*.
Langness, L. L. "Ritual Power and Male Dominance in the New
    Guinea Highlands." In *The Anthropology of Power*.
Levy, R. *Tahitians: Mind and Experience in the Society Islands*.
    Chicago: University of Chicago Press, 1973.
Lindenbaum, Shirley. "Variations on a Sociosexual Theme in
    Melanesia." In *Ritualized Homosexuality in Melanesia*.
————. "A Wife Is the Hand of Man." In *Man and Woman in the
    New Guinea Highlands*.
Meigs, Anna. "A Papuan Perspective on Pollution." *Man* 13
    (1978): 304–18.
Meggitt, M. J. "Male-Female Relations in the Highlands of Aus-
    tralian New Guinea." *American Anthropologist* 66 (1964): 204–
    24.

Ortner, Sherry. "Gender and Sexuality in Hierarchical Societies: The Case of Polynesia and Some Comparative Implications." In *Sexual Meanings.*

Poole, Fitz John Porter. "Transforming Natural Woman." In *Sexual Meanings.*

Shore, Bradd. "Sexuality and Gender in Samoa: Conceptions and Missed Conceptions." In *Sexual Meanings.*

Strathern, Andrew. "Men's House, Women's House: The Efficacy of Opposition Reversal and Pairing in the Melpa Amkor Cult." *Journal of the Polynesian Society* 88 (1979): 37–51.

———. "The Female and Male Spirit Cult in Mount Hagen." *Man* 5 (1970): 571–85.

Tiffany, Sharon. "Introduction: Feminist Perspectives in Anthropology." In *Rethinking Women's Roles.*

Wedgwood, C. H. "The Nature and Function of Secret Societies." *Oceania* 1 (1930): 129–45.

Weiner, Annette. *Women of Value, Men of Reknown.*

———. "Trobriand Kinship from Another View: The Reproductive Power of Women and Men." *Man* 14 (1979): 328–48.

White, Isobel. "Aboriginal Women's Status: A Paradox Resolved." In *Women's Role in Aboriginal Society,* 21–29.

Whiting, B. *Becoming a Kwoma.* New Haven: Yale University Press (Institute of Human Relations), 1941.

Lecture Topics

Ideological Bases of Status Differentiation. In much of Polynesia, men and women were defined in terms of one another, suggesting both the differences that were thought to exist and the complementarity that so frequently was present in practice. Depending on the society, maleness and femaleness were defined as antithetical or complementary. In most cases there were actually elements of both. In those societies that claimed men and women were antithetical, the actual division of labor often emphasized mutual cooperation; in societies whose ideologies suggested complementarity, there were often significant impediments to women's full social participation. In the more extreme cases, for example, Maori men were defined as *tapu,* or sacred, while women were seen as *noa,* or common. Similarly, in Hawaii, perceived differences in sanctity made it impossible for men and women to dine together. Thus, religious notions in one way or another tended to militate against equal participation of men and women in all spheres of social life. Male activities have been given preeminence by anthropologists and by the cultural ideology. Role amgibuities, occasioned by rank or personal predilections, were seen in the Great Women of Tahiti and their male servants, the feminized *mahu* who loyally waited upon their female masters.

While the division of labor was often buttressed by religious notions, it would be inaccurate to suggest that a domestic/public distinction can be applied to Polynesia. Instructors can make this point quite readily using whatever society they are taking as an example. Tiffany has written:

> Single or multiple household ties are not necessarily focused on mother-child relationships. Furthermore, the notion of household in Oceania does not invariably convey the connotation of being "domestic," private or low status. To define the household as "domestic" and activities beyond it as "public" would be a distortion of reality, given the almost daily fluctuations in compositions, as well as the continual flow of goods.

In Melanesia, cultural notions of maleness and femaleness pervade all aspects of social endeavor. Often men and women occupy mutually exclusive spheres. Male initiation ceremonies and/or male cults accompany the rather widespread emphasis on male solidarity and masculine superiority. But Keesing cautions that while sexual polarity may appear similar in different societies, the nature of male/female relations is far from uniform. While in some societies, the ideology emphasizes the differences that exist between males and females, in other areas myth and ritual become vehicles for the expression of fear, hostility, and envy of women. In many, but not all societies, men and women lead separate, distinct lives; men reside in men's houses, while women, viewed as pollutants, spend several days a month in menstrual huts, or in specially demarcated sections of the house. However, even in those cases of active, explicit sexual opposition, it would be a mistake to view women as passive. In 1934–35 Hilde Thurnwald documented the incidence of abortion and birth control.

Socialization and Initiation. In general, the different experiences males and females have over the course of the life cycle results in differential socialization. By and large, young men are prepared for formal ceremonial responsibilities, while young women are trained in household responsibilities. In Polynesia, initiations do not separate men from women or the uninitiated, although the organization and preparation for war may well have served this purpose. In Melanesia and Australia, initiation ceremonies explicitly celebrate masculine strength and control. Throughout

Melanesia, sexual polarity, male biological incompleteness, and ceremonial secrecy are major themes in male cults and male initiation ceremonies. Herdt has pointed out that for many Highlanders growth is seen as natural for women but difficult, and hence subject to cultural manipulation, for men. In the Eastern Highlands, men deliberately imitate women's procreative capacities. Rituals equating semen and breast milk, nosebleeding and menstruation affirm the ultimate superiority of males and masculinity and celebrate their social and sexual power. Yet, while fear and hostility are commonly expressed in ceremonies, the interdependence of men and women may also be proclaimed, as it is by the Siane and the Iatmul.

Lawrence and Meggitt note that the harshness of the ritual ordeal is often related to the degree of hostility between men and women. In the Eastern Highlands, where antagonism is quite intense, male superiority is reaffirmed, while the procedure is less demanding in the Western Highlands where sexual dissatisfaction is not as pronounced. In many cultures, women are excluded from secret societies and thus from ceremonial participation. In others, women have their own secret societies and their own exclusive ceremonial activities (see, e.g., Goodale, White, and Bell). Wedgwood, who studied Malekula (New Hebrides), in which both men and women belong to secret societies, writes:

> We have here therefore not a contest between men as important and women as unimportant but rather a recognition and socialization of the different qualities and of the innate suspicion of an antagonism between the sexes which characterizes the behavior of groups of men and groups of women toward each other.

Explanations. Several theories have been proposed to elucidate the hostility between men and women. Many analysts integrate several theories into complex cosmologies. Others, such as Margaret Mead, suggest that male behavior is understandable in terms of womb envy, or an insufficiently developed male identity. She suggests that the discrepancy between the expectations attendant upon childhood and adulthood provokes a neurotic response among some Melanesian males. Meggitt and Allen explain hostility in terms of the practical political exigencies of marrying into enemy tribes. Langness suggests that warfare, male solidarity, and the appropriation of women's labor make sexual polarity inevitable. Herdt has recently suggested that women's status is higher in high population areas of Melanesia. In these societies, characterized by Big Men and economic exchange, women's contribution to such transactions raises their status in the absence of economically productive activities. Male hegemony is expressed through ritualized homosexuality. Keesing has integrated a variety of approaches to give us the most comprehensive attempt at explanation.

Women and the Life Cycle. The inappropriateness of a public/ private dichotomy for Polynesia can be seen in the increasing prominence of women as they move through the life cycle. Never wholly absent from ceremonial activity, they assume significant responsibilities as they mature past the childbearing years. Moreover, many of the negative connotations and prohibitions attached to femininity are relaxed as women age. In Polynesia, old women often act as mediators between the aboriginal culture and encroaching Western ideals and technology. In Melanesia, postmenopausal women, no longer viewed as pollutants, may occupy powerful positions. In Australia, a woman's prestige also increases as she matures, for she now is able to exert control over her sons-in-law. Goodale also notes that women can obtain some leverage over their husbands by engaging in extramarital affairs.

The Contribution of Women Reconsidered. Recent researchers (Strathern, Weiner, Feil) have all suggested that women play a far more dynamic role in Oceanic society than was previously thought. Weiner, who did field work in the anthropological shrine of the Trobriand Islands, discovered a female world of high finance and prestige that was a surprising complement to the male exchange system whose depiction so dominated the literature. A similar conclusion has been reached by Feil in his analysis of the Enga Tee exchange. Strathern's analysis of Hagen women reveals that women are important intermediaries between their affinal and natal groups. Furthermore, women have the means at their disposal with which to undercut and short-circuit masculine careers. Such potential treachery has also been documented by Miranda for Lau Malaita.

Feil, Weiner, and Strathern do not always agree with one another when they attempt to define and locate the position of women in Melanesian society. But it is significant that women are now the focus of important empirical research.

Discussion Questions
1. Men are isolated in the men's house performing duties and rituals that are culturally prescribed as "male" activities, and women are in the menstrual huts at times

when their female nature is most apparent (menstruation and parturition). Why is it that men perceive it as an honor to go to the men's house, while women are "banished" whey they attend the menstrual hut? In other words, since both institutions create sexual solidarity, why is one viewed as an "honor" to be earned, while the other is seen as a "stigma" to be overcome?

2. What, if any, correlation exists between the presence of a men's house where the men actually reside, and the position of women?

3. Why do women accept the public view of themselves as inferior and dangerous? If they are indeed believed to be so damaging, why don't they spend their time terrorizing, rather than acquiescing to the surrounding men? In other words, why not translate their symbolic potency into actual power?

4. Can a public/private dichotomy be applied to Polynesia? Are male and female roles complementary, asymmetrical, neither, or both?

5. What evidence does Faithorn use to suggest that pollution may apply to men as well as to women? Why is Langness skeptical?

6. Mead suggests that much of the ritual activity of men in Melanesia is an expression of an ill-disguised womb envy. Do you agree? What other explanations are possible to account for male/female hostility?

7. What courses of action are open to women in societies where they are defined as pollutants and men are the dominant actors in political and economic activities?

8. What new light has Weiner's and Strathern's research shed on the position of women in the Pacific?

WOMEN AND MODERNIZATION

The two greatest influences on Pacific Island life have been the advent of missions and the appearance of colonists and colonial administrators. Missionaries and their wives introduced new models into Pacific Island conceptions of womanhood. Women, who were frequently mediums in indigenous Polynesian religious systems, readily became members of church women's groups. While this might appear to be, and indeed in some cases did represent, a lowering of status, the church was influential in local affairs and women's participation in church activities often accompanied pronounced gains in status. In general, however, the ideology of the colonizers had a negative effect on the status of women. The current status of women in Oceania is a complex issue. In many areas their position has deteriorated. Yet there are some aspects of the modern situation that would appear to work to women's advantage.

Research seems to have been most active in Melanesia, where the effects of economic development have been documented in a variety of cultural contexts. The results are both incomplete and, as usual, somewhat contradictory. Gains made by young girls are often accomplished at the expense of older women. In some societies men have become entrepreneurs, while in others women have formed savings associations that provide them with both money and leverage.

Readings for Students

Bell, Diane. "Desert Politics: Choices in the Marriage Market." In *Women and Colonization*, 239–69.

Nash, J. "Women and Power in Nagovisi Society." *Journal de la Societe des Oceanistes* 34 (1978): 119–26.

Reay, Marie. "Politics, Development and Women in the Rural Highlands." *Administration for Developments* (1975): 4–12.

Salmond, Anne, and Amiria Stirling. *Amiria.*

Strathern, Andrew. "Gender, Ideology and Money in Mount Hagen." *Man* 14 (1979): 530–48.

Weiner, Annette. "Stability in Banana Leaves." In *Women and Colonization*, 275–93.

Readings for Instructors

Barwick, Diane. "Outsiders: Aboriginal Women." In *In Their Own Right*, edited by J. Rigg, 85–97. Sydney: Thomas Nelson, 1969.

Bell, Diane. *Daughters of the Dreaming.*

Boutillier, James. "European Women in the Solomon Islands, 1900–1942: Accommodation and Change on the Pacific Frontier." In *Rethinking Women's Roles.*

Finney, Ben R. *Big Men and Business: Entrepreneurship and Economic Growth in the New Guinea Highlands.* Canberra: Australian National University Press, 1973.

Forman, Charles. "Sing to the Lord a New Song: Women in the Churches of Oceania." In *Rethinking Women's Roles*.

Gailey, Christine. "Putting Down Sisters and Wives: Tongan Women and Colonization." In *Women and Colonization*, 294–323.

Gale, Fay, ed. *Women's Role in Aboriginal Society*.

Griffin, Vanessa. "Women's Role in Fiji 'Suva'." The South Pacific Social Science Association.

Mead, Margaret. "Weaver of the Border." In *In the Company of Men*.

Nash, J. "Matriliny and Modernization: The Nagovisi of South Bougainville." *New Guinea Research Bulletin* 55 (1974).

Randall, Shirley K. "United for Action: Women's Fellowships, an Agent of Change in Papua New Guinea." *Point* 2 (1975): 118–31.

Reay, Marie. "Aboriginal and White Family Structure: An Inquiry into Assimilation Trends." *Sociological Review* 11, no. 1 (1963): 19–47.

———. "Women in Transitional Societies." In *New Guinea on the Threshold*, edited by E. R. Fisk, 166–84. Pittsburgh: University of Pittsburgh Press, 1968.

Reeson, Margaret. "Southern Highlands Women in Gospel Perspective." *Point* 2 (1975): 95–101.

Sexton, Lorraine. "Little Women and Big Men in Business: A Goroken Development Project and Social Stratification." *Oceania* 54 (1983): 133–50.

———. "Pigs, Pearlshells, and 'Women's Work': Collective Response to Change in Highland Papua New Guinea." In *Rethinking Women's Roles*.

Sinclair, Karen. "Maori Women at Midlife." In *In Her Prime! A New View of Middle Aged Women*, edited by Judith Brown and Virginia Kerns. Hadley, Mass.: Bergin, 1984.

Tonkinson, Robert. *The Jigalong Mob*. Menlo Park, Cal.: Cummings, 1971.

White, Isobel. "Aboriginal Women in Transition." In *Seminars 1971*. Centre for Research into Aboriginal Affairs, Monash University, 1971.

———. "Aboriginal Women's Status: A Paradox Resolved." In *Women's Role in Aboriginal Society*, 21–29.

Lecture Topics

The Effects of Colonists and Missionaries. The arrival of whalers, missionaries, and finally colonists had an important effect on women in the Pacific. Venereal and other diseases were introduced during this period, affecting the general health and fertility of the population.

The social effects of early contact, especially with missionaries, tended to be rather ambiguous. On the one hand, Pacific women (especially those in Melanesia and Australia) had to confront the dual problems of caste and gender. Gailey claims that early visitors to Tonga devalued women, while Bell asserts that in Australia missionaries now give aboriginal women little recognition. Yet mission churches often have provided women greater opportunities for religious participation than had been true in the traditional culture. In some cases, women have found public voice in new religious movements. In these instances, inspiration has more than compensated for their previous lack of public religious activity.

In Australia, Bell has analyzed changing marriage rules and suggests that women are now at a disadvantage. Dependent on a government that does not recognize their former autonomy, aboriginal women "are forced to the periphery of frontier society from where their only access is sexual." Violence and instability frequently mark the marriages of young women. Summing up the situation for many Pacific women, Bell writes:

> Women were disadvantaged from the outset because of the white male perception of them as domestic workers and sex objects. Aboriginal men have been able to take real political advantage of certain aspects of frontier society, while aboriginal women have been seen by whites as peripheral to the political process.

Women and the Labor Force. The introduction of a wage economy has had differential effects on the status of men and women, transforming their relationship to economic structures and to one another. In general, men gain legitimacy, while women have moved into the labor force in more menial capacities. Even when women are trained as nurses and teachers (as they are in Papua, New Guinea), they abandon these careers when they marry. For the Tiwi in Australia, innovation has been accommodated without severe dislocation; evidence from other areas in Australia would suggest that other tribes have not been so fortunate.

In addition, migrations to urban centers have altered traditional family structure; women frequently find themselves with increased financial and family responsibilities and decreased kin support. Nash's work demonstrates that an ideology of equality may well alienate women from other women and from their own people.

Women's Organizations and Public Participation. An increasingly important public force has been the emergence of women's organizations. Sexton has analyzed a women's savings organization, demonstrating the significance of new forms of female solidarity. In New Zealand, the importance of single-sex committees and of the Maori Women's Welfare League has been documented by many anthropologists. In addition, several scholars have noted that the position of older Maori women has in fact improved in the postcolonial situation. New Zealand, however, appears to be an exception. For the rest of Oceania, it is difficult to say whether such public activities compensate for the general loss of status upon modernization.

Discussion Questions

1. In what ways has the ideology of Western culture influenced the direction change has taken in the Pacific? What happened to the status of women in Oceania when Western ideas and religion were introduced?

2. How has the "Big Man" system prepared men to be entrepreneurs? How has cash cropping affected the position and activities of women?

3. Discuss the importance of female solidarity groups as a buffer against the effects of Western culture contact. Ultimately, how much do these groups enhance the social and economic status of women?

CHAPTER NINE

WOMEN IN SUB-SAHARAN AFRICA

Lance F. Morrow

Study of women's experience in sub-Saharan Africa, dramatically different in many ways from that of women in Western and other cultures, offers important new perspectives on the range of potential female roles in society and the extent to which they are defined not by biology but by economics, power relationships, and institutionalized privilege. The status of women, as a class, varied from almost complete subordination to virtual equality with men in precolonial Africa, but extensive social, economic, and political constraints were the norm. However, as individuals and members of organized groups, women often had substantial independence, influence, decision-making authority, and even institutionally sanctioned power over men. Women assumed more varied and significant public roles in African societies than in most other cultures, and were important as farmers, traders, spirit mediums, chiefs, and, in at least one society, warriors. The traditional bases of their influence and authority have been severely eroded during the colonial and modern periods, and women have been excluded from many of the social and economic opportunities associated with the sweeping reorganization of society since the nineteenth century. Yet women continue to be major forces in all aspects of African life. Study of their past and present experience can illuminate not only the problems and importance of women in African development but also the ongoing, worldwide reevaluation of women's roles in all cultures.

The enormous social, economic, historical, and theoretical importance of African women's experience did not begin to be recognized until about 1960, when growing numbers of women scholars began to question the male biases of mainstream social science research and theory. Although women still rarely figure as independent actors in much of the general literature on Africa, a great deal of exciting work has now been done focusing specifically on women. This research has both contributed to and been influenced by the theoretical and area studies discussed in other chapters of this volume.

This chapter provides a guide, for teachers and students with little specialized knowledge about Africa, to important concepts, issues, and published studies central to understanding African women's diverse experience.

Since African cultures' distinctive approaches to universal human problems often differ considerably from Western concepts, some basic guidelines are provided about the conceptual, institutional, economic, and social context of African women's activities. Only relatively accessible English-language books and journals are considered, and some alternative references are listed where possible. More specialized studies and information about topics not considered here may be found in the general bibliographies and the notes and references of individual works discussed below.

SUBORDINATION AND AUTONOMY IN TRADITIONAL AFRICAN SOCIETIES

Depending on perspective, African women can appear as brutally oppressed, extraordinarily free, or anywhere in between. Traditionally, many Hausa women never left the domestic seclusion of the family compound, Ashanti women often lived apart from their husbands in independent households, and Bakweri women worked in the forest and enjoyed great personal and sexual freedom while their husbands stayed in the villages and occupied themselves with the male domains of cattle tending and politics. While Kanuri women had little authority over economic resources, Bamileke women controlled the major food supplies, and Nupe women's exclusive role in trade and marketing often gave them economic dominance over most men, including their husbands. Sebei women had few legal rights and played little role in public affairs, while Mende women ruled numerous chiefdoms, Dahomean women formed elite military regiments and filled key political offices, and the queen of the Lovedu exercised the highest political as well as religious authority.

Westerners, ignoring the systematic discrimination in their

own cultures, have generally taken African women's heavy physical labor, the custom of polygyny which allowed important men to marry several wives, and the customary marriage gifts (called "brideprice" or "buying a wife" by Europeans) as proof of severe female degradation. However, recent research, with its emphasis on women's active roles in society, has dramatically shifted the focus to women's previously unsuspected social, economic, and political activities and impacts.

Methodological Issues and Approaches

It is important to understand several major sources of confusion in interpreting the conflicting evidence of subordination and autonomy in the lives of traditional African women. These include the extraordinary cultural diversity of Africa, the separation of female and male roles and activities, cultural biases and methodological problems in social science research and interpretation, and insufficient clarity and consistency in applying the analytical concepts of role and status in the published literature.

There is enormous cultural diversity among sub-Saharan African societies, which offers unparalleled opportunities for exploring the broad range of human possibilities both in general social organization and particularly in sex roles and relationships. The low population density and severe environmental barriers to long-distance communications encouraged and protected local cultural innovations, and the position of women varied widely in conjunction with differences in economic organization, autochthonous and imported ideologies, and other social variables. Great care is therefore required in generalizing from one culture to another. Helpful general introductions to the cultural diversity of Africa may be found in:

Bohannan, Paul, and Philip Curtin. *Africa and Africans.* Rev. ed. Garden City, N.Y.: Natural History Press, 1971.

Davidson, Basil. *The African Genius: An Introduction to African Cultural and Social History.* Boston: Little, Brown & Co., 1969.

Maquet, Jacques. *Civilizations of Black Africa.* Revised and translated by Joan Rayfield. New York: Oxford University Press, 1972.

Olaniyan, Richard, ed. *African History and Culture.* London: Longmans, 1982.

Schneider, Harold K. *The Africans: An Ethnological Account.*
Englewood Cliffs, N.J.: Prentice-Hall, 1981.

The systematic separation of women's and men's activities
within individual societies often gave women extensive areas of
virtual autonomy despite male control in other spheres. Women's
work was largely carried out independently from men, according
to different rules and procedures, and often in the context of
their own institutions. Even the marriage relationship usually
involved far less merging of wives' and husbands' personal goals,
social relationships, and economic interests than Westerners expect. There were many overlapping interests and reciprocal obligations between men and women, and institutions such as the
kinship system created powerful bonds, preventing anything approaching full cultural dualism. But sexual segregation in parallel
activities and institutions was a fundamental feature of African
women's experience. While separation of roles and responsibilities
often perpetuated overall sexual inequality, it usually increased
women's autonomy within their own areas.

Although social science concepts and research methods are
indispensable for effective study, it should be recognized that
there are cultural biases and methodological limitations in many
approaches and interpretations that severely hamper understanding of African women's roles and experience. European and
American perceptions of African history and culture have long
been obscured by Western technological, imperial, and racial mythologies, which view departures from European models as primitive, inferior, or immoral. Perceptions of African women's roles
have been further distorted by male researchers' preoccupation
with male-dominated activities like warfare and long-distance
trade, low valuation of women's activities outside of marriage and
the family, reliance on male African informants with biases of
their own, and inability to recognize African women's importance
in economic, political, and social spheres where Western women
have been little represented.

The problem goes beyond faults in research technique to
more fundamental issues of the theoretical models used to define
research questions and interpret results. Students need to understand that research, far from an open quest for truth, is a highly
directive effort to answer previously selected questions that often
reveal more about the interests and worldview of social scientists
than of informants. When researchers' models fail to recognize
and integrate the goals and actions of the entire female half of the

population, the published results inevitably omit essential data and severely distort the actual social process. Students also bring their own models, often based on fallacious popular myths, into the classroom. Learning how to test and reject the spurious facts, interpretations, and cultural assumptions that already color both their own views and many of the sources on women and Africa should be a major course goal.

Several studies drawing on African data have begun to define the problems arising from the almost unisexual male model of social life prevalent in the social sciences, and to point the way toward more inclusive and revealing approaches:

Ardener, Edwin. "Belief and the Problem of Women." In *Perceiving Women,* edited by Shirley Ardener, 1–17. London: Malaby Press, 1975. Noting that women's cosmology and ideology are almost ignored in social anthropology, Ardener attacks "the astounding deficiency of a method, supposedly objective," that fails "to include half the people in the total analysis" (4).

Etienne, Mona, and Eleanor Leacock. "Women and Anthropology: Conceptual Problems." In *Women and Colonization: Anthropological Perspectives,* edited by Etienne and Leacock, 1–24. New York: Praeger Pubs., 1980. Critique of anthropologists' frequent failure to recognize that many restrictive attitudes and practices regarding women observed among Africans were introduced or encouraged by European colonial rule, and hence were not in fact autochthonous and traditional.

Gough, Kathleen. "Nuer Kinship: a Re-Examination." In *The Translation of Culture: Essays to E. E. Evans-Pritchard,* edited by T. O. Beidelman, 79–121. London: Tavistock, 1971. By relying almost exclusively on elite male informants, who promoted an ideal of complete male dominance, Evans-Pritchard's classic study of the Nuer fails to recognize that in practice nearly half of all adult women lived independently without male guardianship, and that women generally had much more influence than the official ideology claimed.

Kinsman, Margaret. " 'Beasts of Burden': The Subordination of Southern Tswana Women, ca. 1800–1840." *Journal of Southern African Studies* 10, no. 1 (October 1983), 39–54. Special Issue on Women in Southern Africa. Male control of economic surpluses and legal and political action combined in a system of inequality where girls were socialized to obedience and independent women were punished with "social ostracism, physical violence, and material deprivation" which "forced them to rationalize their domination by southern Tswana men" (41).

Marshall, Gloria. "In a World of Women: Field Work in a Yoruba Community." In *Women in the Field: Anthropological Experiences*, edited by Peggy Golde, 165–91. Chicago: Aldine Publishing Co., 1970. Discusses and illustrates how field researcher gender determines access to informants and information in African societies with sharply demarcated sex roles (see especially 181–84). Marshall was able to study women's activities much more fully than a male researcher could have, but was herself excluded from many male activities that were important to full understanding.

O'Barr, Jean F. "Making the Invisible Visible: African Women in Politics and Policy." *African Studies Review* 18, no. 3 (December 1975): 19–27. Political scientists, using Western models of politics and women's roles, have failed to recognize African women's traditional political importance. Assumption of a sharp distinction between public and private obscures the extensive overlap between the political and domestic spheres in Africa. Preoccupation with state institutions and processes of government ignores the exercise of power and influence in traditionally decentralized or stateless societies. Historical ignorance of the formerly more extensive political roles of African women, which were suppressed by male colonial administrators, and uncritical acceptance of contemporary African informants' male-oriented political ideologies, further obscure African women's political activity.

Sacks, Karen. *Sisters and Wives: The Past and Future of Sexual Equality*. Westport, Conn.: Greenwood Press, 1979. Chap. 1, "Anthropology Against Women," explores themes in past and present anthropological theory that rationalize male dominance by defining women primarily in terms of their reproductive role. The Introduction and Chap. 2, 3, and 7 present an alternative model in which male-female roles are defined largely by their different relationships to the means of production. The model is then used to clarify women's roles and status in a variety of traditional African state and stateless societies, including the Mbuti, Lovedu, Mpondo, and Buganda.

Lack of clarity and consistency in the definition of roles and status, and limited conceptual tools for reliable comparative studies within and between cultures, continue to pose major problems. Women's status in relation to men varies greatly in different roles, and the woman who acts with complete deference in some situations may assert herself from a position of equality or even superiority in others. Because the situational and cultural variables are so complex, cross-cultural comparison is particularly difficult and subject to qualification. Some African research that highlights the problems and methodologies of defining and comparing women's roles and status includes:

Burton, John W. "Nilotic Women: A Diachronic Perspective." *Journal of Modern African Studies* 20, no. 3 (1982): 467–91. Documents how colonial written sources presented southern Sudan women as insignificant objects of sexual derision even though they actually played important roles both in their own economic and social spheres and in general cultural myths. However, in attacking what he perceives as the "radical feminist social scientists'" Western-biased "search for systems of inequality where the indigenous system lacks an equivalent hierarchy of values and statuses," Burton fails to adequately support the claim that there is an overall "equality and symmetry in gender roles" based not on androgyny but on "an equality that emphasizes and assumes the complementarity of sexual difference" (490–91).

Mbilinyi, Marjorie J. "The 'New Woman' and Traditional Norms in Tanzania." *Journal of Modern African Studies* 10, no. 1 (1972): 57–72. Study of women's role and status requires recognition that African women traditionally assumed many different roles and statuses in different situations and relationships with others.

Oboler, Regina Smith. *Women, Power, and Economic Change: The Nandi of Kenya.* Stanford: Stanford University Press, 1985. Current conceptual tools for evaluating women's position compared with men lack the precision in definition of terms and ability to synthesize complex and conflicting data needed to categorize women's status in individual societies or to support cross-cultural comparisons ("Introduction," 9–16, and Chap. 8, "Sexual Stratification and Socioeconomic Change"). In her study of the Nandi, Oboler models an approach to analyzing women's relative power and autonomy that can accommodate differences between male and female accounts, ideology and practice, and public and private activities. Conflicting previous interpretations of Nandi women as autonomous or subordinate oversimplify the dynamics of female-male relationships. A balance of power exists between the sexes that, though heavily tilted in favor of men, shifts widely in different situations.

Peters, Pauline. "Gender, Developmental Cycles and Historical Process: a Critique of Recent Research on Women in Botswana." *Journal of African Studies* 10, no. 1 (October 1983), 100–22. Special Issue on Women in Southern Africa. A valuable introduction to current issues in research methodology, theory, and interpretation concerning Southern African women.

Sacks, Karen. "An Overview of Women and Power in Africa." In *Perspectives on Power: Women in Africa, Asia, and Latin America,* edited by Jean F. O'Barr, 1–10. Durham, N.C.: Duke University Center for International Studies, Occasional Papers Series, Number 13, 1982. In traditional Africa, women simultaneously had two different status identities. As sisters in their corporate lineages, women had recognized individual identity, property rights, and decision-making roles. As wives living in their husbands' villages, women were ideologically subordinate, dependent on their husbands for access to land, and largely restricted from participation in decision making.

Although awareness of women's social roles is spreading, they are still largely ignored in much of the general literature. Women are barely mentioned in the indexes and tables of contents of most of the newest studies and even revisionist and Marxist approaches, with expanded models that recognize class differences and focus attention on the non-elite, are often oblivious to women as a distinctive social group within society.

The major progress has been in many specialized studies, particularly by Western and African women researchers. Rejecting the old model of women as passive beings playing biologically and socially defined roles, these studies focus on women's individual and collective goals, implementation strategies, constraints and powers, successes and failures, and impact on male activities and the overall functioning of society. Good introductions to the new research may be found in:

Bozzoli, Belinda. "Marxism, Feminism and South African Studies." *Journal of Southern African Studies* 9, no. 2 (April 1983), 139–71. While Marxist discussion of gender inequalities has described "the points at which female oppression and the capitalist mode of production suit each other" (142), it has failed to address women's perspectives and other aspects of female oppression including rape and gender conflicts within families and economic classes.

Cutrufelli, Maria Rosa. *Women of Africa: Roots of Oppression.* Translated by Nicolas Romano. London: Zed Press, 1983. Written from a European, Marxist perspective, the book explores some areas, sources, and methodologies that have received relatively little attention, including modern nationalist exaggeration of some traditional female roles such as motherhood, and traditional and modern women's efforts to assert control over reproduction through contraception and abortion.

Gaitskell, Deborah. "Introduction." *Journal of Southern African Studies* 10, no. 1 (October 1983), 1–16. Special Issue on Women in Southern Africa. Reviews major themes in previous studies of Southern African women, largely done by women researchers, and introduces the six new articles on: British women immigrants; the subordination of Tswana women; women's resistance to pass law controls; negative effects of agricultural changes on women's position; matrilineal supports for women; and major issues in recent research.

Hafkin, Nancy J., and Edna G. Bay, eds. *Women in Africa: Studies in Social and Economic Change.* Stanford: Stanford University Press, 1976. Major interpretive themes are summarized in the editors' Introduction, 1–18. This collection of more recent research supplements and updates the studies in Paulme (below) and further extends the discussion into the colonial and modern periods. Useful as an introductory text.

Hay, Margaret Jean, and Sharon Stichter, eds. *African Women South of the Sahara.* New York: Longman, 1984. Collectively the most comprehensive introduction to the study of modern African women, the individually authored chapters explore women's changing roles and actions in rural and urban economic life, family relationships, voluntary associations, religion and ideology, literature, the arts, politics, national liberation movements, and economic development. Each section highlights the differences as well as patterns in women's experience in various economic and cultural environments throughout all of sub-Saharan Africa including Southern Africa. The studies also illustrate the value of increasingly sophisticated theoretical models in interpreting individual case studies and comparative evidence.

Oppong, Christine, ed. *Female and Male in West Africa*. London: Allen & Unwin, 1983. Useful as an introductory text, particularly for contemporary Africa. The individually authored chapters seek to avoid the "neo-sexist trap" of looking at women in isolation by focusing on "the process of co-operation and complementarity, separation and conflict, communication and coercion—the sexual dynamic" (xv–xvi). Three valuable statistical chapters compare female and male life cycles, work experiences, and migration. The twenty-two case studies explore the separations and connections between women's and men's spheres; how their cooperation and conflict are defined by rights, exchanges, and bargains; female disadvantages in access to opportunities and resources; and women's strategies for gaining autonomy under conditions of rapid social change.

Paulme, Denise, ed. *Women of Tropical Africa*. Translated by H. M. Wright. London: Routledge & Kegan Paul, 1963; Berkeley and Los Angeles: University of California Press, 1971. One of the earliest and most influential efforts to view African women as actors in their own right, this collection of interpretive articles and case studies by women anthropologists still provides a good introduction to the study of women's traditional roles and status. The main issues, evidence, and approaches are summarized in Paulme's Introduction, 1–16.

Robertson, Claire C. *Sharing the Same Bowl: A Socioeconomic History of Women and Class in Accra, Ghana*. Bloomington: Indiana University Press, 1984. Chap. 1, "Women and Socioeconomic Change," critically reviews the dominant theoretical and methodological approaches to study of women's position in African social life, and suggests new approaches that identify important links between class and gender stratification and modes of production. See also Chap. 3, "The Social

Context: Female Strategies in a Male-Dominated System,"
and Chap. 7, "Conclusions."

Steady, Filomina Chioma, ed. "The Black Woman Cross-
Culturally: An Overview." In *The Black Woman Cross-
Culturallly,* Cambridge, Mass.: Schenkman, 1981. Provides
an overview, from an African perspective, of new approaches to the study of African and Afro-American
women's experience.

Strobel, Margaret. "African Women." *Signs* 8, no. 1 (Autumn
1982): 109–31. An excellent update on current issues, interpretations, and published literature on African women, this
comprehensive review essay discusses recent research in the
areas of women's productive and reproductive labor; their
status within kinship, marriage, and legal relationships;
female political roles and activity; and women's position in
ritual, religion, and secular ideology. Although emphasizing
new developments, the references also include many earlier
works, all considered together in logical analytical categories.

Additional sources and topics not considered here may be
found in the following general bibliographical guides:

Hafkin and Bay. "References Cited." In *Women in Africa,* 285–98.
Includes research published up to 1975.

Hay and Stichter. "Bibliography." In *African Women South of the
Sahara,* 195–211. Includes studies published up to 1984.

Kerina, J. M. "Women in Africa: A Select Bibliography." *Africa
Report* 22, no. 1 (1977): 44–50.

Kratochvil, Laura and Shauna Shaw. *African Women: A Select
Bibliography.* Cambridge: African Studies Center, Cambridge
University, 1974.

Murray, Jocelyn. "Women in Africa: A Select Bibliography."
Rural Africana, Current Research in the Social Sciences 29
(Winter 1975–76); 215–29. Special issue: Rural Women:
Development or Underdevelopment?

Oppong, Christine. "References." In *Female and Male in West
Africa,* 374–91. Includes studies through 1980.

Perlman, M., and M. P. Moel. "Analytical Bibliography." In
Women of Tropical Africa, 231–93. Comprehensive collection

through 1960 of annotated references, organized by region, in categories of social and legal status, family life, puberty initiation rituals, women's associations, work, ornaments, political activities, beliefs and rituals, and modern education.

Robertson, Claire C. "Selected Bibliography." In *Sharing the Same Bowl,* 257–92. Comprehensive list of sources on Ghanaian women's experience and extensive coverage of other studies, through 1980.

The new studies of African women being published or reviewed in various journals can usually be located as they appear by consulting such aids as the *Social Sciences Citation Index.* The most important single periodical for keeping up with the field is *Signs: Journal of Women in Culture and Society,* published by the University of Chicago Press.

Methodologically, one of the major challenges, and a central focus of many of the studies discussed here, is identification of the specific economic roles, institutional structures, social relationships, and value systems associated with the subordination or autonomy of women in individual African societies. What specific constraints limit women's activities, and what opportunities are open to them? How differently do women and men define their goals, and what strategies do they pursue? What correlations are there between women's position in different areas of social life, and what determines whether status in one area will effect others? Important areas to consider include: marriage and lineage relationships; economic power and social status; legal and property rights; political representation and strategies; and beliefs, rituals, and cultural values.

Marriage and Lineage Relationships

The traditional African concepts of marriage and the family, which still have great influence except among some of the westernized elite, differ greatly from modern Western norms. In precolonial Africa, the husband-wife relationship, which has such overwhelming emotional importance in the West, was always merely one element—and often not the most important—in a complex web of kinship and social ties. Instead of being a purely personal association, traditional African marriage often served to establish lineage claims over children and to cement political alliances between lineages. Even at the individual level, marriage was primarily viewed as a symbol of status, a vehicle for acquiring children, and a business partnership with a sexually defined division of labor. Most people's closest emotional attachments and personal allegiances usually continued to be with their own kin groups or children rather than with their mates.

Although there was often affection and even romantic attraction, the central organizational purpose of traditional African marriage was to define the roles and reciprocal obligations of the spouses and their extended kin groups. An extremely versatile institution, marriage was often contracted for a far wider range of social and economic purposes than in the West, and several different types of conjugal relationships, involving different kinds or degrees of mutual obligation, were frequently practiced concurrently within the same society. Useful introductions to the different types of marriage relationships, the degree of male dominance and female autonomy, and the factors that affected the dynamics and balance of power in relations between spouses are found in:

Abu, Katherine. "The Separateness of Spouses: Conjugal Resources in an Ashanti Town." In *Female and Male in West Africa*, 156–68.

Bohannan and Curtin. *Africa and Africans*, 101–18.

Etienne, Mona. "Gender Relations and Conjugality Among the Baule." In *Female and Male in West Africa*, 303–19. Excellent case study of a relatively egalitarian society in the Ivory Coast, illustrating the wide range of social and economic factors that influence women's position in marriage.

Hogan, George Panyin. "Marriage, Divorce and Polygyny in Winneba." In *Female and Male in West Africa*, 192–203. An extreme example of sexual dualism, women and men among the Effutu of modern Ghana have traditionally lived largely separate lives. Marriage is duolocal, with both spouses continuing to live in their own lineage compounds, supporting themselves through separate but highly complementary economic activities, and retaining their individual identities and autonomy.

Karanja, Wambui Wa. "Conjugal Decision-Making: Some Data from Lagos." In *Female and Male in West Africa*, 236–41. Even in a Nigerian society where women are economically independent, they are still subject to male domination. Although they usually operate in separate spheres, "at the juncture where they meet . . . the wife is expected to show deference to her husband." Women "defer to men in practically all areas of domestic decision-making," and "men can intrude on women's activities if and when they so desire" (239–40).

Mair, Lucy. *African Marriage and Social Change*. London: Frank Cass & Co., 1969. Repr. from Part I of the *Survey of African Marriage and Family Life*, edited by Arthur Phillips. London: Oxford University Press for the International African Institute, 1953. Detailed descriptions of traditional marriage, residency, and relationship patterns, and some colonial changes.

Radcliffe-Brown, A. R., and Daryll Forde, eds. *African Systems of Kinship and Marriage*. London: Oxford University Press, 1950. The second half of Radcliffe-Brown's Introduction, 43–82, provides a systematic theoretical and comparative overview of the structure of marriage relationships throughout Africa. Other authors in the collection provide a number of detailed studies of kinship and marriage in different types of societies.

White, Luise. "Women in the Changing African Family." In *African Women South of the Sahara*, 53–58. The wide range of women's family relationships with kin as well as by marriage are surveyed in relation to variations in social practices and institutions, such as work roles and responsibilities, marriage age and rights, polygyny, woman-woman marriage, and decision-making authority.

The predominantly social and economic rather than emotional functions of traditional African marriage were reflected in the almost universal requirement for bridewealth or, in some societies, brideservice payments to future wife's guardians in order to obtain the social benefits of marriage. Other types of personal and sexual relationships were often available to both sexes, but payment of bridewealth or brideservice was necessary to create contractual legal and economic obligations. In patrilineal societies, bridewealth exchange established the right to incorporate all children born during the marriage into the legal husband's lineage, regardless of actual paternity or subsequent divorce, unless the bridewealth was repaid.

The bridewealth or brideservice system was one of the principal keys to membership and control of resources in the largely but not exclusively male elite. While discriminatory towards women, the system was based not on purchase of wives as chattels but on establishment of unequal but reciprocal labor and other obligations. Control of domestic labor was the main source of wealth in most of the subsistence-based societies of sub-Saharan Africa because land was plentiful, human numbers and use of animal power were limited by environmental hazards, and women were the primary agricultural producers. With wealth and status largely dependent on the size of the extended household labor pool, lineage heads could demand valuable goods and services as compensation for transfer of female labor and reproductive power through marriage.

Where brideservice was practiced, suitors had to contribute several years of labor to their wives' guardians but were not dependent on economic help from their own parents or lineage heads. In the more numerous bridewealth societies, suitors usually had to serve their own household or lineage heads for years in order to acquire enough valuable spears or cattle to negotiate a marriage agreement. The system gave household and lineage heads powerful controls over the young and poor of both sexes. However, women were particularly disadvantaged in the competition for wealth and power through marriage contracts. In addition to their heavy productive and reproductive responsibilities, other cultural, legal, and economic constraints severely limited their ability to pay bridewealth or brideservice and obtain the advantages of household and lineage head status for themselves.

Although male rhetoric sometimes asserted that payment of bridewealth gave them complete control over their wives, women did not lose their lineage names and identities or become slaves without redress. Husbands acquired contractual rights to specified services, such as providing and preparing food for the immediate household, but these responsibilities were usually limited and at least partially offset by reciprocal male obligations. Useful if sometimes conflicting analyses of the social significance of bridewealth exchange, marriage, and contractual control of wives' and children's labor are presented in:

Bledsoe, Caroline. *Women and Marriage in Kpelle Society.* Stanford: Stanford University Press, 1980. Valuable discussion of the concept of "Wealth in People" (46–80).

Brain, Robert. *Bangwa Kinship and Marriage.* Cambridge: Cambridge University Press, 1972. Control of women through marriage had a great economic importance to influential Bangwa men as a source of productive and reproductive labor (Chap. 5). Women were said to be inferior and expected to act deferentially towards men, but male privileges and ideology were partially balanced by women's domination of agricultural production, control of their own crops, right to act as regents even in paramount chiefdoms, and supporting organizations and associations.

Evans-Pritchard, E. E. "Zande Bridewealth." *Africa* 40, no. 2 (April 1970): 115–24. Among the Zande, Evans-Pritchard concluded, it was not just women, "the real wealth," who were controlled by the institution of bridewealth. Young men could not accumulate the necessary wealth in marriage spears except by working for their fathers or serving their chiefs, and they could not establish independent households without marrying. Women had few legal rights in this patrilineal society, and Zande men sometimes talked as if bridewealth gave them absolute control over their wives.

Gray, Robert F. "Sonjo Bride-Price and the Question of African 'Wife Purchase.'" *American Anthropologist* 62, no. 1 (1960): 34–57. Argues that earlier anthropologists' adoption of "bridewealth" in place of the value-loaded term "wife purchase" obscured the institution's fundamental importance in stimulating the entire economic exchange system. However, Gray fails to document a profit motive (46–47) or to recognize that transfer of women's reproductive power did not imply chattel ownership of the women themselves.

Gulliver, Philip H. "Bride-wealth: The Economic vs. the Noneconomic Interpretation." *American Anthropologist* 63, no. 5 (1961): 1098–1100. Accepts Gray's point that bridewealth sometimes had some economic functions, but emphasizes that the institution had different meanings for different peoples. The Jie and Turkana, for example, use the verb "to give," rather than the word for barter, and an important goal is to give as many animals as possible in order to increase prestige and cement relationships.

Meillassoux, Claude. *Maidens, Meal and Money: Capitalism and the Domestic Community.* Cambridge and New York: Cambridge

University Press, 1981. Meillassoux presents a valuable but very abstract model of how the social control of reproduction through incest taboos, bridewealth, and other institutions placed women and children in a surbordinate position. Key concepts in the discussion on bridewealth (61–74) include the emphasis on compensation for transfer of reproductive power, the role of bridewealth in demonstrating the social prerogatives of those who pay it, and the fact that women are not commodities for exchange because they can never be passed on to third parties.

The role of marriage in establishing lineage relationships and alliances, and the effect of different levels of social stratification and political centralization on wives' status are explored in:

Albert, Ethel M. "Women of Burundi: A Study of Social Values." in *Women of Tropical Africa*, 179–215. In the highly stratified society of Burundi, a powerful East African state, women were classified as minors in law and politics, were largely confined to domestic affairs, and were expected to be deferential to their husbands and men of their own class. However, the hierarchical social structure gave elite women, whose domestic responsibilities often included day-to-day management of an estate, authority over lower-class men.

Brain, Robert. *Bangwa Kinship and Marriage*. Marriages were an important vehicle for establishing alliances between influential men (Chap. 6, "Alliance").

Dupire, Marguerite. "The Position of Women in a Pastoral Society (The Fulani WoDaaBe, Nomads of the Niger)." In *Women of Tropical Africa*, 47–92. The studies by Dupire and Gessain (below) show how marriage served to establish family and lineage connections among both the matrilineal Coniagui and the patrilineal WoDaaBe, who also had different economic bases and roles for women in production.

Gessain, Monique. "Coniagui Women (Guinea)." In *Women of Tropical Africa*, 17–46.

Goody, Jack. "Marriage Policy and Incorporation in Northern Ghana." In *From Tribe to Nation in Africa: Studies in Incorporation Processes*, edited by Ronald Cohen and John Middleton, 114–49. Scranton, Penn.: Chandler Pub. Co., 1970. Shows how intermarriage between lineages and groups was a major factor in cultural assimilation and political integration in traditional African societies.

Green, M. M. *Ibo Village Affairs*. New York: Praeger Pubs., 1964. See particularly Chap. 2, "The Village Group"; Chap. 12, "The System of Exogamy"; and Chap. 13, "The Implications of Exogamy."

Women's influence and autonomy within the conjugal relationship, like marriage's ability to create links between lineages, depended heavily on the strength of wives' continuing ties with their natal kin. The lineage was the fundamental source of identity, support, security, and access to land in traditional African life, and all those who were separated from their kin groups were at a severe economic, political, and psychological disadvantage. Since the custom of exogamy prevented intermarriage within a broadly defined range of kin, one spouse usually had to move into the alien and isolating environment of the other's extended family and possibly distant area or village. Who would move, how far away, and whether they could continue to be involved in the affairs of their own lineages were critical questions in determining women's status in relation to men. These questions overlapped with another basic social variable in defining women's position in marriage: whether kinship and inheritance were defined patrilineally or matrilineally.

Women's independence and influence were usually more limited in patrilocal societies, where wives lived with their husbands' kin groups, and more extensive in matrilocal societies, where couples lived with the wives' kin at least during the first years of marriage, and husbands had less access to the support of their own lineages. Women also had greater autonomy in matrilineal societies, where wives and their brothers filled the authority roles assumed by fathers in patrilineal cultures. In matrilineal descent systems it was men who lived divided lives, alternating between their own kin groups and villages, where they had kinship and political responsibilities, and the lineages and villages of their wives, where they had only conjugal roles and little authority. Divorce was also a much more viable option for women in matrilineal societies, where wives usually had stronger support from their kin groups and often retained custody of their children in conjugal breakdowns. The effect of lineage connections and residency patterns on marriage relationships and women's independence are examined in:

Ember, Melvin, and Carol R. Ember, "The Conditions Favoring
    Matrilocal Versus Patrilocal Residence." *American An-
    thropologist* 73, no. 3 (June 1971): 571–94. Although difficult
    to follow and based on a worldwide sample, the article is
    useful for its statistical correlations among women's status,
    residency patterns, relative contribution to subsistence,
    farming versus herding economies, scale of political integra-
    tion, polygyny, presence of slavery, and warfare.

Fortes, Meyer, "Kinship and Marriage Among the Ashanti." In
    African Systems of Kinship and Marriage, 252–84. Among the
    Ashanti of modern Ghana, a matrilineal people who de-
    veloped a powerful state over several centuries, "there was a
    very high degree of equality between male and female
    members of the lineage" (256). Both men and women could
    own property, nearly half of the population lived in house-
    holds headed by women, and only about a third of all
    married women resided with their husbands. In such a
    matrifocal society, a "person's status, rank and fundamental
    rights stem from his mother, and that is why she is the most
    important person in his life" (264).

Gluckman, Max. *Custom and Conflict in Africa.* Oxford: Basil
    Blackwell, 1956; New York: Barnes & Noble, 1969. Chap. 3,
    "Estrangement in the Family," uses southern and eastern
    African evidence to clarify how wives' and husbands' con-
    tinuing ties with their own kin groups, the only associations
    large enough to ensure support in personal and economic
    crises, reduced the significance of the marriage relationship
    and created complex and sometimes conflicting allegiances.

Richards, A. I. "Some Types of Family Structure Amongst the
    Central Bantu." In *African Systems of Kinship and Marriage*,
    207–51. Discusses variations in women's status in different
    Central African systens of matrilineal descent, and identifies
    residency after marriage and degree of male authority over
    wives' produce and children as key variables in determining
    the power balance between husbands and wives. Concludes
    that wives always have substantial autonomy in matrilineal
    societies.

Schlegel, Alice. *Male Dominance and Female Autonomy: Domestic
    Authority in Matrilineal Societies.* New Haven, Conn.: Human
    Relations Area File Press, 1972.

Schneider, David M., and Kathleen Gough, eds. *Matrilineal Kinship.* Berkeley: University of California Press, 1961. While most of the individual studies pay little attention to the position of women and their options within matrilineal societies, there are useful interpretive chapters by Gough ("Variation in Residence" and "Variation in Interpersonal Kinship Relations") and by David F. Aberle ("Matrilineal Descent in Cross-Cultural Perspective"). See also the Bibliography, 731–53.

Smith, M. F., ed. and trans. *Baba of Karo: A Woman of the Muslim Hausa.* Introduction and notes by M. G. Smith. London: Faber & Faber, 1954. A remarkable first-person account, translated and organized by a Western woman researcher, from an old northern Nigerian woman who had always lived in purdah, secluded in the family compounds. Although excluded from political life and constrained in their mobility and activity, elite Hausa women were free to divorce and otherwise control their relationships. Continuing ties with their own kin, among whom they had greater influence, were more important than their relationships with their husbands.

The custom of polygyny, which allowed the wealthy to marry more than one wife, sometimes forced wives into competition with each other, but often reflected and increased women's economic power and personal independence. Although almost universally condemned as degrading by Western observers, in traditional Africa the effect of polygyny on women and their attitudes toward it varied greatly from society to society. Uncommon in many societies and unknown in some, polygyny was most likely to be practiced where female agricultural productivity was the foundation of the economy, where descent was patrilineal and marriage residence patrilocal, and where there was significant economic stratification. In some societies there was competition and jealousy between co-wives, while in others relations were amicable and first wives often encouraged or even financed additional marriages. Co-wives were often welcomed where there was little competition over children's rights or inheritance, and each wife's freedom to farm or trade on her own account was increased by having separate homesteads or sharing child care and household services owed to the husband. Useful studies of polygyny and its implications for women may be found in:

Boserup, Ester. *Woman's Role in Economic Development.* New York: St. Martin's Press, 1970. See especially Chap. 2, "The Economics of Polygamy."

Brabin, Loretta. "Polygyny: An Indicator of Nutritional Stress in African Agricultural Societies?" *Africa* 54, no. 1 (1984): 31–45. Surveys the literature on polygyny, documents wide variations in conditions and economic and nutritional implications for wives and children, and identifies major variables associated with the differences in the incidence and implications of polygyny in individual cultures.

Clignet, Remi. *Many Wives, Many Powers: Authority and Power in Polygynous Families.* Evanston, Ill.: Northwestern University Press, 1970. The incidence and social implications of polygyny varied widely among different African societies, with the balance of power between wives and husbands shifting according to whether descent was matrilineal or patrilineal, the extent of women's economic independence, and several other variables.

Clignet, Remi, and Joyce A. Sween. "For a Revisionist Theory of Human Polygyny." *Signs* 6, no 3 (Spring 1981): 445–68.

Goody, Jack, ed. "Polygyny, Economy and the Role of Women." In *The Character of Kinship.* Cambridge: Cambridge University Press, 1975.

Smith, M. F. *Baba of Karo.*

Women also took advantage of conjugal social and economic opportunities through the widespread institution of woman/woman marriage, where women assumed male social roles and authority by contracting legal bridewealth marriages with other women. Woman/woman marriages, which have been documented in more than thirty societies throughout Africa and probably existed in many others, were often available to both married and unmarried women who had acquired the necessary personal wealth from farming, inheritance, or trade. Since marriage, with the opportunities it offered for mobilizing the labor of wives and children and building an enduring lineage under one's own name, was regarded as a primary purpose and symbol of wealth and status, woman/woman marriage was accepted by both sexes in the societies where it was practiced as a legitimate goal for successful women. The principal barrier to attaining the advantages of husband and lineage-head status was not ideology but social and economic structures that limited the ability of most women and many young men to acquire the necessary resources. See:

Herskovits, Melville J. "A Note on 'Woman Marriage' in Dahomey." *Africa: Journal of the International African Institute* 10, no. 3 (1937): 335–41.

Krige, Eileen Jensen. "Woman-Marriage, with Special Reference to the Lovedu—Its Significance for the Definition of Marriage." *Africa* 44, no. 1 (January 1974): 11–37. Based on a survey of woman/woman marriage in various African societies and a detailed case study of the Lovedu of South Africa, Kirge's work identifies many different situations where woman/woman marriage was adopted, including raising an heir for a political office, investment of wealth from divining and other sources, inheritance of a wife by a woman, compensation for barrenness, and political affiliation with the ruling queen. As an institution, woman/woman marriage "forms an essential part of, and is closely integrated with, the whole social system in which it is found." Adaptable to many purposes, it reflects "a conception of marriage . . . that is far wider, more comprehensive, less bound up with the sexual needs of the individual partners than in Western society," for it "carries with it no necessary sexual implications for the individuals in whose names it is contracted" (34–35).

Obbo, Christine. "Dominant Male Ideology and Female Options: Three East African Case Studies." *Africa* 46, no. 4 (1976): 371–89. Far from being an aberration, woman/woman marriage was an advantageous and socially acceptable option for women who had the desire and economic resources to live independently.

Oboler, Regina Smith. "Is the Female Husband a Man: Woman/Woman Marriage Among the Nandi of Kenya." *Ethnology* 19 (1982): 69–88.

O'Brien, Denise. "Female Husbands in Southern Bantu Societies." In *Sexual Stratification: A Cross-Cultural View,* edited by Alice Schlegel, 109–26. New York: Columbia University Press, 1977.

Sacks, Karen. *Sisters and Wives,* 76–79.

Other options and strategies pursued by women, and the politics of marriage and community life that defined their actual rather than ascribed roles and status, are only beginning to be studied seriously. Although almost always subject to substantial social, political, and economic constraints, women nevertheless employed a variety of strategies for limiting male control and pursuing their own interests. Some of these strategies operated in the economic and political spheres discussed later, but women also pursued their own interests within the framework of the marriage relationship. Women's domestic strategies are explored in:

Bledsoe, Caroline. *Women and Marriage in Kpelle Society.* Explores the implications of the concept of "Wealth in People" (46–80) and the organization and dynamics of "Traditional Kpelle Marriage" (81–117). Particularly strong in identifying women's strategies as "Seekers of Power" in various relationship situations. Critically evaluates jural and other concepts of marriage and develops a process model of conjugal relationships that recognizes that rules are used selectively to justify individual choices based on rational self-interest ("Conclusion," 173–92).

Cohen, Ronald. *Dominance and Defiance: A Study of Marital Instability in an Islamic Society.* Anthropological Studies no. 6. Washington, D.C.: American Anthropological Association, 1971. Among the Kanuri of Bornu, a kingdom near Lake Chad with strong Islamic influences from trans-Saharan trade, women relied on restriction of personal services to partially offset their husbands' advantages in age and control of economic resources. Withholding of food and sexual relations were often-used strategies, while women's continuing links with their own kin made divorce a viable threat.

Collier, Jane Fishburne. "Women in Politics." In *Woman, Culture, and Society,* 89–96. Explores the conflicting strategies of wives, who gain increased control of family affairs by encouraging their husbands to set up independent households, and of mothers and mothers-in-law, who achieve influence for themselves and their children by keeping the extended family together in a large and powerful kin group.

Lamphere, Louise. "Strategies, Cooperation, and Conflict Among Women in Domestic Groups." In *Woman, Culture, and Society,* 97–112. Identifies women's strategies in countering male family authority and gaining maximum social and economic benefits for themselves and their children. Important factors influencing wives' strategies include the overlap between the social and domestic spheres, the presence or absence of polygyny, availability of trade and other economic options, their own age and the maturity of their children, and whether the society is matrilineal or patrilineal, matrilocal or patrilocal.

Tanner, Nancy. "Matrifocality in Indonesia and Africa and Among Black Americans." In *Woman, Culture, and Society,* 129–56. A comparative study of matrifocality, defined as "the cultural elaboration and valuation, as well as the structural centrality, of mother roles within a kinship system" (154). The Igbo (Ibo) people of southeastern Nigeria provide the primary African example.

Economic Power and Social Status

The economic position of women in many traditional African societies was much stronger than in most other cultures. Women were usually the primary producers in hoe agriculture, the major mode of subsistence production in the vast tsetse fly regions where cattle raising and plow agriculture were impossible, and they dominated local trade and markets in many areas. A substantial part of married women's agricultural production was obligated for support of their husbands and children, but their trading profits were commonly regarded as their own private property and in some societies it was not unusual for women to become independently wealthy. Where they had important roles in the production and distribution of resources, women normally had considerable status and influence both within the family and in the wider community. However, a number of economic constraints, particularly men's control of land and domination of the most profitable or prestigious sectors of the economy, frequently made it difficult for women to either take full advantage of the social and economic opportunities available to the wealthy or to compete effectively with men for public office and recognized political power.

Some of the most important variables to consider in studying women's economic roles and power are the importance of female contribution to subsistence, the extent of women's control over the products of their labors, their rights to own and inherit land and property, and their access to the most profitable and prestigious areas of production. The overall balance of economic power between women and men should also be weighed along with the extent to which the dominant ideology and institutions of the society allowed even women who achieved wealth to claim important offices and privileges. Useful comparative and theoretical introductions to these issues are found in:

Boserup, Ester. *Woman's Role in Economic Development.* Chap. 1, "Male and Female Farming Systems," analyzes the division of labor in African hoe agriculture, contrasts these results with the pattern in other nonindustrialized areas of the world where plow agriculture is practiced, and discusses the correlation between population pressure and sex roles in farming. Chap. 2, "The Economics of Polygamy," draws correlations between work output and women's status.

Goody, Jack, and Joan Buckley. "Inheritance and Women's Labour in Africa." *Africa* 43, no. 2 (April 1973); 108–21. Using data from *The Ethnographic Atlas,* Goody and Buckley demonstrate that women were the primary cultivators in 53 percent of sub-Saharan African societies, women and men contributed equally in 26 percent, and men were the principal contributors in only 18 percent. Female dominance in agriculture was significantly correlated with either matrilineal inheritance or the type of patrilineal inheritance where property is divided among male children on the basis of their mother's status or the land she farmed.

Gough, Kathleen. "The Origin of the Family." In *Toward an Anthropology of Women,* 51–76. Compares the role of women in African and other hunting-gathering societies (see especially 62–73).

Henn, Jeanne K. "Women in the Rural Economy: Past, Present, and Future." In *African Women South of the Sahara,* 1–18. Good general introduction to women's varied and changing economic roles and the correlations between economic power and other social variables such as type of political organization, descent and inheritance, modes of production, and control of resources and profits. The contradictory ways in which colonial and modern changes increased women's economic options in some areas while limiting them in others are also surveyed.

Martin, M. Kay, and Barbara Voorhies. *Female of the Species.* New York: Columbia University Press, 1975. Comparative statistical studies, from Africa, and other societies, of the position "Woman the Gatherer"; Chap. 8, "Women in Horticultural Society"; Chap. 9, "Women in Agricultural Society'" and Chap. 10, "Women in Pastoral Society."

Sacks, Karen. "Engels Revisited: Women, the Organization of Production, and Private Property." In *Woman, Culture, and Society,* 207–22. Comparative evidence from four African societies suggests that women's position tends to decline as class differentiation increases, because male ability to avoid reproductive and childrearing responsibilities makes men more adaptable to the specialized needs of a ruling elite.

Sanday, Peggy R. "Female Status in the Public Domain." In *Woman, Culture, and Society,* 189–206. Establishes a statistical correlation betwen variations in women's economic contribution and their overall status.

Schneider, Harold K. *Livestock and Equality in East Africa: The Economic Basis for Social Structure.* Bloomington: Indiana University Press, 1979. Illuminates the general relationship between economic systems of production and exchange and social structures of kinship, marriage, status, and political organization. Discusses women in many social capacities ("as labor," "exchange of," "rights in" "Pawnship," "land tenure," etc.), though primarily from a male perspective. Suggests that in East Africa matrilineal and matrilocal social systems have been associated with low economic productivity and limited moveable wealth, unlike some West African experience.

A number of case studies explore the complex relationship between women's economic roles and their social influence and status in individual societies. These examples also highlight the wide variations in women's economic options and strategies in different environments and systems of production.

Clark, Carolyn M. "Land and Food, Women and Power, in Nineteenth Century Kikuyu." *Africa* 50, no. 4 (1980): 357–70. Precolonial politics among the Kikuyu of modern Kenya were dominated by senior males, who gained wealth and power by acquiring wives and using their agricultural surplus to attract male followers. Women, however, were often able to influence decision making, despite the rhetoric of male dominance, because they not only produced most of the subsistence resources of the society but they also had the authority to allocate their produce between household use and provisions for their husbands' male followers.

Draper, Patricia. "!Kung Women: Contrasts in Sexual Egalitarianism in Foraging and Sedentary Contexts." In *Toward an Anthropology of Women,* 77–109. Argues that male-female relations among the !Kung of southern Africa are highly egalitarian in the traditional hunting-gathering economy, but become less egalitarian when !Kung adopt a sedentary pastoral life.

Green, M. M. *Ibo Village Affairs,* Chap. 4, "The Economic Side of Village Life," and Chap. 14, "Women's Work." Describes women's control of food production, distribution, and market trading among the Ibo (Igbo) people of the densely populated rainforest of southeastern Nigeria. "It is the women who own us," a male informant said (174).

Hill, Polly. "Hidden Trade in Hausaland." *Man* 4, no. 3 (September 1969): 392–409. Even northern Nigerian Hausa women, who live within the seclusion of their husbands' compounds, are economically independent. By exploiting the freedom from male interference afforded by seclusion, they dominate the trade in staple grains and peanuts. Marriage obligates husbands to provide support and wives to perform specified domestic services, but they conduct their business activities independently and "a wife's economic autonomy is often sufficient to insulate her from her husband's poverty" (398). Secluded women traders invest their profits in credit associations and livestock, and mobilize political influence to block establishment of public markets that might threaten the female-dominated house trade.

Kaberry, Phyllis M. *Women of the Grassfields: A Study of the Economic Position of Women in Bamenda, British Cameroons.* London: Her Majesty's Stationery Office, 1952. Examines all aspects of the economic position of women in a small-scale agricultural society, including "Control of Crops" (Chap. 6). Concludes that although "in the formal kinship structure women are subordinate to the authority of the male head of the household," in practice women have extensive rights because "in the last resort the men are dependent on the competence, goodwill, and feeling of moral responsibility of the women for the bulk of the food supply" (103).

Nadel. S. F. "Witchcraft in Four African Societies: An Essay in Comparison." In *Cultures and Societies of Africa,* edited by Simon Ottenberg and Phoebe Ottenberg, 407–20. New York: Random House, 1960. Reprinted from *American Anthropologist* 54 (1952): 18–29. In Nupe, an important northern Nigerian kingdom, women's control of markets and trade gave them economic dominance over most men, who were mainly peasant farmers. The result was a radical role reversal in which husbands were often heavily dependent on and in debt to their wives, who assumed such important and nominally male roles as providing family feasts and paying the bridewealth for sons' marriages. In order to pursue their market interests, Nupe trading women commonly left their children in care, practiced contraception and abortion, and strictly limited their domestic obligations despite male demands.

Sudarkasa, Niara. *Where Women Work: A Study of Yoruba Women in the Marketplace and in the Home.* Anthropological Papers no. 53. Ann Arbor: Museum of Anthropology, University of Michigan, 1973. Detailed description of the sexual division of labor among the Yoruba people of southwestern Nigeria, where men are the primary food producers and women dominate regional as well as local trade. Women and men pursue separate careers, which prevents men from demanding extensive household services: "What can be said when a wife has her work to do just as her husband has his? If the women stop trading, the men won't be able to meet all the responsibilities" (131). However, men retain some economic and other advantages over women.

Legal and Property Rights

Women's legal and property rights varied with their economic and social autonomy. In many pastoral and mixed economies where their subsistence and commercial contributions were less important, women were legally classified as minors and had access to judicial action only through male representatives. But in most agricultural societies, where women were primary producers, they had legal standing and extensive rights. Some of the key factors in determining women's legal position were property rights and land tenure, inheritance rights, legal and customary protection from assault and abuse, and access to legal redress for crimes and damages. Studies that explicitly discuss women's legal and property rights in traditional African societies include:

Dupire, Marguerite. "The Position of Women in a Pastoral Society." In *Women of Tropical Africa.* See especially 77–88. WoDaaBe women, in a male-dominated West African pastoral society, had inferior personal property rights, received much smaller shares of an inheritance than their brothers, and could not take legal action in their own names. However, men's discretionary power over the use and distribution of property was limited by clearly defined social obligations to their wives and children.

Goldschmidt, Walter. *Sebei Law.* Berkeley: University of California Press, 1967. Among the Sebei, a pastoral East African people, women's general legal position was far inferior to men's (40–78). Murder of women was not as serious an offense as murder of men, though the incidence was also much lower (93–95, 102–3). Incest and rape were prohibited, and the law paid little attention to most adultery by either sex, but wife-beating was legal. Ownership of cattle and land, the principal sources of wealth, was vested in men, who also had joint authority over the sale of crops produced by their wives (143–60). Male legal control was somewhat limited by extra-legal community norms, the need to encourage wives' agricultural productivity, and male fear of the supposed magical knowledge and power of women (108–28, 154–55).

Hay, Margaret Jean, and Marcia Wright, eds. *African Women and the Law: Historical Perspectives.* Boston University Papers on Africa no. 7. Boston: Boston University African Studies Center, 1982. A collection of papers focusing on women's traditional legal position and activity and the changes that occurred during colonial rule.

Kaberry, Phyllis M. *Women of the Grassfields.* See especially 117–44. Among the agricultural peoples of Bamenda in Cameroon, all land tenure was merely usufruct based on traditional norms and reciprocal obligations rather than personal ownership (29–52). Male chiefs had exclusive authority to allocate farmland, but women's preeminence in agricultural production and their claims as lineage members gave them land as well as personal property rights that were nearly equal to men's in practice if not in legal theory.

Klima, George. "Jural Relations Between the Sexes Among the Barabaig." In *Women and Society: An Anthropological Reader,* edited by Sharon W. Tiffany, 145–62. Montreal and St. Albans, Vt.: Eden Press, 1979.

Uchendu, Victor C. *The Igbo of Southeast Nigeria.* New York: Holt, Rinehart & Winston, 1965. In the densely populated agricultural society of the Ibgo (Ibo), land was owned by individuals rather than corporate lineages. While women sometimes owned land, normally they could not inherit title. But, as major contributors to subsistence, women had recognized rights to the use of land and to control of its produce (22–24, 50), and they could leave their husbands at will, summon them to court, take leases and honorary titles, and control their own sometimes extensive trading profits and capital.

Political Representation and Strategies

The status of women in social and political organization varied widely. Political offices were largely reserved for men in most societies, and women were sometimes excluded from all formal participation in public life and decision making. Yet women often had considerable influence, and in many societies they had recognized political and constitutional roles, representation, and positions. Important variables included ability to participate in public forums, representation in council or at court, access to political office, and control of important economic resources. Also crucial was the level of female solidarity and ability to mobilize public support, and the presence or absence of independent women's organizations paralleling those of men.

O'Barr, Jean. "African Women in Politics." In *African Women South of the Sahara,* 140–55. A good introduction to women's traditional political roles, the chapter surveys the institutional forms and limits of their political power in the societies where women held public office and had recognized political representation. In many other societies where they did not have institutionalized representation, the broadly overlapping boundaries between the public and private spheres still allowed ambitious women to significantly influence political decision making.

Women's associations based on age grades, market women's groups, secret societies, and a sense of common interest in competition with men gave women significant group support and some institutionalized voice in public affairs in many societies where explicitly political offices were dominated by men.

Ardener, Shirley. "Sexual Insult and Female Militancy." In *Perceiving Women*, 29–53. Among the Kom of Cameroon and many other peoples throughout Africa, women traditionally responded to abuse, assault, and especially sexual insult by mobilizing other women to collectively demand redress and impose sanctions, which usually included social ostracism, vulgar gestures, destruction of property, and sometimes mass beatings. Although the offenders were usually male, the fact that women who sexually insulted other women were similarly sanctioned confirms that women mobilized not only to support each other but ultimately to assert their collective dignity and rights as women.

Bellman, Beryl L. "The Social Organization of Knowledge in Kpelle Ritual." In *The New Religions of Africa,* edited by Bennetta Jules-Rosette, 39–56. Norwood, N.J.: Ablex Pub. Corp., 1979.

Bujra, Janet M. "Introductory: Female Solidarity and the Sexual Division of Labour." In *Women United, Women Divided: Cross-Cultural Perspectives on Female Solidarity,* edited by Patricia Caplan and Janet M. Bujra, 13–45. London: Tavistock, 1978. Using case studies from Africa and elsewhere, Bujra develops a model of the economic and social conditions and consequences of female solidarity.

Green, M. M. *Ibo Village Affairs.* Chap. 15, "Groups Based on Place of Marriage," and Chap. 16, "Groups Based on Place of Birth," provide a detailed description of women's associations among the Ibo, and how they represented women's interests and contributed to the general social and political organization of the community.

Leis, Nancy B. "Women in Groups: Ijaw Women's Associations." In *Woman, Culture, and Society,* 223–42. Compares the position of women in two Ijaw communities in the Niger Delta region of Nigeria, one with active and influential women's associations and one without, and identifies some of the social factors associated with the development of such organizations in traditional African societies.

Llewelyn-Davies, Melissa. "Two Contexts of Solidarity Among Pastoral Maasai Women." In *Women United, Women Divided*, 206–37. Among the Maasai people of Kenya, the authority of male elders was maintained by a hierarchy of age-grade organizations and male ownership of the cattle on which the economy was based. When women united to protect other women who committed adultery with men from prohibited junior age grades, they were implicitly challenging the whole discriminatory social order by asserting their equality and freedom to choose their own partners. However, when women exercised their ritual power to punish individual men who had supposedly endangered their fertility by minor social improprieties, female solidarity reinforced the social values associated with the subordination of women.

MacCormack, Carol P. "Sande: The Public Face of a Secret Society." In *The New Religion of Africa*, 27–37. The all-female Sande society of Liberia and Sierra Leone, an independent women's institution, operates in parallel with complementary male organizations to maintain the social order. With affiliated chapters of the Sande society in nearly every village, membership counteracts the isolating effects of patrilocal residence after marriage. Although the largely male Poro society is more directly concerned with political affairs, "The decisions of Sande officials are no less fundamental to the survival of the population than decisions made by Poro officials, and executive strategies operated by Sande officials can be as overtly political as those made by the Poro" (37). Since young women come under the tutelage of Sande leaders for several years before marriage, important officials of the society like Madam Yoko, a powerful nineteenth-century Mende chief, can strongly influence their choice of husbands, thus establishing political alliances with both families in a strategy unavailable to male leaders.

Richards, J. V. O. "Some Aspects of the Multivariant Socio-Cultural Roles of the Sande of the Mende." *Canadian Journal of African Studies* 9, no. 1 (1975): 103–13.

Women's strategies often had an important indirect influence on political decision making, even in societies where they had no official political representation, through their critical involvement in family and lineage politics. In polygynous African societies where kinship alignments and personal connections were the glue of politics, and chiefs sought to build alliances by marrying wives from as many important lineages as possible, women's maneuvering as wives and mothers of potential heirs could define the focus and sometimes decisively affect the outcome of political competition. Some of the dynamics and implications of women's private political activity are explored in:

Collier, Jane Fishburne. "Women in Politics." In *Woman, Culture, and Society*, 89–96. Even where women are barred from political office, "the men who compete for political prizes operate in a world where women are also seeking to maximize desired ends" (89). Women as well as men ultimately seek power, influence, wealth, and security, though the social and institutional constraints within which each operates force them to pursue their interests in different ways. In patrilocal societies, where men seek power by attracting a following of co-resident kin, ambitious women maneuver for influence by pressuring their husbands to establish independent households, and compete with their co-wives to help their own sons inherit a greater share of the lineage's wealth and power. While male informants commonly dismiss women's domestic quarrels as personal pettiness, both sexes know that their power and status are affected by the outcome of women's struggles, thus making women major actors in the political process.

Other examples of women's ability to influence public events even when formally excluded from the political sphere are described in the previously cited studies by Gessain, Dupire, Albert, Kaberry, Uchendu, and Goldschmidt.

Women filled major political offices in many other societies where they directly participated in political decision making to an extent unparalleled in modern Western history. See:

Aidoo, Agnes Akosua. "Asante Queen Mothers in Government and Politics in the Nineteenth Century." In *The Black Woman Cross-Culturally*, 65–77. Reconstructs the political and constitutional role of the queen mother in the Asante kingdom, and traces the political career and immense historical influence of three queen mothers who held office during the turbulent years of the mid-nineteenth century.

Hoffer, Carol P. "Madam Yoko: Ruler of the Kpa Mende Confederacy." In *Woman, Culture, and Society,* 173–87. Describes the rise and rule of a major female chief among the Mende peoples of Sierra Leone, where women "have enjoyed high office, as lineage heads, heads of secret societies, and chiefs, for centuries" (187).

Krige, E. J., and J. D. Krige. *The Realm of a Rain-Queen: A Study of the Pattern of Lovedu Society.* London: Oxford University Press, 1943. Reconstructs the social and political system of a southern Africa society in which supreme authority was vested in a woman, the queen.

Laurentin, Anne. "Nzakara Women (Central African Republic)." In *Women of Tropical Africa,* 121–78. See especially 121–37. Discusses the rise and power of female chiefs in a strong West African kingdom.

Lebeuf, Annie M. D. "The Role of Women in the Political Organization of African Societies." In *Women of Tropical Africa,* 93–119. Surveys both the explicitly political roles of women and the various social organizations that represented their interests in many communities. Valuable bibliography.

Miller, Joseph C. "Nzinga of Matamba in a New Perspective." *Journal of African History* 16, no. 2 (1975): 201–16. Nzinga, who became the ruling queen of a powerful state in what is now Angola during the seventeenth century, attained a dominant position despite local opposition to centralized authority and male reluctance to accept the legitimacy of a female ruler.

Sweetman, David. *Women Leaders in African History.* London: Heinemann, 1984. Describes, with little analysis, the careers of twelve women who held high office and influenced the history of important African societies over several centuries.

The separation and parallelism of female and male roles and activities in traditional social and economic life extended to political organization, where women often had their own semi-autonomous social institutions and political offices. Female titleholders usually had responsibility for managing and adjudicating women's affairs and representing their interests at the community council or chief's court, and in many states also checked and balanced the actions of male chiefs, counsellors, and kings.

Awe, Bolanle. "The Iyalode in the Traditional Yoruba Political System." In *Sexual Stratification*, 144–60. Among the Yoruba, a major trading people of southwestern Nigeria, women as a group had official public representation through a variety of institutions including the office of the Iyalode, an influential woman appointed to the ruler's council of chiefs, who functioned as the leader and spokesperson for the women of the city. The Iyalode had her own court and council of subordinate female chiefs to make decisions and adjudicate disputes connected with women's dominant role in trade and markets as well as domestic concerns. Their roles were complementary to those of the male chiefs; the Iyalode participated in all the judicial and political affairs of the royal council, and some Iyalode were major political powers in their states.

Fortes, M. "Kinship and Marriage Among the Ashanti." In *African Systems of Kinship and Marriage*, 252–83. In the matrilineal society of the Ashanti state women had great political influence, with the queen mother having the power to nominate the new king and advise him on his conduct in office.

Gluckman, Max. "The Lozi of Barotseland in North-Western Rhodesia." In *Seven Tribes of Central Africa*, edited by Elizabeth Colson and Max Gluckman, 1–93. Rev. ed. Manchester: Manchester University Press for the Institute of Social Research, University of Zambia, 1959. Because political authority was believed to be an attribute of the royal lineage, including women as well as men, female members of the lineage held important political offices. The senior woman titleholder, called the "Princess Chief," ruled half the country from a separate capital, which paralleled the king's establishment in the other half. (See especially 21–29).

Kuper, Hilda. *An African Aristocracy: Rank Among the Swazi.* London: Oxford University Press for the International African Institute, 1947. See especially 40–45, 54–60, 72–74, 88–103, 169–72, 197–229. In the Swazi kingdom, an important southern African state founded in the late eighteenth century, political and ritual power were divided between the king and queen mother. Although he was vested with ultimate authority, she had far-reaching powers to advise and check the abuses of the king.

Lombard, J. "The Kingdom of Dahomey." In *West African Kingdoms in the Nineteenth Century*, edited by Daryll Forde and P. M. Kaberry, 70–92. London: Oxford University Press for the International African Institute, 1967. Describes the role of the elite female regiments that guarded the king, and of the senior women at the royal court who paralleled and reviewed the functions of the male ministers of state.

Mba, Nina Emma. *Nigerian Women Mobilized: Women's Political Activity in Southern Nigeria, 1900–1965*. Research Series No. 48. Berkeley: Institute of International Studies, University of California, 1982. Surveys women's important political as well as economic roles in the precolonial societies of southern Nigeria (1–37). Through a variety of traditional institutions, influential women made decisions and exercised authority with great autonomy in a largely separate but culturally recognized women's world. Other women held powerful positions or exercised great informal influence in the general politics of their societies.

Okonjo, Kamene. "The Dual-Sex Political System in Operation: Igbo Women and Community Politics in Midwestern Nigeria." In *Women in Africa*, 45–58. Describes the traditional dual political system of the Igbo (Ibo), where "each sex manages its own affairs, and women's interests are represented at all levels," in contrast to the Western pattern where politics has been defined as a male sphere and women have had to take on male roles in the few instances where they are allowed to participate (45).

Beliefs, Rituals, and Cultural Values

The central importance of women, their reproductive power, and the ordering of sex roles and relationships in traditional African ideologies have often been poorly understood because the general problems arising from inadequate models and reliance on male informants are magnified when working in the intangible realm of ideas. Observational techniques focusing on activities and interactions, which normally provide a check on informants' accounts, are of limited applicability in studying beliefs and values, while male researchers are often excluded from women's rituals.

Even where good studies have been done, the evidence is often contradictory and difficult to interpret. In most societies both sexes acknowledged the concept that women's public behavior should be deferential to men as a class and especially to their husbands, though in many of the same communities women were publicly recognized as having important social and political roles. In the male-dominated societies where they were excluded from public affairs, women and women's activities were sometimes referred to with derision by men, but at other times those same men expressed great fear of women's supposed supernatural powers.

Understanding women's position in the ideological framework of a society requires recognition that ideas about sex and sex roles are always situational, contradictory, laden with symbols, emotionally charged, and inextricably enmeshed with personal anxieties and self-interest. Key questions to consider in determining the social meaning of ideological statements and rituals involving women are the sex of the speakers or actors, whether they are in mixed or single-sex groups, how women and men define themselves ideologically, and their individual and collective self-interest. Also consider the extent of institutionalized separation of female and male roles, the congruence between professed values and actual behaviors, the role of the official ideology in rationalizing the distribution of social and political power, and male and female efforts to gain advantage by reinterpreting existing dogmas or introducing imported ideologies. Theoretical and methodological approaches for exploring these issues are suggested in:

Ardener, Edwin. "Belief and the Problem of Women." In *Perceiving Women*, 1–17. Men and women define themselves and their relationships to each other and to nature in such different terms that anthropologists must employ new types of evidence as well as new models in order to understand the female worldview. Analysis of the symbolic content of women's rituals, as in Ardener's study of female initiation rites, provides a powerful method for reaching beyond politically sanctioned male interpretations to understand women's perspectives.

———. "The 'Problem' Revisited." In *Perceiving Women*, 19–27. Develops the concept of "muted groups," which may include children and subordinate classes of men as well as women, to clarify how major elements of a society may be rendered publicly inarticulate and almost invisible by a dominant ideology used to rationalize the authority and worldview of a political elite.

Gottlieb, Alma. "Sex, Fertility and Menstruation Among the Beng of the Ivory Coast: A Symbolic Analysis." *Africa* 52, no. 4 (1982): 34–47. Taboos prohibiting menstruating women from many public activities do not always indicate inferior status and degradation. By examining other activities not prohibited to menstruating women, and those that are also prohibited to men, Gottlieb shows that among the Beng neither women nor menstruation are regarded as inherently polluting. Instead menstruation is valued as a crucial aspect of human fertility, and pollution is considered to occur from activities of either sex that create an improper conjunction of human and forest or field fertility.

Background information about traditional African beliefs and values, with some attention to women's roles and concerns, is provided in:

Dorson, Richard M. *African Folklore*. Garden City, N.Y.: Anchor Books, 1972. See especially 399–418, 449–67, 528–61. Folktales were one of the most important expressions of traditional African beliefs and values in all spheres of life. Many stories in this anthology throw light on the position of women and relations between the sexes.

Mbiti, John S. *African Religions and Philosophy.* London: Heinemann, 1969. See particularly 92–148 on the processes of first creation, kinship, birth and childhood, initiation, and marriage.

In ideology as in other areas, women normally had higher status where they had significant economic power. Where men were economically and politically dominant, women were forced into subordinate ritual roles as well, while societies in which both sexes made important contributions commonly had more egalitarian systems of belief and ritual.

Bellman, Beryl L. "The Social Organization of Knowledge in Kpelle Ritual." In *The New Religions of Africa*, 39–56. Among the peoples of Liberia and Sierra Leone, where women were economically important and often became chiefs, Bellman and MacCormack (below) both found women's position in ideology and ritual to be fully comparable with men's. This equality was expressed institutionally through the joint supervision of community morals and actions by the male Poro and female Sande societies.

Bisilliat, Jeanne. "The Feminine Sphere in the Institutions of the Songhay-Zarma." In *Female and Male in West Africa*, 99–106. In the patrilineal, patrilocal culture of the Songhay in modern Mali, where men have almost complete economic and political control, women have been ignored and disparaged in public ideology and social ritual, with women's perspective being represented only through private ritual and myth. "The female roles, although important, are consigned to the imaginary sphere and omitted in masculine discourse." Men are "aware of this feminine side of things," but "to maintain a coherent image of themselves and their institutions, they are obliged to dismiss it as meaningless" (106).

MacCormack, Carol P. "Sande: The Public Face of a Secret Society." In *The New Religions of Africa*, 27–37.

Mendonsa, Eugene L. "The Position of Women in the Sisala Divination Cult." In *The New Religions of Africa*, 57–66. The restricted economic roles and political exclusion of women among the Sisala of northern Ghana were reflected in the ideologically important divinition cults where women could participate at the lowest levels but could never attain special titles or decision-making authority.

Richards, Audrey I. *Chisungu: A Girls' Initiation Ceremony Among the Bemba of Northern Rhodesia*. London: Faber & Faber, 1956. Discusses the supernatural powers and complex ritual roles assigned to women among the Bemba, a matrilineal and matrilocal people who established a powerful kingdom during the nineteenth century. Although not an egalitarian society, the strong support of their lineages gave women power in domestic relations, while identification of noble rank with particular matrilineages gave elite women direct and indirect political power. In this context the Chisungu female initiation ceremonies organized by women were important not only for their role in preparing girls for marriage but also as a reflection and support of the entire Bemba social structure.

Strobel, Margaret. "Women in Religion and in Secular Ideology." In *African Women South of the Sahara*, 87–101. Women's roles in traditional African initiation ceremonies, spirit possession cults, and other religious activities reflected and reinforced both the overall ideology of women's inferiority and the value of their activities within their special social and economic spheres.

In some societies where women had economic and social importance, dogma and ritual were controlled by men to maintain an ideology of male dominance. In other communities where women had great economic power, the theory of male supremacy was effective only at the level of myth and psychological rationalization.

Nadel, S. F. "Witchcraft in Four African Societies." In *Cultures and Societies of Africa*, 407–20. Among the Nupe of northern Nigeria, women's control of trade effectively gave them economic independence and sometimes dominance over their husbands. Male frustration and fear were reflected in an ideology of witchcraft, which asserted that all witches were women, who were symbolically assumed to be led by the official head of the women traders. The belief system thus provided a rationalization for men, unable to assert their economic or personal authority, to use their secret societies for intermittent and largely ineffectual attempts to intimidate women through witchcraft eradication campaigns. However, attribution of exclusive powers of witchcraft to women gave them a further threat with which to resist men's attempts to assert authority over their wives.

O'Laughlin, Bridget. "Mediation of Contradiction: Why Mbum Women Do Not Eat Chicken." In *Woman, Culture, and Society*, 301–18. Ideologically based control of particular types of resources (especially prestige goods and agricultural surpluses, and to some extent the biological productivity of women) gave men a degree of dominance in a society in which women as well as men were major producers.

Where actual male authority more nearly approached the claims of official ideology, women's interests and influence found some expression through ritual and the performing arts. Rituals where social conflicts were acknowledged and subordinate males as well as females criticized and exchanged roles with their social superiors served to periodically relieve tensions, validate the social order, and remind those in dominant positions of their reciprocal obligations. The supernatural powers associated with reproduction and other aspects of women's lives provided a more regularly accessible vehicle for women as a class to assert their rights and punish male or female violators, and for individual women to gain status and economic rewards through ritual observances of spirit possession. Music and dance, where both sexes participated on a largely equal basis, provided both an outlet for female expression and an affirmation of fundamental cultural unity in some male-dominated societies.

Ardener, Shirley. "Sexual Insult and Female Militancy." In *Perceiving Women*, 29–53.

Berger, Iris. "Rebels or Status-Seekers? Women as Spirit Mediums in East Africa." In *Women in Africa*, 157–81. In parts of East Africa where women's participation in other ritual as well as political activity was very restricted, largely female spirit possession cults increased women's leverage in resisting male dominance, "offered large numbers of women initiates an unusual degree of authority in ritual situations and provided smaller numbers with long-term positions of high status" (157).

Gluckman, Max. *Custom and Conflict in Africa*, Chap. 5, "The Licence in Ritual." Describes and analyzes rituals of rebellion and role reversal in which women donned male clothing and weapons and herded cattle while men and boys stayed inside to avoid harassment.

Kilson, Marion. "Ritual Portrait of a Ga Medium." In *The New Religions of Africa*, 67–79. Offers a case study of one woman's success in acquiring wealth and status as a recognized medium for a god.

Llewelyn-Davies, Melissa. "Two Contexts of Solidarity Among Pastoral Maasai Women." In *Women United, Women Divided*, 206–37. Among the Maasai of Kenya, women had little economic or political power, but the blessings organized by women every four years to ensure fertility and the health of children provided an opportunity to impose sanctions on men who beat or had prohibited sexual relationships with women. However, even this power was limited by the senior male council's authority to withhold permission for the blessings.

Onwuejeogwu, Michael. "The Cult of the 'Bori' Spirits Among the Hausa." In *Man in Africa,* edited by Mary Douglas and Phyllis Kaberry, 279–305. Garden City, N.Y.: Anchor Books, 1971. Excellent example of how female control over the system of spirit mediumship, and economic and political exploitation of individual spirit possessions, allowed women to periodically escape the female seclusion of a partially Islamicized culture, counter the authority of their husbands, and defy the male economic and political dominance established by the devoutly Muslim Fulani conquerors in the early nineteenth century.

Ottenberg, Simon. "Artistic and Sex Roles in a Limba Chiefdom." In *Female and Male in West Africa,* 76–90. In the male-dominated society of the Limba in Sierra Leone, it is only in music and dance that there is "equality of sex, so that in the very heart of the aesthetic life principles of separatism and sex status tend to disappear, and there is a joining of the sexes. . . . It is in the musical events that the aesthetic solidarity of the society is found" (89).

Where women exercised direct political authority they necessarily performed major rituals similar to those of male chiefs and kings:

Krige, J. D., and E. J. Krige. "The Lovedu of the Transvaal." In *African Worlds: Studies in the Cosmological Ideas and Social Values of African Peoples,* edited by Daryll Forde, 55–82. London: Oxford University Press for the International African Institute, 1954. Describes the religious concepts and mythology underlying the power of a ruling queenship.

The organizational separation of women's and men's spheres of activity in most African societies was reflected in highly dualistic cosmologies.

Griaule, Marcel, and Germaine Dieterlen. "The Dogon of the French Sudan." In *African Worlds,* 83–110. The mythology of the Dogon people of the upper Niger River provides probably the most comprehensive and systematic formulation of the widespread concept of dualistic opposition between the masculine and feminine principles in Africa.

Odugbesan, Clara. "Femininity in Yoruba Religious Art." In *Man in Africa,* 201–13. Examines women's role in the religious art and ritual of the Yoruba people of southwestern Nigeria, where "the imagery of male and female" was used to express "the dualistic element of the natural or cosmological order" (210).

OBSTACLES, OPPORTUNITIES, AND STRATEGIES IN COLONIAL AND MODERN AFRICA

African women have been active participants in the revolutionary changes during the past century of colonial contact and independent development. Although Western influences and colonial rule accelerated and altered the processes of social change, much of the impetus came from indigenous individuals and interest groups' efforts to exploit all available opportunities for their own purposes. African society has always been dynamic, with major migrations, technological innovations, economic growth, and enormous creativity in social and political organization. Women's varied and important roles in precolonial culture reflected their continued involvement and impact in these ongoing processes of African development. In the nineteenth- and twentieth-century African experiences with colonial contact, the slave trade, industrial technology, urbanization, the international capitalist economic system, and large-scale bureaucratic institutions have also been powerfully influenced by women's activities even while they have altered the framework of women's lives.

The complex dynamics by which women's actions have both affected and been constrained by the transformations of the last century will be considered here in analytical categories similar to those used in studying their experience in traditional society: methodological issues and approaches; economic change and social status; legal and property rights; marriage, kinship, and urbanization; political representation and strategies; and beliefs, rituals, and cultural adaptation. The colonial and modern periods will be treated together because the major social and economic changes affecting women are continuing processes that often began before the establishment of direct colonial rule and are far from complete today.

Methodological Issues and Approaches

The experience of women as a class, largely ignored in most studies of traditional life, has received even less notice in the standard literature on colonial contact and modern development. Research emphasis on colonial policy, the nationalist movements, institution building, and macroeconomic trends has focused attention on general processes and aggregate national statistics, with little attention to basic distributive questions about which sectors of the population benefitted, which lost, how much, and how the social costs and benefits could be allocated more equitably. At a more fundamental level, the underlying research models have been severely distorted by four untested assumptions: that development of national economies and political institutions is inherently good and beneficial to all; that most economic and political changes are sex-neutral in their effects; that women's needs and interests are basically similar to and subsumed by men's; and that participation of women in technological, economic, and organizational innovations is only marginally important for national development.

Discovery that these assumptions—which still shape African and international development planning—are fundamentally wrong is one of the major contributions of recent research on African women's experience. While both sexes have experienced the traumas of cultural disruption and some of the benefits of the new technologies and organization introduced during the colonial and modern periods, men and women have not encountered the same problems or participated equally in the benefits. Whatever their aggregate value for society as a whole, few technological, economic, or political changes are truly neutral in their implications for specific individuals and interest groups. In many African societies, where women traditionally had important roles and powers, their overall position compared with men has probably worsened during the last century because of the decline in sex-role separation, loss of traditional political rights, and restricted access to Western education and the modernizing sectors of government and the economy. Since women are still the primary subsistence producers in most of Africa, the obstacles they face in taking advantage of the new techniques and opportunities severely inhibit increases in economic productivity and the achievement of national development goals.

Women's traditional options and powers have been eroded at the same time that they have been excluded from many of the new roles and opportunities open to men. Colonial administrators from the male-dominated societies of nineteenth- and early twentieth-century Europe commonly ignored African women leaders and institutions and replaced them with male warrant chiefs, civil servants, and administrators. Where European law and civil codes were introduced, with their classification of women as legal minors, their legal and political rights were restricted. Women have had less access to the Western-style education required for good jobs in government and the cash economy, and replacement of male colonial administrators with male African politicians since independence has done little to increase women's options.

Despite the obstacles confronting them, African women have shown at least as much initiative as men in exploiting the opportunities and innovations accessible to them. Women in traditional authority roles made great efforts, despite European discrimination, to persuade or compel colonial administrators to recognize their positions and form alliances. Where traditional prestige crops or products were male prerogatives, women often led the way in adopting technical innovations. When large-scale labor migration drew many adult males to distant mines and cities for long periods, women took on important new roles in economic production and social decision making. Women also energetically exploited the opportunities that, while usually not as rewarding as those open to men, were created by the growth of trade and urbanization and the weakening of traditional social restraints.

Understanding the dynamics of innovation and its significance for African women requires analytical approaches that go beyond evaluation of general processes and aggregate economic data to systematic study of the kinds of opportunities actually available to different segments and interest groups within society. Basic questions that should be asked at every point include:

1. Were women in positions to participate in the introduction and control of all, some, or no innovations?

2. Did women and men have equal access to use of the new technologies and other opportunities? What obstacles limited women's participation?

3. How did both sexes perceive their options and what were their objectives and strategies?

4. How did social and economic innovation affect women's position both in absolute terms and relative to men?

5. How are women's actions, in exploiting the opportunities available to them, affecting modern African cultural and economic development?

Useful introductions to the issues surrounding African women's involvement and experience in the social, economic, and political changes of the last century include:

Boserup, Ester. *Woman's Role in Economic Development.* Uses comparative evidence from Africa, Asia, the Middle East, and Latin America to show how women's position has deteriorated with modernization, economic development, and urbanization. See particularly "Loss of Status Under European Rule," "Women in a Men's World," "Industry: From the Hut to the Factory," "The Educated Woman," "Women in the Urban Hierarchy," "Urban Job Opportunities for Women" and the Bibliography.

Bossen, Laurel. "Women in Modernizing Societies." *American Ethnologist* 2, no. 4 (November 1975): 587–601. Presents cross-cultural evidence that the process of economic modernization is reducing women's autonomy and equality in farming, trade, and other areas.

Dobert, Jargarita, and Mwanganga Schields. "Africa's Women: Security in Tradition, Challenge in Change." *Africa Report* 17 (July–August 1972): 14–20. Women's secure if somewhat subordinate position in precolonial societies has been undercut by shifts in the balance of labor productivity as men have been taught improved farming methods and new technologies while women have been left to operate almost exclusively with traditional methods.

Mullings, Leith. "Women in Economic Change in Africa." In *Women in Africa*, 239–64. Argues that women's position is being progressively undercut by major structural changes such as the sale of communally held land to individuals (mainly male, because men have greater access to cash income), increasing concentration of wealth and class stratification, and restriction of women's access to the nontraditional growth sectors of the economy.

Pellow, Deborah. *Women in Accra: Options for Autonomy.* Algonac, Mich.: Reference Publications, 1977. See especially the theoretical discussion of "Perspectives on Autonomy" in Chap. 1.

Remy, Dorothy. "Underdevelopment and the Experience of Women: A Nigerian Case Study." In *Toward an Anthropology of Women*, 358–71.

Robertson, Claire C. *Sharing the Same Bowl.* Chap. 1, "Women and Socioeconomic Change," and Chap. 7, "Conclusions," discuss standard and alternative models of social and economic change.

Robertson, Claire C., and Martin A. Klein, eds. *Women and Slavery in Africa.* Madison: University of Wisconsin Press, 1983. Valuable collection of pioneering studies of how women were affected by and participated in the nineteenth- and early twentieth-century African slave trade, including the internal and export trades and the use of slaves within labor-hungry African societies. Robertson and Klein's introduction, surveying "Women's Importance in African Slave Systems," presents the major issues and findings, showing that women's lives were especially vulnerable to the disruption caused by the trade, that female slaves had a much higher economic value than males, and that some African women entrepreneurs used the trade and slave labor for their own economic advantage.

Van Allen, Judith. "Women in Africa: Modernization Means More Dependency." *The Center Magazine,* Center for the Study of Democratic Institutions, Santa Barbara, Cal. (May–June 1974): 60–67. Modernization makes women more dependent on men because of the breakdown of a clearly defined economic role and sphere for women.

Additional information and bibliographic references about African women's experience during the colonial and independence periods may be found in the footnotes and bibliographies of the individual studies cited throughout, and the following general references:

Buvinić, Mayra et al. *Women and World Development: An Annotated Bibliography.* Overseas Development Council under the auspices of the American Association for the Advancement of Science, 1976.

Newman, Jeanne S. *Women of the World: Sub-Saharan Africa.* Washington, D.C.: U.S. Department of Commerce, Bureau of the Census, 1984. Presents demographic and economic data about women in many countries and regions of Africa during the 1970s, including population distribution and change, literacy, education, economic activity, marital status and living arrangements, fertility, and mortality. Good bibliography and discussion of the types and value of the census data available regarding women.

Saulniers, Suzanne Smith, and Cathy A. Rakowski. *Women in the Development Process: A Select Bibliography on Women in Sub-*

Saharan Africa and Latin America. Austin: Institute of Latin American Studies, University of Texas, 1977. Includes pre-colonial, colonial, and modern Africa, with sections divided by region on general status, social attitudes, family roles and status, legal position, religion, education, political roles, women's organizations, economic position, and development. Also general references on women in society and women in the development process.

Tinker, Irene et al., eds. *Women and Development: An Annotated Bibliography.* New York: Wiley, 1976. Though worldwide in scope, there are many references to women in Africa.

Economic Change and Social Status

Study of women's role and experience in technological and economic change should include agriculture, production, trade, economic strategies, and development planning. Good general introductions to these issues, which also include more detailed studies of a variety of specialized topics, include:

Bay, Edna G., ed. *Women and Work in Africa.* Boulder, Colo.: Westview Press, 1982. Bay's introduction discusses the theoretical implications of the individual studies, which explore aspects and problems in women's economic position on the margins of the modern development process, the ideological and value conflicts associated with economic change, the discriminatory effects of development policies on women, and current and future prospects for women in the role conflicts among fertility, child care, and employment.

Beneria, Lourdes, ed. *Women and Development: The Sexual Division of Labor in Rural Societies.* New York: Praeger Pubs., 1982. Useful theoretical and comparative studies from Africa, Asia, and Latin America. See particularly Benería's chapter on "Accounting for Women's Work," dealing with the lack of data, especially in non-wage subsistence and domestic production, about women's work and needs.

Dauber, Roslyn, and Melinda L. Cain. *Women and Technological Change in Developing Countries.* American Association for the Advancement of Science. Selected Symposium Series no. 53. Boulder, Colo.: Westview Press, 1981. Separately authored chapters offering broad theoretical and comparative perspectives and detailed case studies dealing with Africa and other Third World areas. Chap. 6, by Ann Seidman, dis-

cusses "Women and the Development of 'Underdevelopment': The African Experience."

Guyer, Jane I. "Women in the Rural Economy: Contemporary
Variations." In *African Women South of the Sahara*, 19–32.
Illustrates differences in women's economic roles and options in representative rural economies dominated by
subsistence farming, established cash-crop production, male
labor migration, and plantation agriculture.

Lewis, Barbara. "The Impact of Development Policies on
Women." In *African Women South of the Sahara*, 170–82.
Excellent survey of the complex and contradictory ways
economic and technological changes in general, and national
development policies in particular, have affected women's
economic opportunities and quality of life. Major policy
alternatives that make development projects harmful or
beneficial to women are identified through specific case
studies.

Nelson, Nici, ed. *African Women in the Development Process.*
London: Frank Cass, 1981. Reprint of a special issue of the
Journal of Development Studies 17, no. 3 (1981). Ten separate
studies of key issues and individual cases about women's
experience in the development process throughout Africa.

Oboler, Regina Smith. *Women, Power, and Economic Change.* Excellent case study of colonial and modern changes in Nandi
gender roles and relationships, marriage and other life-cycle
milestones, and production and control of resources. Because land, cash crops, wage-paying jobs, and education are
dominated by men, incorporation in the cash economy has
produced "a growing economic gap between the sexes,
shown in the disparity between the value of resources
controlled by men and those controlled by women" (235).

Robertson, Claire C. *Sharing the Same Bowl.* See especially chaps.
titled "The Historical Context: Accra and Economic
Change," "The Social Context: Female Strategies in a Male-
Dominated System," "Decline in the Terms of Trade: A
History of Four Trades," and "Changes in the Female Heir-
archy: Access to Capital and the Impact of Formal
Education."

As the primary agricultural producers in most African societies, women have carried the main burden for increasing

subsistence production to feed the growing rural population and support and subsidize low paid male migrant labor in industrial and commercial farming areas. Women have also shown great initiative in expanding cash crop production for export. However, nearly all government cash crop development programs have focused on male farmers, and very little support has been channeled into improving subsistence productivity. Women farmers have also suffered from transfer of land title to male owners through land reform projects, lack of access to improvement loans that require land title as collateral, and discriminatory exclusion from agricultural extension services. Women's problems and initiatives in taking advantage of new farming methods and market opportunities, and the negative effects of sexual discrimination in agricultural support on national development and food production, are described in:

Bryson, Judy C. "Women and Agriculture in Sub-Saharan Africa: Implications for Development (an Exploratory Study)." *Journal of Development Studies* 17, no. 3 (1981): 29–46. Reprinted in *African Women in the Development Process*, edited by Nici Nelson, 29–46. Women's predominance in unpaid agricultural subsistence production allowed and subsidized involvement of males in the developing cash industrial and export economy. However, failure to recognize and invest resources in women's agricultural production has resulted in widespread and sometimes severe decline in food availability and nutrition, which threatens to undermine development efforts in many countries.

Fortmann, L. "The Plight of the Invisible Farmer: The Effect of National Agricultural Policy on Women in Africa." In *Women and Technological Change in Developing Countries*. American Association for the Advancement of Science, Selected Symposia Series no. 53 (1981): 205–14.

Okeyo, Achola Pala. "Daughters of the Lakes and Rivers: Colonization and the Land Rights of Luo Women." In *Women and Colonization*, 186–213. In Kenya, traditionally inalienable land held in common by lineages, with definite use rights by women, is gradually being transferred only to males through individual titles that permit sale without protection for women's rights.

Oppong, Christine, Christine Okali, and Beverly Houghton. "Woman Power: Retrograde Steps in Ghana." *African Studies Review* 18, no. 3 (December 1975): 71–84. Although women

as well as men farm independently and strive to develop
their holdings, women's child care, domestic responsibilities,
and limited access to land make them less successful as
farmers.

Ottenberg, Pheobe. "The Changing Economic Position of
Women Among the Afikpo Ibo." In *Continuity and Change in
African Cultures,* edited by William R. Bascom and Melville J.
Herskovits, 205–23. Chicago: University of Chicago Press,
1959. Afikpo Ibo women took advantage of the introduction
of cassava and the increased safety of regional trade after
establishment of colonial rule to become economically independent of their husbands, who were slower to utilize the
new opportunities because the yams traditionally produced
by men were a prestige crop that supported male status.
"What is man?" an elderly woman said. "I have my own
money" (215).

Stamp, Patricia. "Perceptions of Change and Economic Strategy
Among Kikuyu Women of Mitero, Kenya." *Rural Africana* 29
(Winter 1975–76): 19–43. Despite problems of decreasing
fertility of the land, reduced support from husbands working as migrant laborers in the cities, and increased living
costs, Kikuyu women have generally raised their agricultural
productivity, gained increased incomes through cash crops,
and become more economically independent of husbands'
control. "Women are as concerned to compete for money as
men," and their strategies include use of modern agricultural techniques, information sharing through church
and cooperative organizations, and education for their children.

Staudt, Kathleen. "Agricultural Productivity Gaps: A Case Study
of Male Preference in Government Policy Implementation."
Development and Change 9, no. 3 (1978): 439–57. Women
farmers in Kenya are as likely as men to adopt agricultural
innovations but receive much less government training,
loans, and other services from exclusively male agricultural
agency staff who follow custom in discussing public affairs
only with men. Where agricultural services are limited,
women have been able to keep up with new techniques
through women's associations, but this support is inadequate
where intensive development efforts expand services.
Women's relative productivity has also declined where they

do not have access to enough land, exclusively owned by men under land reform procedures, to risk innovations without endangering their basic responsiblity to feed their families.

————. "Women Farmers and Inequities in Agricultural Services." *Rural Africana* 29 (Winter 1975–76): 81–94.

In the production of goods for domestic consumption and trade, women have traditionally been major suppliers, and the introduction of manufactured goods has frequently threatened or destroyed their economic independence. Although generally excluded from exploiting new opportunities in the developing industrial cash economy by official policy and limited access to wage work or other methods of accumulating capital, women have become important providers of goods and services in the informal exchange economy. They have also played a major role in subsidizing economic development and corporate profits through their agricultural and other supports for migrant male labor in mines, farms, and cities.

Chauncey, George, Jr. "The Locus of Reproduction: Women's Labour in the Zambian Copperbelt, 1927–1953." *Journal of Southern African Studies* 7, no. 2 (April 1981): 135-64. Independent and married women, who provided food and services for African miners at extremely low cost, were vital to the success of the colonial mining companies competing with South African industries for cheap labor. Many women earned enough by providing traditional goods and services to attain economic independence, despite periodic company efforts to control their activities, and thousands of women came from rural areas to take advantage of the new opportunities.

Etienne, Mona. "Women and Men, Cloth and Colonization: The Transformation of Production-Distribution Relations Among the Baule (Ivory Coast)." In *Women and Colonialization*, 214–38. Cloth production for trade, a prestigious and economically important activity, was traditionally a cooperative effort where husbands did the weaving and wives grew the cotton, spun the thread, and controlled the final product. Introduction of large-scale commercial cotton growing and manufactured thread during the colonial period eliminated women's productive role and control of wealth, and reduced their reciprocal relationships with their husbands to economic dependency.

Mueller, Martha. "Women and Men, Power and Powerlessness in Lesotho." *Signs* 3, no. 1 (Autumn 1977): 154–66. While there is a traditional pattern of female subordination in Lesotho, women's options, goals, and relationships are more profoundly affected by the economic, social, and political dominance of South Africa, which stifles the local economy, forces men into international labor migration, and drives women from the public sphere into household subsistence production and dependence on their husbands' earnings in South Africa.

Stichter, Sharon. "Women and the Labor Force in Kenya 1895–1964." *Rural Africana* 29 (Winter 1975–76): 45–67. Important study of how African women took over all aspects of subsistence agricultural production in rural areas and subsidized low wages and male labor migration for colonial export farms and processing industries. Women's unpaid subsistence labor was so important to the colonial economy that they were excluded from government measures to force men into wage labor. During the same period women also accounted for a substantial increase in African cash crop production.

Trade and marketing have been major economic activities of women in many West African societies for centuries, and they have continued and sometimes substantially expanded their operations during the colonial and modern periods. In some cases, expanded trade has increased women's economic and personal independence and reduced the control of husbands and kin groups. However, lack of access to capital and decreased assistance from husbands and lineages in the support and care of children make it difficult for many women to move beyond petty local trade in low-margin items into the more profitable long-distance trade in commodity and manufactured products.

Brooks, George E., Jr. "The *Signares* of Saint-Louis and Gorée: Women Entrepreneurs in Eighteenth-Century Senegal." In *Women in Africa*, 19–44. Women's efforts to exploit the new economic opportunities began with some of the earliest contacts with Europeans. By adapting their traditional trading skills, women in Senegal succeeded in dominating trade between the two cultures for more than a century, while attaining great social and political leverage and creating a sophisticated new Afro-European culture.

Bujra, Janet M. "Women 'Entrepreneurs' of Early Nairobi." *Canadian Journal of African Studies* 9, no. 2 (1975): 213-34. Recognizing the opportunities offered by the rapid growth of Nairobi at the beginning of the twentieth century, women from many societies throughout Kenya came seeking personal freedom and economic advantage. With the help of women already there, they used beer brewing and prostitution to accumulate the capital to buy houses for rent to male migrant workers, because "Property was indeed a firmer base for long term security than marriage" (224). Some women became wealthy enough to adopt children or pay bridewealth and contract woman/woman marriages to establish their own lineages.

McCall, D. "Trade and the Role of Wife in a Modern West African Town." In *Social Change in Modern Africa,* edited by Aidan Southall, 286–99. London: Oxford University Press for the International African Institute, 1961. Ashanti women in Ghana have dominated trade since colonial rule as men's traditional trading commodities lost importance and their preferential access to Western education allowed them to move into prestigious and well-paying administrative and commercial jobs. By developing trade and abandoning farming, where their husbands had partial authority over their produce, women became economically independent, while by moving into the expanding urban areas they escaped traditional lineage and family controls.

Mintz, Sidney W. "Men, Women, and Trade." *Comparative Studies in Society and History* 13, no. 3 (July 1971): 247–69. Although in a few areas like Dakar, Senegal, women traders have been able to develop the capital to invest in large-scale trade, most women operate at the margins of the cash economy and are unable to expand into more profitable areas. Lack of land ownership, which is predominantly vested in men, is a major barrier for women traders because property is usually the only possible collateral for loans and advances by Western export-import companies. Colonial and modern encouragement for men to produce cash crops for the export trade also gives them an advantage over women traders.

Robertson, Claire. "Ga Women and Change in Marketing Conditions in the Accra Area." *Rural Africana* 29 (Winter 1975–76): 157–71. Ga women still dominate local trade in cloth, meat, vegetables, prepared foods, and small hardware, but cheaper or more prestigious imported goods have driven them out of production, and declining demand for beads and pressure from better-capitalized male competitors in long-distance trade have restricted them to less profitable local markets.

Simms, Ruth. "The African Woman as Entrepreneur: Problems and Perspectives on Their Roles." In *The Black Woman Cross-Culturally*, 141–68.

A variety of strategies has been used by women to overcome threats to their traditional economic activities as well as obstacles to their participation in current opportunities, including mass demonstrations, women's associations, and educational efforts to join the new elite. Each of these strategies has its own difficulties, but all have been successful at times.

Mass protests and demonstrations have been used more often and more effectively than has been recognized, in part because male colonial officials often assumed that the women were either acting irrationally or under the direction of men. In many cases traditional women's networks and tactics provided the model for action even though the goals and scale were different.

Ardener, Shirley. "Sexual Insult and Female Militancy." In *Perceiving Women*. See especially 36–40.

Ifeka-Moller, Caroline. "Female Militancy and Colonial Revolt: The Women's War of 1929, Eastern Nigeria." In *Perceiving Women*, 127–57. Not just a reaction to colonial taxes on marketing, the "riots that climaxed a decade of female militancy had their roots in the emergence of female wealth at a time when colonial rule buttressed and strengthened traditional male dominance" (145).

O'Barr, Jean F. "Making the Invisible Visible." *African Studies Review* 18, no. 3 (December 1975). See especially 21–22.

Van Allen, Judith. "'Aba Riots' or Igbo 'Women's War'? Ideology, Stratification, and the Invisibility of Women." In *Women in Africa*, 59–85. British colonial threats to Igbo (Ibo) women's established economic interests sparked one of the major

West African rebellions against colonial rule. Although the absence of male involvement showed that women's interests were the issue, the male biases of the British commission of inquiry prevented it from recognizing women's leadership or claims. The official report assumed that they had merely been agents of men, so women as a group were denied any redress in the administrative reforms that followed.

Women's networks and associations, already noted in the studies by Staudt, Stamp, and Bujra above, continue to be major factors in women's economic strategies and successes. Although of crucial importance, women's agricultural, mutual aid, land purchase, and other associations are limited in their effectiveness by women's general problems of insufficient capital, education, managerial skills, and political experience.

Ladipo, Patricia. "Developing Women's Cooperatives: An Experiment in Rural Nigeria." In *African Women in the Development Process*, 123–36. The agricultural cooperative system in Nigeria was developed to assist male farmers, and women are severely handicapped in organizing cooperatives by lack of education, unfamiliarity with administrative procedures and machinery, limited cash, and male feelings that the women are intruding in male activities. While these disadvantages have hindered development of women's co-ops, the women involved have shown great determination and learned important new skills for functioning in the modernizing economy.

Lewis, Barbara C. "The Limitations of Group Action Among Entrepreneurs: The Market Women of Abidjan, Ivory Coast." In *Women in Africa*, 135–56.

Nelson, Nici. " 'Women Must Help Each Other': The Operation of Personal Networks Among Buzaa Beer Brewers in Mathare Valley, Kenya." In *Women United, Women Divided*, 77–98.

Pittin, Renée. "Houses of Women: A Focus on Alternative Life-Styles in Katsina City." In *Female and Male in West Africa*, 291–302.

Wachtel, Eleanor. "A Farm of One's Own: The Rural Orientation of Women's Group Enterprises in Nakuru, Kenya." *Rural Africana* 29 (Winter 1975–76): 69–80.

Wipper, Audrey. "Women's Voluntary Associations." In *African Women South of the Sahara,* 59–86. Describes how women's involvement in different types of traditional and modern associations has provided significant mutual support and a basis for collective action which partially counterbalance male dominance in many social and political institutions.

Western-style education is a key to wealth and power, and considerable numbers of women have attempted to move into the new elite through technical training and education. While clerical and teaching positions were reserved for men during much of the colonial period, women are now entering those fields in substantial numbers. A small number of women have also established themselves in professional fields such as law and medicine. Generally, however, women have had much less access to education at all levels, and the finishing-school type of training they have often received has failed to provide them with marketable skills. Family and child care responsibilities, lack of social acceptance, and discrimination in hiring have further limited women's access to well-paying business and government positions.

Adams, Lois. "Women in Zaire: Disparate Status and Roles." In *Comparative Perspectives of Third World Women: The Impact of Race, Sex, and Class,* edited by Beverly Lindsay, 55–77. New York: Praeger Pub. 1980. Despite constitutional statements of equality, women are forced into subordinate roles and economic dependence on men by limited educational and employment opportunities and heavy procreative and child care expectations. During the 1970s only 3 percent of women in the city of Lubumbashi were classified as employed. The legal code required married women to have their husbands' permission to work, and the International Women's Year was called "The Year of the Momma" in Zaire.

Barthel, Diane L. "The Rise of a Female Professional Elite: The Case of Senegal." *African Studies Review* 18, no. 3 (December 1975): 1–17.

Biraimah, Karen Coffyn. "The Impact of Western Schools on Girls' Expectations: A Togolese Case." In *Women's Education in the Third World: Comparative Perspectives,* edited by Gail P. Kelly and Carolyn M. Elliott, 188–200. Albany: State University of New York Press, 1982. Men dominated school administration and teaching staff, and female students' academic abilities and career prospects were viewed as inferior even though girls actually did nearly as well as boys. However the girls themselves had high educational and career expectations, and the discriminatory faculty attitudes and lack of female role models were partially offset by the girls' desire to get good jobs to support themselves, disregard for teaching as a career, and high awareness of important Togolese women with prestigious careers as role models.

Boserup, Ester. *Woman's Role in Economic Development.* "The Educated Woman" and "The Design of Female Education," Chaps. 7 and 12, analyze women's education and access to professional and other jobs in Africa, Asia, and Latin America. "Women in the Urban Hierarchy," Chap. 8, shows that while women participate extensively in the modern administrative and business sectors, they are rarely in positions of authority.

Human Resources Development Division, African Training and Research Center for Women, United Nations Economic Commission for Africa. "Women and National Development in African Countries: Some Profound Contradictions." *African Studies Review* 18, no. 3 (December 1975): 47–70. See particularly 59–62.

Leith-Ross, S. "The Rise of a New Elite Among the Women of Nigeria." In *Africa: Social Problems of Change and Conflict,* edited by Pierre L. VandenBerghe, 221–29. San Francisco: Chandler Pub. Co., 1965.

Lindsay, Beverly. "Issues Confronting Professional African Women: Illustrations from Kenya." In *Comparative Perspectives of Third World Women,* 78–95. Professional women in the developing business and governmental sectors face many obstacles compared with men. Far fewer school spaces are available for girls, and they are increasingly channeled into primary school teaching, nursing, and other lower status fields. The percentage of women at the national university declined from 1966 to 1977, and very few study engineering and other important technical fields. In employment women have suffered from legal restrictions and inequalities, use of sex-segregated job titles to hire women at lower pay scales, and male attitudes that assign women sole responsibility for child care and domestic tasks.

McSweeney, Brenda Gael, and Marion Freedman. "Lack of Time as an Obstacle to Women's Education: The Case of Upper Volta." In *Women's Education in the Third World*, 88–103. Women spend many more hours a day working than men, and have much less personal and free time. Girls of most ages work almost twice as many hours as boys. Labor-saving devices can reduce the time required for some traditional tasks, but much of the time saved goes for other household needs instead of education.

Mbilinyi, Marjorie J. "The 'New Woman' and Traditional Norms in Tanzania." *Journal of Modern African Studies* 10, no. 1 (1972). See especially 57–60. With colonialism and modernization, the division of labor between women and men has shifted in the subsistence economy, with women taking on many male tasks but men rarely engaging in women's work. Conversely, women are largely excluded from assuming new roles in the much more profitable and influential modernizing sectors of government and the economy by limitations on Western-type education and traditional values of male superiority and dominance.

Oppong, Christine, Christine Okali, and Beverly Houghton. "Woman Power." *African Studies Review* 18, no. 3 (December 1975). See especially 79–81.

Robertson, Claire C. "The Nature and Effects of Differential Access to Education in Ga Society." *Africa* 47, no. 2 (1977): 208–19.

Schuster, Ilsa. "Perspectives in Development: The Problem of Nurses and Nursing in Zambia." In *African Women in the Development Process*, 77–97. As the first generation of Western-trained but traditionally socialized professional and semi-professional women, nurses experience major conceptual conflicts between African and Western medical procedures and role conflicts between traditional and modern expectations about the place of young women in society.

Vandra, Masemann. "The 'Hidden Curriculum' of a West African Girls' Boarding School." *Canadian Journal of African Studies* 8, no. 3 (1974): 479–94.

Yates, Barbara A. "Church, State and Education in Belgian Africa: Implications for Contemporary Third World Women." In *Women's Education in the Third World*, 127–51.

Girls were excluded from educational opportunity in Zaire throughout the colonial period. By 1960 girls constituted only 20 percent of primary school enrollment, and only 4 percent of secondary school students. Catholic missionary-dominated education restricted girls to a domestic training curriculum designed to socialize them as good wives and mothers on a European patriarchal model. Prevented from learning marketable skills or the French language, Zairian women were also excluded from almost all jobs in government service and the developing cash economy.

Development planning, supposedly for the general public good, has usually ignored or harmed women's interests. Most planning and governmental support have focused on relatively large projects, which require more capital than most women have access to, and very little has been done at the level of local subsistence or small cash crop farming. Planners' emphasis on aggregate national economic performance rather than on distribution, and introduction of Western demographic assumptions about male heads of households, have also put women at a competitive disadvantage with men for governmental and international assistance. Although women have overcome some of these disadvantages through their own support networks, discrimination against women in planning hurts not only them but also the overall economic development of their countries. Good introductions to these complex issues include:

Beneria, Lourdes. "Conceptualizing the Labor Force: The Underestimation of Women's Economic Activities." In *African Women in the Development Process,* 10–28. Development studies and national statistics on production, labor force participation, and incomes employ market value definitions of economic activity and productive labor that systematically exclude or undervalue women's contribution to subsistence production. Alternative "use value" models that recognize the importance of domestic labor and its contribution to the cash economy are essential.

Caplan, Pat. "Development Policies in Tanzania—Some Implications for Women." In *African Women in the Development Process,* 98–108. Government policies that treat families as unified productive units and assign land title and other authority to husbands as heads of households are undercutting women's traditional land rights and economic autonomy and reducing wives to legal and economic dependency.

Dey, Jennie. "Gambian Women: Unequal Partners in Rice Development Projects?" In *African Women in the Development Process*, 109–22. Agricultural development programs direct resources to males on the assumption that husbands control land, production decisions, and finances. However, many Mandinka women own or have use rights to bottom land and have traditionally dominated rice production. Their exclusion from major rice irrigation projects has increased women's economic dependency on their husbands and deprived the development projects of vital rice-growing expertise.

Elliott, Carolyn M. "Theories of Development: An Assessment." *Signs* 3, no. 1 (Autumn 1977): 1–8. General overview of the principal development theories.

Human Resources Development Division. "Women and National Development in African Countries." *African Studies Review* 18, no. 3 (December 1975): 47–70. Surveys women's major economic activities and shows how lack of educational, training, and planning support in those areas creates or reinforces many of the principal development problems planners are concerned with.

Lewis, Barbara. "Women in Development Planning: Advocacy, Institutionalization and Implementation." In *Perspectives on Power*, 102–20. Excellent review of how women have been disadvantaged by colonial and modern development planning, and of the problems and advantages of alternative strategies for assisting women in the development process. Major issues include not only the types of projects that are most effective, but also whether or when it is better to target assistance directly to women or to attempt to include women on an equal basis in general development projects.

Lewis, Shelby. "African Women and National Development." In *Comparative Perspectives of Third World Women*, 31–54. Summarizes planners' and critics' perspectives and assumptions about the status of African women and the barriers that have limited their participation in national development.

Nelson, Nici. "Mobilizing Village Women: Some Organisational and Management Considerations." In *African Women in the*

Development Process, 47–58. Effectiveness in organizing economic development projects for women requires both involvement of women in the central planning process and recruitment and training of women as local field service staff and volunteer project leaders. Locally oriented research on women's activities and needs, and sensitivity to cultural values about women's public roles are also essential.

Palo, Achola O. "Definitions of Women and Development: An African Perspective." *Signs* 3, no. 1 (Autumn 1977): 9–13. Most African development planning is irrelevant to village life because it fails to develop its priorities on the basis of local community perceptions of need.

Rogers, Barbara. *The Domestication of Women: Discrimination in Developing Societies.* New York: St. Martin's Press, 1979. Critically examines the quantitative techniques and activities of the international development agencies and shows how they systematically discriminate against women. Critical questions about relative need and equity in the distribution of services are concealed by nearly total reliance on such aggregate measures as GNP, paid (usually male) labor rather than unpaid (usually female) subsistence production, and head of household census data in which women are classified as dependents. Cost-benefit analysis also distorts because its concern with total costs and total benefits fails to consider that benefits often go to one group (mainly male) while costs are allocated to another (chiefly female).

Wipper, Audrey. "Introduction: The Underside of Development." *Rural Africana* 29 (Winter 1975–76): 1–18. Special issue: Rural Women: Development or Underdevelopment? Develops the case, in reviewing the various studies included in the issue, that so little has been done to promote development in the areas of principal concern to women that in some ways they have actually experienced negative changes or "underdevelopment."

Legal and Property Rights Changes

The legal position of women has changed greatly during the colonial and modern periods through the introduction of Western legal concepts and the codification and redefinition of customary law. In some urban areas the prohibition of polygyny and vesting of wives with certain property rights in ordinance marriages under European law have benefitted some women. In rural areas, however, colonial administrators' preference for working with male headmen and chiefs meant that women's traditional rights were ignored when customary legal principles were codified. Administrators also usually supported rural chiefs' efforts to maintain male control and economic advantages by barring women from working and marrying independently in the cities. Colonial and modern land registration programs, which transfer title from kin groups to individual men, jeopardize women's traditional use rights to land and give male farmers and businesspeople a great competitive advantage in raising capital by selling or using land as collateral for loans.

Since independence, the definition of "head of household" as exclusively male in census data and planning projects has largely excluded women from participation in many national and international development programs. With courts and legal practice a predominantly male sphere, the legal rights women do possess are frequently not enforced. In racially segregated and discriminatory South Africa, African women are further disadvantaged by legal prohibitions that confine them to overcrowded reserves, limit their ability to work and own land, and prevent them from moving to the cities and taking advantage of urban opportunities.

Bohmer, Carol. "Modernization, Divorce and the Status of Women: Le Tribunal Coutumier in Bobodioulasso." *African Studies Review* 23, no. 2 (September 1980): 81–90. Customary law heavily favors men in divorce, child custody, and other domestic disputes, but women's legal disadvantages are magnified by the hostile and discriminatory conduct of the courts.

Chauncey, George, Jr., "The Locus of Reproduction." *Journal of Southern African Studies* 7 (April 1981): especially 149–63. The traditional male elite, working through the native authority councils, lobbied and collaborated with colonial administrators to keep marriageable women and young men seeking wives under the authority of the women's fathers in the rural areas. Thousands of single women evaded the regulations and moved to the mines and towns where they could support themselves and control their own relationships.

Dagadzi, Veronique. "Law and the Status of Women in Togo: Discrimination against Women in Togo." *Columbia Human Rights Law Review* 8, no. 1 (Spring-Summer 1976): 295–310. One of the few women lawyers and judges in Togo, Dagadzi demonstrates that both custom and law treat women as inferior to men, and "in all areas of endeavor rules and customs have been developed to insure the dominant position of the male" (p. 295). Women's legal status is improving, though customary discrimination has been little challenged by the courts.

Hay, Margaret Jean, and Marcia Wright, eds. *African Women and the Law.* For effects of ordinance marriage and codification of customary law on women see especially "Women's Rights in Law and Practice: Marriage and Dispute Settlement in Colonial Lagos," by Kristin Mann; "Making Customary Law: Men, Women and Courts in Colonial Northern Rhodesia," by Martin Charnock; "Justice, Women and the Social Order in Abercorn, Northeastern Rhodesia, 1897–1903," by Marcia Wright; and "The Articulation of Legal Spheres," by Sally Engle Merry.

Luckham, Yaa. "Law and the Status of Women in Ghana." *Columbia Human Rights Law Review* 8, no. 1 (Spring-Summer 1976): 69–94. Ghanaian law relating to women's rights and obligations, particularly regarding family and inheritance issues, is extremely complex. Major differences exist between traditional and Muslim law, customary law as interpreted by the courts, and Ordinance law. Comprehensive reform has been limited by lack of data about the operation and effects of legal practices, opposition of vested male and lineage interests, and the general difficulty of changing social practice through legal mandate and adjudication.

Maina, Rose, V. W. Muchai, and S. B. O. Gutto. "Law and the Status of Women in Kenya." *Columbia Human Rights Law Review* 8, no. 1 (Spring-Summer 1976): 185–206. Women's rights and powers vary widely between customary, religious, and statute law. Although women have various legal protections, they "are legally less privileged than are men and this explains much of their subservient position in society" (p. 185).

Okeyo, Achola Pala. "Daughters of the Lakes and Rivers." In *Women and Colonization,* 186–213. Women's traditional land rights and economic opportunities are being jeopardized by colonial and modern transfers of lineage lands to individual male ownership.

Rogers, Barbara. *The Domestication of Women.* Legal and quasi-legal administrative definitions of "head of household" and "productive labor" effectively exclude women from participation in national and international development projects.

Simons, H. J. *African Women: Their Legal Status in South Africa.* Evanston, Ill.: Northwestern University Press, 1968. Detailed analysis of the implications of "separate development," customary and civil marriage law, women's legal rights and disabilities, and the legal discrimination associated with apartheid.

Tadesse, Zenebeworke. "The Impact of Land Reform on Women: The Case of Ethiopia." In *Women and Development: The Sexual Division of Labor in Rural Societies,* 203–22.

Vellenga, Dorothy Dee. "Who Is a Wife? Legal Expressions of Heterosexual Conflicts in Ghana." In *Female and Male in West Africa,* 144–55.

Marriage, Kinship, and Urbanization

Although most Africans do not live in cities, many live in towns and all are affected by the economic and social forces of the urban areas. Capitalist commerce and production, male labor migration, new if not more equal female options in towns, and the breakdown of family economic units as young adults leave for education and opportunity in the cities are progressively altering the social and economic significance of marriage and kinship relationships. These changes have benefitted or harmed women in various ways, depending on their options in traditional society and their access to new opportunities. The long history and large scale of female migration indicates that towns and commercial centers are widely perceived as offering improved opportunities.

A number of studies describe how women have taken advantage of urban options to increase their economic and personal independence. Other research emphasizes the loss of traditional lineage support systems, the limited job opportunities, and the increasing dependence on husbands' or lovers' economic support experienced by women in cities. Part of the discrepancy in inter-

pretation is attributable to economic and cultural differences between particular individuals and urban areas, with women faring
better where descent is matrilineal, relations between the sexes are
traditionally fairly equal, local trade is dominated by women, and
there are strong women's associations to offset the loss of kinship
connections.

Women's migration to towns, and their experience there, are
described in:

Bryden, Lynn. "Women at Work: Some Changes in Family
   Structure in Amedzofe-Avatime, Ghana." *Africa* 49, no. 2
   (1979): 97–111. The pattern of women's migration to urban
   areas has changed from accompanying husbands to seeking
   independent education or work, and "Adult women are
   recognized as women rather than wives and as individual
   adult members of society" (107). Although lower educated
   and paid than men, migrant women also normally work in
   jobs requiring regular hours. However, inadequate urban
   child care has forced many migrant women to adapt traditional foster home practices and have their young children
   brought up by parents or kin in rural villages.

Bujra, Janet M. "Women 'Entrepreneurs' of Early Nairobi."
   Canadian Journal of African Studies 9 (1975): 213–34.

Gugler, Josef. "The Second Sex in Town." *Canadian Journal of
   African Studies* 6, no. 2 (1972): 289–302. Reprinted in *The
   Black Woman Cross-Culturally*, 169–84.

Little, Kenneth. *African Women in Towns: An Aspect of Africa's
   Social Revolution.* Cambridge: Cambridge University Press,
   1973. Describes female migrants' experience in cities, including economic activity, women's associations, political
   influence, and the range of sexual relationships from prostitution to marriage. Overemphasizes sexual activity and
   relationships with men at the expense of women's independent goals and strategies.

Mandeville, Elizabeth. "Poverty, Work and the Financing of
   Single Women in Kampala." *Africa* 49, no. 1 (1979): 42–52.
   Many single women in Kampala, Uganda cannot support
   themselves and their children from work alone. Oppressed
   by poor education and contacts, the primary burden of child
   support and care, and severe discrimination, non-elite
   women migrants to the city are confined to the most unsta-

ble and lowest paying jobs. Trade and market production, formerly an important source of income, are no longer economically viable or socially respectable. Many single women must therefore depend on gifts from lovers to supplement their earnings, though this support is usually limited and unreliable.

Obbo, Christine. *African Women: Their Struggle for Economic Independence.* London: Zed Press, 1980. Provides a comprehensive recent overview, from an East African perspective, of women's experience and strategies in towns.

Remy, Dorothy. "Underdevelopment and the Experience of Women: A Nigerian Case Study." In *Toward an Anthropology of Women,* 358–71. Although town women use many adaptive strategies, the capitalist urban economy "undermines the customary economic activities of women while at the same time failing to train or provide a supporting infrastructure that would enable women to provide for their own economic security" (371).

Robertson, Claire C. "Women in the Urban Economy." In *African Women South of the Sahara,* 33–52. Despite job discrimination and other obstacles, women are increasingly moving into towns. Women's occupations in both the formal and informal labor markets are described, and the individual experiences of a market trader, prostitute, secretary, and domestic servant from different parts of Africa are examined to illustrate how women have sought to exploit new options and cope with severe economic and social pressures in the urban environment.

Schuster, Ilsa M. Glazer. *New Women of Lusaka.* Palo Alto, Cal.: Mayfield, 1979.

Sudarkasa, Niara. "Women and Migration in Contemporary West Africa." *Signs* 3, no. 1 (Autumn 1977): 178–89. Most migrants are either young women travelling with husbands or older women who are widowed, divorced, or barren. Nearly all are seeking clerical jobs or trade opportunities. When both husbands and wives are migrants, isolated from family and lineage connections, they often became more interdependent.

The structural framework and functions of marriage and kinship ties are changing drastically as the economic and social conditions that gave rise to traditional institutions are replaced by new economic and social forces. The role and value of marriage as a vehicle for organizing relationships and economic cooperation have been undercut and partially replaced by bureaucratic social and political institutions and the operation of the market economy. Children have increasingly become an economic burden rather than an asset because of their limited ability to contribute to non-subsistence production and the high costs of educating them to function in the cash economy. And the traditionally valued stability of marriage and other permanent, highly structured social relationships has often become disfunctional and unmaintainable under the pressure of enormously increased mobility, the concentration of economic production and opportunity in distant urban and industrial areas, and the individual isolation and impersonality of town life.

Aldous, Joan. "Urbanization, the Extended Family, and Kinship Ties in West Africa." In *Africa: Social Problems of Change and Conflict,* 107–16.

Brabin, Loretta. "Polygyny: An Indicator of Nutritional Stress in African Agricultural Societies?" *Africa* 54, no. 1 (1984): 31–45. The declining availability of land and other modern changes are undermining the agricultural economic base that made polygyny feasible in many traditional societies, leaving wives with reduced economic autonomy and ability to feed themselves and their children. Where women are largely excluded from jobs in the expanding cash economy by limited education, child care responsibilities, and other restrictions, wives and children in polygynous households often suffer economic and nutritional stress.

Bukh, Jette. *The Village Woman in Ghana.* Uppsala: Scandinavian Institute of African Studies, 1979. General economic changes have altered the economic functions and importance of the household, and therefore of marriage. There are more female-headed households because of the breakdown of traditional marriage and male labor migration, and almost half of all men and women over eighteen are unmarried. Children, formerly an important economic asset, have become a burden because of school time and costs and the probability of their leaving the family unit at maturity. Men, often working far away as migrant laborers, increasingly have little desire to acknowledge and support children, leaving women with primary or total responsibility. Labor migration and work in the cash economy have also reduced the economic interdependence of wives and husbands.

Douglas, Mary. "Is Matriliny Doomed in Africa?" In *Man in Africa*, 123–37. Concludes from study of several societies that have recently switched from matrilineal to patrilineal inheritance that the change is prompted not so much by development of a cash economy and differentiated wealth as by competition for scarce land and resources in traditional societies with declining economies.

Gough, Kathleen. "The Modern Disintegration of Matrilineal Descent Groups." In *Matrilineal Kinship*, 631–52. Finds evidence that matrilineal systems of kinship, which are often associated with relatively high status for women, disintegrate faster than patrilineal systems through contact with the highly individualistic capitalist market processes.

Harrell-Bond, Barbara E. *Modern Marriage in Sierra Leone: A Study of the Professional Group*. The Hague: Mouton, 1975. The Western model of romantically based, monogomous marriage that has been adopted by the elite conflicts so severely with cultural norms that very extensive adaptation will probably be necessary. See particularly chaps. on "The Composition and Social Background of the Professional Group" (35–60), "Stereotypes of Traditional and Western Marriage and Family Life" (61–83), "The Legal Setting of Marriage" (84–123), "Choosing a Marriage Partner" (157–95), "The Organization of Domestic Life and Family Relationships" (196–222), "Marital Conflicts and Their Resolution" (223–49), "Attitudes Towards Sex, Family Limitation and the Use of Contraceptives" (250–78), and "Prospects for Marriage among the Professional Group" (279–95). Useful "References" (333–39).

Harrington, Judith A. "Nutritional Stress and Economic Responsibility: A Study of Nigerian Women." In *Women and Poverty in the Third World*, edited by Mayra Buvinić, Margaret A. Lycette, and William Paul McGreevey, 130–56. Baltimore: Johns Hopkins University Press, 1983. Many women, who traditionally breastfeed babies for 1½ to 2 years before weaning to reduce infant mortality, suffer chronic nutritional stress but must still work long hours to provide basic child and household support.

LeVine, Robert A. "Sex Roles and Economic Change in Africa." In *Black Africa: Its Peoples and Their Cultures Today*, edited by

John Middleton, 174–80. London: Macmillan, 1970. Explores the social and psychological stresses women and men experience as sex roles change.

Lloyd, P. C. *Africa in Social Change.* Harmondsworth, England: Penguin Books, 1969. Chap. 7, "The Family," identifies elements of continuity and change in relationships between wives and husbands of the new elite. Many traditional customs, such as bridewealth and separation of female and male activities, have continued in modified form.

Oppong, Christine, Christine Okali, and Beverly Houghton. "Woman Power." *African Studies Review* 18, no. 3 (December 1975). Urban mobility and decreasing kinship ties, which often prevent women from sharing child care responsibilities with other kin and co-wives, make it increasingly difficult for mothers to work and compete with men for jobs (71–72). Urban professional women are constrained by traditional expectations and lack of support from their husbands.

Oppong, Christine, and Wolf Bleek. "Economic Models and Having Children: Some Evidence From Kwahu, Ghana." *Africa* 52, no. 4 (1982): 15–33. Decisions about family planning are complicated by the primacy of kinship over marriage ties, the marginality of husbands in a matrilineal society, the frequency of divorce, the sharing of child care with kin, the limited availability of birth control, and the importance of education and mobility in women's and men's struggles to support themselves and improve their lot.

Robertson, Claire. "Ga Women and Socioeconomic Change in Accra, Ghana." In *Women in Africa,* 111–33. Poorly educated, non-elite women in Accra still dominate local trade, but their economic position has declined as husbands provide less support for children, more children survive, and growing educational and capital requirements make it harder to compete in trade. Better-educated "women working in offices have to contend with sexual overtures from male co-workers, who regard such 'emancipated women' as fair game" (133).

Ware, Helen. "Polygyny: Women's Views in a Transitional Society, Nigeria 1975." *Journal of Marriage and the Family* 41 (February 1979): 185–95.

Weinrich, A. K. H. *Women and Racial Discrimination in Rhodesia.* Paris: United Nations Educational, Scientific and Cultural

Organization, 1979. See particularly Chap. 3, "Changes in
Family Structure," and Chap. 4, "The Changing Function of
Bridewealth."

The pattern of relationships and the balance of power between women and men, wives and husbands, have changed profoundly in response to the rapid, ongoing transformation of
economic life and social structure. Women's options have expanded substantially, and in some cases they have been able or
forced to take on roles and decision-making responsibility traditionally claimed by men. However, these new roles have often
merely added to women's already disproportionately heavy work-
load, and male economic and political advantages have often
allowed them to appropriate much of the profits and benefits of
women's increased productivity. Women have also been severely
restricted in exploiting many of the most rewarding new opportunities. Although the balance shifts widely in individual situations, women's overall autonomy and power relative to husbands
and men in other social and personal relationships has often
substantially declined.

Several questions should be considered in evaluating the
somewhat conflicting studies of changes in women's independence and dependence in marriage and personal relationships. To
what extent did women gain acknowledged and effective authority along with responsibility? What degree of equality was
there in the resources available to husbands and wives? How were
child care responsibilities distributed, and how available was outside support? Were public policy and legal rights equitable?

Abbott, Susan. "Full-Time Farmers and Week-End Wives: An
Analysis of Altering Conjugal Roles." *Journal of Marriage and
the Family* 38, no. 1 (February 1976): 165–74. Wives acquire
great decision-making power in domestic affairs, despite
traditional values of male dominance, whenever they gain
control of economic resources through cash crops or their
husbands' absences as migrant laborers.

Bledsoe, Caroline. *Women and Marriage in Kpelle Society.* See
particularly "Transition to a Cash Economy" (118–72).

Clignet, Remi. *Many Wives, Many Powers.* Chap. 8, "Social Change
and Domestic Power Structures," explores how social change
is affecting the position of wives in polygynous households.

Colson, Elizabeth. "Family Change in Contemporary Africa." In
Black Africa, 152–58. Eastern and southern African women's

independence is increased by male labor migration, which
has given women control both of their children and the
property of their husbands, and by urban trading opportunities, which have allowed many women to escape lineage
and family controls and support themselves and their children without husbands.

Gordon, Elizabeth. "An Analysis of the Impact of Labour Migration on the Lives of Women in Lesotho." In *African Women in
the Development Process*, 59–76. Up to 60 percent of married
women in Lesotho have husbands working in South Africa.
While some observers have argued that women have gained
decision-making authority, many older women with large
families experience substantial stress in handling male livestock management roles along with their own child care and
farming responsibilities. Although both wives and husbands
are involved in family decision making, women contine to be
subject to disapproval and punishment if their decisions
contravene their husbands' instructions or wishes.

Izzett, Alison. "Family Life Among the Yoruba, in Lagos,
Nigeria." In *Social Change in Modern Africa*, 305–15. Analyzes
advantages and disadvantages for women in different types
of relationships with men in highly mobile urban environments.

Karanja, Wambui Wa. "Conjugal Decision-Making: Some Data
from Lagos." In *Female and Male in West Africa*, 236–41.

Lewis, Barbara C. "Economic Activity and Marriage Among
Ivoirian Urban Women." In *Sexual Stratification*, 161–91.
Surveys the relationship between economic autonomy and
freedom from husbands' control among urban women in
the Ivory Coast. Most women worked, the uneducated as
traders and those with some secondary education as salaried
workers, and most kept control of their earnings instead of
combining them in a joint budget with their husbands.

Mann, Kristin. "The Dangers of Dependence: Christian Marriage Among Elite Women in Lagos Colony, 1880–1915."
Journal of African History 24 (1983): 37–56. Christian marriage initially attracted the Western-educated elite because of
colonial socialization, and elite women because of better
inheritance rights, monogamy, the concept that husbands
should support wives, and lack of socially acceptable opportunities for women to support themselves. However, by

1900 it was clear that elite men, who gained important
benefits from polygyny and traditional marriage relationships, would not fully accept the middle-class European
marriage model, and elite women began searching for ways
to reestablish their economic independence.

Robertson, Claire C. *Sharing the Same Bowl*, Chap. 6, "Social
    Aspects of Deprivation: Change in Marriage and Depen-
    dency Patterns, Help from Dispersed Family Members"
    (177–225).

Smock, Audrey Chapman. "The Impact of Modernization on
    Women's Position in the Family in Ghana." In *Sexual Strat-
    ification*, 192–214. Erosion of women's traditional economic
    and social independence, because of inferior access to West-
    ern-style education and jobs in the modern sectors of
    government and the economy, is creating a "new pattern of
    relationships where the wife increasingly becomes an appen-
    dage of her husband"(211).

Southall, Aidan. "The Position of Women and the Stability of
    Marriage." In *Social Change in Modern Africa*, 46–66. Despite
    male political dominance, ordinary "women who move out
    of traditional contexts simply assert themselves in a practical
    manner, rejecting in their own lives the traditionally held
    male standard for women, choosing their own mates, and
    supporting themselves independently"(53).

Sudarkasa, Niara. "Female Employment and Family Organization
    in West Africa." In *New Research on Women and Sex Roles at the
    University of Michigan*, edited by Dorothy G. McGuigan, 48–
    63. Ann Arbor: University of Michigan Center for Con-
    tinuing Education of Women, 1974. Reprinted in *The Black
    Woman Cross-Culturally*, 49–63.

Verdon, Michel. "Divorce in Abutia." *Africa* 52, no. 4 (1982): 48–
    66. Traditional and Christian marriage rituals have disap-
    peared entirely among the Ewe of southern Ghana since
    1945, as labor migration and school attendance undermined
    parental control over daughters' marriages and society be-
    came increasingly mobile and individualistic. Without
    significant economic functions, the marriage contract no
    longer plays an important role in bridging the separate
    social and economic worlds of women and men. Divorce has
    long been common because wives have strong kinship ties

and land use rights in their parental homesteads and keep custody of young children. Now, although women and men live together for extended periods, over 90 percent of these limited relationships break up as individuals' needs change through their life cycles.

Political Representation and Strategies

The traditional political roles and dual-sex political institutions of African women, which reflected their extensive economic power and social organization in many societies, were largely ignored or suppressed by colonial administrators despite the concept of indirect rule. Most existing states were allowed to continue operating with few internal changes, but women were severely disadvantaged in attempting to maintain or strengthen their political positions through contacts with Europeans or colonial recognition of their local political authority. Male colonial officials, coming from European cultures in which women had no official political roles, usually negotiated only with male chiefs and titleholders, whose main concerns were to preserve and sometimes expand their own authority within their societies. Female institutions and offices were normally abolished or excluded from legal and political recognition, and the traditional system of separate activities and representation, which had given many women substantial political autonomy and influence, was officially abandoned.

Women responded vigorously to the colonial threat to their traditional rights and powers with a variety of strategies. In the few societies with female paramount chiefs, some women titleholders successfully maneuvered to overcome colonial biases and retain their positions. In a few other societies with male-dominated politics, less tradition-bound women effectively exploited the opportunities for alliance and trade afforded by European contact to expand their political power. However, in most societies women's traditional political roles and interests were disregarded. Their greater losses in political influence and status compared with men often prompted women to take the lead in militant opposition to colonial rule.

Hoffer, Carol P. "Madam Yoko: Ruler of the Kpa Mende Confederacy." In *Woman, Culture, and Society*, 173–87. Madam Yoko, aided by the long tradition of female chiefs among the Mende of Sierra Leone, was one of the few women leaders who was in a position to exploit precolonial contacts with expanding British economic and political agents to consolidate and extend her own political power.

————. "Mende and Sherbro Women in High Office." *Canadian Journal of African Studies* 6, no. 2 (1972): 151–64. Retaining their political influence through the transition from colonial rule to an independent national government, Mende and Sherbro women continued to hold ten of the eighty-one chiefdoms in Sierra Leone in 1970.

Mba, Nina Emma. *Nigerian Women Mobilized.* A comprehensive study, using archival sources and interviews with leading participants, of Nigerian women's political interests, strategies, and actions from colonial rule to national independence. Mba provides comparative insight and new detail on the colonial exclusion of women from both traditional and new political roles (Chap. 2), and traditionally based mass protests against restrictive policies (Chaps. 3–5).

Miller, Joseph. "Nzinga of Matamba in a New Perspective." *Journal of African History* 16 (1975): 201–16. Probably the best-known example of a woman in a society with no tradition of female rulers using early contact with Europeans to acquire and buttress political power.

O'Barr, Jean. "African Women in Politics." In *African Women South of the Sahara,* 140–55. Because women's traditional political rights and powers were generally more drastically curtailed than men's by European colonial governments, women often played leading roles in the resistance to colonial rule. Women also participated significantly in subsequent nationalist movements, but their political contributions and interests were little recognized after independence except where equality of rights was a central principal of the nationalist struggle.

Okonjo, Kamene. "Women's Political Participation in Nigeria." In *The Black Woman Cross-Culturally,* 79–106. Suggests a model for including women in the study of modern African politics, and explores the past and current political involvement of women in Nigeria.

————. "Sex Roles in Nigerian Politics." In *Female and Male in West Africa,* 211–22. Explores the precolonial, colonial, and post-independence political experience of women among the Hausa, Yoruba, Edo, and Igbo (Ibo) peoples of Nigeria, showing how women's roles and influence have declined.

Sacks, Karen. "An Overview of Women and Power in Africa." In *Perspectives on Power,* 1–10. Interpretations of change in African women's position have gone through three phases: what colonialism supposedly did for women, what it did to them, and finally what women have done in resisting colonial restrictions and exploiting new opportunities. Colonial authorities damaged women's interests and rights by transferring collective lineage property and powers to individual males, excluding women from important governmental and economic opportunities, and increasing responsibility for subsistence production. As a result, women often initiated or participated extensively in mass opposition to colonial rule.

Smock, Audrey Chapman. "Ghana: From Autonomy to Subordination." In *Women: Roles and Status in Eight Countries,* edited by Janet Zollinger Giele and Audrey Chapman Smock, 173–216. New York: Wiley, 1977. Contrasts women's substantial though usually subordinate political roles in traditional society (175–78) with their limited and decreasing political representation since independence in 1957 (205–8). Concludes that the personal independence, economic power, and social and political position of traditional Ghanaian women "have frequently been undermined by the course of Ghana's modernization. Ghanaian society seems to be moving away from the traditional separation of male and female spheres of work and social relations into a new and more sexually integrated situation in which women are less separate and less equal" (211).

Van Allen, Judith. " 'Sitting on a Man': Colonialism and the Lost Political Institutions of Igbo Women." *Canadian Journal of African Studies* 6, no. 2 (1972): 169–82. Describes the precolonial political institutions and power of Igbo (Ibo) women in Nigeria, and shows how British colonial administrators ignored their traditional political roles and excluded them from representation in the modern institutions that were gradually introduced.

Wipper, Audrey. "Riot and Rebellion Among African Women: Three Examples of Women's Political Clout." In *Perspectives on Power,* 50–72. Compares three examples of women's violent mass political action: Kenya in 1922, Nigeria in 1929,

and the British Cameroons in 1958–59. All were prompted
by colonial actions that threatened women's interests, and all
utilized traditional forms of militant collective protest including derisive rejection of male leadership and authority
and affirmation of women's importance and rights. Common problems included lack of an organizational and
ideological base for sustained political action after the initial
protests, and lack of recognition and rewards for the leaders.

Women's participation in the independence movements and
subsequent national politics has been significant. Women's organizations and political mobilization have played important roles in
developing mass political parties and pressuring colonial admin-
istrations throughout West, Central, and East Africa. In southern
Africa, where colonial and European settler regimes have attempted to suppress African political aspirations by force, women
have provided vital support and leadership in the resistance and
independence movements.

Goodwin, June. *Cry Amandla: South African Women and the Question of Power.* New York: Africana Publishing Co., 1984.
Goodwin provides vivid accounts, based on intensive individual interviews, of Afrikaner, English, and African women's
attitudes and actions regarding apartheid. Ordinary African
women, partially radicalized by their daily experiences, describe their frustration, anger, and involvement in public
and clandestine resistance. Political organizers describe their
battles, detention, torture, and continued underground
struggle.

Lapchick, Richard E. "The Role of Women in the Struggle
Against Apartheid in South Africa." In *The Black Woman
Cross-Culturally,* 230–61.

Lapchick, Richard E., and Stephanie Urdang. *Oppression and
Resistance: The Struggle of Women in Southern Africa.* Contribu-
tions in Women's Studies no. 29. Westport, Conn.:
Greenwood Press, 1982.

Mba, Nina Emma. *Nigerian Women Mobilized.* Women were politically active during colonial rule in new women's political
organizations and pressure groups like the Nigerian
Women's Union (Chap. 6), local government (Chap. 7), and
nationalist political parties and the independence movement

(Chap. 8). Major themes include use of traditional concepts of association and tactics for new purposes, the continued separation of women's and men's political activities, continuity in leadership styles, and emphasis on redress of grievances rather than revolutionary change (Chap. 9).

O'Barr, Jean F. "Pare Women: A Case of Political Involvement." *Rural Africana* 29 (Winter 1975–76): 121–34. Women in the Pare district of Tanzania became involved in politics during the 1940s when they mobilized large demonstrations supporting demands for repeal of colonially sanctioned taxes. Encouraged by this experience and the absence of many men because of labor migration, Pare women continued to be politically active and many have held lower-level political offices since independence.

Rivkin, Elizabeth Thaele. "The Black Woman in South Africa: An Anzanian Profile." In *The Black Woman Cross-Culturally,* 215–29.

Van Allen, Judith. *"Memsahib, Militante, Femme Libre:* Political and Apolitical Styles of Modern African Women." In *Women in Politics,* edited by Jane S. Jaquette, 304–21. New York: Wiley, 1974.

Walker, Cherryl. *Women and Resistance in South Africa.* London: Onyx Press, 1982. A detailed study based on archival research and interviews with women activists of "the development of a women's movement of South Africa, within the context of the national liberation movement, from 1910 to the early 1960s" (vii). South African women developed a number of political organizations between 1920 and 1939, and women played an important role in voicing and organizing political resistance to racial and sexual discrimination and oppression from 1939 to 1953. During the 1950s and early 1960s the Federation of South African Women provided important national leadership.

However, women's public recognition, policy influence, and direct access to political office and power within African independence movements and national governments have been severely limited by cultural traditions of public deference, erosion of women's relative economic position, and colonial biases in favor of male African leaders. Women have been further handicapped by disproportionately heavy subsistence production and child care responsibilities and less access to Western-style education. More-over, the Western-based political ideologies and methods of or-ganization adapted by the nationalist movements emphasize male roles and leadership models, and male political leaders have ig-nored, co-opted, and sometimes publicly attacked movements to end discrimination and address women's needs. Where exclusively male military regimes have been established, women's influence in the political decision-making process has been further reduced.

By restricting women's involvement and representation in development planning and political decision making, these struc-tural and political obstacles have hindered national development and deprived women of participation and leadership in the de-velopment of the rights, services, and programs that are defining current opportunities and the future social and political order.

Mbilinyi, Marjorie J. "The 'New Woman' and Traditional Norms in Tanzania." *Journal of Modern African Studies* 10, no. 1 (1972). See especially 65–72 and the attitudes of male politi-cians about the mildly reformist Marriage Act of 1971.

Rogers, Susan G. "Efforts Toward Women's Development in Tanzania: Gender Rhetoric vs. Gender Realities." In *Women in Developing Countries: A Policy Focus*, edited by Kathleen A. Staudt and Jane S. Jacquette, 23–41. New York: Haworth Press, 1983. Despite extensive official rhetoric about the importance of ending the subordination and oppression of women in Tanzania, government programs have failed to address the unequal social structure of gender relations or to materially improve the conditions of women's lives in the rural areas. Economic and social progress for women con-tinues to be impeded by many constraints such as the granting of land title to men and traditional male claims to most of the profits from women's agricultural production.

Smock, Audrey Chapman. "Ghana: From Autonomy to Subor-dination." In *Women: Roles and Status in Eight Societies.* See especially 205–8. Identifies the main structural disadvan-tages that have restricted women's participation in modern politics in Ghana despite their precolonial autonomy and political importance.

Staudt, Kathleen A. "The Umoja Federation: Women's Coopta-tion Into a Local Power Structure." *Western Political Quarterly* 33, no. 2 (1980): 278–90. Created by a Kenyan district chief to mobilize women's assistance in a land reform project during the 1950s, the Umoja Federation partially legitimized women's involvement in public affairs and provided a framework for women to assert their concerns and influence. However, inadequate support and restrictions imposed by the district chiefs also contributed to the collapse of Umoja, suggesting that "empowerment for women must occur either in a context in which women do not depend on men as mediated recipients of collective goods, or under redistributive regimes that consciously restructure economic and sex disparities" (290).

Wipper, Audrey. "The Maendeleo ya Wanawake Organization: The Co-Optation of Leadership." *African Studies Review* 18, no. 3 (December 1975): 99–120.

———. "The Politics of Sex: Some Strategies Employed by the Kenyan Power Elite to Handle a Normative-Existential Discrepancy." *African Studies Review* 14, no. 3 (December 1971): 463–82. Women were active in the nationalist opposition to colonial rule but became disillusioned by male politicians' failure to carry out the rhetoric of sexual as well as racial egalitarianism after independence. A small women's civil rights movement demanded equity but male leaders used their control of party and governmental offices to neutralize its demands by ceremonial recognition, tokenism, support for conservative leaders in the women's movement, broken promises, and arguments that women were not aggressive enough and did not "behave like a man" (477).

Since women's political disabilities are largely a product of discriminatory social values, structural inequalities, and institutionalized male privileges, adoption of socialist and other egalitarian ideologies has made little difference in women's actual political opportunities and benefits. Only where the experience of guerrilla warfare against colonial regimes elevated political consciousness and mandated complete national mobilization have women moved extensively into leadership positions and serious efforts have been made to address women's concerns and eliminate discriminatory attitudes and practices in social as well as economic and political life.

Brain, James L. "Less Than Second-Class: Women in Rural Settlement Schemes in Tanzania." In *Women in Africa*, 265–82. Although Tanzania has adopted an egalitarian socialist approach to development, women have not benefitted equally in government-sponsored rural development collectives where all land rights and profits are allocated to husbands, and women are expected to do all domestic tasks while working the same hours in the fields as men.

Davies, Miranda, comp. *Third World—Second Sex: Women's Struggles and National Liberation. Third World Women Speak Out.* London: Zed Press, 1983. Includes policy statements, official documents, and personal accounts about women's needs and activities in various African countries and national liberation movements, on topics ranging from political strategies to female circumcision.

Mullings, Leith. "Women and Economic Change in Africa." In *Women in Africa,* 239–64. Finds that the growth of capitalist-based economic concentration and class stratification is reducing women to a more subordinate position, despite some short-term gains, because they are being excluded from the nontraditional growth sectors of the economy. Only in a few revolutionary socialist societies such as Guinea-Bissau and the People's Republic of Mozambique, where sexual equality is a major political goal and women fill important positions of authority, are women's long-term prospects bright.

Organization of Angolan Women. *Angolan Women Building the Future: From National Liberation to Women's Emancipation.* Translated by Marga Holness. London: Zed Press, 1984. Describes the position and problems of women in colonial society, current and proposed changes in government policy and programs, and additional needs. Primarily a position statement and call for action, the book illustrates the far-reaching changes in traditional values as well as colonial practice that revolutionary African women with a high level of social consciousness consider essential for full equality.

Storgaard, Birgit. "Women in Ujamaa Villages." *Rural Africana* 29 (Winter 1975–76): 135–55. Identifies the government policies and local customs that prevent women from gaining equality of opportunity in the Tanzanian rural development schemes.

Urdang, Stephanie. *Fighting Two Colonialisms: Women in Guinea-Bissau.* New York: Monthly Review Press, 1979. The removal of traditional and colonial practices that discriminate against women, including forced marriage, polygyny, and denial of

divorce rights, was adopted as a major goal of the independence movement in order to promote equity and more
efficient national development. Eleven years of guerrilla
warfare raised political consciousness and gave many women
political experience and power. Urdang's research in the
countryside after independence found extensive improvements in women's rights and opportunities.

————. "The Role of Women in the Revolution in Guinea-
Bissau." In *The Black Woman Cross-Culturally*, 118–39.

————. "Women in Contemporary National Liberation Movements." In *African Women South of the Sahara*, 156–69.
Comparison of the armed anticolonial struggles in Mozambique, Angola, Guinea-Bissau, Zimbabwe, and Namibia
shows that ideological commitment to comprehensive social
as well as political change resulted in far more inclusion of
women in political leadership and decision making than in
most other countries.

African women have struggled to compensate for exclusion
from political office and benefits, and to advance their specific
constituency interests within local and national interest-group
competition, through a variety of women's associations. Some of
these have been highly informal, with few functions beyond protecting prostitutes and other women forced to operate on the
legal margins of the economy from police interference and exploitation. Other women's associations have developed into influential public education and lobbying organizations. These
political associations and campaigns have adapted both traditional
and Western models for women's political organization with some
success. However, cross-cutting ethnic, family, and class interests
severely hinder united political action to address women's common economic and political disadvantages.

Little, Kenneth. *West African Urbanization: A Study of Voluntary
Associations in Social Change.* Cambridge: Cambridge University Press, 1965. Chap. 7, "The Position of Women,"
describes several types of associations organized to protect
women and promote their interests.

Nelson, Nici. "Women Must Help Each Other." In *Women United,
Women Divided*, 77–98.

Staudt, Kathleen A. "Class and Sex in the Politics of Women
Farmers." *Journal of Politics* 41, no. 2 (1979): 492–512. Class-

based differentiation in educational goals, experience of discrimination, and economic interests among women in Kenya mean that non-elite women's needs are often poorly represented by the elite women who have political influence. Hence, "without a recognition of class based interests and divisions within and among members of women's organizations, issues voiced as 'women's issues' may serve mainly to entrench the ideas and material situations of an elite class, and do little to alter the status of most women" (512).

———. "Sex, Ethnic, and Class Consciousness in Western Kenya." *Comparative Politics* 14, no. 2 (1982): 149–67. While women in Kenya experience common disadvantages compared with men, including inferior education and agricultural services and exclusion from land ownership, their ability to pursue those interests through common political action is severely hindered by growing economic and class differentiation. Elite women with organizational skills and political influence identify more with the political status quo and the interests of their families than with the economic interests of the majority of women.

Steady, Filomina Chioma. "Protestant Women's Associations in Freetown, Sierra Leone." In *Women in Africa*, 213–37. West African Christian women's organizations, originally oriented toward religious and social activities, are beginning to support women's interests in public issues.

Strobel, Margaret. "From *Lelemama* to Lobbying: Women's Associations in Mombasa, Kenya." In *Women in Africa*, 183–211. Analyzes organizational efforts by East African Muslim women to promote social as well as political goals.

———. "Women's Wedding Celebrations in Mombasa, Kenya." *African Studies Review* 18, no. 3 (1975): 35–45.

Beliefs, Rituals, and Cultural Adaptation

Religious activity and innovation have long been vehicles for expression among the politically disenfranchised. African women have played important roles in the development of syncretistic religious movements that, while often not egalitarian, have promoted social change and cultural adaptation throughout the colonial and modern periods. Borrowing and modifying concepts and practices from Islam and Christianity as well as traditional beliefs, these religions provide a foundation for personal identity, community organization, and mutual support that can substitute for inflexible kinship ties and transcend the ethnic diversity of town environments. By providing information, contacts, and support groups, religious associations have helped many women migrate to the cities, cope with urban pressures, and take advantage of new social and economic opportunities. By bridging lineage and ethnic differences, women's religious activity and associations have played a major role in developing pluralistic urban and national cultures throughout Africa.

Bujra, Janet M. "Women 'Entrepreneurs' of Early Nairobi." *Canadian Journal of African Studies* 9 (1975). See especially 226–29. Women migrants to Nairobi during the first decades of the twentieth century nearly all converted to the tolerant local form of Islam because it offered membership in a supportive community and sometimes provided helpful patrons.

Constantinides, Pamela. "Women's Spirit Possession and Urban Adaptation in the Muslim Northern Sudan." In *Women United, Women Divided,* 185–205. A relatively traditional healing cult spread throughout northeastern Africa, the *zaar bori,* "provided one of the prime bases for such female solidarity as exists in the urban areas, and . . . it has played an important role in women's adaptation and integration into multi-ethnic urban society" (185).

Jules-Rosette, Bennetta. "Changing Aspects of Women's Initiation in Southern Africa: An Exploratory Study." *Canadian Journal of African Studies* 13, no. 3 (1980): 389–405. Identifies important parallels in traditional female initiation rituals among Bemba, Shona, and Ngoni women and the women's purity rites in a widespread indigenous Christian church.

———. "Women in Indigenous African Cults and Churches." In *The Black Woman Cross-Culturally,* 185–207.

Jules-Rosette, Bennetta, ed. *The New Religions of Africa,* Chaps. 5–11. Discusses women's roles in a wide variety of indigenous African, syncretistic, and Muslim churches, sects, and religious movements.

Steady, Filomina Chioma. "Protestant Women's Associations in Freetown, Sierra Leone." In *Women in Africa,* 213–37.

Sibisi, Harriet. "How African Women Cope with Migrant Labor in South Africa." *Signs* 3, no. 1 (Autumn 1977): 167–77.

Suggests that several kinds of spirit possession treated by women diviners are responses to social tensions associated with the absence of local Zulu men and the periodic presence of nonlocal male workers because of labor migration.

Strobel, Margaret. *Muslim Women in Mombasa, 1890–1975.* New Haven: Yale University Press, 1979. Through changes in wedding rituals and cooperative effort in dance groups and other associations, women in Mombasa, Kenya have gradually overcome class and ethnic divisions and have developed a more integrated and supportive female subculture. Women have played a major role in pulling together the various strands now amalgamated into the general Swahili culture of the region.

————. "Women in Religion and in Secular Ideology." In *African Women South of the Sahara,* 87–101. After reviewing contradictory elements of subordination and autonomy in women's traditional ideological and ritual position, Strobel shows how conflicts about women's social roles and influence have continued to be important issues in the introduction and adaptation of Christianity and to a lesser extent Islam.

————. "Women's Wedding Celebrations in Mombasa, Kenya." *African Studies Review* 18, no. 3 (December 1975): 35–45.

Secular literary and artistic expression by and about women, although little studied, also reflects and illuminates the ongoing changes in women's social, economic, and political experience. Good general introductions to women in African art and literature are provided in:

Aronson, Lisa. "Women in the Arts." In *African Women South of the Sahara,* 119–39. Women's artistic expression in the production of textiles, pottery, basketry, and ritual objects, more than in the performing arts, reflects the separation and interdependence of women's and men's work. These differences have been perpetuated, sometimes in new forms, by the sexually differentiated effects of colonial and modern changes in economic opportunities.

LaPin, Deirdre. "Women in African Literature." In *African Women South of the Sahara,* 102–18. Literary expression by and about African women reveals a growing consciousness of the difficulties and inequities they face and rising aspirations for personal and social change.

CONCLUDING NOTE

The culturally innovative and diverse traditional heritage and revolutionary modern economic and social changes that are shaping African life today can provide models and opportunities for dramatic advances in the roles, status, and productivity of women. However, inequitable values and practices in all areas of social, economic, and political life continue to harm women and national development. These problems are being perpetuated by discriminatory social structures and power relationships built into the modernization process through the granting of land title to males, limited educational and employment opportunities for women, male-oriented development planning, and male domination of political offices and decision making.

If not reversed soon, these one-sided policies may undermine movement toward a more equitable and rewarding future for both women and men for generations. Neither the productivity nor the well-being of women, who constitute half the full-time labor force, can be rapidly increased by replacing specific traditional constraints with a new and more restrictive system of inequality that institutionalizes male dominance and female dependency in all areas of life. Once embedded in the family, educational, employment, and power structures of the emerging industrially based social order, the modernized pattern of sexual discrimination may become as resistant to change in Africa as it has been in the Western countries that have already been struggling painfully through the industrial and bureaucratic transformation of society.

CHAPTER TEN

WOMEN IN LATIN AMERICA

Muriel Nazzari

A study of women in Latin America must start by recognizing their present and past diversity. Sexism and role differentiation mark the reality of present-day women in Latin America, in addition to stark class cleavages and ethnic and cultural differences within a context of expanding industrialization and agribusiness under varying degrees of political repression. Such diversity prompts the question of whether there is in fact a commonality of oppression among women in Latin America.

The analysis of the condition of women in Latin America lies within the larger debate about the origin of Latin America's underdevelopment. Why is Latin America underdeveloped at all, when it experienced European colonization four and a half centuries ago and established independent democratic republics in the early nineteenth century? Some early hypotheses to explain underdevelopment, such as the influence of the Catholic Church and the survival of feudal attitudes, have sometimes been used to explain the inferior position of women in Latin America. A new framework for the analysis of underdevelopment emerged from dependency theory, which explains the underdevelopment of nations and regions by their unequal relationships to the world market. Variations of dependency theory have influenced many studies of how processes of change have affected women in Latin America.

The condition of women in different classes, times, and places throughout Latin America's history cannot be explained solely by economic processes, however. Cultural and ideological factors have their significance, and women's role in reproduction undoubtedly affects women's opportunities in both positive and negative ways.

Because of differing interpretations of the present and past of Latin America, and because of the four-hundred-year span since initial European colonization, feminist scholarship confronts a very complex field when it embarks on the study of Latin American women.

General Readings on Latin America

Individual essays from the anthologies listed below are annotated under the appropriate topic. The periodicals listed here are entire issues or issues with special sections on women in Latin America.

Journal of Family History 3, no. 4 (Winter 1978).

Journal of Interamerican Studies and World Affairs 17, no. 4 (November 1975).

Journal of Marriage and the Family 35 (May 1973).

Lavrin, Asuncion, ed. *Latin American Women: Historical Perspectives.* Westport, Conn.: Greenwood Press, 1978.

Nash, June, and Helen Icken Safa, eds. *Sex and Class in Latin America.* Brooklyn, N.Y.: J. F. Bergin, 1980.

Pescatello, Ann, ed. *Female and Male in Latin America: Essays.* Pittsburgh: University of Pittsburgh Press, 1973.

Rohrlich-Leavitt, Ruby, ed. *Women Cross-Culturally: Change and Challenge.* The Hague: Mouton, 1975.

Signs 3, no. 1 (Autumn 1977). The same group of essays is in Wellesley Editorial Committee, eds. *Women and National Development: The Complexities of Change.* Chicago: University of Chicago Press, 1977.

Signs 5, no. 1 (Autumn 1979).

Women in Latin America: An Anthology from Latin American Perspectives. Riverside, Cal.: Latin American Perspectives, 1979.

WOMEN IN COLONIAL TIMES

The study of women in Latin America can commence with their history. The Iberian conquest of America provides a useful starting place. Contrary to the stereotypical view, the European conquerors and colonizers were accompanied by some women. A rare surviving letter from a woman who went with the expedition that founded Buenos Aires in 1536 provides an excellent introduction to the experience of Spanish women in the Conquest.

de Guevara, Isabel. "Hardships and Bravery in the Conquest of the Rio de la Plata." In *Women in Latin American History,* edited by June Hahner. Los Angeles: University of California Latin American Center, 1976.

Spanish women had an influence far exceeding their numbers in early colonial times because they were related by ties of blood or marriage to the ruling colonizers. For their role as transmitters of Spanish culture in the process of colonization see:

Lockhart, James. "Spanish Women and the Second Generation." Chap. 9 in *Spanish Peru, 1536–1560: A Colonial Society.* Madison: University of Wisconsin Press, 1968.

An excellent primary source for class use that illuminates aspects of Spanish colonial women's lives is:

Lockhart, James, and Enrique Otte, eds. and trans. *Letters of People of the Spanish Indies: Sixteenth Century.* Cambridge: Cambridge University Press, 1976. See especially "An Encomendero's Establishment," Chap. 11; "The Tanner and His Wife," Chap. 17; "The Troubadour," Chap. 18; "The Nephew," Chap. 19; "The Garden and the Gate," Chap. 20; "The Woman as Settler," Chap. 21; "The Farmer," Chap. 22; "The Petty Dealer," Chap. 23; "How a Governor Operates," Chap. 29; "The Petty Administrator," Chap. 30.

The issue of whether a commonality of experience existed among women of different classes in Spanish colonial society is addressed in:

Burkett, Elinor C. "In Dubious Sisterhood: Class and Sex in Spanish Colonial South America." In *Women in Latin America: An Anthology from Latin American Perspectives.* Burkett argues that women shared the norm of what was expected of them by male-imposed social standards, but that in their interaction, class differences were more important than gender commonalities.

The majority of women in colonial times, however, were Indians, and by the second generation many of them were *mestizos*—children of Spaniards and Indians. The origins of this process can be found in:

Morner, Magnus. "The Conquest of Women." In *History of Latin American Civilizations: Sources and Interpretations,* edited by Lewis Hanke, vol. 1, 137–41. New York: Little, Brown & Co., 1973.

IMAGES AND STATUS OF LATIN AMERICAN WOMEN

The rape of indigenous women, part of the violence of the conquest, contrasted with the deliberate use of strategic marriage alliances, such as those between noble Inca women and Spaniards. Amerindian women were not just passive victims, however. They were able to maneuver and make a place for themselves in early colonial society. See:

Burkett, Elinor C. "Indian Women and White Society: The Case of Sixteenth Century Peru." In *Latin American Women.* Burkett describes the active economic role of women in pre-conquest Inca society; the disruption caused by the conquest which affected rural women more than it did rural men; and the varied productive activities Indian women performed in urban colonial Peru, manipulating the Spaniards' need for domestic servants and sexual companions.

The possibilities open to Indian women while their sex was in short supply disappeared as a highly stratified society came into being. Two studies comparing the roles of women in pre-conquest Aztec and Inca societies, and the effects of Spanish colonization are:

Etienne, Mona, and Eleanor Leacock, eds. *Women and Colonization: Anthropological Perspectives.* New York: Praeger Pubs., 1980. See especially "Aztec Women: The Transition from Status to Class in Empire and Colony," by June Nash; and "Andean Women Under Spanish Rule," by Irene Silverblatt.
Nash uses Aztec historical traditions to show that women's position worsened under Aztec conquest and the transformation into a stratified military society. Even so, she finds that women retained more rights and played a more important role than subsequently under Spanish rule.

Silverblatt studies the complementarity of roles of men and women in the society of Andean people conquered by the Incas, showing how the Inca society extracted surplus without hindering the self-sufficiency of the productive unit. Under Spanish rule, however, the complementarity of roles was transformed into the subordination of women to men.

Spanish women in early colonial Latin America were largely integrated into society through the institutions of the family, convents, and retirement homes. Retirement houses and convents filled a societal role as safe places for undesirable or excess women. Decent destitute widows, women without dowries, battered or separated wives, or women who had violated the norms of society, such as deflowered young girls or adulteresses, could join retirement houses. Convents provided shelter to wealthy widows and a positive role to those women not destined for marriage. See:

Lavrin, Asuncion. "Women and Convents: Their Economic and Social Role in Colonial Mexico." In *Liberating Women's History: Theoretical and Critical Essays,* edited by Berenice A. Carroll. Urbana: University of Illinois Press, 1976.

Soeiro, Susan. "The Feminine Orders in Colonial Bahia, Brazil: Economic, Social, and Demographic Implications, 1677–1800." In *Latin American Women.*

———. "The Social and Economic Role of the Convent: Women and Nuns in Colonial Bahia, 1677–1800." *Hispanic American Historical Review* 54, no. 2 (May 1974).

To the individual woman a convent should provide a viable alternative to marriage with the possibility of an active life and a certain degree of freedom. The great seventeenth-century poet, intellectual, and even feminist, Sor Juana Inez de la Cruz, deliberately rejected marriage to become a nun because of her thirst for knowledge. Her singular life is analyzed in:

Paz, Octavio. "Juana Ramirez." *Signs* 5, no. 1 (Autumn 1979).

A translation selection of Sor Juana's work is in:

"Life and Sufferings of an Intellectual in Colonial Mexico." In *Women in Latin American History.*

Her biography is in:

Henderson, James, and Linda R. Henderson. *Ten Notable Women of Latin America*. Chicago: Nelson-Hall, 1978.

The diversity of colonial women's lives is studied in:

Lavrin, Asuncion. "In Search of the Colonial Woman in Mexico: The Seventeenth and Eighteenth Centuries." In *Latin American Women*.

The ways women were integrated into colonial society through the family can be found in:

Coutourier, Edith. "Women in a Noble Family: The Mexican Counts of Regla, 1750–1830." In *Latin American Women*. Coutourier demonstrates how some female members of a noble Mexican family had opportunities to exercise power and participate in economic activities.

Courtourier, Edith, and Asuncion Lavrin. "Dowries and Wills: A View of Women's Socioeconomic Role in Colonial Guadelajara and Puebla." *Hispanic American Historical Review* 59, no. 2 (May 1979). Research in wills and dowries shows that Spanish colonial women had a certain degree of security and independence in economic matters.

Duke, Cathy. "The Family in Eighteenth-Century Plantation Society in Mexico." *Annals of the New York Academy of Science* 292 (1977). This paper analyzes the family as a vehicle to consolidate or better people's position in society, whether in the landowning class, or as workers, artisans, or even slaves.

Russell-Wood, A. J. R. "Female and Family in the Economy and Society of Colonial Brazil." In *Latin American Women*.

The family was not a static institution throughout the three centuries of Spanish and Portuguese rule of Latin America, however. Demographic studies of the family and households in late colonial Latin America show processes of change and regional variations. See:

Arrom, Silvia. "Marriage Patterns in Mexico City, 1811." *Journal of Family History* 3, no. 4 (Winter 1978). Arrom shows that Mexican men and women did not marry much younger than their European counterparts, that many men and women never married, and that marriage practices varied by race.

Hagerman Johnson, Ann. "The Impact of Market Agriculture on Family and Household Structure in Nineteenth-Century Chile." *Hispanic American Historical Review* 58, no. 4 (1978). This paper analyzes the changes in household structure that accompanied the transformation from subsistence to market agriculture. In the mid-eighteenth century the conjugal family was the most prevalent household in regions dedicated to subsistence agriculture. As agriculture became more and more commercialized and men migrated in the nineteenth century, the female-headed family became very common in small holdings. The complex household, with several unrelated members, became common on the large estates.

Kuznesof, Elizabeth. "The Role of the Female-Headed Household in Brazilian Modernization: São Paulo, 1765 to 1836." *Journal of Social History* 13, no. 4 (Summer 1980). Kuznesof suggests that the large proportion of female-headed households (44.7 percent of the urban households in 1802) was a consequence of a low sex ratio due to outmigration of males and the transformation of household production from subsistence agriculture to home-based crafts and industries produced mostly by women.

Ramos, Donald. "Marriage and the Family in Colonial Vila Rica." *Hispanic American Historical Review* 55, no. 2 (May 1975). This study of the 1804 census in a Brazilian mining town finds that marriage seems to have been an institution of the upper classes, as the lower classes show a majority of female-headed households and consensual unions.

As colonial societies became caste societies in which race was the principal defining factor, a family strategy to better the possibilities of its descendents by contracting marriage with whiter mates emerged. This is studied in:

Martinez-Alier, Verena. *Marriage, Class and Colour in Nineteenth-Century Cuba: A Study of Racial Attitudes and Sexual Values in a Slave Society.* Cambridge: Cambridge University Press, 1978.

———. "Elopement and Seduction in Nineteenth-Century Cuba." In *Past and Present* 55 (May 1972).

LATIN AMERICAN WOMEN SEE THEMSELVES

The classic view is that even in the twentieth century, pervasive machismo defines women's passive roles in the family and in Latin American society as a whole. That women's situation is much more complex is seen in:

Flynn, Patricia, Aracelly Santana, and Helen Shapiro. "Latin American Women, One Myth—Many Realities." In *NACLA: Report on the Americas* 9, no. 5 (September–October 1980).

Studies of the images of women in Latin American literature point to the contradictions between image and reality.

Flora, Cornelia Butler. "The Passive Female and Social Change: A Cross-Cultural Comparison of Women's Magazine Fiction." In *Female and Male in Latin America*. Flora carries out a comparative study of fiction directed to different classes in the United States and Latin America, finding that while fiction for middle-class American women does not present the heroine as holding a paying job, its Latin American counterpart does. Her general conclusion, however, is that both North American and Latin American fiction represent females as passive while males are active.

———. "Pentecostal Women in Colombia: Religious Change and the Status of Working-Class Women." *Journal of Interamerican Studies and World Affairs* 17 (November 1975). In this essay Flora makes an interesting comparison between the ideology and practice of the Catholic and Pentecostal Churches in relation to women. She contrasts the Catholic Church's exaltation of the Virgin Mary and saints with the Pentecostal proclamation of the priesthood of all believers (including women). Comparing the practice of each church, she finds a more balanced sex ratio in the Pentecostal, but no women in the strictly male hierarchy as in the Catholic Church. But the Pentecostal Church has a very active women's organization, which gives women a medium for participation. She concludes that women who join the Pentecostal Church gain in individual status, but that whether women in that setting have a better collective status than in the Catholic Church remains to be seen.

Gissi Bustos, Jorge. "Mythology About Women with Special
    Reference to Chili." In *Sex and Class in Latin America*. This
    article studies how machismo as an ideology is transmitted
    through the authoritarian structures of the family and the
    Church, and internalized by men and women alive.

Jacquette, Jane S. "Literary Archetypes and Female Role
    Alternatives." In *Female and Male in Latin America*. Jac-
    quette studies literary roles in Peruvian literature,
    concluding that it is precisely in role differentiation that
    women find their power because of the continuing
    strength of the family as an institution. She finds that
    even the principle of chastity acts as a means to power.

Pescatello, Ann. "The Brasiliera: Images and Realities in the
    Writings of Machado de Assis and Jorge Amado." In
    Female and Male in Latin America. As a historian, Pescatello
    studies how two Brazilian novelists show class distinctions
    in their characters according to race and color, and evoke
    a passive feminine ideal, especially for the middle and
    upper classes.

Schmidt, Steffen W. "Women in Colombia: Attitudes and
    Future Perspectives in the Political System." *Journal of
    Interamerican Studies and World Affairs* 17, no. 4 (November
    1975). Schmidt claims that women of the ruling class in
    Colombia routinely manage men and that a large propor-
    tion are professionals. He makes the point that contrary to
    the North American stereotype, Latin America is *not*
    permeated by "macho" men and passive women. To
    confirm this he cites the responses of Colombians asked to
    name important women. Instead of naming beauty
    queens, they named women politicians.

Stevens, Evelyn P. Marianismo: The Other Face of Machismo."
    In *Female and Male in Latin America*. Stevens argues that
    marianismo, the cult of female superiority, which derives
    from the cult of the Virgin Mary, is a source of strength
    for women, who use it to wield a certain power while
    outwardly conforming to the submissive role prescribed by
    machismo.

WOMEN IN POLITICS

Women in Latin America have participated in different aspects of the political process, leading scholars to question how the

norm of passivity and dependence is reconciled with such activity.

Chaney, Elsa M. "Women in Latin American Politics: The Case of Peru and Chile." In *Female and Male in Latin America*. Chaney argues that women act in government and politics as an extension of their maternal role, as *supermadres*.

Jacquette, Jane. "Female Political Participation in Latin America." In *Sex and Class in Latin America*. Jacquette criticizes North American political scientists who study the political participation of women in Latin America exclusively at the formal level of voting practice, without considering that political action in Latin America can consist of many other kinds of activity, permitting female influence within informal settings and accepted sex-role differentiation. She argues against the stereotype of the "conservative" woman in the face of women's participation in guerrilla movements, mining strikes, and peasant revolts, and calls for revised notions of participation in terms of class and cultural differences.

Yet the fear of women as conservative voters existed in Latin America itself and led Magda Portal, a Peruvian radical of the 1930s, to oppose women's suffrage. See:

"The Place of Women in a Peruvian Reform Party." In *Women in Latin American History*.

In addition, women have been successfully mobilized for conservative aims, as discussed in:

Mattelart, Michele. "Chile: The Femine Version of the Coup D'etat." In *Sex and Class in Latin America*. Mattelart studies the active role of women in the fall of Allende. Campaigns by the opposition stressed women's corporate identity and maintained the myth of the eternal feminine, both mobilizing and containing the movement that resulted.

Women's involvement with Peronism exemplifies their political strength in working for nonconservative causes.

Hollander, Nancy Caro. "Women: The Forgotten Half of Argentine History." In *Female and Male in Latin America*. Hollander describes the role of women in the work force in Buenos Aires from the turn of the century, and the changing status that culminated in their intense political participation in the separate women's branch of the Peronist party under the direction of Eva Peron. Peronism was a populist regime with a strong working-class base, and Hollander has shown that women's electoral support came from precisely this sector.

————. "Women Workers and Class Struggle: The Case of Argentina." *Latin American Perspectives* 4 (Winter–Spring 1977). Here Hollander analyzes the dialectic between women and Peronism. Although women joined the Peronist party massively in the 1940s and 1950s, the party never challenged the oppression of women as women; instead it reinforced the norm that women's place is in the home.

Eva Peron herself never challenged the subordination of women to men. See her biography in:

Navarro, Maryssa. "The Case of Eva Peron." In *Women and National Development*.

Despite the fact that most Latin American women have not challenged subordination of women to men, they do understand and feel it. See:

Safa, Helen Icken. "Class Consciousness Among Working-Class Women in Latin America: Puerto Rico." In *Sex and Class in Latin America*. Safa studies women in shantytowns in Puerto Rico, finding that though many of them work outside the home, they see themselves primarily as wives and mothers, and understand their sexual oppression much better than their class oppression.

Many Latin American women, however, have understood their class oppression and have participated in revolutions, uprisings, and labor protests.

Hahner, June. "Anarchists, Labor and Equality for Women." In *Women in Latin American History*. Hahner reproduces selections from an article written by three São Paulo seamstresses in the early twentieth century exhorting their sisters to lose their apathy in labor disputes because women are the most exploited workers.

Nash, June. "Resistance as Protest: Women in the Struggle of Bolivian Tin-Mining Communities." In *Women Cross-*

Culturally. Nash analyzes women's organized resistance to authority as a feminine form of protest women take up when the level of exploitation becomes intolerable. She observes, however, that with victory women return to being "protected" and men fail to recognize the importance of women's role in the struggle.

Rivera, Maria A. Irias de, and Irma Violeta Alfaro de Carpio. "Guatemalan Working Women in the Labor Movement." In *Women Cross-Culturally.* The authors' description of a protest movement of female workers in a Guatemalan garment factory belies the traditional view of women's passivity toward their economic exploitation.

Women are not very visible, however, in the general political arena of Latin America.

Blachman, Morris J. "Selective Omission and Theoretical Distortions in Studying the Political Activity of Women in Brazil." In *Sex and Class in Latin America.* Blachman argues that part of this lack of visibility is due to the myopia of the observer. For example, he points out that both North and Latin American Scholarship have ignored the existence of a feminist movement in Brazil that contributed to the granting of the vote to women in 1932. He also argues that interest group theory does not provide the correct theoretical framework to analyze the structural constraints on women's political participation, instead blaming the victims.

Some Latin American women have been able to break through the structural constraints that hold back their active political participation. Some have even reached positions of leadership.

Barrios de Chungara, Domitila, with Moema Viezzer. *Let Me Speak: Testimony of Domitila, a Woman of the Bolivian Mines.* New York: Monthly Review Press, 1978. Domitila, the wife of a miner and mother of seven, went to the Women's Year Tribunal in Mexico City in 1975, representing the Housewives' Committee of a militant mining center in Bolivia. This is the account of her life, her opinions, and her struggle for social justice.

Blay, Eva Alterman. "The Political Participation of Women in Brazil: Female Mayors." *Signs* 5, no. 1 (Autumn 1979). Blay analyzes the careers of sixty women who were elected mayors in Brazil between 1972 and 1976. She finds that this occurred concurrently with a reduction of municipal power in relation to central power, in districts in which male outmigration produced a majority of women. A few of these mayors belong to the haute bourgeoisie and use their position as a power base as their male counterparts do, but a majority belong to the petit bourgeoisie. They are teachers, nurses, etc., who are striving for better social conditions. Blay concludes that we can no longer maintain that the political participation of women comes about only when the economic and industrial structure has expanded. The cases she studies show that women's participation can occur even if the level of development is low.

Bunster, Ximena. "The Emergence of a Mapuche Leader: Chile." In *Sex and Class in Latin America.* Bunster studies the life of a woman leader in the Mapuche invasion of the lands that had been unrightfully torn from them years before.

FEMINISM IN LATIN AMERICA

Feminist movements of varying intensity and appeal have existed since the second half of the nineteenth century in many parts of Latin America.

Chaney, Elsa M. "Old and New Feminists in Latin America: The Case of Peru and Chile." *Journal of Marriage and the Family* 35, no. 2 (May 1973). Chaney points out that in both countries feminists were mostly from middle or upper-middle classes, and that women's achieving the right to vote did not result in their increased political participation.

Hahner, June E. "Feminism, Women's Rights and the Suffrage Movement in Brazil." *Latin American Research Review* 15, no. 1 (1980). Describes the early twentieth-century feminist movement.

———. "The Early Feminist Press in Brazil." In *Women in Latin American History.* Provides excerpts of early feminist writings.

———. "The Nineteenth-Century Feminist Press and Women's Rights in Brazil." In *Latin American Women.* In this essay

Hahner studies the first Brazilian feminist journal, which appeared in 1852, and various other periodicals edited by women during the following decades. They emphasize the need for better education for women based on the recognition of women's intellectual equality with men and for the end of women's virtual slavery.

Little, Cynthia Jefress. "Education, Philanthropy and Feminism: Components of Argentine Womanhood, 1860–1920." In *Latin American Women.* Describes how elite Argentine women used philanthropic organizations, the push for education, and feminism to widen their roles and advocate their rights.

———. "Moral Reform and Feminism: A Case Study." *Journal of Interamerican Studies and World Affairs* 17, no. 4 (November 1975). Studies the life of Paulina Luisi (1875–1950), an early female surgeon, who struggled for female suffrage and social hygiene and against prostitution and venereal disease.

Mota, Vivian M. "Politics and Feminism in the Dominican Republic: 1931–1945 and 1966–1974." In *Sex and Class in Latin America.* Mota analyzes how feminists in the Dominican Republic were principally women of the elite classes, who achieved limited goals, such as the right to vote, precisely because they supported the status quo, therefore broadening the dictator's support.

Schmink, Marianne. "Women in Brazilian Abertura Politics." *Sings* 7, no. 1 (Autumn 1981). Schmink studies Brazilian feminist groups of the seventies, independent working-class women's organizations, and the attempt to coordinate the two movements, which culminated in the Second Congress of São Paulo Women held in 1980. Schmink views the tensions and contradictions that emerged between the different women's groups as the result of the differences among social classes.

Stevens, Evelyn P. "The Prospects for a Women's Liberation Movement in Latin America." *Journal of Marriage and the Family* 35, no. 2 (May 1973). Stevens believes that Latin America will not experience a feminist movement like that of post-industrial societies because of the inequality due to continued exploitation. She feels that as long as middle-

and upper-class women have domestic servants, they will
not feel the need to demand change.

FAMILY PATTERNS IN CONTEMPORARY
LATIN AMERICA

That women in Latin America are passive, submissive, and
confined to the family is both a stereotypical outsider's view and
an internalized ideal that molds Latin American women's views of
themselves and society. The congruence, if any, between the
cultural definition of the female role and social reality is studied
by:

Youseff, Nadia H. "Cultural Ideals, Feminine Behavior and
    Family Control." *Comparative Studies in Society and History*
    15, no. 3 (June, 1973). Youseff makes a comparative study
    between the Middle East and Latin America, two regions
    that share the ideal of a patriarchal social structure that
    reinforces women's subordination within the family. Within
    such a society, women seem to have no roles outside of
    marriage, so that it is logical to expect that most women
    will marry, and marry young. Youseff's study demon-
    strated that the Middle East conforms to the expected
    pattern, while in Latin America women do not marry
    young and many never marry. Eighteen percent of women
    between thirty and sixty-four in Latin America are single.
    They are not necessarily celibate, and there is a high rate
    of illegitimacy, which is practically nonexistent in the
    Middle East.

Thus there are different mating arrangements in Latin
America besides legitimate marriage and the traditional nuclear
family. Several hypotheses that use industrialization as a variable
to show the adaptive aspect of different kinship arrangements are
presented in:

Cancian, Francesca M., Louis Wolf Goodman, and Peter H.
    Smith. "Capitalism, Industrialization and Kinship in Latin
    America: Major Issues." *Journal of Family History* 3, no. 4
    (Winter 1978).
    Essays studying different examples of kinship arrangements
in the same issue of *Journal of Family History* are:

Deere, Carmen Diana. "The Differentiation of the Peasantry and Family Structure: A Peruvian Case Study."

Smith, Raymond T. "The Family and the Modern World System: Some Observations from the Caribbean."

Studies of alternative mating patterns include:

Brown, Susan E. "Lower Economic Sector Female Mating Patterns in the Dominican Republic: A Comparative Analysis." In *Women Cross-Culturally.* Brown distinguishes the single-mate pattern from the multiple-mate pattern. She concludes that women using the single-mate pattern are slightly better off in terms of traditional wealth indices, while those who use the multiple-mate pattern do better in the sense that they have more personal contentment, freedom to manage money, to break up unions, and to use mother-daughter dyads as coping mechanisms.

Nieves, Isabel. "Household Arrangements and Multiple Jobs in San Salvador." *Signs* 5, no. 1 (Autumn 1979). Nieves shows the effectiveness of consanguinal household arrangements (such as adult sisters living with their mothers and their children) in helping lower-class women simultaneously fulfill their roles as mothers, housewives, and providers.

The relation between the ideal norm and actual practice is studied in:

Maynard, Eileen. "Guatemalan Women: Life Under Two Types of Patriarchy." In *Many Sisters: Women in Cross-Cultural Perspective,* edited by Carolyn J. Matthiasson. New York: The Free Press, 1974. Maynard studied two groups, ladino and Indian, which shared the ideal of machismo in which men strove for many sexual conquests and many children, and women are relegated to the home. In the ladino community, men practiced serial monogamy, abandoning their mates and children. Because women had to support their children, they became virtual career women, contradicting the norm. In the Indian community, the ideal of machismo also includes a commitment to supporting one's family, providing women with more emotional and economic security. Although marriage is an economic partnership and all women are active outside the home, there is more congruence between ideal and actual patterns, and more rigidity.

FERTILITY AND POPULATION CONTROL

The question of population control is important to an understanding of women in Latin America because of the common idea that excessive population growth is one of the causes of poverty and underdevelopment in Latin America.

Kinzer, Nora Scott. "Priest, Machos and Babies: Or Latin American Women and the Manichean Heresy." *Journal of Marriage and the Family* 35, no. 2 (May 1973). This article challenges the common assumption that the opposition of the Catholic Church to birth control, together with the continued existence of machismo, are responsible for the growing population of Latin America. Kinzer argues that high female unemployment and illiteracy explain high birth rates.

Latin American regions vary widely in rates of population growth. The countries of the Southern Cone—Argentina, Uruguay, and Chile—have had relatively low birth rates since the beginning of the twentieth century.

Elu de Lenero, Maria del Carmen. "Women's Work and Fertility." In *Sex and Class in Latin America*. Lenero studies how Latin American women have been conditioned to value their roles as mothers and may have difficulty accepting impersonal population control programs which consider women to be reproductive machines in need of better contraceptive techniques. Lenero also makes the point that Mexico has a labor surplus and would not be able to absorb a great number of women into the work force.

Gimenez, Martha. "Population and Capitalism." *Latin American Perspectives* (Fall 1977). Gimenez argues that Latin America's problems are not due to population growth but to the consequences of imperialist capitalist development. She rejects, however, the assumption that population is no problem for Latin America.

Mass, Bonnie. *Population Target: The Political Economy of Population Control in Latin America.* Toronto: Latin American Working Group, 1976.

————. "Puerto Rico: A Case Study of Population Control." *Latin American Perspectives* 4 (Fall 1977). Studies sterilization projects in Puerto Rico.

McCoy, Terry, ed. *The Dynamics of Population Policy in Latin America.* Cambridge, Mass.: Ballinger, 1974. This book includes an essay by Stycos, "Politics and Population Control in Latin America," and one by Jose Consuegra, "Birth Control as a Weapon of Imperialism," which argues that the concept of population explosion is a diversionary tactic against those who point out the injustice and inequality of Latin American society. He argues that population explosion is not an obstacle to development by comparing the population density of Latin America, twelve inhabitants per square kilometer, to Europe's ninety, and Asia' sixty-three.

WOMEN IN THE WORK FORCE

Class differences must be considered when studying Latin American women. It must be emphasized that middle- and upper-class women, who are a part of the cosmopolitan, internationally linked ruling sectors of the large Latin American cities, are not so different from their United States counterparts, except that there may be proportionately more professionals among them and they usually have domestic servants to perform housework.

Cohen, Lucy M. "Women's Entry to the Professions in Colombia: Selected Characteristics." *Journal of Marriage and the Family* 35, no. 2 (May 1973). In this analysis of the career experiences of one hundred Colombian professional women thirty-five to forty-nine years old, Cohen finds that the encouragement and support of family members, especially husbands, was an important factor. These women maintain flexible roles that do not conflict with traditional norms.

Kinzer, Nora Scott. "Sociocultural Factors Mitigating Role Conflicts of Buenos Aires Professional Women." In *Women Cross-Culturally.*

————. "Women Professionals in Buenos Aires." In Female and Male in Latin America. In these articles, Kinzer provides data showing that the University of Buenos Aires (in a country with one-tenth the population of the United States) graduated in 1965 ten times the number of women dentists graduated from United States universities and proportionately more women doctors, lawyers, architects, and engineers. Based on interviews with practicing professional women, the author finds that they have supportive husbands and parents and domestic help that minimizes any adverse effects of their professional duties on their families.

Yet the cosmopolitanism, leisure, and opportunity of the upper- and upper-middle-class Latin American women is countered by the difficulties and poverty facing the majority of Latin American women. To undertand their problems it is helpful to try to enter into their lives. An excellent start is provided by:

Bunster, Ximena, "Talking Pictures." Signs 3, no. 1 (Autumn 1977). Bunster's use of photography to elicit information about Peruvian working women's feelings and aspirations results in a poignant depiction of the harsh reality of their lives.

An example of the ways in which women cope in the daily round of poverty can be found in:

Child of the Dark: The Diary of Carolina Maria de Jesus. New York: Dutton, 1962.

Women in Latin American History includes an excerpt from Child of the Dark, entitled "Life in a Brazilian Slum." It also includes two selections by Oscar Lewis: "A Prostitute in San Juan de Puerto Rico" (from La Vida: A Puerto Rican Family in the Culture of Poverty, San Juan and New York, New York: Random House, 1966); and "A Mexican Peasant Woman Remembers" (from Pedro Martinez: A Mexican Peasant and His Family, New York: Random House, 1965).

No study of Latin American women can ignore domestic servants, as they constitute a majority of female wage workers and provide the necessary infrastructure for the freedom and opportunities of middle- and upper-class women. Most of the servants in the large Latin American urban centers are migrants from the countryside or small towns. See:

Orlansky, Dora, and Silvia Dubrovsky. *The Effects of Rural-Urban Migration on Women's Role and Status in Latin America.* UNESCO Reports and Papers in the Social Sciences no. 41. Paris: UNESCO, 1978. This study demonstrates that there is a majority of women among the rural-urban migrants in Latin America and that most of them become domestic servants. It analyzes the expulsive factors of stagnation and change in rural areas that result in the differential migration of women and it examines the function of private domestic service in the Latin American economy.

For more studies on women migrants and domestic servants see:

Jelin, Elizabeth. "Migration and Labor Force Participation of Latin American Women: The Domestic Servants in Cities." In *Women and National Development* and *Signs* 3, no. 1 (Autumn 1977). Jelin studies domestic service as a prolongation of women's usual household activities. Jelin argues that domestic service functions like subsistence agriculture, in which crops grown for consumption are occasionally commercialized. Women perform for pay that which they would usually do anyhow. Jelin has not found sufficient evidence to prove that it is a channel for upward mobility. She has, however, found a correlation between the presence of a domestic in a house and the mistress's ability to enter the labor force or be a professional.

Rubbo, Anna, and Michael Taussig. "Up Off Their Knees: Servanthood in Southwest Columbia." *Michigan Discussions in Anthropology* 3 (Fall 1977). The authors analyze domestic service as the result of 1) industrialization, which increases the number of middle-class families that need servants, and 2) expanding agribusiness, which drives people off the land, thereby supplying servants. The authors argue that the servant relationship is a means of maintaining class stratification within the family. They do not find any evidence in Colombia that domestic service serves as a means of upward mobility.

Smith, Margo. "Domestic Service as a Channel of Upward
Mobility for the Lower-Class Woman: The Lima Case." In
Female and Male in Latin America. Smith studies rural
women who migrate to the city and enter domestic
service, arguing that they achieve a limited upward
mobility. She describes how the young migrants progress
from lower-paying general domestic work to specializations
in domestic service (cooks, nannies) while at the same time
demanding and receiving further training or education.
She shows that most ex-servants progress through marriage to at least an upper-lower-class status, and that their
children are consistently better educated than they were
and only rarely become servants.

Studies relating domestic service to both housework and the
larger capitalist economy are:

Arizpe, Lourdes. "Women in the Informal Labor Sector: The
Case of Mexico City." In *Women and National Development*
and *Signs* 3, no. 1 (Autumn 1977). Arizpe argues that it is
necessary to reconceptualize women's work, since domestic
service is part of GNP while the same labor carried out at
home or on an informal part-time basis is considered
outside the economic system. She describes the limited
opportunities for women of the lower and lower-middle
classes in Mexico City, their unemployment and low wages,
and shows how the availability of jobs in domestic service
is used to dismiss female unemployment. Unable to find
work in the regular work force, women turn to work in
the informal sector, which includes all kinds of personal
services (washing clothes, housecleaning, physical recrea-
tion or language classes, dressmaking), the elaboration of
food or crafts for sale, street vending, and even prostitution.

Jelin, Elizabeth. "The Bahiana in the Labor Force in Salvador,
Brazil." In *Sex and Class in Latin America*. Jelin includes
women's household production (housework) in this study
of women's participation in the labor force of Salvador,
thereby challenging conventional definitions of what constitutes "economic activities," "economically active
population," and "participation in the labor force."

The importance of housework to the system as a whole is
argued in:

Larguia, Isabel, and John Dumoulin. "Aspects of the Condition of Women." *NACLA Report* 9, no. 6 (September 1975). Larguia and Dumoulin analyze the importance of housework in the reproduction of the labor force and the condition of women.

Saffiotti, Heleieth. "Women, Mode of Production and Social Formations." *Latin American Perspectives* 4 (Winter-Spring 1977). Saffiotti argues that the domestic labor of women is a precapitalist working relation essential to capitalism because it reproduces labor power with no cost to the system.

The ramifications of the lack of opportunity for women in the labor force are studied further in:

Lustig, Nora, and Teresa Rendon. "Female Employment, Occupational Status, and Socioeconomic Characteristics of the Family in Mexico," *Signs* 5, no. 1 (Autumn 1979). This study of wives of men with different incomes and occupations found that, contrary to the authors' hypothesis, the lower the husband's income, the less likely was the wife's participation in waged labor.

Safa, Helen Icken. "The Changing Class Composition of the Female Labor Force in Latin America." *Latin American Perspectives* 4(Fall 1977). Safa shows that an expansion of the tertiary sector in urban Latin America especially benefits middle-class women. The reduced employment in the primary and secondary sectors leads her to conclude that working-class women may be experiencing decreasing opportunities.

Further information about how women's participation in the work force has varied with the progress of industrialization in Latin America can be found in:

Arizpe, Lourdes, and Josefina Aranda. "The Comparative Advantages' of Women's Disadvantages: Women Workers in the Strawberry Export Agribusiness in Mexico." *Signs* 7, no. 2 (Winter 1981). This paper shows how companies achieve a "comparative advantage" precisely from the social and economic disadvantages that drive Mexican women to accept low wages and unstable working conditions.

Gonzalez Salazar, Gloria. "Participation of Women in the Mexican Labor Force." In *Sex and Class in Latin America.* This study demonstrates that women are concentrated in the lower-paid jobs in the Mexican labor force.

Madeira, Felicia R., and Paul Singer. "Structure of Female Employment and Work in Brazil 1920–1970," *Journal of Interamerican Studies and World Affairs* 17, no. 4 (November 1975). This study demonstrates that in the Brazilian process of dependent development, men gained opportunities in modern agriculture and manufacturing while women remained in primitive agriculture and lost their market for handicrafts, which competed with manufacturers. Women did, however, gain opportunities in the increased clerical work brought about by development.

Miranda, Gloria Vasques de. "Women's Labor Force Participation in a Developing Society: The Case of Brazil." In *Women and National Development* and *Signs* 3, no. 1 (Autumn 1977). Miranda shows that the process described by Madeira and Singer had a different impact on lower-class women than on middle- and upper-class women. It was the lower class uneducated women who lost job opportunities in agriculture and handicrafts, while only educated middle- and upper-class women benefitted with the rise in clerical openings.

Safa, Helen Icken. "Runaway Shops and Female Employment: The Search for Cheap Labor." *Signs* 7, no. 2 (Winter 1981). Studies the ambiguous consequences for women of the greater opportunities for low-paying jobs that come to Mexico with export-processing industries.

Saffiotti, Heleieth. "Relationships of Sex and Social Class in Brazil." In *Sex and Class in Latin America.* This essay contains much information about women's participation in the work force, and also studies the effect of wage labor on women's ability to make decisions within the family.

IMPACT OF MODERNIZATION
ON THE CONDITION OF WOMEN

Feminist scholars studying Latin American women have had to address the issue of whether modernization through industrialization or the spread of capitalist agriculture improves the condition of women and brings them equality with men. A comparison between pre- and postindustrial conditions is made easier by the fact that industrialization is still occurring in many regions of Latin America. An example of the authors who argue that industrialization can improve women's situation is:

Rosen, B. C., and A. La Rais, "Modernity in Women: An Index of Social Change in Brazil." *Journal of Marriage and the Family* 34, no. 2 (May 1972).

Several authors, on the contrary, have concluded that industrialization or the introduction of capitalist agriculture leads to the deterioration of women's position.

Bossen, Laurel. "Women in Modernizing Societies." *American Ethnologist* 2 (1975). Bossen analyzes a community in Guatemala, finding that Western institutions and modern capitalism tend to increase sexual inequality.

Chaney, Elsa M., and Marianne Schmink. "Women and Modernization: Access to Tools." In *Sex and Class in Latin America.* Chaney and Schmink use access to tools to measure change in women's status due to development and modernization. They find that women's limited access to modern tools results in their relative "unproductivity."

Chinchilla, Norma S. "Industrialization, Monopoly Capitalism and Women's Work in Guatemala." In *Women and National Development* and *Signs* 3, no. 1 (Autumn 1977). Chinchilla describes how industrialization in Guatemala did not draw women into manufacturing industries, and how it resulted in proportionately smaller numbers of female workers in industries traditionally considered female. Chinchilla argues that industrial growth, once "the liberal panacea to poverty and backward ideas about 'women's place,' becomes linked to increased poverty and feudal patriarchy."

Mintz, S. "Men, Women and Trade." *Comparative Studies in Society and History* 13 (1971). Mintz demonstrates that the process of industrialization and modernization associated with women's incorporation into urban wage labor actually reduces the economic power of women, who in some peasant societies in Latin America play important roles as traders.

Rubbo, Anna. "The Spread of Capitalism in Rural Colombia: Effects on Poor Women." In *Toward an Anthropology of*

Women, edited by Rayna R. Reiter. New York: Monthly Review Press, 1975. Rubbo found that women lost in the transition from peasant to proletarian.

Schmink, Marianne. "Dependent Development and the Division of Labor by Sex: Venezuela." In *Latin American Perspectives* 4 (Winter-Spring, 1977). Schmink studies how the introduction of imperialist capital intensifies the division between men and women, maintaining women as a reserve army of labor in backward modes of production and restricting their participation in the labor force or the labor movement.

Modernization, industrialization, and capitalist agriculture affect the position of women in complex and ambiguous ways. Some scholars who have reacted against simplistic arguments on one side or the other are:

Aguiar, Neuma. "The Impact of Industrialization on Women's Work Roles in Northeast Brazil." In *Sex and Class in Latin America.* Aguiar argues that industrialization merely reproduces the inequality that exists between men and women in a rural setting.

Bourque, Susan C., and Kay Barbara Warren. *Women of the Andes: Patriarchy and Social Change in Two Peruvian Towns.* Ann Arbor: University of Michigan Press, 1981. Studying individual women's lives in two Peruvian towns that are experiencing different degrees of social change, Bourque and Warren analyze both the economic and cultural institutions that maintain women's subordination to men and the resourcefulness with which women cope and struggle.

———. "Compesinas and Comuneras." *Journal of Marriage and the Family* (November 1976).

Deere, Carmen Diana, "Changing Social Relations of Production and Peruvian Peasant Women's Work." In *Women in Latin America.* Deere argues against the idealization of the position of women in precapitalist societies in this study of the effects on women of the end of servile relations on Peruvian haciendas. She demonstrates that conditions for women both improved and deteriorated through this process. Women were no longer subject to the unlimited demands on their labor and they achieved a greater degree of autonomy and decision-making power, but within a context of peasant impoverishment. Those women whose economic conditions improved because they worked in cooperatives did not, however, participate more in the decision-making process.

Leon de Leal, Magdalena, and Carmen Diana Deere. "Rural Women and the Development of Capitalism in Colombian Agriculture." *Signs* 5, no. 1 (Autumn 1979). Leal and Deere compare four different regions of Colombia to show that the sexual division of labor does not vary in a mechanistic way with changes in the relations of production, but responds to both economic and ideological factors. They show how women have functioned as a labor reserve for labor intensive seasonal work, and that women's increased agricultural work is related to decreasing farm size and greater poverty.

Rothstein, Frances. "Two Different Worlds: Gender and Industrialization in Rural Mexico." In *New Direction in Political Economy: An Approach from Anthropology*, edited by Madeleine B. Leons and Frances Rothstein. Westport, Conn.: Greenwood Press, 1979, Rothstein observes that proletarian couples in the community she studied evince an asymmetrical relationship not present in peasant couples. She suggests that "the values that today temper equality are reflections of the alternatives available in the capitalist present and not remnants of the pre-industrial past." At the same time she shows that the proletarian family has a better standard of living and lower infant mortality than peasant families. People in San Cosme believe that women who stay at home are "more modern," and domesticity is not devalued. The basis for future devaluation, however, is laid as the difference between male and female spheres widens.

Shapiro, Judith. "Sexual Hierarchy Among the Yanomama." In *Sex and Class in Latin America*. Shapiro also argues against an idealization of primitive communities. She shows that among the Yanomama, the world of women is restricted in scope, while that of men embraces religious activities and relations with nearby villages. Though male dominance is rooted in kinship relations between brothers-in-

law, Shapiro argues that its results for women are similar
to those of more complex societies.

Young, Kate. "Modes of Appropriation and the Sexual Division
of Labor: A Case Study from Oaxaca, Mexico." In
Feminism and Materialism: Women and Modes of Production,
edited by Annette Kuhn and Ann Marie Wolpe. London:
Routledge & Kegan Paul, 1978. Young analyzes the
changes in the division of labor between the sexes in a
small Mexican community as a result of the influx of
circulation capital. She finds that the results of women
were contradictory and varied according to the socioeconomic position of the household in the community. She
therefore concludes that economic status was as important
a variable as sex, and that certain changes reinforced
women's reproductive role because of families' increased
need for wage laborers.

LATIN AMERICAN WOMEN UNDER SOCIALISM

Because socialists have maintained that the transition to socialism would lead to women's emancipation, feminist scholars
have viewed the Cuban experiment with special interest. Cuban
women themselves seem to perceive a positive change. See:

Randall, Margaret. *Cuban Women Now: Interviews with Cuban
Women.* Toronto: Women's Press, 1974.

Yet Cuban women also understand the objective and subjec-
tive limitations to radical change. See

"Women in Revolutionary Cuba: Interview with Vilma Espin."
In *Women in Latin American History.* The president of the
Federation of Cuban Women here analyzes the progress
Cuban women have experienced and the goals still to be
achieved.

A different view is that of:

Purcell, S. K. "Modernizing Women for a Modern Society." In
Female and Male in Latin America. Purcell argues that the
positive changes for women in the Cuban Revolution

derive only from the process of modernization and from the Revolution's need for labor power.

The liberating potential for women in revolutionary mobilization is studied in:

Azicri, Max. "Women's Development Through Revolutionary Mobilization: A Study of the Federation of Cuban Women." *International Journal of Women's Studies* 2, no. 1 (1979). This article examines the achievements and shortcomings of the Federation of Cuban Women and its role in the incorporation of women into the labor force, the education of women, the participation of women in politics, and the creation of the Family Code.

Olesen, Virginia. "Confluences in Social Change: Cuban Women and Health Care." *Journal of Interamerican Studies and World Affairs* 17, no. 4 (November 1975). Oelsen argues that it is due to women's wide participation in health care brigades, the literacy campaign, and other volunteer activities promoted by the Federation of Cuban Women that sex roles are slowly changing.

Though hundreds of day care centers were built, Cuban working women still found themselves saddled with a second shift—housework to be performed when they returned home. Cuba was the first socialist nation in the world to address this problem with a law, the Family Code, which specifies that husband and wife are equally responsible for the support of the family and the performance of household tasks and child care. This process is described in:

King, Marjorie. "Cuba's Attack on Women's Second Shift, 1974–1976." In *Women in Latin America*.

Despite this law, problems remain in the struggle for women's equality in Cuba. An update to Margaret Randall's first book that reflects both the successes and remaining problems women face is:

Randall, Margaret. *Women in Cuba: Twenty Years Later.* New York: Smyrna Press, 1981.

Good analyses of the situation of women in Cuba in the mid-seventies are:

Bengelsdorf, Carollee, and Alice Hageman. "Emerging from Underdevelopment: Women and Work in Cuba." In *Capitalist Patriarchy and the Case for Socialist Feminism,* edited by Zillah R. Eisenstein. New York: Monthly Review Press, 1979.

Casal, Lourdes. "Revolution and *Conciencia:* Women in Cuba." In *Women, War and Revolution,* edited by Carol Berkin and Clara M. Lovett. New York: Holmes and Miers, 1980. Casal argues that women's complete equality has not yet been achieved in Cuba because of the persistence of prejudice and machismo due to the inevitable time lag between structural and ideological change.

Croll, Elizabeth. "Women in Rural Production and Reproduction in the Soviet Union, China, Cuba, and Tanzania: Socialist Development Experiences" and "Women in Rural Production and Reproduction in the Soviet Union, China, Cuba, and Tanzania: Case Studies." *Signs* 7, no. 2 (Winter 1981). In these articles Croll argues that though ideological constraints persist in these countries, economic considerations are the principal barrier to the elimination of women's second shift. Because socializing reproductive activities (housework and child care) is so very expensive, socialist countries first emphasize capital accumulation.

Nazzari, Muriel. "The 'Woman Question' in Cuba: An Analysis of the Constraints to Its Solution." *Signs* 8, no. 3 (Spring 1983). This essay argues that the Cuban choice of systems of distribution and work incentives has negative consequences for the position of women in the workforce and within the family.

The study of women in Latin America illuminates the complexity of the subject "woman," demonstrating that there are no easy answers to the concerns of feminist scholarship. For North American students it is broadening to discover the limitations of sweeping generalizations about the condition of women and to feel the challenge to further exploration. The following sources are excellent guides for additional course development or independent research.

Balmori, Diana. "A Course in Latin American Family History." *The History Teacher,* 14, no. 3 (May 1981).

Hahner, June E. "Bibliographical Survey of Writings on Latin American Women." In *Women in Latin American History.*

Knaster, Meri. *Women in Spanish America: An Annotated Bibliography from Pre-Conquest to Contemporary Times.* Boston: G. K. Hall, 1977. Covers the literature through 1974.

————. "Women in Latin America: The State of Research, 1975." *Latin American Research Review* 11, no. 1 (1976). Updates her earlier bibliography.

Lavrin, Asuncion. "Women in Latin American History." *The History Teacher* 14, no. 3 (May 1981).

Navarro, Maryssa. "Research on Latin American Women." *Signs* 5, no. 1 (Autumn 1979). Especially valuable regarding research by Latin American scholars.

Soeiro, Susan. "Recent Work on Latin American Women: A Review Essay." *Journal of Interamerican Studies and World Affairs* 17, no. 4 (November 1975).

A good book to consult for a synthesis of Latin American history is:

Burns, E. Bradford. *Latin America: A Concise Interpretive History.* Englewood Cliffs, N.J.: Prentice-Hall, 1972.

CHAPTER ELEVEN

WOMEN IN THE ISLAMIC MIDDLE EAST AND NORTH AFRICA

Margot I. Duley

There is an enormous amount of literature on the status of women in the Islamic religion and on Islamic women's formal rights and relationships. Most of the scholarship, however, can be divided according to two contending interpretations of what is being described. On the face of it, it seems impossible to reconcile the divergent viewpoints.

Vern Bullough, for example, in surveying attitudes toward women cross-culturally, is unsparing in his depiction of how women are regarded in Islam: Islam has "strong misogynistic tendencies"; and it considers women as a "sexual object of the man as well as a somewhat helpless pawn to her own passion," attitudes institutionalized by seclusion, veiling, and clitoridectomy to control female sexuality.[1]

This viewpoint is not well received by many scholars from the cultures it attacks. Much Western scholarship, including that by feminists, is regarded with suspicion: it is done by outsiders who directly or indirectly represent imperialist powers and speak from a Judeo-Christian tradition which is itself misogynist. "Middle Eastern women have been the object of the most malicious campaign of defamation in human history, a campaign that was initiated in early anti-Muslim theological tracts," claims Muhsin Mahdi, director of the Center for Middle Eastern Studies at Harvard.[2]

The scholarship is thus more than usually bedeviled by biases. Western antagonism toward Islam contends with Islamic cultural revivalism and a tendency to idealize; scholars fail to distinguish between the letter and spirit of the original Qur'ānic injunctions and subsequent social developments. And all of this is overlaid by the now familiar sins of omission and commission of nonfeminist scholars.

In fairness to Bullough, he does not present Islam's misogyny as unique. He is equally and rightly critical of every great religious tradition. Other writers have not been as scrupulous. Western writings on the Middle East in general and on women in particular have long been marred by polemical overtones, dating from medieval justifications for the crusades; continuing in nineteenth- and twentieth-century justifications for Western imperialism; and present to this day in American views of Middle Eastern politics, the oil crisis, and the Arab-Israeli conflict. Instructors should be forewarned of the degree to which their students are likely to share these anti-Arab feelings, and to be prepared to challenge enduring stereotypes. In this heated atmosphere the question of "the status of women" has often been a pawn in scholarship, linked on both sides to justifications of who was more or less "civilized." We may now be at an historical juncture where Arab and Western feminists can painfully cut through their respective cultural biases, and rebuke the patriarchy on both sides of the divide for their self-serving commentaries.

Not that feminist scholarship itself has been free of certain overemphases. Some feminists see the veil and seclusion as evidence of total subjection and humiliation and largely ignore the historical achievements of Muslim women. Others refuse to depict women as passive actors and emphasize, perhaps overemphasize, female power, especially in domestic spheres. The division of opinion often breaks down along national lines, with Western feminists tending to highlight women's subjection and Middle Eastern women tending to stress women's power. The polarities in this debate have the merit of correcting one another's criticisms. In more recent work one can perhaps detect a greater meeting of minds.

A further caution should be suggested. In constructing a unit on women in the Islamic Middle East and North Africa, instructors should guard against portraying a spurious homogeneity. Islam adapted to and interacted with a wide variety of ecological, economic, and cultural environments. Within nations the divergences between city and village, between settled agriculturalists and nomads, and especially between classes make generalization difficult. Likewise, differences between nations cannot be ignored, ranging from Marxist, revolutionary South Yemen to monarchist Saudi Arabia, or from fundamentalist Iran, rooted in

Persian culture, to socialist Algeria, whose Arab roots were scarred by French colonialism.

Despite the difficulties, careful generalizations are possible, and the following bibliography attempts to depict both the details of local conditions and commonalities between regions. This unit is divided into five parts: women and Islam, village and pastoral societies, selected social issues that range from polygamy to women's power in their societies, the impact of national development on women, and feminism.

General Background Sources

The choice of works in this bibliography is highly selective. First, only books or articles that are fairly commonly available have been included—chiefly, books published within the last twenty-five years and articles from major journals. Second, only works in the English language are listed. Finally, selections are restricted to those that best illustrate the theoretical and interpretive framework developed earlier in this guide.

The instructor or student in search of a more comprehensive bibliography will find a number of excellent ones. The following general work has a special section on women in Islamic cultures.

Buvinić, Mayra. *Women and World Development: An Annotated Bibliography.* Washington, D.C.: Overseas Development Council, 1976.

Recent bibliographies specifically on women in the Middle East that are more or less accessible include:

Ahdab-Yehia, May, and Mary Rihani. *A Bibliography of Recent Research on Family and Women in the Arab States.* Beirut: Institute for Women's Studies in the Arab World, Beirut University College, 1976.

Gulick, John, and Margaret Gulick. *An Annotated Bibliography of Sources Concerned with Women in the Middle East.* Princeton, N.J.: Princeton Near East Paper no. 17, 1974.

Meghdessian, Samita Rafidi. *The Status of the Arab Woman: A Select Bibliography.* Compiled under the auspices of the Institute for Women's Studies in the Arab World, Beirut University College, Lebanon. Westport, Conn.: The Greenwood Press, 1980. Some 1,600 entries cover materials on the twentieth century published since 1950 in Western languages. Listings include books, journals, theses, dissertations, conference proceedings, and unpublished papers, making it particularly useful as a research tool. There are five thematic sections plus specialized bibliographies on nineteen Arab nations.

Al-Quzzaz, Ayad. *Women in the Middle East and North Africa: An Annotated Bibliography.* Austin: University of Texas Press, 1978. This bibliography contains over 200 English-language titles, indexed by country and topic.

Raccagni, Michelle. *The Modern Arab Woman: A Bibliography.* Metuchen, N.J.: Scarecrow Press, 1978. Contains over 3,000 entries including books, articles, and dissertations in Western languages (principally French and English) as well as Arabic. This bibliography is particularly valuable for its inclusion of sections by country on Arab feminism.

Van Dusen, Roxann. "Bibliography: Women in the Near East." In *Integrating Women into National Economies: Programming Considerations with Special Reference to the Near East.* Near East Bureau, U.S. Agency for International Development, 1977.

———. "The Study of Women in the Middle East: Some Thoughts." *Middle Eastern Studies Association Bulletin* (May 1976): 1–20.

In her excellent bibliographies Roxann Van Dusen makes the point that scholarship on women in the Near East and North Africa is mainly an underground literature or occasional papers produced for institutes, government agencies, or conferences. It has yet to reach a broad audience, as the publishing sources of several of the bibliographies listed here illustrate.

Four recent, complementary works provide a good general overview of Middle Eastern and North African women. Taken together they provide rich classroom sources.

Beck, Lois, and Nikki Keddie, eds. *Women in the Muslim World.* Cambridge: Harvard University Press, 1978. This volume contains thirty-three original essays on women in the Muslim world from a variety of historical periods and disciplinary perspectives. A number of the essays are cited below.

Fernea, Elizabeth Warnock, and Basima Quattan Bezirgan, eds. *Middle Eastern Muslim Women Speak.* Austin: University of Texas Press, 1977. Through poetry, prose, biography, auto-biography, oral history, and anthropology the voices of

Middle Eastern women, both historical and contemporary, are heard.

Minai, Naila. *Women in Islam: Tradition and Transition in the Middle East.* New York: Seaview Press, 1971. Minai, who is a U.N. correspondent, was born in Turkey and educated in France and the United States. She combines an historical review with current events including the Islamic revival. Individuals come alive through biographies of famous and ordinary Muslim women. There is also information on early feminists.

ᐸ *Women's Studies International Forum* 5, no. 2 (1982). Special Edition: Women and Islam. Azizah al-Hibri, Guest Editor. A provocative collection of nine scholarly articles, mostly by Arab women, brings a feminist perspective to such questions as the status of women in pre-Islamic and early Islamic society, the evolution of Islamic patriarchy, and feminism in the Middle East. This volume is indispensable to an understanding of the contemporary dialogue between Muslim feminism and Islam, and for its challenge to Western stereotypes about Muslim women.

Finally, the Institute for Women's Studies in the Arab World, Beirut University College, P.O. Box 13-5053, Beirut, Lebanon publishes occasional papers as well as *Al-Raida,* a journal about women in Arab societies. This publication, a testimony to scholarly determination in increasingly difficult circumstances, provides book reviews, critiques of research, and news of current interest about women in the Middle East. Subscriptions are $18.00 per year payable to Beirut University College, which also has a U.S. office at 475 Riverside Drive, Room 1846, New York, NY 10115.

WOMEN AND ISLAM

Debates about the role and status of women throughout the Middle East and North Africa occur largely within the framework of Islamic law. The great exception to this generalization is Turkey, which declared Islamic family law abolished and replaced it with a secular civil code in 1926, under the leadership of Kemal Ataturk.

Legal pronouncements concerning women are of several types, with varying degrees of authority. The most authoritative injunctions are contained in the Qur'ān, the word of God revealed to the Prophet Mohammad. The *hadiths,* or sayings attributed to the Prophet, are of varying degrees of authority. Some were recorded a few years after the death of the Prophet, others were recorded centuries later or are inconsistent. Religious scholars classify the hadiths in categories ranging from certain to false. Whole schools of legal and theological interpretation turn on whether a hadith is considered authoritative or not. The Qur'ān and the hadiths form the *shariah,* or law, for Muslims.

The debate about women's role in Islam thus turns on which hadiths are to be believed, how particular words in the Qur'ān and a hadith are to be interpreted, and which legal school is to be followed. Though religous fundamentalists staunchly resist any changes in Islamic law as it has evolved over the centuries, reformers have found ample justifications for changes by reexamining texts. Maliki legal theorists in Tunisia, for example, sanctioned a series of sweeping reforms governing divorce and outlawing polygamy in 1956, under the presidency of Habib Bourguiba.[3]

Regardless of the letter of the law and the authenticity of particular hadiths, a key issue for scholars and reformers is Islam's early spirit. Hence much attention is paid in the literature to the Prophet Mohammad's role as a social reformer in the context of sixth-century Arabia.

Useful works that delineate the social context are:

Levy, Reuben. *The Social Structure of Islam.* Cambridge: Cambridge University Press, 1965.

Watt, W. Montgomery. *Mohammad at Medina.* Oxford: Clarendon Press, 1962. See especially J. Excursus: "The Reform of the Social Structure" and "Marriage and the Family in Pre-Islamic Times."

Two recent articles, both by Muslim feminists, which examine the status of women in pre-Islamic Arabian society (the age of Jahiliyyah or ignorance) are:

al-Hibri, Azizah. "A Study of Islamic Herstory: Or How Did We Ever Get Into This Mess?" *Women's Studies International Forum* 5, no. 2 (1982): 207–19. al-Hibri's original essay provides, as she says, "preliminary data" for the rewriting of Arab history from a feminist perspective. In her

analysis of pre-Islamic Arabia she concludes that the
Prophet Mohammad's progressive views on women were
greatly influenced by surviving traces of an earlier but
dying matrilineal and matrilocal culture. This society had
been replaced, especially in the north, by a harsh
patriarchy based on the patrilineal tribe. Male takeover
occurred as a result of the acquisition of new technologies
in trade and warfare. Nevertheless, women (as is evident
in the personalities and activities of the Prophet's own
wives) still possessed vigorous characters and participated
in politics, theological disputes, and even battles. The
Islamic record, she asserts, if one returns to Qur'ānic
sources, was "one brave and successful attempt at the time,
to undercut Patriarchy and to regain for women some of
their lost rights" (214).

el Saadawi, Nawal. "Woman and Islam." *Women's Studies
International Forum* 5, no. 2 (1982): 193–206. el Saadawi
also argues that "the greater recognition accorded by the
Prophet and early Islam to the rights of women was the
direct result of the comparatively higher position occupied
by the Arab woman in the pre-Islamic era" (196). She also
outlines the active roles that women took in the pre-
Islamic and early Islamic eras.

Regardless of the original thrust of Islamic law regarding
women's status, the indisputable fact remains that inequalities are
now embodied in legal codes. While the Prophet Mohammad
placed limitations on polygamy, guaranteed married women's
property rights, and entrenched female inheritance rights, there
were other respects in which women from early Islamic times (*how
early is, we shall see, a matter of dispute*) were not considered
equal to men in family law. Women inherited one-half the share of
men in family property; child custody, though initially vested in
the mother, reverts to the father after the child reaches a certain
age, with girls staying with their mothers longer than boys; laws of
divorce were unequal; and there were numerous religious injunctions on female modesty and obedience to men.

Conservative Islamic scholars and many Western Orientalists
argue that these disparities in status are Qur'ānic or reflect the
Prophet's intent. Works in English that give the conservative view
are:

Abdul-Rauf, Muhammad. *The Islamic View of Women and the
Family.* New York: Speller, 1977.

Fischer, Michael J. "On Changing the Concept and Position of Persian Women." In *Women in the Muslim World.* 193–97. A succinct summary of the conservative apologia for the place of women is contained in this article.

A' La Maududi, Abdul. *Purdah and the Status of Women in Islam.* Translated and edited by Al-Ash'ari. Lahore: Islamic Pub., 1972. Maududi, writing from a Sunni fundamentalist perspective, argues that male control of women and their seclusion is divinely ordained and indispensable to the proper functioning of society. Although this book was published in Pakistan, which is not geographically part of the Middle East, it does share the Hanafi family law tradition with Syria, Iraq, and Egypt.

The vigorous reformist counterattack to traditionalist views began in the nineteenth century, and continued in the twentieth when nationalists sought to ease the conflict between literalist interpretations and the needs of modernizing states attempting to rid themselves of Western colonialism. Change in the status of women was seen by reformers as necessary for national regeneration. Unfortunately, little of this literature is available in English.

The works of Qasim Amin (1865–1908), a French-educated Egyptian lawyer and judge, are considered landmarks in the development of Arab feminism. His *Emancipation of Women* was published in 1899, provoking a storm of controversy to which he replied with *The New Woman* in 1901. Those works still arouse hostility among religious conservatives. Overviews of Qasim Amin's life and work can be found in:

Cole, Juan Ricardo. "Feminism, Class and Islam in Turn-of-the-Century Egypt." *International Journal of Middle East Studies* 13 (1981): 387–407. Qasim Amin and the debate on women are placed within the context of the emergence of new social classes in Egypt.

Mikhail, Mona, ed. "Qasim Amin, the Champion Pioneer of the Emancipation of Women." In *Images of Arab Women,* Chap. 2. Washington, D.C.: Three Continents Press, 1979.

Contemporary reform arguments that are available in English and are broadly representative of more liberal views are:

Khan, Mazhar ul Haq. *Purdah and Polygamy: A Study in Social Pathology of the Muslim Society.* Peshawar: Nashiren-e-Ilm-o-Tariqiyet, 1972.

Rahman, Fazlur. "The Status of Women in Islam: A Modernist
Interpretation." In *Separate Worlds: Studies of Purdah in
South Asia,* edited by Hanna Papanek and Gail Minault,
Chap. 11. Delhi: Chanakya Pubs., 1982.

Though the earliest generation of feminists was male, by the
early twentieth century Muslim women made powerful arguments on behalf of reforms within the Islamic tradition. One such
feminist was Nazirah Zein Ed-Din, a Lebanese Muslim whose
father Sa'id Bey headed the Lebanese Court of Appeals and who
encouraged her theological studies. She published *Removing the
Veil and Veiling* in 1928. So erudite were her arguments that her
critics concluded the book was written by a group of nine men,
including missionaries and lawyers, as a method of undermining
Islam. See:

Ed-Din, Nazirah Zein. *"Removing the Veil and Veiling:* Lectures
   and Reflections Towards Women's Liberation and Social
   Reform in the Islamic World." Translated by Salah-Dine
   Hammoud. Reprinted in *Women's Studies International Forum*
   5, no. 2 (1982): 221–26.

More recently, Muslim feminists have taken the first steps in
reevaluating Muslim history and theological development in light
of modern historical techniques and textual criticism. Azizah al-
Hibri, for example, calls for an examination of the ways in which
"patriarchy co-opted Islam after the death of the prophet."[4] Her
own article, discussed above, contains a delineation of how pas-
sages in the Qur'ān were interpreted "loosely and out of context
in support of a vicious patriarchal ideology." She reviews prevailing Islamic views on polygamy and divorce in light of careful
readings of texts, and claims that the intent of the Qur'ān has been
distorted in the males' favor.
  One key passage from the Qur'ān deserves attention here, for
it illustrates both the dynamics of the debate and something of the
technical and scholarly challenge facing the reformer. Central to
the conservative argument about male superiority is a verse from
the Qur'ān that is usually translated as follows: "Men are in charge
of women, because Allah hath made the one of them to excel the
other, and because they spend of their property (for the support
of women)."[5] However, Azizah al-Hibri claims this is closer to the
original intent: "Men are 'qawwamūm' over women in matters
where God gave some of them more than others, and in what they

spend of their money." She goes on to argue that "the word 'qawwamūn' is a difficult word to translate. Some writers translate it as 'protectors' not 'maintainers.' However that is not quite accurate. The basic notion . . . is one of moral guidance and caring" (217).

A fascinating process of theological evolution, which reinforces al-Hibri's claim that the Prophet Mohammad's original message was distorted by later generations, is depicted in:

Smith, Jane I., and Yvonne Y. Haddad. "Eve: Islamic Image of Woman." *Women's Studies International Forum* 5, no. 2 (1982): 135–44. The way in which Eve's nature is portrayed has profound implications for Muslim (and Christian) views of women as a sex. Smith and Haddad point out that though Adam is in some ways depicted in the Qur'ān as more important (he alone is taught names and given the covenant as part of a prophetic mission), nevertheless both Adam and his wife, Eve, are asked to live in Eden and warned not to eat of the tree of immortality. "Both members of the primordial pair are [seen as] equally responsible in the sequence of events that resulted in the banishment . . ." (135). Later tradition, however, depicts Eve as culpable and created out of Adam's rib, thus justifying her subservience and male control.

Recent scholarship is also rediscovering the important contributions that women made to the development of Islamic religious traditions. Although the Qur'ān considered women equal in the eyes of God, and although women prayed in mosques and became religious scholars in the early years of Islam, much of this history was lost or forgotten as local patriarchal norms gradually excluded women. Even in later years, however, women participated in religion in several ways:

Mernissi, Fatima. "Women, Saints, and Sanctuaries." *Signs* 3, no. 1 (Autumn 1977): 101–12. This article is part of a growing body of knowledge that articulates the role of women in anti-establishment religious arenas, in this case a Moroccan saint's sanctuary, which functions as an informal women's association.

A complementary article studies a Sufi area of Morocco and outlines the role of women in determining with which saints a family will affiliate:

Dwyer, Daisy H. "Women, Sufism, and Decision-Making in Mo-
    roccan Islam." Chap. 29 in *Women in the Muslim World.*

Women also made important contributions as saints, particularly in mystic orders. Rabi'a al-Adawiyah (712–801),
important in the development of early Sufism, is perhaps the most
famous. The Sufis' quest was for direct union with the divine
through a passionate love of God. In this intensely personal spiritual life, there was no distinction between male and female. Thus,
in Islam as in other religious traditions, we find women attaining
equality with men outside the confines of formal orthodoxy (see
Chapter 5, "Women and Religion," above).

Fernea, Elizabeth Warnock, and Basima Quattan Bezirgan.
    "Rabi'a the Mystic," Chap. 4 in *Middle Eastern Muslim Women
    Speak.* Contains part of an earlier biography by Margaret
    Smith. *Rabi'a the Mystic and Her Fellow-Saints in Islam.* Cam-
    bridge: Cambridge University Press, 1928.

Schimmel, Annemarie. "Women in Mystical Islam." *Women's Stud-
    ies International Forum* 5, no. 2 (1982): 145–51. Schimmel
    points out that women have been venerated as saints and
    accepted as teachers in the Sufi tradition, and it was women
    who introduced the concept of pure love into Islamic mys-
    ticism.

In the earlier centuries of Islam, women also attained emi-
nence as scholars. Women were licensed to teach religion as late as
the early thirteenth century, and female scholars were cited as
authorities until the seventeenth century. For further discussion,
see:

Fernea, Elizabeth Warnock, and Basima Quattan Bezirgan. In-
    troduction in *Middle Eastern Muslim Women Speak,* xxvii–
    xxviii.

Goldziher, Ignaz. *Muslim Studies.* Translated by S. M. Stern and
    C. R. Barber. London: Allen & Unwin, 1970.

Levy, Reuben. *Social Structure of Islam,* 133.

Finally, an article that synthesizes much of the research on
women's involvement in religion in a concise and readable way
should be mentioned:

Beck, Lois. "The Religious Lives of Muslim Women." In *Women in Contemporary Muslim Societies,* edited by Jane I. Smith, 27–60. East Brunswick, N.J.: Bucknell University Press, 1980.

Despite the achievements of women in Islam in earlier times, and despite their continuing membership in mystic orders, particularly in Turkey and in North Africa to this day, there is no doubt that a conception of separate and unequal has rigidified over time. This inferior status receives strong sanction from religious fundamentalists and is enshrined in their interpretations of Islamic law. According to Nadia Youssef, an Egyptian sociologist, "By the standards of the twentieth century, the religious sanctioning of polygamy and concubinage, divorce at will by the husband, guardianship of children to the father, unequal female inheritance, unequal weight to the legal testimony of women, are hardly consonant with a woman's equitable position in the modern world" (*Women and Work in Developing Societies,* 100). Discussions of Islamic legal reform are found in:

Coulson, Noel, and Doreen Hinchcliffe. "Women and Law Reform in Contemporary Islam." Chap. 1 in *Women in the Muslim World.* A good overview of modern reforms involving five areas of Islamic law: capacity to marry, polygamy, divorce, custody of children, and succession.

Dorph, Kenneth Jan. "Islamic Law in Contemporary North Africa: A Study of the Laws of Divorce in the Maghreb." In *Women's Studies International Forum* 5, no. 2 (1982): 169–82. A comparison of the diverse trends in interpretation, indicating something of the plasticity of tradition among Maliki theorists in Tunisia, Algeria, and Morocco.

Eposito, John L. *Women in Muslim Family Law.* Syracuse, N.Y.: Syracuse University Press, 1982. An excellent extended treatment of Islamic family law, both traditional and modern, with suggested avenues of reform that draw on traditional Islamic legal reasoning.

Pastner, Carroll McC. "Access to Property and the Status of Women in Islam." In *Women in Contemporary Muslim Societies,* 146–85. Drawing a distinction between "access to property" and actual control, Pastner argues that "managerial rights on the part of the father, brother, or husband provide a major means of distraction from Muslim females rights of property disposal."

White, Elizabeth H. "Legal Reform as an Indicator of Women's Status in Muslim Nations." Chap. 2 in *Women in the Muslim World*. Though somewhat dated, this valuable article ranks Muslim nations according to the extent to which they have reformed traditional laws affecting women, as of 1974.

VILLAGE AND PASTORAL SOCIETIES

The literature on the status of women in village and pastoral societies contains numerous statistical and descriptive gaps. Women as a group have been neglected by many male anthropologists, and the custom of seclusion makes it difficult for even the unbiased social scientist to gather information. Recent studies that give more than passing reference to women may nevertheless be recommended, to read in conjunction with the theoretical works on the status of women in Part I. Women in the Islamic world share common characteristics with their sisters in other plow agricultural systems and pastoral societies.

Village Studies. While the forces of tradition remain powerful in rural society, villages themselves have undergone change in the last century and should not be presumed to be static. With the penetration of world markets to the countryside, and domestic industrialization, villages have become increasingly stratified by class and their largely self-sufficient economies have been increasingly oriented to the demands of outside markets. The literature on modern villages can be usefully examined in the light of Ester Boserup's theme that men and women may be affected disparately by economic change (see "Traditional Modernization Theory and the Status of Women" in Chapter 3, above).

Ammar, Hamed. *Growing Up in an Egyptian Village: Silva, Province of Aswan*. New York: Octagon Books, 1954.

Antoun, Richard. *Arab Village: A Social Structural Study of a Trans-Jordan Village*, Chap. 3. Bloomington: Indiana University Press, 1977.

Celarie, Henriette. *Behind Moroccan Walls*. Translated by Constance Lilly Morris. Freeport, N.Y.: Books for Libraries, 1970. Repr. of 1931 edition.

Davis, Susan Schaefer. "Working Women in a Moroccan Village." Chap. 20 in *Women in the Muslim World*. This article focuses on women who fall outside the norm—women in a village who work as wage laborers. Davis analyzes the effects of different occupations (seamstress, clothes washer, teacher, witch, field laborer, and prostitute, among others) on female status.

Fernea, Elizabeth Warnock. *Guests of the Sheik*. Garden City, N.Y.: Doubleday, 1965. An account of an American woman's attempt to gain acceptance from women of El Nahra, a village in southern Iraq, by adopting local traditions. The work contains insights into the role and status of women.

Fernea, Robert. *Shaykh and Effendi*. Cambridge: Harvard University Press, 1970. Robert Fernea presents a more formal, anthropological account of life in El Nahra.

Martin, M. Kay, and Barbara Voorhies, eds. "Women in Agricultural Society." Chap. 2 in *Female of the Species*. New York: Columbia University Press, 1974. This chapter combines a valuable theoretical description of the status of women in agricultural societies from an anthropological perspective, with a detailed study of the status of women in Daghara (El Nahra) based on the work of Robert Fernea and Elizabeth Fernea.

Peters, Emrys L. "The Status of Women in Four Middle East Communities." Chap. 16 in *Women in the Muslim World*. A valuable discussion of variations in the status of women under different socioeconomic circumstances (particularly modes of property ownership and labor demands), which highlight the limitations of discussing "a" status for women in Islam. Peters's article also discusses restrictions on some female behavior (for example, in the choice of marriage partner) in the context of parallel restrictions on male behavior. Examples are drawn from both nomadic and village societies.

Simmons, John, ed. *Village and Family: Essays on Rural Tunisia*. New Haven, Conn.: Human Relations Area File, 1974.

Vielle, Paul. "Iranian Women in Family Alliance and Sexual Politics." Chap. 22 in *Women in the Muslim World*. Based on

fieldwork in an Iranian village, Vielle's article depicts
peasant ideologies concerning sexuality and illustrates that
the formal property rights of women under Islamic law
are, in practice, often ignored.

Besides these accounts by outsiders, travelers, and anthropologists, there are a number of valuable short personal
histories, told by village women themselves.

Fernea, Elizabeth Warnock, and Basima Quattan Bezirgan.
    "Zahrah Muhammad: A Rural Woman of Morocco," and
    Umm Ahmad: A Village Mother of Egypt." Chaps. 13 and
    14 in *Middle Eastern Muslim Women Speak.*

Huston, Perdita. *Message from the Village,* Chaps. 3, 4, 6. New
    York: The Epoch B Foundation, 1978.

Pastoral Societies. Studies of women in pastoral societies are
comparatively sparse, a particularly regrettable fact for the student of women in Islamic societies because a large proportion of
modern pastoralists are nominally Muslim. Pastoral societies exist
in ecologically marginal areas of the Middle East, and often ignore Islamic orthodoxy. Examination of pastoral societies are
fascinating both in their own right and for the insight they bring
to the study of the relative impact of Islamic ideology and environmental conditions on the status of women.

Beck, Lois. "Women Among Qashqa'i Nomadic Pastoralists in
    Iran." Chap. 17 in *Women in the Muslim World.* Beck
    outlines a "surprising degree of symmetry and equality
    between the sexes" in a subsistence economy where
    women's and men's work activities are integrated, and the
    basic economic unit is a small nuclear family. Islamic law
    has only a marginal impact on the status of Qashqa'i
    women.

Chatty, Dawn. "Changing Sex Roles in Bedouin Society in Syria
    and Lebanon." Chap. 19 in *Women in the Muslim World.*
    This essay delineates the changes in male and female roles
    generated by a technological shift from the use of the
    camel to the use of trucks.

Martin, M. Kay, and Barbara Voorhies. "Women in Pastoral
    Society." In *Female of the Species.* This chapter summarizes
    research on women in pastoral societies, and concludes

that it is difficult to find common patterns of social adaptation. The authors discuss the complex interaction of three factors (the relative influence of Islam, prior cultural history, and specific ecological necessities) on the status of women among pastoralists.

Nelson, Cynthia, ed. "Women and Power in Nomadic Societies of the Middle East." In *The Desert and the Sown: Nomads in the Wider Society* 43–59. Berkeley: University of California Institute of International Studies, 1973. An important early article that points out the importance of women in power relationships and of ties between women in the maintenance of camp groups.

Tapper, Nancy. "The Women's Subsociety Among the Shahseran Nomads of Iran." Chap. 18 in *Women in the Muslim World*. Tapper outlines the social relationships and rankings among women that only partially conform to male ascription, and describes the life histories and activities of several female leaders.

SELECTED SOCIAL ISSUES

Seclusion

A complex and symbiotic interaction of a number of factors underlies the seclusion of Muslim women. Seclusion, the veil, clitoridectomy, and infibulation (described in more detail below) are linked with cultural concepts of family honor in which the female's sexual honor, or *'ird,* is to be guarded by her male relatives at all costs. Women are regarded as sexually aggressive and, hence, liable to behave dishonorably if left alone with men. This concept is, of course, linked to the necessity of protecting inheritance lines and controlling the transfer of property.

Descriptions of the Muslim view of female sexuality can be found in:

Bullough, Vern L. *The Subordinate Sex.* Baltimore: Penguin Books, 1973.

el Saadawi, Nawal. *Women and Sex.* Beirut. 1972. A pioneering work, less available than Bullough, but well worth the effort to locate. el Saadawi's outspoken feminism led to her dismissal as Egyptian Director of Public Health. In this, her most controversial book, she discusses female sexuality, Arabic notions of chastity, and analyzes the relevance and shortcomings of Western feminism to the Arab world. el Saadawi attempts to reconcile feminist, socialist, and reformist Muslim perspectives.

The ability of a society or an individual family to practice seclusion of women depends on an economy in which male relatives are able to provide economic support for women at all times. The practice of female seclusion also reduces the labor participation rate outside the home, and therefore presupposes an economic surplus and specialization of labor. The degree and thoroughness of seclusion commonly varies by class. Historically, the upper class, best able to sustain the practice economically, was more restrictive than the lower class, though in contemporary times this is not invariably the case. Parallel examples of female seclusion, or *purdah,* can be found in Mediterranean Europe, India, and China.

Several anthropological studies of seclusion are of particular importance. (Chapter 6 also discusses seclusion practices, albeit in South Asia.)

Ahmed, Leila. "Western Ethnocentrism and Perceptions of the Harem." *Feminist Studies* 8, no. 3 (Fall 1982): 521–34. A provocative response to Western feminists who see women in seclusion as submissive, cardboard characters.

Antoun, Richard T. "On the Modesty of Women in Arab Muslim Villages: A Study in the Accommodation of Traditions." *American Anthropologist* 70 (1968): 67–97.

Dobkin, Marlene. "Social Ranking in the Woman's World of Purdah: A Turkish Example." *Anthropological Quarterly* 40 (1967): 65–72.

Papanek, Hanna. "Purdah: Separate Worlds and Symbolic Shelter." *Comparative Studies in Society and History* 15, no. 3 (1973): 289–325. Analyzes seclusion in terms of "separate worlds," and the "symbolic shelter" of women who are seen as vulnerable to the outside world. Chapter 6, "Women in India," above, contains a description of Papanek's argument.

Pastner, Carroll McC. "Accommodations to Purdah: The Female Perspective." *Journal of Marriage and the Family* 36, no. 2

(1974): 408–14. Provides important insights on how women, even within a secluded culture, strike back at male authority.

Youssef, Nadia H. "The Status and Fertility Pattern of Muslim Women." Chap. 3 in *Women in the Muslim World*. Youssef's thought-provoking article does a great deal more than its title suggests. In addition to examining correlations between GNP, child death rates, female status, and fertility, Youssef provides a compelling discussion of the relationship between female honor, female seclusion, and the lack of social and economic incentives for Muslim women to seek options outside of marriage. She argues that only when the traditional family can no longer economically sustain its women in seclusion, due to the impact of industrialization, rising consumer expectations, and the expense of raising children, will women's roles widen.

Abu-Zahra, M. "On the Modesty of Women in Arab Muslim Villages: A Reply." *American Anthropologist* 72 (1970): 1079–92. Debates Antoun's argument on the meaning of certain female social behaviors.

Polygamy

Polygamy, like seclusion, has a complex cultural meaning. The religious laws underlying the practice are discussed in Watt, Levy, and Khan, among others listed above.

Boserup, Ester. "The Economics of Polygamy." Chap. 2 in *Woman's Role in Economic Development*. New York: St. Martin's Press, 1970. Boserup's work correlates the incidence of polygamous marriage, which ranges from 4 percent in Egypt to 33–50 percent of all marriages in sub-Saharan Africa, to the economic value of women in agricultural production. Though Boserup is mainly concerned with Africa south of the Sahara, she provides valuable insights into the institution of polygamy in general.

Genital Mutilation

Of all the cultural practices affecting women in the Muslim world, none has provoked more heated contemporary criticism, particularly from Western feminists, than female circumcision. The custom predates Islam, and was reported as early as the fifth century B.C. by Herodotus. It is now found in parts of the Middle East, North Africa, and sub-Saharan Africa. It should be noted that female circumcision is not a "Muslim" practice. It is not required by the Qur'ān, and it has flourished in a wide range of religious and cultural settings including parts of Latin America, Sri Lanka, and among theists as well as Muslims in certain areas of sub-Saharan Africa. Clitoridectomy was also practiced by physicians in nineteenth-century Europe, and indeed was recommended as recently as the 1930s to prevent "self-abuse" and to cure certain "female disorders."

Female circumcision is of three types, varying regionally: partial clitoridectomy (misnamed "sunna" excision), involving the excision of part of the clitoris; total clitoridectomy, which also sometimes involves the excision of the labia minora; and infibulation, or Pharaonic circumcision, consisting of clitoridectomy and excision of both the labia minora and the inner walls of the labia majora, which are then sutured together, leaving a small opening for the passage of urine and menstrual flow. These procedures reduce or abolish a woman's capacity for sexual pleasure and are rationalized as a method of controlling women's aggressive sexuality. They also serve to ensure female monogamy by making sex unpleasurable and to protect inheritance lines. Though the operation is usually depicted as a method of ensuring heterosexual marital fidelity (Hayes), it may well also function as a method of controlling lesbianism in sex-segregated societies (Barry, Rich).

Barry, Kathleen. *Female Sexual Slavery,* 163–64. Englewood Cliffs, N.J.: Prentice-Hall, 1979.

Hayes, Rose D. "Female Genital Mutilation, Fertility Control, Women's Role and the Patrilineage in Modern Sudan." *American Ethnologist* 2, no. 4 (1975): 617–33.

Rich, Adrienne. "Compulsory Heterosexuality and Lesbian Existence." *Signs* 5, no. 4 (Summer 1980): 640.

el Saadawi, Nawal. *The Hidden Face of Eve: Women in the Arab World.* Translated and edited by Sherif Hetata. Boston: Beacon Press, 1980.

Many medical complications result from genital mutilation, both immediately and later, during childbirth. The operations are often performed by village midwives under unsanitary conditions, although female circumcision also occurs under modern medical conditions.

Hosken, Fran P. *The Hosken Report: Genital/Sexual Mutilation of Females*. Boston: Women's International Network News, 1978. This controversial account has stirred international activity. Periodic updates on the campaign to eliminate or modify the practice through U.N. agencies, some Middle Eastern and African governments, and women's groups may be found in the quarterly editions of *WIN News*, 187 Grant St., Lexington, MA 02173, edited by Hosken, a leader in the campaign.

Sanderson, Lilian Passmore. *Against the Mutilation of Women*. London: Ithaca Press, 1981. Treading through ideological minefields, Sanderson manages a balanced yet committed treatment of the issues surrounding genital mutilation, including current political controversies, practices, history and geography, effects, explanations of, and attempts to eradicate the practice, especially in the Sudan.

American and European efforts to eliminate genital mutilation by lobbying international health and development agencies have met with mixed reactions from Arab and African feminists. Nawal el Saadawi, who has written and campaigned against traditional practices, accuses Westerners of cultural blindness for failing to point out that clitoridectomy has occurred in many cultures including the West, and for presenting it as an "Islamic" practice, thus fueling anti-Arab racism. A number of Arab (and African) feminists believe their task is made harder by outside interference and argue that because the practice of genital mutilation arises in a context of extreme poverty and lack of education, it is inseparable from the demand of the less developed nations for a new international economic order. Western feminists are accused of having too narrow a field of vision, and of indirectly profiting from the oppressive economic and political power of their own imperialist societies.

The complexities of the debate, in which anti-Western, anti-capitalist, antifeminist, pan-feminist, socialist, and nationalist currents swirl together, can be discerned in *WIN News* and in:

Mathu, Njambi. "Women: Female Circumcision." *1980 Copenhagen Conference*, no. 5. Available through InterPress Service, c/o International Women's Tribune, 305 E. 46 St., 6 floor, New York, NY 10017.

Savané, Marie Angélique. "Genital Mutilation: A Statement by the Association of African Women for Research and De-

velopment (AAWORD)." *Resources for Feminist Research* 9, no.
1 (March 1980): 8–9.

Power Versus Powerlessness

Much of the recent literature on the status of women in the
Middle East and North Africa has been revisionist. Whereas earlier writers emphasized the control men exercise over women, and
stressed the paradigm of wifely obedience and seclusion and
manly sexual bravado and superiority, a number of recent scholars emphasize the areas in which women exercise power.

Sweet, Louise E. "In Reality: Some Middle Eastern Women." In
    Many Sisters: Women in Cross-Cultural Perspective, edited by
    Carolyn J. Matthiasson, 379–97. New York: The Free Press,
    1974. An early dissenter from the paradigm of complete
    obedience, Sweet argues that the veil and a legal bias toward
    corporate lineage are not evidences of subordination. Seclu-
    sion, she says, is for protection, and the law is aimed at
    protection of the family unit. Women occupy important
    managerial roles in the household, indirectly influence polit-
    ical decisions, and occupy complementary roles with men.
    Most of Sweet's assertions are based on a field study she
    made in the village of Toqaan, Syria from 1953 to 1954.

Three more recent works that also stress elements of female
power are:

Maher, Vanessa. *Women and Property in Morocco: Their Changing
    Relation to the Process of Social Stratification in the Middle Atlas.*
    Cambridge: Cambridge University Press, 1975. This book is
    based upon research in Akhdar and neighboring towns in
    the Middle Atlas from 1969 to 1971. Among the subjects
    discussed are religious justifications for women's nonpar-
    ticipation in the public sphere, the idea of women as
    dangerous to men, social relationships among women fos-
    tered by their segregated roles, different forms of marriage
    and their relationship to the marketplace economy, and
    divorce and property. Maher argues that, although women
    are economically ultimately dependent on men and are
    excluded from public roles, they are not entirely powerless,
    because they rely on female associates and uterine kinship
    ties as channels of economic and social help.

Mernissi, Fatima. *Beyond the Veil: Male-Female Dynamics in a Modern Muslim Society.* New York: Wiley, 1975. Mernissi argues that there is no belief in female inferiority in Islamic society and that "the whole system is based on the assumption that the woman is a powerful and dangerous being. All sexual institutions (polygamy, repudiation, sexual segregation, etc.) can be perceived as a strategy for containing her power" (xvi). She sees the Muslim social order as destructive and limiting to men as well as women, for a man's honor is external, dependent upon his ability to control his kinswomen's honor, and this control is increasingly difficult as the forces of modernization break down seclusion (by education and work outside of the home). Modernization is thus perceived as an "emasculating phenomenon" (97) by the male.

Nelson, Cynthia. "Public and Private Politics: Women in the Middle Eastern World." *American Ethnologist* 1, no. 3 (1974): 551–63. Like Maher, Nelson looks beneath the surface of Muslim life and finds areas of power held by women.

Finally, any discussion of female power is misleadingly incomplete without an examination of the class variable in women's authority. Women in a landed upper-class family, for example, are likely by indirect influence to wield more power over even public policy than a male landless laborer can directly. Elite women's networks can also be important in maintaining the position of their class as a whole. Two articles that discuss the female networks of dominant families are:

Aswad, Barbara C. "Key and Peripheral Roles of Noblewomen in a Middle Eastern Plains Village." *Anthropological Quarterly* 40 (1967): 139–52.

———. "Women, Class and Power: Examples from the Hatay, Turkey." Chap. 23 in *Women in the Muslim World.*

An historical examination of variations in women's power and status by class is contained in:

Dengler, Ian C. "Turkish Women in the Ottoman Empire: The Classical Age." Chap. 11 in *Women in the Muslim World.*

These works provide a needed redress to the distorted view of the Muslim woman as a helpless pawn and victim and man as

an all-powerful overseer. But they raise many question: Can separate ever truly be equal? Who defines who will be protected? And
can domestic complementarity ever rival public participation and
control of the broader socioeconomic order in terms of status,
power, and privilege? Evidence of female networking and indirect influence may be signs of resistance, not control; and fear of
the female at a cultural level, while no doubt discomfiting to the
male psyche, may be as destructive an ideology as pedestal worship, for neither cultural construct accepts women on their own
terms.

WOMEN AND DEVELOPMENT

The Middle East and North Africa present a patchwork of
differential impacts of modernization upon the condition of
women. Countries diverge widely in the gap between male-female
literacy rates and school enrollments. In the latter case the discrepancy is often more pronounced in grade school than at the
college level, for daughters of the middle and upper-middle
classes have been better able than poor women to avail themselves
of broadened opportunities. There are important class differences on virtually every measure of development. Nationally,
women's college enrollments range from an astonishing high of
60 percent of the total in Kuwait to a low of 7 percent in Saudi
Arabia; women's labor force participation rates vary from 48
percent of the workforce in Egypt to 1 percent in Saudi Arabia.
Whatever the degree of change, rarely have expanded options
been in response to an autonomous feminist or women's movement. The motivating forces have been the needs of national
development and the degree to which nationalists saw changes in
the status of women as accomplishing their goals. Fifteen Arab
countries have an offical, government-sponsored women's movement. Short overviews of current women's rights issues are contained in:

Youssef, Nadia H. "Women in the Muslim World." In *Women in
    the World: A Comparative Study*, edited by Lynne B. Iglitzin
    and Ruth Ross, 203–17. Santa Barbara, Cal.: Clio Books,
    1976.
Morgan, Robin. *Sisterhood is Global*. Garden City, N.Y.: Double-
    day, 1984.

The literature on particular measures of women and development (education, work, political participation, health, fertility) can easily be traced in the general bibliographies listed above. Books describing the impact of nationalism, urbanization, and workforce participation on female status are discussed below. The great bulk of research on women and development focuses on the modern period, and there is a consequent danger of seeing the current situation as "fixed." Two important articles that provide a rare historical perspective, focusing on women's economic participation, should be noted:

Tucker, Judith. "Decline of the Family Economy in Mid-Nineteenth Century Egypt." *Arab Studies Quarterly* 1 (1979): 245–71.

———. "Problems in the Historiography of Women in the Middle East: The Case of Egypt." *International Journal of Middle East Studies* 15 (1983): 321–36.

Colonialism and Nationalism

The impact of colonialism and rising nationalism upon the status of women in the Middle East and North Africa is complex and multilinear. Colonial powers frequently enacted legislation along European lines, and the new Western schools, together with jobs in the modern business sector and government offices, were sometimes open to women.

Nationalists reacted in divergent ways to these changes. Some argued that changes in the status of women were essential to national regeneration (see "Women and Islam," above). In Egypt, starting with the establishment of a school for midwives in the 1830s, and continuing with the Egyptian Constitution of 1956 under President Nasser, women played an important part in nation building. In Turkey, as well, Ataturk's secularist nationalism placed great emphasis on women's legal rights and education. For further information see:

Cosar, Fatma Mansur. "Women in Turkish Society." Chap. 5 in *Women in the Muslim World*.

Fernea, Elizabeth, and Basima Quattan Bezirgan. "Excerpts from Memoirs and the Turkish Ordeal by Malidé Edib Adivar, Turkish Nationalist." Chap. 11 in *Middle Eastern Muslim Women Speak*.

Mikhail, Mona. "The Beginnings of the Professional Woman in Egypt." Chap. 6 in *Images of Arab Women.*

Smock, Audrey Chapman, and Nadia H. Youssef. "Egypt: From Seclusion to Limited Participation." In *Women: Roles and Status in Eight Countries,* edited by Janet Zollinger Giele and Audrey Chapman Smock, 35–79. New York: Wiley, 1977.

Another result of the intervention of foreign powers (including the United States) into the region was the alliance of nationalism with tradition. As Fatima Mernissi puts it, "Modern changes were identified as the enemy's subtle tools for carrying out the destruction of Islam" (*Beyond the Veil,* xix). Instances of this reaction are widespread, from the fundamentalist clergy in modern Iran to the traditionalist assumptions about women in "Arab socialist" Libya. And in less dramatic forms, governments throughout the area recognize Islam as the ideology of the family in otherwise secular legal codes.

The traditionalist backlash to women's liberation when it is associated with Westernization and imperialism is best documented in English in the case of Algeria.

Boals, Kay. "The Politics of Cultural Liberation: Male-Female Relations in Algeria." In *Liberating Women's History,* edited by Berenice A. Carroll, 194–211. Urbana: University of Illinois Press, 1976. Boals discusses the "politics of cultural liberation" of oppressed groups (including the colonized, American blacks, women, and homosexuals), and applies her theoretical insights to the specific case of Algeria. In Algeria, reform in the status of women is inhibited by a nationalist need to affirm the traditional Algerian heritage and culture. Reforms, insofar as they have occurred (as in education), are propelled by the needs of economic development, rather than by a desire for male-female equality.

Fernea, Elizabeth, and Basima Quattan Bezirgan. "Interviews with Jamilah Buhrayd, Legendary Algerian Hero," and "Excerpts from Les Algériennes by Fadéla M'rabet, Modern Algerian Journalist." Chaps. 16 and 20 in *Middle Eastern Muslim Women Speak.*

Gordon, David C. *Women of Algeria: An Essay on Change.* Cambridge: Cambridge University Press, 1968.

Minces, Juliette. "Women in Algeria." Chap. 7 in *Women in the Muslim World.* Contains a short overview of women's role during the Resistance, as well as statistics current to the mid-1970s.

Traditionalism, however is only part of the complexity of the forces shaping national politics in the Middle East and North Africa today. In South Yemen the Marxist government has made changes in the opportunities available to women a central issue in national development.

Myntti, Cynthia. *Women and Development in Yemen Arab Republic.* Eschborn: German Agency for Technical Cooperation, 1979.

Molyneux, Maxine. "Legal Reform and Socialist Revolution in Democratic Yemen: Women and the Family." *International Journal of the Sociology of Law* 13, no. 2 (May 1985): 147–72.

A special and tragic case of women's changing roles under the impact of nationalism is that of the Palestinians driven from their homelands. Works on Palestinian women, as distinct from the overall Palestinian question, are rare. See:

Antonius, Soraya. "Fighting on Two Fronts: Conversations with Palestinian Women." Chap. 5 in *Third World, Second Sex: Women's Struggles and National Liberation,* Miranda Davis. edited by London: Zed Press, 1983. Conversations with five women, ranging in age from twenty-two to sixty-five, who are actively involved in the Palestinian struggle and in the struggle to liberate women from traditional norms.

Bendt, Ingela, and James Downing. *We Shall Return: Women of Palestine.* London: Zed Press, 1982. This recent book gives a detailed depiction of the daily life of women in the Rashidiyeh refugee camp in southern Lebanon before the Israeli invasion uprooted them once again. The authors outline how the Palestinian struggle has affected both young and old women. While the older women have mixed feelings about the changes induced in their traditional roles, the young see the revolution not only as an assertion of Palestinian rights but also as a liberating influence from traditional social practices.

The struggle for women's rights, though inextricably linked with nationalism, has been greatly aided by the existence of separate women's organizations who keep the issue alive in the post-independence period. A good comparative overview is contained in:

Fluehr-Loban, Carolyn. "The Political Mobilization of Women in the Arab World." In *Women in Contemporary Muslim Societies*, 235–52. A comparative treatment of the Sudan, Egypt, Algeria, the Palestinian movement, Iraq, and the People's Republic of Yemen. Algerian backsliding is seen in part as due to the lack of a separate women's organization.

Impact of Urbanization

Early literature on development often contained the facile assumption that female seclusion would die out in urban areas, and that the broader educational opportunities and wider horizons in cities and towns would induce a rapid rise in female status as women entered the modern sector. Recent literature challenges these assumptions, and points to the persistence of tradition in most urban areas, especially among the working and middle classes who form the bulk of the population. Two exceptions to this generalization should be noted. In Kuwait, a city-state, vast oil revenues, accelerating modernization, and mass education of women have precipitated rapid change. Another current exception is socialist South Yemen, on the southern tip of the Arabian peninsula.

Gulick, John, and Margaret E. Gulick. "The Domestic Social Environments of Women and Girls in Isfahan, Iran." Chap. 25 in *Women in the Muslim World*. This article points to the persistence of seclusion among both migrant and city-born women, including those who received an education.

Joseph, Suad. "Women and the Neighborhood Street in Borj Hammoud, Lebanon." Chap. 27 in *Women in the Muslim World*. A discussion of female street networks and behavior in a working-class neighborhood.

Makhlouf-Obermeyer, Carla. *Changing Veils*. Austin: University of Texas Press, 1978. Based on fieldwork in Yemen, this work examines the lives of urban women and the complexities of both continuity and change.

el-Messiri, Sawsan. "Self-Images of Traditional Urban Women in Cairo." Chap. 26 in *Women in the Muslim World*. A useful article, especially as Cairo contains both highly educated, Westernized, elite women and *banat al-balah*, or "daughters of the country," who preserve traditional attitudes.

Mohsen, Safia K. "The Egyptian Woman: Between Modernity and Tradition." In *Many Sisters*, 37–58. The author, herself an Egyptian, argues that the conservatism of both women and men retards significant changes in the status of women. The article contains detailed information about current legal reforms and the debate surrounding them in Egypt, as well as information about Egyptian feminists up to the mid-1970s, but recent events have made some of the information dated.

Molyneux, Maxine. "Women and Revolution in the People's Democratic Republic of Yemen." *Feminist Review* 1, no. 1 (1979): 5–19. This article consists primarily of interviews with three members of the General Union of Yemeni women. Under the dual impact of a war of national liberation in which women participated and Marxist-Leninist ideology, women in South Yemen have actively entered the paid workplace and transformed their traditional roles. Change has been further aided by a shortage of male workers.

Nath, Kamla. "Education and Employment Among Kuwaiti Women." Chap. 8 in *Women in the Muslim World*. Vast oil revenues, the absence of a strong religious class, and a dominant and adaptive maritime trading class have combined, according to Nath, to produce striking changes in female opportunities.

Sedghi, Hamideh. "Women in Iran." In *Women in the World: A Comparative Study*, 219–28. The author surveys formal reforms in the status of women prior to the Islamic revolution of 1979 and concludes that "the secular influence of the West, intermingled with the Islamic tradition, provides a slightly different form for masculine domination than was found during the [historical] Islamic period."

Women and Work

A key issue in the development literature is the question of women and work, and specifically the degree to which women's labor participation should be taken into account in planning. Development literature has traditionally depicted women's participation in the paid labor force in the Middle East and North Africa as the lowest in the world. Comparative work has sought an explanation.

Youssef, Nadia H. *Women and Work in Developing Societies.* Youssef compares labor participation rates in the Middle East and Latin America, which share many cultural attitudes about female and family honor, family control, and suspicion about the intermingling of the sexes in the work force. Latin America has higher female labor participation rates because, Youssef argues, indigenous Indian norms were shattered by the European conquest, and because the Catholic Church emphasized female education, religious participation, and charity, modifying familial controls among the upper class. In the Middle East, however, systems of familial control of women remain relatively unscathed by outside forces.

Recent writing, however, modifies the terms of the discussion of labor participation rates. Both Roxann Van Dusen and Elizabeth Fernea point out that the focus on nonagricultural labor outside the home excludes from the statistics the entire informal market system and women's home industries—sewing, weaving, embroidery, factory piece work, garden vegetables, kitchen products, small animal husbandry, paid child care, midwifery, and paid domestic labor. Further, some village studies do not confirm government statistics about low female participation even in agricultural labor. Governments in the Middle East and North Africa, as elsewhere, must redefine the concept of economic activity in framing development plans and in measuring the impact of industrialization, for there is considerable evidence that capitalism had had a negative impact on female home workers, at least in the initial stages of industrialization.

Fernea. Elizabeth, Basima Quattan Bezirgan. *Middle Eastern Muslim Women Speak,* xxvi–xxvii.

Nasr, J. Abu, and N. Khoury, eds. *Women, Employment and Development in the Arab World.* Institute for Women's Studies in the Arab World, Beirut University College. Berlin: Mouton, 1985.

Van Dusen, Roxann A. "Integrating Women into National Economies: Programming Consideration with Special Reference to the Near East." Office of Technical Support. Near East Bureau. U.S. Agency for International Development. Washington, July 1977.

FEMINISM

There is as yet no comprehensive work on feminism in the Middle East and North Africa from either an historical or contemporary perspective. The English sources, such as they are, are best for Egypt, which has a long-established feminist movement.

Arab men played an important role in the development of the early feminist movement (see "Women and Islam," above). The motivation for improving the status of women was national regeneration in the wake of nineteenth-century military defeats. The term "liberation" for women has strong political connotations throughout the Arab world. The first schools for women were Western ones, and the feminist movement has often been perceived as being under the influence of foreigners. Arab feminist literature is at pains to say it wants liberation with men, and not from men. Arab feminists also stress that they do not want to mechanically imitate Western, and particularly American, ways. The American woman is seen as oppressed by her objectification into a sex object. (American feminists are sometimes held responsible for Western sexual mores, and "loose women" are equated with feminism.) Some Arab feminists have taken up the veil again, partly to distance themselves from the perceived tenets of Western feminism, partly as an affirmation of women's dignity, and partly to stress indigenous roots. In Iran, of course, under the Khomeini regime, there has been no choice; in some other instances, however, the act has been voluntary.

The uneasy position of feminists in the Arab world is complicated further by current world events. The Israeli military presence, backed by the United States, coupled with the Arab defeat in the Seven Days' War, has provided a powerful stimulus to the rise of traditionalism. Secularist, reform ideologies are blamed by traditionalists for Arab weakness in the face of Western economic and military incursions. In this polarized atmosphere, conservatives see female emancipation as a particularly threatening symbol of forced change.

Ali, Parveen Shaukat. *Status of Women in the Muslim World.* Lahore: Aziz Pubs., 1975. This work has a rare and valuable comparative perspective, discussing feminist movements in Egypt, Turkey, Iran, and Pakistan.

Araba, Bahiga. *The Social Activities of the Egyptian Feminist Union.* Cairo: Elias Modern Press, 1973.

Fernea. Elizabeth, and Basima Quattan Berzigan. "Huda Sh'arawi, Founder of the Egyptian Women's Movement." Chap. 12 in *Middle Eastern Muslim Women Speak.*

Marsot, Afaf Lutfi al-Sayyid. "The Revolutionary Gentlewomen in Egypt." Chap. 13 in *Women in the Muslim World.*

Mikhail, Mona. "Nabawiyya Musa's Quest: A Woman's Lonely Voice," and "Nawal Al Saadawy: A Contemporary Militant's Position." Chaps. 3 and 5 in *Images of Arab Women.*

Philipp, Thomas. "Feminism and Nationalist Politics in Egypt." Chap. 14 in *Women in the Muslim World.*

al-Sa'id, Aminah. "The Arab Woman and the Challenges of Society." Chap. 22 in *Middle Eastern Muslim Women Speak.*

Sanasarian, Elizabeth. *The Women's Rights Movements in Iran: Mutiny, Appeasement and Repression from 1900 to Khomeini.* New York: Praeger Pubs., 1982.

Sidki, Bahigat Rashid. *The Egyptian Feminist Union, Now the Huda Sh'arawi Association.* Cairo: Anglo-Egyptian Bookshop, 1973.

The women's movement has generally consisted of upper-class leaders and members. It has also frequently been under government control, especially in one-party states. A short description of the General Arab Women's Federation, established in 1944, can be found in *Al-Raida*, 3, no. 31 (February 1, 1985): 8–9. This officially sanctioned wing has as its aims "achieving Arab Unity and working towards the liberation of the occupied Arab territories" as well as "combatting discriminatory attitudes towards women."

Fundamentalist reaction has been a serious problem for Arab feminists, and its continuing importance should not be diminished. Even South Yemen, reportedly, has had to slow its pace of change somewhat in the face of potential backlash. Yet the more spectacular events should not obliterate the very real evidence of a feminist resurgence in a number of Arab countries. Women's studies programs have proliferated in the past decade: Beirut

College, Lebanon; Cairo University and Al-Azhar in Egypt; Centre de Documentation des Sciences Humaines, Wahran, Algeria; The University of Jordan; Kuwait University; and the General Federation of Iraqi Women have all sponsored studies.

The number of women's voluntary associations has doubled. The issue of integrating women into development—and serious questioning of the meaning of development itself—is being debated vigorously. In 1975 President Habib Bourguiba of Tunisia gave assent to a new marriage code abolishing both divorce by repudiation and polygamy, making Tunisia the first Islamic country to ban polygamy. In 1984 Algerian women, after years of quiescence, took to the streets and forced substantive revisions in a new Personal Status Code that deals with divorce, inheritance, polygamy, and other aspects of personal law (*Al-Raida*, 11).

Further advances according to Rose Ghurayyib, the editor of *Al-Raida*, will "require a peaceful atmosphere to insure their growth." War has directly "impeded women's liberation movement in Lebanon, Iraq, Iran, Libya and other Arab countries. A larger proportion of refuges, illiterates and poor, are women. Violence against them is linked to the violence of war. The participation of Arab women in peace movements and conferences, locally or internationally is an imperative task." If an American feminist asks an Arab feminist if global sisterhood is possible, she is likely to provoke another probing question: What effort have American feminists made to understand their own country's role in the region? American feminists sometimes see this query as a hostile sidestep away from "women's issues"; an Arab feminist will likely see it as fundamental to a dialogue.

Notes

1. Vern L. Bullough, *The Subordinate Sex* (Baltimore: Penguin Books, 1973), pp. 134–35.

2. Muhsin Mahdi, foreword to *Middle Eastern Muslim Women Speak*, ed. Elizabeth Warnock Fernea and Basima Quattan Bezirgan (Austin: University of Texas Press, 1977), p. xi.

3. See Kenneth Jan Dorph, "Islamic Law in Contemporary North Africa: A Study of the Laws of Divorce in the Maghreb," *Women's Studies International Forum* 5, no. 2 (1982): 169–82.

4. Editorial, *Women's Studies International Forum* 5, no. 2 (1982): vi.

5. Translation from Mohammed Marmaduke Pickthall, *The Meaning of the Glorious Koran* (New York: New American Library, Mentor Books, 1953). Reprinted in *Middle Eastern Muslim Women Speak*, p. 16.

NOTES ON CONTRIBUTORS

Susan E. Diduk is an Instructor in Sociology and Anthropology at Denison University. She did her graduate work at Indiana University. Her field work in the Republic of Cameroon focused on changing gender roles under the impact of development.

Margot I. Duley received her Ph.D. in History from the School of Oriental and African Studies, University of London. Formerly the Associate Director of the Honors Program, University of Michigan, she is currently Director of Women's Studies and Associate Professor of History and Women's Studies at Denison University. Her current research is on international feminism.

Mary I. Edwards received a Ph.D. in English from the University of Michigan. She was the Associate Director of the National Endowment for the Humanities Curriculum Development Project at the University of Michigan, and a faculty member at the Residential College. She has since moved into the educational side of business and is manager of sales development for Levi Strauss and Company.

Lance F. Morrow received his Ph.D. in African History from Duke University. His specialization is precolonial Southern Africa. He is the former Associate Director of the Residential College, University of Michigan. Currently he is the Associate Dean of Students at the College of Wooster.

Muriel Nazzari, the Argentine-born daughter of American Methodist missionaries, expects to receive her Ph.D. in Latin American History from Yale University in fall 1986, when she will also be joining the history faculty of Indiana University at Bloomington as Assistant Professor. Her research has concentrated on women in Latin American history.

Karen Sinclair received her Ph.D. in Anthropology from Brown University. She is Professor of Anthropology and Associate Director of Women's Studies at Eastern Michigan University. Her research interests are Maori women, and women, religion and social change.

The Feminist Press at the City University of New York offers alternatives in education and in literature. Founded in 1970, this non-profit, tax-exempt educational and publishing organization works to eliminate sexual stereotypes in books and schools and to provide literature with a broad vision of human potential. The publishing program includes reprints of important works by women, feminist biographies of women, and nonsexist children's books. Curricular materials, bibliographies, directories, and a quarterly journal provide information and support for students and teachers of women's studies. In-service projects help to transform teaching methods and curricula. Through publications and projects, The Feminist Press contributes to the rediscovery of the history of women and the emergence of a more humane society.

FEMINIST CLASSICS FROM THE FEMINIST PRESS

Antoinette Brown Blackwell: A Biography, by Elizabeth Cazden. $19.95 cloth, $9.95 paper.

Between Mothers and Daughters: Stories Across a Generation. Edited by Susan Koppelman. $8.95 paper.

Brown Girl, Brownstones, a novel by Paule Marshall. Afterword by Mary Helen Washington. $8.95 paper.

Call Home the Heart, a novel of the thirties, by Fielding Burke. Introduction by Alice Kessler-Harris and Paul Lauter and afterwords by Sylvia J. Cook and Anna W. Shannon. $8.95 paper.

Cassandra, by Florence Nightingale. Introduction by Myra Stark. Epilogue by Cynthia Macdonald. $3.50 paper.

The Changelings, a novel by Jo Sinclair. Afterwords by Nellie McKay; and by Johnnetta B. Cole and Elizabeth H. Oakes; Biographical Note by Elisabeth Sandberg. $8.95 paper.

The Convert, a novel by Elizabeth Robins. Introduction by Jane Marcus. $6.95 paper.

Daughter of Earth, a novel by Agnes Smedley. Afterword by Paul Lauter. $7.95 paper.

A Day at a Time: The Diary Literature of American Women from 1764 to the Present, edited and with an introduction by Margo Culley. $29.95 cloth, $12.95 paper.

The Defiant Muse: French Feminist Poems from the Middle Ages to the Present, a bilingual anthology edited and with an introduction by Domna C. Stanton. $24.95 cloth, $9.95 paper.

The Defiant Muse: German Feminist Poems from the Middle Ages to the Present, a bilingual anthology edited and with an introduction by Susan L. Cocalis. $24.95 cloth, $9.95 paper.

The Defiant Muse: Hispanic Feminist Poems from the Middle Ages to the Present, a bilingual anthology edited and with an introduction by Angel Flores and Kate Flores. $24.95 cloth, $9.95 paper.

The Defiant Muse: Italian Feminist Poems from the Middle Ages to the Present, a bilingual anthology edited by Beverly Allen, Muriel Kittel, and Keala Jane Jewell, and with an introduction by Beverly Allen. $24.95 cloth, $9.95 paper.

The Female Spectator, edited by Mary R. Mahl and Helene Koon. $8.95 paper.

Guardian Angel and Other Stories, by Margery Latimer. Afterwords by Nancy Loughridge, Meridel Le Sueur, and Louis Kampf. $8.95 paper.

I Love Myself When I Am Laughing... And Then Again When I Am Looking Mean and Impressive, by Zora Neale Hurston. Edited by Alice Walker with an introduction by Mary Helen Washington. $9.95 paper.

Käthe Kollwitz: Woman and Artist, by Martha Kearns. $7.95 paper.

Life in the Iron Mills and Other Stories, by Rebecca Harding Davis. Biographical interpretation by Tillie Olsen. $7.95 paper.

The Living Is Easy, a novel by Dorothy West. Afterword by Adelaide M. Cromwell. $8.95 paper.

The Other Woman: Stories of Two Women and a Man. Edited by Susan Koppelman. $8.95 paper.

Mother to Daughter, Daughter to Mother: A Daybook and Reader, selected and shaped by Tillie Olsen. $9.95 paper.

Portraits of Chinese Women in Revolution, by Agnes Smedley. Edited with an introduction by Jan MacKinnon and Steve MacKinnon and an afterword by Florence Howe. $5.95 paper.

Reena and Other Stories, selected short stories by Paule Marshall. $8.95 paper.

Ripening: Selected Work, 1927–1980, by Meridel Le Sueur. Edited with an introduction by Elaine Hedges. $8.95 paper.

Rope of Gold, a novel of the thirties, by Josephine Herbst. Introduction by Alice Kessler-Harris and Paul Lauter and afterword by Elinor Langer. $8.95 paper.

The Silent Partner, a novel by Elizabeth Stuart Phelps. Afterword by Mari Jo Buhle and Florence Howe. $8.95 paper.

Swastika Night, a novel by Katharine Burdekin. Introduction by Daphne Patai. $8.95 paper.

These Modern Women: Autobiographical Essays from the Twenties. Edited with an introduction by Elaine Showalter. $4.95 paper.

The Unpossessed, a novel of the thirties, by Tess Slesinger. Introduction by Alice Kessler-Harris and Paul Lauter and afterword by Janet Sharistanian. $8.95 paper.

Weeds, a novel by Edith Summers Kelley. Afterword by Charlotte Goodman. $7.95 paper.

A Woman of Genius, a novel by Mary Austin. Afterword by Nancy Porter. $8.95 paper.

The Woman and the Myth: Margaret Fuller's Life and Writings, by Bell Gale Chevigny. $8.95 paper.

Women and Appletrees, a novel by Moa Martinson. Translated from the Swedish and with an afterword by Margaret S. Lacy. $8.95 paper.

The Yellow Wallpaper, by Charlotte Perkins Gilman. Afterword by Elaine Hedges. $3.95 paper.

OTHER TITLES FROM THE FEMINIST PRESS

Black Foremothers: Three Lives, by Dorothy Sterling. $8.95 paper.

But Some of Us Are Brave: Black Women's Studies. Edited by Gloria T. Hull, Patricia Bell Scott, and Barbara Smith. $12.95.

Complaints and Disorders: The Sexual Politics of Sickness, by Barbara Ehrenreich and Deirdre English. $3.95 paper.

The Cross-Cultural Study of Women. Edited by Margot Duley-Morrow and Mary I. Edwards. $29.95 cloth, $12.95 paper.

Feminist Resources for Schools and Colleges: A Guide to Curricular Materials., 3rd edition. Compiled and edited by Anne Chapman. $12.95 paper.

Household and Kin: Families in Flux, by Amy Swerdlow et al. $8.95 paper.

How to Get Money for Research, by Mary Rubin and the Business and Professional Women's Foundation. Foreword by Mariam Chamberlain. $6.95 paper.

In Her Own Image: Women Working in the Arts. Edited with an introduction by Elaine Hedges and Ingrid Wendt. $9.95 paper.

Integrating Women's Studies into the Curriculum: A Guide and Bibliography, by Betty Schmitz. $9.95 paper.

Las Mujeres: Conversations from a Hispanic Community, by Nan Elsasser, Kyle MacKenzie, and Yvonne Tixier y Vigil. $8.95 paper.

Lesbian Studies: Present and Future. Edited by Margaret Cruikshank. $9.95 paper.

Moving the Mountain: Women Working for Social Change, by Ellen Cantarow with Susan Gushee O'Malley and Sharon Hartman Strom. $8.95 paper.

Out of the Bleachers: Writings on Women and Sport. Edited with an introduction by Stephanie L. Twin. $9.95 paper.

Reconstructing American Literature: Courses, Syllabi, Issues. Edited by Paul Lauter. $10.95 paper.

Salt of the Earth, screenplay by Michael Wilson with historical commentary by Deborah Silverton Rosenfelt. $5.95 paper.

Witches, Midwives, and Nurses: A History of Women Healers, by Barbara Ehrenreich and Deirdre English. $3.95 paper.

With These Hands: Women Working on the Land. Edited with an introduction by Joan M. Jensen. $9.95 paper.

Woman's "True" Profession: Voices from the History of Teaching. Edited with an introduction by Nancy Hoffman. $9.95 paper.

Women Have Always Worked: A Historical Overview, by Alice Kessler-Harris. $8.95 paper.

Women Working: An Anthology of Stories and Poems. Edited and with an introduction by Nancy Hoffman and Florence Howe. $8.95 paper.

For free catalog, write to The Feminist Press at the City University of New York, 311 East 94 Street, New York, N.Y. 10128. Send individual book orders to The Feminist Press, P. O. Box 1654, Hagerstown, MD 21741. Include $1.75 postage and handling for one book and 75¢ for each additional book. To order using MasterCard or Visa, call: (800) 638-3030.